RECOMMENDED BED & BREAKFASTS™ SERIES

RECOMMENDED

Bed & Breakfasts™
CALIFORNIA

ELEVENTH EDITION

Kathy Strong

INSIDERS' GUIDE®

GUILFORD, CONNECTICUT
AN IMPRINT OF THE GLOBE PEQUOT PRESS

*With special appreciation to the innkeepers for their assistance
and good wishes; may your winter Mondays all be "full."*

To buy books in quantity for corporate use
or incentives, call **(800) 962–0973, ext. 4551,**
or e-mail **premiums@GlobePequot.com.**

INSIDERS' GUIDE®

Copyright © 1984, 1986, 1988, 1990, 1992, 1995, 1998, 2000, 2002, 2004, 2006 by
Morris Book Publishing, LLC

Insiders' Guide is a registered trademark of Morris Book Publishing, LLC.
Recommended Bed & Breakfasts is a trademark of Morris Book Publishing, LLC.

Text design by Nancy Freeborn
Interior illustrations: See page ix for credits.

ISSN: 1539-3526
ISBN-13: 978-0-7627-4058-1
ISBN-10: 0-7627-4058-2

Manufactured in the United States of America
Eleventh Edition/First Printing

Contents

Introduction

Selecting the right B&B for your vacation or business journey is a personal matter, one that needs to fit your trip expectations perfectly. Though the stay may be brief—maybe just a night or two—it will live on in your memory for many years to come. If especially memorable, the stay will be lived privately over and over again. Deciding where to stay, where this experience will live up to your expectations, is an important choice. This guide will help you find your most memorable stay yet!

The eleventh edition of *Recommended Bed & Breakfasts California* is a must for any avid B&B traveler or for those who are considering sampling this exciting and personal way of touring the state. This thoroughly updated edition includes new information on inns listed previously plus entries on nearly two dozen new establishments— nearly 400 in all! The new bed- and-breakfast offerings in this edition provide some fun twists on the B&B approach to traveling, as well as wide diversity. For instance, you'll find a Central Valley ranch built in 1902 where you can pick your own oranges for morning juice; an inn on a ten-acre Arabian horse farm; a bed-and-breakfast along an airstrip on a Northern California 1940s military blimp base; a beachside inn that hosts professional tennis tournaments; a relaxing Sedona-style inn in an open desert setting; a bed-and-breakfast experience that allows you to take a bay cruise without ever leaving your "room"; a famous artist's barn complete with original "artist's wall"; a contemporary inn overhanging a lake; an astronomy-lover's dream bed-and-breakfast with state-of-the-art telescope observatory and indoor heated pool; a Tuscan-style villa entrenched in vineyards; a French chateau with wine-tasting cellar; a historic lighthouse on its own little island; and many more.

Recommended Bed & Breakfasts California invites you to venture out of your predictable and perhaps dull traveling routine and discover this gracious world of individuality, comfort, and warmth, where you can indulge your dreams of opulence for a day or step back in history to relive days gone by. Sounds like a large promise? You'll find it isn't once you've ventured into the unknown, for the underlying message in *Recommended Bed & Breakfasts California,* whether you're discovering a gold-rush hotel, a picturesque Victorian house, or a glass-enclosed suite overhanging the

Pacific, is the certainty of a highly personalized and comfortable stay. After all, in this rapid-paced, computerized life nearly everyone is searching for a world that moves more slowly and relates more personally.

Recommended Bed & Breakfasts California encourages you to experience these overnight adventures, as varied and vast as the California scenery. If you've already sampled bed-and-breakfast travel here, you're undoubtedly yearning for more, for it's an exciting discovery that gives a whole new dimension to touring the "sunshine" state. Although bed-and-breakfast is hardly new (it was born and is practiced widely in Europe, is synonymous with New England America, and is about thirty years old in California), it is still gaining momentum and popularity in the West. And, as always, California has its own unique qualities to lend to and blend with the old, established traditions known to bed-and-breakfast travel. That's where *Recommended Bed & Breakfasts California* shines as the adventure it truly is.

If bed-and-breakfast travel is such a glorious and fulfilling experience, then why, you may ask, is it currently enjoyed by only a small (albeit rapidly growing) portion of the traveling community? One explanation is that the majority of bed-and-breakfast establishments in the state are still in their infancy, having mushroomed in the countryside and cityside in the last two decades faster than anyone could have predicted. The second reason is ironic yet true. Bed-and-breakfast travel is so varied in California that many travelers are timid about pioneering into this unknown territory, which seemingly lacks uniformity in any respect. If you are one of these reluctant but curious pioneers, *Recommended Bed & Breakfasts California* will help you to become a courageous explorer discovering those special places in and about California's alluring valleys, peaks, deserts, and coastlines, reserving confidently and arriving enthusiastic about the very differences you are about to find. The following pages will guide the most cautious of you through the sometimes confusing and overwhelming aspects of what to expect, what to ask, and what to watch for, culminating with a detailed "What to Ask the Innkeeper" for especially easy reference.

The "Bed & Breakfasts in California Directory" herein contains nearly 400 California B&B establishments and is the largest, most up-to-date directory available. An at-a-glance list of features with each B&B listing offers basic information about that particular establishment to help you narrow your search in any specific geographic area. But *Recommended Bed & Breakfasts California* highly recommends that you personally contact each establishment you are considering, check out their Web sites, and request a brochure and/or additional information. The aim of this book is to present you with a guide to a variety of B&B destinations and let you choose. A routine B&B to one person may be a fantasy-come-true to another! The descriptions of the bed-and-breakfasts are as accurate as possible. Sometimes, however, situations and/or owners change, and if you should find any accommodation not measuring up to your expectations, the author would very much appreciate your letting her know. Most bed-and-breakfast travelers find, however, that once they know what to expect, disappointments are rare.

So, venture out to one of California's few remaining frontiers. The experiences you will have are sure to add spice and spirit to your travel and, above all, restore your belief that personal comforts, individuality, and hospitality are still part of California living.

The prices and rates listed in this guidebook were confirmed at press time. We recommend, however, that you call establishments before traveling to obtain current information.

Illustrations

■ Illustrations in this book have been reproduced from establishments' brochures or literature, with the permission of the establishment. Special credit and thanks are given to the following individuals, agencies, or inns: the Gosby House, Carol Simmons Ragle; Heritage Park Bed & Breakfast Inn, Eldon Anderson; the Brakey House Bed and Breakfast, Sara Fine; Ten Inverness Way, Jacquetta Nisbet; the Darling House, Daniel R. Dicicco; Camellia Inn, Sonoma County Atlas of 1877; Hope-Merrill & Hope-Bosworth Houses, Steve Doty; Beazley House, Mandy Fisher; Philo Pottery Inn, Brian McFann; the Stanford Inn and Spa by the Sea, Larry Eifert; Joshua Grindle Inn, Dick Smith; Elk Cove Inn and Spa, Judith Brown; Old Thyme Inn; Christmas House Bed & Breakfast Inn, Bill Baldwin; the Raford House Inn, Robert Matson; Heritage Inn, the Publicity Mill; Old Town Bed & Breakfast Inn; the Gingerbread Mansion Inn; Howard Creek Ranch; Mendocino Hotel & Garden Suites; Whitegate Inn; Harbor House Inn; North Coast Country Inn; Haydon Street Inn; Calderwood Inn; Scarlett's Country Inn; Wine Way Inn; Erika's Hillside; the Wine Country Inn; Magliulo's Rose Garden Inn; Victorian Garden Inn; Napa Inn; the Old World Inn; the Feather Bed; the American River Inn; Court Street Inn; the Robin's Nest Bed and Breakfast; Marina Inn B&B; Petite Auberge; Centrella Inn; Old Monterey Inn; the J. Patrick House; Bayview Hotel Bed & Breakfast; Green Gables Inn; the Babbling Brook Inn; the Gables Wine Country Inn; the Hidden Oak; Zaballa House, Corky Wahl; the Goose & Turrets B&B, Alex Koronatov; the Chateau Tivoli; Chaney House; Inn on Summer Hill, Janice Blair; Channel Road Inn; Red Castle Inn, D. R. Graffis; the Inn on Mt. Ada; Strawberry Creek Inn; Pelican Cove Inn; Gerstle Park Inn, Bill Bates; Stanyan Park Hotel; Evergreen, Jane Cameron; the Artists' Inn and Cottage, Janet Margani; the Bissell House; the Seal Beach Inn and Gardens; the Willows Historic Palm Springs Inn; the Bed & Breakfast Inn at La Jolla; Gold Mountain Manor Historic B&B; Sutter Creek Inn; the Shore House at Lake Tahoe; the Cottage Inn; Inn at Shallow Creek Farm; Amber House; Piety Hill Cottages; the Emma Nevada House; Poppy Hill Bed & Breakfast; Jamestown Hotel—A Country Inn; the Wedgewood Inn; Johnson's Country Inn; Imperial Hotel; the Cain House; Ben Maddox House; 1898 Chalfant House; Château du Sureau, Peter Ledger; Cliff Crest; Chateau Victorian; the Martine Inn; the Gate House Inn; Cypress Inn, Bob Bates; the Briarwood Inn; Trojan Horse Inn; Sonoma Hotel; Cavanagh Inn, Dina Farris; Churchill Manor Bed & Breakfast; Cedar Gables Inn; Blue Violet Mansion; Grape Leaf Inn; Gaige House Inn; Foothill House; Cottage Grove Inn; the Shelford House; Glenelly Inn & Cottages, Claudia Wagar; Zinfandel House, Joanne Yates; the Lost Whale Inn, Vicky

Smith; Sea Rock Inn; Mendocino Village Inn; the Headlands Inn; Agate Cove Inn; McCloud B&B Hotel; the John Dougherty House, Jay Graham; the Daly Inn; Harbor House Inn, Bob Bates; Quail Mountain; Lake Oroville Bed and Breakfast; the Groveland Hotel, Barbara Hansen; Deer Creek Inn; Grey Gables Inn, Mike Walsh; Coxhead House; Roughley Manor Bed & Breakfast Inn; Apples Bed & Breakfast Inn; the Old Turner Inn; Alpenhorn Bed and Breakfast; Windy Point Inn; Petit Soleil; the Artists' Barn; Fensalden; Sandpiper House Inn; Abigail's Elegant Victorian Mansion; the Carter House; Hotel Carter; the Shaw House Inn; Country Inn; the Lodge at Noyo River; Jenner Inn & Cottages; Glendeven Inn; the George Alexander House; La Belle Époque; Rancho Caymus Inn; Melitta Station Inn; Pygmalion House; the Coloma Country Inn; Columbia City Hotel; Dunbar House, 1880; the Chichester-McKee House; Vizcaya; Rose Garden Inn; the Victorian on Lytton; Abella Garden Inn; Happy Landing Inn; Sandpiper Inn; Vagabond's House Inn; the Carmel Valley Lodge; the Jabberwock; Pacific Grove Inn; Seven Gables Inn; Garden Street Inn; Kern River Inn Bed & Breakfast; the Ballard Inn; Julian Hotel; Pine Hills Lodge; Hotel Nipton; the Cottage; the Bath Street Inn; the Upham Hotel & Garden Cottages.

PART ONE

Exploring California's Bed & Breakfasts

The Variety of California's
Bed & Breakfast Establishments

■ Drawing from Europe's popular and quaint *pension,* enterprising and always innovative Californians have produced a bounty of that intimate and hospitable form of lodging in almost every imaginable size, style of architecture and furnishings, and location. In other words, you name it, and a California bed-and-breakfast has it (or will very soon!). To give you an idea of the creative bed-and-breakfasts awaiting you, let's explore a sampling.

SIZE AND TYPE

The size of bed-and-breakfast establishments ranges from the large inn, with as many as fifty rooms, to the small private home, with one or two rooms. Some of the inns contain amenities associated with hotels, and, indeed, some were at one time traditional hotels or boardinghouses. Within these you may find restaurants, pools, spas, large lounges, full business services, and other hotel-type offerings. Smaller homes make up the majority of bed-and-breakfast establishments in the state and were originally, for the most part, single-family homes. Each inn is operated primarily as a bed-and-breakfast business with more businesslike hours, staffing, policies, and routine in general than is usually found in a private-home situation.

A cottage or guesthouse may be found in conjunction with an inn or may be an overnight rental all by itself in back of a private home. This separate dwelling provides more privacy, often is more family-oriented, and sometimes offers cooking facilities.

Although local zoning regulations that discourage bed-and-breakfast use in residential areas are on the rise, private homes offering from one to four bed-and-breakfast accommodations still exist in large numbers around the state. A few private homes with guest rooms, primarily those that remain independent from referral agencies, are listed in the directory in this book. But the bulk of home listings can be found by contacting one of the several agencies, also listed in this book, that specialize in finding you bed-and-breakfast accommodations in private homes for either a membership or placement fee or at no cost to you at all.

Architecture and Period

The California concept of the B&B ranges architecturally from an 1888 Eastlake Victorian mansion to a 1920s Italian stone villa with Gothic arches, to a real working lighthouse, to a new Cape Cod or Mediterranean structure overlooking the Pacific. In other words, you'll find a bed-and-breakfast representative of almost every type of California's architecture, whether it be turn-of-the-twentieth-century, Gothic, Tudor, early frontier, contemporary, or brand-new built to look old. You'll also discover bed-and-breakfasts with unusual historic uses, such as a 1920s yacht club, a 1903 senator's home that was host to presidents, and a former lifesaving station overlooking the Pacific.

Furnishings and Accessories

Just as the architecture of California bed-and-breakfasts varies, the furnishings within also provide variety and, sometimes, surprises. Many B&B travelers assume "bed-and-breakfast" is equivalent to "antique." True, many of the bed-and-breakfasts concentrate on re-creating the past in California, often in a style consistent with the establishment's turn-of-the-twentieth-century or late-1800s vintage. But some bed-and-breakfast owners choose an eclectic decorating style, often blending harmoniously the old and new to create a very individual feel. Some establishments feature guest rooms that not only carry out different themes, but also offer quite different decors. The unusual and elaborate room themes at a noteworthy California B&B may take the prize for originality: Guests may choose to "depart" to a foreign country of desire by selecting a guest room in the appropriate theme in this vintage railroad depot–turned–B&B.

Family heirlooms, pottery or paintings, and the innkeeper's hobbies, such as a rare doll collection, add a personal touch to many establishments. One Southern California B&B decorates individual guest rooms around the artist's work displayed in that room. Though the decor is endlessly varied, you'll find a common element in all the bed-and-breakfasts statewide: a desire to provide a hospitable and comfortable environment, whether it is accomplished with fresh flowers, candy, a decanter of wine or sherry, fresh fruit, bright and cheerful wall coverings, or soft and inviting colors and patterns.

Bed & Breakfast Settings

The bed-and-breakfast concept is synonymous with the "country inn," but many of California's B&Bs have sprung up in cities and downtown areas. These "urban inns" are a mixture of hotels and former factories turned bed-and-breakfast, large homes or mansions, row houses, and even private homes and cottages offering a room or two. *Convenience* is the key word in this urban setting, for the tourist and businessperson alike. Fine restaurants, civic centers, shopping, and cultural events are often just a walk away. Many of the city establishments that were once hotels also offer a wider range of services, such as telephones, television, and business-meeting facilities.

Nestled among lilacs and ancient oaks or perched atop a mountain with patchwork fields stretched out for miles, the bed-and-breakfast in the country offers diverse, and often rural, settings. Many Western ranches in the state have adopted bed-and-breakfast traits while also offering the ranch-style amenities of animals, casual dress, and hearty meals. California's rapidly growing wine industry goes hand-in-hand with its expanding B&B business, as shown not only in the number of bed-and-breakfasts surrounding wineries, but also by the many B&Bs on the vineyard grounds. What could be more characteristic of California bed-and-breakfast travel than the opportunity to sleep and breakfast among verdant vines and oak barrels, sampling the latest harvest in your room before retiring?

Residential-area B&Bs range from tree-lined Victorian neighborhoods to a California 1950s tract to a custom wood-and-glass structure reaching out to the Pacific Ocean. You'll find mansions and estates and modest private homes located in all sorts of residential areas, some more rural than others, but all with something special to offer.

Finding the Right Bed & Breakfast

Scouting the Whereabouts of Bed & Breakfasts

The directory in this book is the most complete guide currently available to bed-and-breakfast establishments in California. Of course, new B&Bs are opening constantly as this idea gains greater and greater popularity from seashore to desert, from mountains to cities. For that reason, if you care to stay completely abreast of new finds, you'll want to keep a watchful eye on other sources as well.

Travel Publications

To the delight of bed-and-breakfast travelers, travel articles in newspapers and magazines are focusing more and more on bed-and-breakfasts these days. Many new establishments gain their audience this way, so openings are often announced in travel editors' columns or the "Letters to the Travel Editor" section on Sunday.

Tourist Bureaus

If you're traveling to a specific area and want an update on possible new bed-and-breakfasts, a call, letter, or visit to the local chamber of commerce or tourist center is usually a good start. These offices keep up with new businesses in general, especially those that cater to the tourist. Often they will distribute a brochure, if available, on the inn.

Referrals and Associations

Following the directory in this book is a listing of referral agencies based in California and primarily involved in B&B accommodations within the state. These referral agencies work in a variety of ways: Some choose to charge the inn or home owner for each room they book; others require a membership fee, usually annual, which gives the member a descriptive listing of their offerings from which to choose; and still others sell the listings only, and you handle the booking arrangements. Some of these referral agencies deal only with selected inns, but a majority offer listings in private homes. Indeed, more home B&Bs choose this alternative rather than soliciting guests on their own. The private homes listed in this directory are those that do not rely solely on a referral agency for their trade.

The bed-and-breakfast associations also listed following the directory in this book are organizations formed by the innkeepers within that region. The associations have many and varied functions, such as forming guidelines for member inns, advertising jointly, and offering referrals, but all of the groups mentioned in this guide publish or give out the names of their association members. Most of these associations will send you a brochure or pamphlet with the names and descriptions of their member inns and require only that you first send a self-addressed stamped envelope. Several of the associations now offer toll-free numbers for a quick referral.

Of course, let's not overlook the very valuable "personal referral" when searching for new B&Bs. Bed-and-breakfasts survive mainly on word of mouth, and a new establishment's opening spreads among innkeepers and avid B&B–goers like fresh butter on a steaming hot croissant. So when staying at a bed-and-breakfast, talk to your fellow guests and pump your innkeeper for new information. It's by far the most delightful way to enlarge your directory.

What You Should Ask about a Bed & Breakfast

What could be less personal than contacting some anonymous person 2,000 miles away by dialing an even more anonymous "800" number and reserving a room in a chain motel by answering a quick, memorized list of questions? We have all performed this rather mindless act (perhaps hundreds of times), and it is simple to guess we are apt to receive the same impersonal greeting upon our arrival. We know what the room will look like except for the rather unexciting surprise of what the color scheme will be this time. If guessing the color of the bedspread and drapes is the most intrigue you derive from travel, then you're in for *thrills* traveling B&B style in California! Right from the moment you place your first call or receive a handwritten response to your inquiry, you'll discover researching B&Bs is not only easy to do, but also fun—as long as you know what sorts of things to ask. For, before traveling to a California bed-and-breakfast, you get to ask the questions and mold your stay into the adventure and experience for which you've been longing.

Description of the B&B

By studying the directory in this book, you may have a good idea which establishments in any given area you would like to know more about. If time allows, you may want to write a note briefly stating your specific questions; or if you are in a hurry, you will want to call the establishment directly and speak with the innkeeper or clerk. You will notice that some B&Bs have facsimile (fax) machines and/or e-mail for quick responses. You will also notice that many inns offer Web sites; if you are an Internet user, be sure to glance at the inn's site. In either case, you will most likely be delighted with the very personal and warm response you receive. A common trait among innkeepers is their basic fondness for people, and this results in a gracious and helpful attitude. They are eager to answer your smallest question. If you telephone your innkeeper at a busy moment (the phone always rings when he or she is just about to serve perfect three-minute eggs to ten guests), ask him or her to call you back. Generally, the busiest times are during breakfast and early evening, but since some innkeepers close at midday to take care of cleaning, shopping, washing, and the like, it is difficult to guess the best time to call—just keep trying.

Whether writing, phoning, or e-mailing, be sure to request a brochure, rate card, postcard, or whatever descriptive pieces are available. A brochure or Web site is the B&B's best tool for informing you and saving both of you time. One of the most common questions an innkeeper hears is "Can you tell me about your inn?" Because the very nature of a bed-and-breakfast is its uniqueness and individuality throughout, from its hand-sewn quilts to its teddy bear collection, the question can be overwhelming. In comes the brochure or Web site, the most convenient and descriptive way of telling you about all the little extras, as well as the cost, rules, and policies.

Accommodations

Although the trend in California B&Bs is oversize beds (king or queen) due to guests' demands in the last decade, you may want to double-check just in case a larger bed is important to you or if you prefer twin beds. Some inns have compromised by putting a larger bed and twin in the same room, which also satisfies requests for three to a room. But this situation is not common, and rollaway beds are not always available, so be sure to check. Some inns will offer a special rate for three traveling together in exchange for allowing three to a room, especially during off-peak times. No matter what the size, comfort is usually a foremost consideration, and the beds are often outfitted with delicate sheets and plump comforters for an unforgettable night's rest.

Shared baths: Those persons about to venture into B&B travel for the first time are usually the most hesitant about the next topic: the "shared bath." It actually prevents some people from experiencing many places they would have otherwise cherished. The majority of California B&Bs in this directory offer all private baths, but shared-bath situations do exist. "Shared bath" is not as easily defined as "private bath," because there are several degrees of "sharing" to be found. For instance, many shared-bath accommodations have within the guest room itself a "vanity area," generally consisting of a sink, mirror, electrical outlet, and appropriate towels and soap. Vanity areas cut down considerably on the use of the baths by allowing you to complete the more time-consuming tasks of shaving, applying makeup, brushing teeth, fixing hair, and so on in your own room. If sharing the bath worries you, be sure to ask about the ratio of rooms to a bath. Often it is as low as two rooms to one bath or perhaps four rooms to a bath, but even the latter is rarely a problem. Remember, too, that bed-and-breakfast travelers are, for the most part, a very considerate lot who know to leave the bath promptly and as neat as when they entered. If you're still skittish, most establishments do offer some private, if not all private, bath accommodations. But if you do insist on a private bath, be sure to peek at the shared baths before you leave. You may be pleasantly surprised to find them elegant and spacious or decorated authentically with claw-foot tubs, pedestal sinks, and pull-chain toilets. A few California inns offer twin claw-foots for bathing side by side!

Wheelchair access: Many cities and counties in California have adopted strict building and operating requirements for the wheelchair-bound guest at bed-and-breakfast inns, but the rules are far from uniform and rarely apply to private residences. If climbing stairs is the main concern, be sure to specify downstairs accommodations if available. The inn's ability to accommodate a wheelchair guest is noted with an icon below the address of the establishment. Because this relates to wheelchair-equipped units primarily, please check with the individual inn for possible accommodations "with assistance." For quicker reference refer to the index listing of establishments that offer wheelchair access.

Rules and Policies

You'll discover many similarities in the rules and general policies of bed-and-breakfast establishments throughout the state. But you're also sure to find some exceptions and "bending of the rules." Bed-and-breakfasts can do that because they're dealing on such a personal level. The more professional the establishment, however, the more rigid it will tend to be regarding key policies, especially those regarding smoking and pets, which affect other guests.

Children: A recent amendment to the federal Civil Rights Act prohibits bed-and-breakfast and other lodging establishments from discriminating against children. For this reason there is no reference in this book to each B&B's policy regarding children. It is important to note, however, that many California B&Bs are not equipped to handle small children easily, and a great many establishments cannot accommodate more than two people in a room. Guests traveling with children should therefore check carefully with the B&B regarding specific arrangements. There is a listing of B&Bs in the index in this guide that are especially family-friendly; these inns do not represent the only B&Bs accommodating children, but rather those that go out of their way to make families welcome with amenities such as cribs, strollers, or children's activities. Of course, you will discover many fine inns that are perfect for family travel and offer many wonderful adventures for children, such as sleeping lofts, playrooms, nature trails, and backyard play areas.

Smoking: Smoking is a controversial subject everywhere these days. Most of the B&Bs in this directory do not allow smoking inside the establishment (as indicated with an icon below the establishment's address); several others permit smoking only in specific rooms. This policy should be spelled out in the establishment's literature, but if not, be sure to ask. If you are a smoker, please abide by the rules of the house to avoid embarrassment to yourself and your obliging innkeeper. Try to keep in mind that a no-smoking policy is often due to a variety of factors that include the protection and longevity of delicate fabrics and expensive antiques as well as the proximity of areas and the general risks involved. Be warned that some B&Bs that prohibit smoking charge guests for deodorizing rooms that have been smoked in.

Pets: There are a sprinkling of exceptions to the "no pets" rule at bed-and-breakfasts listed in this book. Either refer to the "Features" listing under each B&B or, for quick reference, check the index section at the back of the book. If you plan to travel with a pet, be sure to check all rules in advance, because even those establishments that allow pets sometimes have restrictions or special accommodations reserved for guests with pets. Unless otherwise stated in "Features" or in the index, pets are not allowed.

Days and Hours of Operation, Minimum Stays

Some bed-and-breakfasts operate nearly as motels/hotels—open seven days a week, management on duty twenty-four hours, and so forth—but this is far from the norm. Indeed, some are open only when business is there, some only on weekends, and some only during certain seasons. Therefore it is important to determine if a particular establishment is open for business when you care to visit, as well as if a minimum stay is required. It is not unusual for a B&B to require a minimum stay of two nights during peak times: weekends, holidays, and special local events. Also, it is critical to indicate your approximate time of arrival so that proper arrangements are made for your check-in, especially if you are arriving later or earlier than the establishment's normal check-in hours.

Rates

If you're traveling bed-and-breakfast style in California on the premise that you'll save a lot of money—sorry! You'll discover that many California inns are actually very similar in cost to the nicer hotels in the same area; however, don't overlook all the extras you receive traveling B&B style. You probably will decide it is a bargain of sorts. Also, the rates in private homes are generally lower than those in the local hostelries, so genuine bargains do exist. In fact, in this edition you will find a symbol with those bed-and-breakfasts that represent the "best buys" in their area. Look for the (Best Buy) icon if you are traveling on a budget, yet don't want to sacrifice quality.

Some bed-and-breakfasts charge a flat fee per room, whereas others will give a separate rate for single occupancy, averaging about $5.00 less than the double fee. Because commercial business is not the mainstay of most bed-and-breakfast establishments, many do not offer commercial rates. If you are traveling on business, do make the request. More and more establishments are beginning to realize the value of the business patron and are offering a special rate, especially in urban areas and on weekdays. You will find a handy listing of business services available at each B&B in the "Features" listing.

It is not unusual for a bed-and-breakfast to offer special room rates at different times of the year: lower midweek rates, winter or off-season reductions, weekly discounts, and holiday increases. Often this information is not stated on the rate card, so be sure to inquire.

The tax imposed on lodging in California is referred to as "bed tax," and this tax amount varies from area to area, ranging anywhere from 8 percent to as high as 20 percent of the room rate, with the average being around 10 percent. Rates quoted for bed-and-breakfast accommodations are "without tax," so be sure to ask for the total amount when making advance payment for your lodging.

Deposits: To secure a reservation, many establishments require that the first night's stay be paid in advance; others require that the entire stay be paid for before arrival. When credit cards are accepted, the credit card number can usually be taken for confirmation. It is important to ask what form of payment is acceptable at your bed-and-breakfast because many establishments deal only in cash and checks.

Cancellations: Because a majority of bed-and-breakfasts in California operate on a relatively small scale compared with hotels and motels, they must also impose much stricter cancellation policies. Most B&Bs offer a total refund if a cancellation is made within a certain amount of time prior to your stay, ranging from forty-eight hours to seven days. The cancellation policy should be stated clearly in the establishment's literature. If it isn't, be sure to ask. If circumstances require that you cancel your reservation at the last minute, do notify your B&B immediately. If the room remains vacant, you may be charged, although most innkeepers will be lenient for extenuating circumstances or may move your stay to another agreed-upon date. A handful of B&Bs will charge you a cancellation fee for time and trouble regardless of when the cancellation was made.

Other Considerations

Breakfast: Breakfast is, of course, a common element in all the B&Bs around, but it can take many delicious forms. Some establishments serve an "extended continental breakfast," consisting of juice, fruit, coffee or tea, and baked goods, but the trend is certainly toward a full, often gourmet, cuisine. A "full" breakfast might add eggs, pancakes, waffles, or crepes to the above; a simpler continental fare might delete the fresh fruit. Guests may delight in such breakfast delicacies as stuffed French toast, lemon-shirred eggs, apple-ricotta pancakes, or fried apples.

If *where* breakfast is served is important to you, be sure to ask. Many establishments with a dining room serve all guests there during a certain period of time, such as from 8:00 to 10:00 A.M. Some offer both the dining room (or parlor) and patio, as well as in-room service, whereas others offer only the latter. Some B&Bs literally offer "breakfast in bed," but most in-room breakfasts are served at a specific time on a table in the room. Breakfast in your room can be fun, but many avid B&B travelers delight in the communal dining situation, which allows for interesting exchanges with fellow guests and innkeepers.

Refreshments: Although it's not a requirement for being defined as a bed-and-breakfast, many B&Bs in California offer refreshments apart from breakfast—and they have found many ways of accomplishing this pleasant repast. You'll discover anything from wine and hors d'oeuvres in the evening to an in-room basket of goodies to cookies and tea at midday. Many B&Bs now offer late-evening desserts in addition to evening or afternoon light snacks.

Televisions, telephones, and transportation: Contrary to common belief, many California B&Bs do have television in the rooms. In fact, many of the newer inns have provided televisions, VCRs, or DVDs in each guest room. When available, televisions are usually cleverly concealed in an armoire. Some inns offer televisions in a lounge area.

Telephones are found more commonly in the inn/hotel situation and also are becoming more frequent in smaller B&Bs. Indeed, many of the new establishments in this directory offer in-room phones or jacks—some even with voice mail.

Because most B&Bs are small operations, transportation service is often not available, but some will pick up at airports, train depots, or bus stations with prior notice. Those that do not are usually happy to assist in arranging alternative ways of getting you there via bus or taxi. Parking availability at your B&B is an important question, especially at those in San Francisco or other urban areas where there may be an additional charge for parking.

Special Arrangements

Bed-and-breakfasts, with all their inherent charm, are catching on as attractive places to hold small functions such as weddings, receptions, business retreats, and reunions. Some establishments do not encourage group functions, whereas others are eager to arrange and assist in the various details. Special services for conferences, weddings, or small meetings are listed in the "Features" guide found under each listing.

Because California B&Bs provide ideal settings for special times such as birthdays, honeymoons, and anniversaries, many establishments offer champagne or some other very special provision, often on a complimentary basis, with prior notice. If you are staying on such an occasion, be sure to mention it when making your reservation.

Reserve, Pack, and Arrive with Confidence—Then Enjoy

Reserving, Confirming, and Arriving

When traveling bed-and-breakfast style in California, a reservation is almost a must in that some establishments operate only on advance reservations, but all prefer and recommend this method. Don't allow this fact to dissuade you from a spur-of-the-moment trip, because cancellations do occur, and B&Bs need a high occupancy rate to survive. Do make it a habit to reserve as early as possible to avoid disappointment, however, because it is not unusual for a B&B to be booked several weeks (even months) ahead, especially on weekends. Not only are you apt to obtain a reservation early, but you also will have a better pick of the guest accommodations: that cozy fireplace room or the bed that "the general" slept in.

The Reservation and Deposit

You may reserve your room by phone, e-mail, or mail, but in any case, be specific. Less confusion is apt to arise if you choose to call, which allows for clear, immediate deposit instructions from your B&B, backup room selections, and a quick acknowledgment of a vacancy. Once an accommodation is decided upon, the next step is the deposit that will secure your reservation. Many establishments, especially those that do not accept credit cards, require either the first night's tariff or the amount for the entire stay in advance. On the average this amount is due within five to seven days from the date the reservation is made. If you forget, you may discover your room has been given away. On your deposit check be sure to indicate the dates of your stay as a cross-check and an easy reference. If your B&B accepts credit cards, usually Visa or MasterCard, then often the number and date of expiration will hold your reservation. If you need to cancel and do not notify your innkeeper, do not be surprised to find the amount on your next charge-account statement. Actually, many hotels operate similarly. In defense of bed-and-breakfasts, every room is crucial to financial prosperity when working on such a small scale, and B&Bs are among the few lodging establishments that will loyally hold that room for you no matter what unless they hear otherwise.

Confirmation and Arrival

Upon receiving your check or after noting your charge number, the B&B should send you a confirmation note, usually handwritten, along with a brochure if you do not already have one. Included somewhere should be the "rules of the house," and you should read these carefully, especially points regarding their cancellation policy, smoking, and check-in times.

When you reserve your room, make it clear what time you plan to arrive. Bed-and-breakfasts often close as early as 8:00 P.M. and may also close around midday. Late arrivals can usually be handled efficiently with advance warning; early arrivals may at least be able to leave luggage and freshen up with prior arrangements.

Another item to keep in mind when placing your reservation is advance tour or dinner arrangements that your B&B host might be happy to handle for you. If there is a special event or very popular dining spot in town, ask if the B&B would handle reservations for you ahead of time. Some B&Bs now cater dinners with advance notice.

Emergency Provisions

As pleasant as bed-and-breakfast travel is in California, problems and emergencies can arise. To avoid a panic situation, be sure to acquaint yourself with emergency provisions upon checking in: Is there a resident manager? Where can he or she be found after closing time? Is an emergency phone available and where? If no resident manager is on the premises, how can the owners be reached? Are phone numbers posted? Ask whom you should see if you lose your key in the night or the toilet backs up or your next-door guests decide to have an all-night party. The chances are good that you will have a marvelous, romantic stay without a hint of a problem, but it is good to be prepared.

A common problem centers on the security of the B&B, which often involves lock-ing doors up tight at a certain time of the night. If you find yourself arriving late with-out notifying the bed-and-breakfast, then look for a late-box with a key or a number to call or just knock loudly! Of course, you should always call when possible if you're arriving later than the indicated office hours. If you're a guest already and you lose your key, the same applies. As a note, keys are handled quite differently at various establishments. Some issue you a key to your room and the front door, others just to the front door if your guest room has an inside latch. Still others deal with no keys at all.

Checking Out

Most bed-and-breakfast check-outs, like motels and hotels, are at 11:00 A.M. or noon. If you haven't paid in full, do so, and also remember to return the keys. Always bid farewell personally and sign the guest book if you like. It's great fun to read the guest book, too. Should you tip? Some B&Bs ask that you do not tip, but others leave that up to the guest; it is rarely expected. Do what pleases you, but add a name if the tip is for a specific person (otherwise the housekeeper may assume it is just for her or him). Some B&B travelers prefer more creative tipping such as a bottle of wine or a bouquet of flowers for the host. As a bed-and-breakfast owner, my favorite gratuity was always a heartfelt note of thanks with a promise to return.

Packing for Your Stay at a Bed & Breakfast

Just two words of advice here: Pack lightly! A recent California University survey on state bed-and-breakfasts reveals the average stay to be two nights, so most likely you won't pack for a week unless you're in transit. In that case, prepare ahead with a small suitcase for your B&B stop and leave the rest in the car. It is not at all unusual to discover your beautiful, antique-filled room is missing a closet, and in its place are a few ornate brass hooks or perhaps a tiny turn-of-the-twentieth-century armoire. Of course, some B&Bs have lovely, large closets, but you might want to check, if you're traveling with an entire wardrobe.

Once you've determined how much to tote, you'll need to give thought to what to bring along. When you're sharing the bath, a robe of some sort is a necessity. Some gracious inns do supply a robe if you forget yours, but you wouldn't want to depend on that. A small cosmetic or toiletry bag for sundry items also will make your "trip down the hall" much more efficient and comfortable. Although most guest rooms will have a mirror, and indeed many are equipped with full vanity/sink areas, it is wise to carry a stand-up travel mirror. Then, if the bath is occupied or you are nervous about taking a few extra minutes on your coiffure, you can proceed in the privacy of your room.

If you plan to travel with a supply of cold drinks or refreshments and your accommodations do not include a refrigerator, then ask about using the establishment's own refrigerator. Some places will offer happily, whereas others prefer not to extend this service due to several factors. Motels and hotels have trained the California traveler into the "ice-machine habit," but not one such machine exists in the state's B&B offerings. A few of the larger inn/hotels may have an ice dispenser, but your "ice machine" will most likely be a carton of cubes brought out graciously by the innkeeper at your request.

Enjoying Your Stay to the Fullest

The grand, spiraling staircase may conjure up childhood fantasies of sliding down its smooth walnut banister, and the painted, carved carousel horse in the parlor has your mind wandering to playful, simpler times. Yet a California bed-and-breakfast can do more than bring back nostalgic thoughts, especially if you prepare to enjoy all it has to offer.

Enjoying a bed-and-breakfast can be an end in itself, but often you'll want to explore its setting as well. As your own "personal tourist bureau," the B&B is ideally suited to recommend and even chart out a day's or week's activities. Many establishments are equipped with area brochures, maps, and, most important, are managed by an innkeeper or a host with very knowledgeable ideas of what's worthwhile.

To give you a start on some interesting things to do on your visit, you will discover some suggestions or advice on nearby attractions as you read about bed-and-breakfast selections in this edition of the book. See the category labeled "Nearby" in the "at-a-glance" information in each B&B profile as well as the sidebars that highlight special attractions. We hope they will give you some ideas to make your stay especially memorable.

The Breakfast

The breakfast is a most enjoyable other half of the B&B, and it's great fun to discover the unique ways different establishments accomplish this meal. As discussed earlier, locales of breakfasts can vary from in-bed trays to formal dining rooms, and the types from juice and croissants to homemade country feasts. To make the most of your breakfast, check your options and try several over the length of your stay. Be sure to mention any special dietary requirement upon arrival. The personal touch at a B&B mirrors the desire to please whenever possible. Don't be surprised to find a copy of the morning paper alongside your coffee cup.

Refreshments and Other Offerings

Picture yourself arriving at your bed-and-breakfast destination exhausted from a long drive; the next thing you know, a chilled glass of wine or a hot cup of tea is there to soothe your traveler's woes. Or perhaps you are escorted to your room to freshen up and presented with a basketed "care package" of fresh fruit or cookies. Or you go downstairs in the late afternoon to gather with fellow guests for champagne, hors d'oeuvres, and warm conversation. Many establishments offer late-night snacks or after-dinner desserts. In any circumstance, the refreshment offering practiced by most California B&Bs is a most enjoyable and welcome gesture.

Breakfast is not necessarily the only meal offered by California bed-and-breakfasts. With advance notice many establishments will pack a homemade picnic lunch for your day's outing or will prepare a special gourmet dinner. Of course, many of the larger inn/hotels have their own adjoining restaurants that are open to guests and the public on a regular basis.

The Extras

The extra services you'll find at California B&Bs are almost too numerous to mention, as you are sure to notice when reading the descriptions in this edition, checking what is listed under "Features," or referring to the indexes. In terms of recreation and relaxation, you'll find bicycles for exploring (both on a complimentary basis and rentals), spas, saunas, hot tubs, and pools—all a part of the California scene. Turn-of-the-twentieth-century gazebos, lawn croquet, tennis, ponds, creeks, and flower-filled gardens abound in both country and urban settings. Some inns offer such extras as dance or cooking lessons, bay cruises, touring in vintage autos, massages, private beaches and coves, and fishing or whale-watching expeditions.

Within your bed-and-breakfast, you'll almost always find some sort of sitting room, parlor, or library with comfy nooks, lots of reading material, and, at times, a television, radio, or player piano. These relaxation spots often feature a fireplace to sit by or challenging board games for one or more.

The newest diversions at California's B&Bs involve "theme" weekends. Guests may participate in a weekend-long murder mystery and rendezvous for clues at midnight at the gazebo; get married or renew their wedding vows with flowers, cake, and all the trimmings; or participate in a special performance of Dickens's *A Christmas Carol.*

Guest-Room Frills

Within the privacy of your room, you may discover a decanter of sherry, fruit, or candies to satisfy your cravings. Many B&B accommodations include refrigerators, wet bars, and even whole kitchens for you to stock with your favorites. With an emphasis on comfort, it is not unusual to find yourself relaxing in beds adorned with plush comforters, down pillows, and fancy sheets. Ask for extra blankets or pillows if you like. If you enjoy reading in bed, then ask for a reading light; ask for an alarm clock for a special wake-up time. If your room has a fireplace, check to be sure it's working, and find out how to use it. Some establishments prefer to start your fire for you or may have simple instructions available. You may return from the evening out to discover that a sweet elf has lovingly turned down your bed and left an elfin treat of candies or sherry, freshened your towels, and maybe even shined your shoes!

What to Ask the Innkeeper

1. **Choosing your bed-and-breakfast**
   Request a brochure, rate card
   Check policies regarding smoking, credit cards, cancellations
   Minimum-stay requirement
   Days and hours of operation, arrival time

2. **Reserving with confidence**
   Total deposit required? When?
   Form of payment accepted
   Confirmation received
   Late or early arrival
   Advance tour or dinner reservations
   Parking
   How to get there
   Public transportation, pickup service

3. **Packing for your stay**
   Robe
   Tote
   Refrigerated food

4. **Checking in and out**
   Breakfast options
   Emergency provisions
   Office hours
   Keys
   Guest book

5. **Enjoying your stay**
   Personal tourist information
   Refreshment time
   Picnics, lunches, dinners
   Bicycles

Spas, saunas, pools, hot tubs

Patios, gardens, gazebos

Parlor/library: books, games, fireplaces, pianos

Shared bath: bubble bath, robes, cleaning supplies

Room comforts: reading lights, alarm clocks, extra pillows/blankets, refreshments, fireplace use

Telephone

Television

Fax machine

Computer hookups

Business or meeting services

PART TWO

Directory of Bed & Breakfasts in California

How to Use the Directory

Geographic Areas: All the B&B establishments listed in the directory have been categorized geographically into one of the following six areas, each displayed with a map highlighting pertinent communities and described in a brief list of things to do and see:

Northern California: Northernmost California, primarily the north coast and redwood country

California Wine Country: Napa and Sonoma Counties

California Gold Country: Sacramento and adjoining Gold Country, including Tahoe and the Sierra foothills

San Francisco Bay Area: The city and surrounding Bay communities

Central California: Santa Cruz–Monterey Bay south through San Luis Obispo County and the San Joaquin and Owens Valleys

Southern California: Santa Barbara County south through San Diego

Use this legend when reading the maps in this book.

LEGEND:
— Freeway Route
— Highway Route
● Listed City or Town
○ Location Reference
◉ LARGER CITY

Individual Listings: Each bed-and-breakfast listing in the directory is followed by basic information about that particular B&B.

Reading the Features:

1. *Inn*—Operates primarily as a bed-and-breakfast inn
2. *Inn/Hotel*—An inn as well as a hotel, usually offering other services such as an adjoining restaurant
3. *Cottage*—Usually a small cabin in back of a home or an inn
4. *Home*—A private home renting from one to four rooms (most bed-and-breakfast homes can be found by checking with the referral agencies at the end of this directory)

Number of Guest Rooms: This is the total number of units available and may include cottages as well as suites.

Rates: Rates have been categorized in the following fashion based upon double occupancy, on-season rates per day before tax:

$:	up to $110
$$:	$111 to $185
$$$:	$186 to $250
$$$$:	$251 and up

Smoking:
Limited—Permitted only in certain rooms.

 Not allowed inside the establishment (most establishments have provisions for *outside* smoking).

Children: (See information on page 9.)

Credit Cards: Most of the B&Bs in this guide accept credit cards. If they do not, it will be indicated in the "Features" information.

Pets: Some B&Bs in this directory do accept pets, but most require advance permission and may have some restrictions. If pets are accepted, it will be indicated in the "Features" information, or refer to the indexes in the back of the book.

♿ This symbol indicates establishments that are equipped for wheelchair users. Check with the establishment for possible access "with assistance." For easy reference to establishments with wheelchair access, refer to the indexes in the back of the book.

Best Buy This symbol represents the "best buys" in each section of the book. These bed-and-breakfast establishments have been selected for their budget value based upon maintenance of quality with relatively inexpensive rates for that area of the state.

Innkeepers and/or Owners: This refers to key people to contact for information or reservations.

To Trinidad

To McCloud and Mount Shasta

299

EUREKA

Samoa

Ferndale

3

REDDING

Scotia

36

101

1

101

Pacific Ocean

99

To Chico

Westport

101

5

Fort Bragg

20

Little River

Mendocino

Albion

Ukiah

20

Lucerne

Elk

Philo

Boonville

128

Point Arena

1

Gualala

101

N

Guerneville

Scale in Miles

Jenner

116

0 10 20 30 40 50

Freestone

Occidental

To Sacramento

To San Francisco

NORTHERN CALIFORNIA

Rugged coastlines, isolated stretches, "Cape Cod" villages, steep mountains, giant redwoods, old lumber and fishing towns, and farm-land are the essence of California's scenic northern section. The inland areas here, housing towns such as Boonville and Garberville, are marked by warmer, drier weather, orchards, and the mighty redwood forests. The Skunk Train, which departs near coastal Fort Bragg, travels the redwood area as a popular tourist attraction. The nineteenth-century coastal towns of Mendocino and Little River offer dramatic cliffs with ocean-view bluffs, meadows, rocky beaches, and architecture reminis-cent of a New England fishing village. Farther north, Eureka beckons visitors with its renovated nineteenth-century Old Town boutiques. To the northeast, ancient redwoods lead a path to majestic Mount Shasta, a paradise of natural scenic splendor. Colorful gardens, artists' gal-leries and craft shops, water recreation, and bountiful driftwood collec-tions are all a part of Northern California, a year-round travel destination.

ALBION RIVER INN

3790 North Highway 1
P.O. Box 100
Albion, CA 95410

♿ ⊘ $$–$$$$

▪ The Albion River Inn is an attractive assemblage of New England–style cottages on ten secluded acres overlooking the scenic ocean bluffs of the Mendocino coast. The ocean-front accommodations are located in some private cottages, but mainly in two- or four-room cottages. The individually decorated guest rooms are tastefully appointed with a mixture of contemporary and country decor, and all offer spectacular ocean views. All the rooms feature wood-burning fireplaces; twelve have tubs-for-two or spas. Guests are welcomed in their rooms with complimentary specialty coffees and teas and a bottle of local wine. A full breakfast from the inn's excellent restaurant is served only to guests. The inn's popular cliff-top restaurant is open nightly and boasts a highly acclaimed selection of local delicacies. The front lawn is a popular site for weddings and parties.

PHONE: (707) 937–1919 or (800) 479–7944 (Northern California only)
FAX: (707) 937–2604
WEB SITE: www.albionriverinn.com
FEATURES: inn/cottages; 22 rooms; in-room phones; fax; computer hookups; catering; dinners available; weddings
NEARBY: ocean recreation
INNKEEPER: Debbie Desmond
OWNERS: Flurry Healy and Peter Wells

FENSALDEN

33810 Navarro Ridge Road
P.O. Box 99
Albion, CA 95410

⊘ $$–$$$$

▪ Built originally in the 1860s as a stagecoach stop and tavern, and later used as a farmhouse, this inviting inn is situated on twenty acres of meadowland sweeping downward to the ocean. The inn's Norwegian name translates appropriately to "land of the mist and sea." The B&B is composed of a main house, a separate house near the 1890s water tower, and a

PHONE: (707) 937–4042 or (800) 959–3850
FAX: (707) 937–2416
WEB SITE: www.fensalden.com
FEATURES: inn/cottage; 8 rooms; fax; copier; computer hookups; conference/meeting area; weddings
NEARBY: ocean recreation
INNKEEPER/OWNER: Lyn Hamby

bungalow; balconies and porches face the ocean. The interiors of the B&B are a pleasant melding of antique and traditional decor punctuated with fine art. Special touches in the guest rooms, all with private baths and fireplaces, include handmade pottery sinks and impressive ocean and countryside views. Home-baked breads and muffins, fruit, freshly squeezed juice, and coffee or tea complement the full breakfast and are served in the "Tavern Room." Refreshments are served at sunset in this tranquil and inspiring spot.

ANDERSON CREEK INN

12050 Anderson Valley Way
P.O. Box 217
Boonville, CA 95415

♿ ⊘ $$–$$$

Located on sixteen acres of land at the junction of two streams and surrounded by mountains and grazing llamas and sheep is this quiet ranch-style B&B in Anderson Valley. The five spacious guest rooms, three with fireplaces, offer unique views of the serene countryside, as well as individual and elegant decor. All rooms contain king-size beds and private baths; the suite-size Meadow Room boasts a fire-

PHONE: (707) 895–3091 or (800) 552–6202
FAX: (707) 895–9466
WEB SITE: www.andersoncreekinn.com
FEATURES: home; 5 rooms; swimming pool; pets allowed; family friendly
INNKEEPERS/OWNERS: Jim and Grace Minton

place and opens out to the pool and spa. Complimentary hors d'oeuvres are served each evening. A full breakfast, carefully prepared with fresh ingredients, is provided each morning. Guests can relax in the inn's pleasant main room with fireplace and use the outdoor pool. Tours to nearby wineries can be arranged.

ELK COVE INN AND SPA

6300 South Highway 1
P.O. Box 367
Elk, CA 95432

 $$–$$$$

Beautifully secluded, atop a bluff overlooking a mile of beachfront, is the main house of this B&B inn. The main structure dates from 1883, when it served as the executive guesthouse of the L. E. White Lumber Company. At present, it still houses guests, with three accommodations upstairs in the main house, four luxurious guest suites, and four cabins behind the house. All accommodations have private baths, and there are fluffy bathrobes, down comforters, rocking chairs, and fresh flowers from the garden. The upstairs rooms of this Victorian retreat have dormer windows with 8-foot window seats that reveal spectacular views of the ocean; these rooms share a cozy parlor and roof deck. The cottages all afford ocean views, and most have skylights. The suites, on the main floor of the house, include the Lumber Baron's Suite, which offers both a king-size and twin-size bed, a gas fireplace, and a private entrance off the front porch. A multicourse gourmet breakfast is served in the ocean-front dining room and is highlighted by farm-fresh products. Guests enjoy a secluded beach, numerous scenic trails, a living room with fireplace, and an alfresco hot tub. A Victorian-style gazebo with breathtaking views of the ocean is a popular whale-watching spot. The inn has the luxurious Coastal Day Spa, offering massage therapy and skin treatments.

PHONE: (707) 877–3321 or (800) 275–2967

FAX: (707) 877–1808

WEB SITE: www.elkcoveinn.com

FEATURES: inn/guesthouses; 14 rooms, cottages, spa suites; in-room massage; day spa; fax; computer hookups; catering; meeting areas

NEARBY: beach/ocean; shops; restaurants

INNKEEPERS: Ron Gratzinger and Margaret Sowers

OWNER: David Lieberman

GREENWOOD PIER INN

5928 South Highway 1
P.O. Box 336
Elk, CA 95432

♿ ⊗ $$–$$$$

▓ This eclectic assemblage of eleven bluff-top cottages, set among carefully designed English-style gardens, offers unsurpassed marine views. Isabel invitingly decorates accommodations, mostly suites. All have private baths, two-person Jacuzzi tubs, and private decks; most have fireplaces. The contemporary Cliffhouse boasts a spiral staircase leading to the bath with black marble tub-for-two and a panoramic sea view. The main New England–style house contains the Aerie Suite with marble fireplace, extra sleeping loft, and private deck. The complimentary continental breakfast is delivered to the room. Resident chef Kendrick supervises the restaurant, open for breakfast, lunch, and dinner.

PHONE: (707) 877–9997 or (800) 807–3423
FAX: (707) 877–3439
WEB SITE: www.greenwoodpierinn .com
FEATURES: inn/cottages; 14 rooms/cottages; hot tub; restaurant/lounge; shops; in-room massages; pet friendly; meeting areas; weddings
NEARBY: Greenwood State Beach; seal- and whale-watching; horseback riding; golf
INNKEEPERS/OWNERS: Kendrick and Isabel Petty

GRIFFIN HOUSE AT GREENWOOD COVE

5910 South Highway 1
P.O. Box 190
Elk, CA 95432

⊗ $–$$$

▓ This turn-of-the-twentieth-century inn offers private, cozy cottages, some with views of the ocean and cove. The individual cottages transport guests into the past. Some units feature sitting rooms or decks overlooking the ocean; all have private baths and wood-burning stoves. Breakfast is always unique and features a variety of egg and meat dishes, delivered to the cottage door. Guests receive a complimentary split of wine upon arrival. An Irish pub and restaurant are located on the property.

PHONE: (707) 877–3422
FAX: (707) 877–1853
WEB SITE: www.griffinn.com
FEATURES: inn/cottages; 7 rooms; fax; copier; in-room workspace; computer hookups; catering; pub and restaurant on premises
NEARBY: ocean
INNKEEPER/OWNER: Leslie Griffin Lawson

HARBOR HOUSE INN

5600 South Highway 1
P.O. Box 369
Elk, CA 95432

♿ ⊘ $$$$

The entirely redwood-constructed main building of this 1916 Craftsman-style inn sits on a bluff overlooking a once-busy lumber port. In this tranquil setting accommodations are offered in the redwood structure as well as in adjacent cottages. All guest quarters host private baths and fireplaces and have private-beach rights. Guests at the small inn are served both breakfast and a four-course dinner in the ocean-view restaurant, which has received a *Wine Spectator* Award of Excellence, as a part of the overnight stay, making the B&B a moderate splurge. (The dinners, which include fish from their waters and home-grown vegetables, are available to the public by reservation.) Fragrant flower gardens, vegetable gardens, and the inn's own laying hens add rustic charm.

PHONE: (707) 877–3203 or (800) 720–7474
WEB SITE: www.theharborhouseinn.com
FEATURES: inn/cottages; 6 rooms, 4 cottages; dinner included; in-room heating; in-room massage available; private beach
NEARBY: beach/ocean
INNKEEPER: Ken Krauss
OWNERS: Sam and Elle Haynes

SANDPIPER HOUSE INN

5520 South Highway 1
P.O. Box 189
Elk, CA 95432

⊘ $$–$$$$

This small country inn sits serenely on the edge of rugged bluffs above Greenwood Cove, offering magnificent views of rock formations and the Pacific. Cottage gardens surround the house and lead to a private beach in the cove below. The California Craftsman–style house was built in 1916 by the Goodyear Redwood Lumber

PHONE: (707) 877–3587 or (800) 894–9016

WEB SITE: www.sandpiperhouse.com

FEATURES: inn; 5 rooms; in-room massages

NEARBY: beach/ocean; hiking; Mendocino Village

INNKEEPERS/OWNERS: Althea and Edward Haworth

Company and displays the beauty of redwood construction of days gone by. The interior of the inn is filled with the warmth of redwood paneling and traditional furnishings mixed with antiques. The five guest accommodations all include comfortable sitting areas, queen-size beds with down comforters, feather pillows, fresh flowers from the garden, private baths, and compact refrigerators; all but one suite offer ocean views. The Headlands Room, decorated in shades of ivory, green, and burgundy, is reached by way of winding staircase; guests can walk through French doors onto a private patio with sweeping ocean vistas. The gourmet breakfast, served in the inn's formal dining room, includes fresh fruit and a main course, such as Finnish pancakes or feta zucchini soufflé, served with breakfast meats. A tea cart with home-baked cookies and breads is rolled out each afternoon; evening refreshments include sherry and homemade spiced pecans by the living-room fireplace.

ABIGAIL'S ELEGANT VICTORIAN MANSION

1406 "C" Street
Eureka, CA 95501

⊗ $–$$$$

■ This Queen Anne–influenced Eastlake Victorian mansion is a National Historic Landmark and is well noted for its turn-of-the-twentieth-century opulence and ornate architecture. Built in 1888, the carefully preserved and restored 4,000-square-foot home offers four unique guest rooms to B&B travelers and serves as a living-history museum for the era. Inside, the inn boasts wallpaper from Bradbury and Bradbury, wool carpets, the mansion's original wood trim, gas and electric lighting fixtures, custom-made Lincripta and Anaglypta wall and ceiling coverings, and a mixture of 1890s family antiques and reproduction pieces. A tuxedoed butler and hosts in period attire greet guests and serve afternoon refreshments and ice-cream sodas. The morning fare includes freshly squeezed juice, fruit, cereals, baked

PHONE: (707) 444–3144

FAX: (707) 442–5594

WEB SITE: www.bbhost.com/eureka-california

FEATURES: inn; 4 rooms; massages, sauna available; laundry; air-conditioning; in-room phones; fax; copier; computer hookups; meeting area

NEARBY: historic district; redwoods; ocean

INNKEEPERS/OWNERS: Doug and Lily Vieyra

fruit in sauce, home-baked breads, rolls, and croissants. The innkeeper/chef, trained by four-star chef Jacques Julien, uses only the finest and freshest of ingredients, most of which come from the inn's own organic orchard and garden. Guests enjoy the inn's parlors, library, and sitting room along with its veranda, croquet field, bicycles, and fleet of antique touring cars available for guided tours of historic Eureka. Swedish massages and Finnish saunas are also available in the hospitable inn, as well as complimentary bay cruises and evening shows of vintage films at the mansion. Laundry service is also complimentary. French, Dutch, and German are spoken.

THE CARTER HOUSE

301 "L" Street
Eureka, CA 95501

♿ ⊘ $$–$$$$

▮ This B&B, an enclave of four luxurious Victorians, calls itself "a modern tribute to the

PHONE: (707) 444–8062 or (800) 404–1390

FAX: (707) 444–8067

WEB SITE: www.carterhouse.com

FEATURES: inn; 9 rooms, cottages, suites; in-room phones; in-room televisions (most); in-room VCRs; fax; copier; computer hookups; in-room workspace; catering; meeting/conference rooms; restaurant

NEARBY: historic district; redwoods; ocean

INNKEEPERS/OWNERS: Mark and Christi Carter

splendor of Victorian architecture." The main four-story structure, carefully built in 1991 from 1884 house plans, is just that. Throughout the light and airy interior are choice Victorian antiques, marble and polished hardwood floors, Oriental carpets, contemporary paintings and ceramics, and fresh flowers. The inn's common areas include three open parlors with marble fireplaces and bay windows with inspiring views. The tastefully decorated guest rooms feature down comforters, some carved headboards, and quality antiques; the deluxe suite has a Jacuzzi, separate dressing room, and fireplace. Next door at the Bell House, a restored 1880 Victorian, there are additional luxury suites with whirlpool baths and fireplaces. The full breakfast is a highlight at the inn and is served across the street in the Hotel Carter's main dining room. Specialties might include tarts with various fillings, eggs with sauces, muffins hot from the oven, and garden-fresh breakfast fruits and vegetables. Late-afternoon refreshments and bedtime goodies also tempt guests.

THE DALY INN

1125 "H" Street
Eureka, CA 95501

⊗ $–$$

▥ The stately, white Colonial Revival mansion was built in 1905 by Cornelius Daly, one of the family founders of the Daly Brothers Department Stores. The home has been beautifully restored to its original elegance with four wood-burning fireplaces, Victorian gardens, and a third-floor Christmas Ballroom. The five guest rooms at the inn are furnished with queen or twin beds and turn-of-the-twentieth-century antiques. Annie Murphy's Room, overlooking the Victorian garden and fish pond, was the master bedroom of the Daly home; it contains a fireplace and a French oak bedroom suite ornamented with gold ormolu. The Victorian Rose Suite is a three-room suite decorated with white wicker furnishings and dramatic black floral wall coverings and fabrics; this popular bridal suite includes a bedroom, a sitting room, and a spacious bath. The Guest Room was the Dalys' guest room; the hospitable interiors include a hand-carved bedroom set from Belgium and a bath with the original claw-foot tub. The full breakfast is highlighted by the inn's freshly baked goods and is served in the formal dining room by fireside, in the more casual sunlit breakfast room, or on the garden patio. Wine and hors d'oeuvres are served each evening at the inn.

PHONE: (707) 445–3638 or (800) 321–9656

WEB SITE: www.dalyinn.com

FEATURES: inn; 5 rooms; fax; copier; computer hookups; in-room workspace; meeting area

INNKEEPERS/OWNERS: Donna and Bob Gafford

Tour the "Palaces" of the Barons

Eureka, a lumbering city on Humboldt Bay, is the chief port between the San Francisco Bay and the Columbia River. But the ornate Victorian dwellings that once housed lumber barons make touring Eureka a treat.

Wander the streets of the renovated nineteenth-century Old Town with its interesting shops, restaurants, and art galleries. Three- and six-hour tours of the city's commercial and Victorian residential districts are offered daily all year. For information about the tours call (800) 400–1849 or (707) 445–2117.

For those wanting to go at their own pace, a map is available for driving past more than one hundred vintage residences. For the self-guided tour, call the Greater Eureka Chamber of Commerce at (800) 356–6381 or (707) 442–3738, or log on to www.eurekachamber.com.

HALCYON INN BED AND BREAKFAST

1420 "C" Street
Eureka, CA 95501

♿ ⊘ $–$$

▪ This charming 1920s Craftsman-style home was named in honor of the legendary bird that calmed the winter solstice seas for mariners. After three years of intensive restoration, which began in 1996, the charming home reflects the warmth and love of its owners. All rooms have private baths, queen-size beds, and antiques or reproductions. The Garden View Room also has a terrific view of the bay. The full breakfast might include Belgian waffles or baked-apple pancakes. Afternoon tea/coffee is served on request, and the guest refrigerator is always stocked with soft drinks and water. The home is within easy walking distance of the historic town of beautifully maintained Victorian mansions.

PHONE: (707) 444–1310 or (888) 882–1310

FAX: (707) 444–9010

WEB SITE: www.halcyoninn.com

FEATURES: home; 3 rooms; in-room televisions (2 rooms) and VCRs; computer hookups

NEARBY: forest, ocean, historic Old Town Eureka

INNKEEPERS/OWNERS: Mary and Ike Floyd

HOTEL CARTER

301 "L" Street
Eureka, CA 95501

♿ ⊗ $$–$$$$

▦ A stay at this intimate hotel holds
many surprises. The B&B looks authenti-
cally Victorian, but it is really a 1986
reproduction of an inn that formerly graced Old Town Eureka. The newer version
tastefully blends European country pine antiques with modern-day comforts such as
whirlpool tubs, televisions, and telephones. The individually decorated rooms and
luxury suites boast light and airy color schemes, some fireplaces and views, and an
abundance of artwork. The inn/hotel is noted for its cuisine: both the complimentary
four-course breakfast as well as the din-
ners offered in its renowned restaurant,
Restaurant 301, which specializes in local
seafood. The restaurant operates Thurs-
day through Sunday. The hotel, along with
the neighboring Carter House bed-and-
breakfast, maintains its own organic gar-
dens, providing the produce used in its
gourmet recipes. Guests may take guided
tours of the gardens and, if they wish,
help harvest the vegetables, herbs, and
edible flowers for dinner or breakfast.
The stay at Hotel Carter also includes late-
afternoon wine and hors d'oeuvres.

PHONE: (707) 444–8062 or (800)
404–1390
FAX: (707) 444–8067
WEB SITE: www.carterhouse.com
FEATURES: inn/hotel; 23 rooms/suites;
air-conditioning; in-room phones; in-
room televisions and VCRs; fax; copier;
in-room workspace; computer
hookups; conference/meeting areas;
catering; dinners available
NEARBY: historic district; ocean; red-
woods
INNKEEPERS/OWNERS: Mark and Christi
Carter

OLD TOWN BED & BREAKFAST INN

1521 Third Street
Eureka, CA 95501

⊗ $$

▦ Built in 1871, this pastel-painted
inn was the original home of the Carson family and is the last remaining

structure of the historic Bay Mill. The Greek Revival Victorian was moved to its present location near the Carson Mansion in 1915. The restored inn, which underwent major renovations in 1998 and 2000 (more fireplaces and period wall coverings were added), offers four guest rooms all with private baths; the Lavender Room, the inn's largest, features a king-size brass feather bed with down comforter, a glass-front woodstove, a private bath with claw-foot tub and shower, and lots of lavender and white lace. One room can accommodate a family of four. The inn's decor combines period pieces with homey touches. The antique claw-foot tubs are outfitted with bubble bath and "rubber duckies." The inn serves a country gourmet breakfast, with fresh fruit, French toast, and Southwest bread pudding, served family-style around the antique oak table; coffee, tea, and baked goods are available in late afternoon.

PHONE: (707) 443–5235 or (888) 508–5235
FAX: (707) 442–4390
WEB SITE: www.oldtownbnb.com
FEATURES: inn; 4 rooms; in-room televisions and VCRs; in-room workspace; fax; copier; computer hookup; library
NEARBY: historic district; redwoods; ocean
INNKEEPERS/OWNERS: Steve and Karen Albright

THE SHIP'S INN

821 "D" Street
Eureka, CA 95501

⊗ $$–$$$

▧ Step back in time to those seafaring days in a cozy, relaxing atmosphere befitting Eureka's Victorian seaport, just blocks from Old Town and the new boardwalk. Built in 1882 by a master ship builder for Capt. Samuel Brandt, this gracious Victorian home has a nautical flagpole standing in front as a landmark. Three guest rooms offer distinct decor, from the Mission Room with shades of Frank Lloyd Wright to the garden fantasy of the Rose Garden Room with its bay window overlooking the peaceful view. Each room offers a king or queen bed with cozy down comforters, fireplace, private bath, robes, and a TV/VCR. Breakfast is served in the dining room, or, upon request, have a private

PHONE: (707) 443–7583 or (877) 443–7583
WEB SITE: www.shipsinn.net
FEATURES: inn; 3 rooms; computer hookups; afternoon tea on arrangement
NEARBY: Old Town Eureka; redwoods; ocean
INNKEEPER/OWNER: Genie Wood

breakfast served in your room. Visit the Fireside Room for quiet reflection, relaxation, reading, writing letters, playing games, or listening to soft music. Enjoy the quiet sanctuary of the garden, with a deck and waterfall. A new addition is the peaceful Zen garden. Make reservations for an afternoon tea, with an assortment of teas and delicate tea sandwiches such as salmon and cream cheese, deviled ham, and tuna puffs, served with carrot sticks, Belgian chocolates, and more! An evening reception is held on the first Saturday of each month, featuring the talent and inspiration of a local artist. Meet the artist, enjoy refreshments, and tour the inn. Works are on display throughout the inn all month long and are available for purchase.

THE GINGERBREAD MANSION INN

400 Berding Street
P.O. Box 40
Ferndale, CA 95536

⊗ $$–$$$$

▓ This storybook Queen Anne–Eastlake-style Victorian mansion with turrets, gables, and "gingerbread" galore is surrounded by colorful English gardens. Guests enjoy the turn-of-the-twentieth-century elegance of four parlors with two fireplaces and eleven large and romantic guest rooms, all with private baths. The guest rooms have been outfitted with exquisite furnishings, wall coverings, fireplaces, and Victorian floral carpets. Four feature claw-foot tubs in the rooms. Both the Gingerbread Suite and the Fountain Suite offer two tubs for his-and-her bubble baths! The inn's most opulent offering is the Empire Suite, featuring a marble walk-in shower with three shower heads and five massage sprays. Before-breakfast trays of coffee and tea may be taken into the rooms. A full gourmet breakfast, featuring fruit with Devon cream, is served in the formal dining room overlooking the garden. Guests at this inn are pampered with afternoon tea, cakes, and chocolates; bathrobes and bubble bath; and even boots and umbrellas when it rains!

PHONE: (707) 786–4000 or (800) 952–4136
FAX: (707) 786–4381
WEB SITE: www.gingerbread-mansion.com
FEATURES: inn; 11 rooms; some in-room phones; some in-room televisions; fax; copier; in-room computer hookups
NEARBY: historic district; redwoods; ocean
INNKEEPERS/OWNERS: Robert and Juli McInroy; Vince and Sue Arriaga

THE SHAW HOUSE INN

703 Main Street
P.O. Box 1369
Ferndale, CA 95536

⊗ $–$$$

▓ This gabled, Gothic-style house was built by the town's founder in 1854. The exterior is enhanced by two old-fashioned porches, bay windows, and numerous balconies. Rooms inside are decorated with wall coverings, antiques, art, and memorabilia; all rooms have private baths. The Honeymoon Room offers an unusual canopied ceiling plus a bath with claw-foot tub and shower; the Fountain Suite has a fireplace and parlor. Tea is served by the fire in the library, and the homemade full breakfast is enjoyed in the dining room of the house. Breakfast favorites include mouthwatering scones and French bread pudding with homemade berry sauce. Shaw House, the oldest B&B in California, is listed on the National Register of Historic Places.

PHONE: (707) 786–9958 or (800) 557–SHAW
FAX: (707) 786–9758
WEB SITE: www.shawhouse.com
FEATURES: inn; 8 rooms; in-room computer, modem, and fax
NEARBY: Victorian village; redwoods; ocean; Bear River Casino
INNKEEPER/OWNER: Paula Bigley

THE ATRIUM

700 North Main Street
Fort Bragg, CA 95437

⊗ $$

▓ Located in the heart of historic Fort Bragg, the restored home is surrounded by colorful gardens and decorated in antique furnishings. The nine guest rooms all have private baths and such amenities as down comforters, flannel sheets, CD players, and television/DVDs. Try the Interlude room, a romantic hideaway with a fireplace and king-size bed; the Buttercup

PHONE: (707) 964–9440 or (800) 287–8392
FAX: (707) 964–1770
WEB SITE: www.atriumbnb.com
FEATURES: inn; 9 rooms; special events; newspaper; DVD library; in-room televisions and DVD players
NEARBY: shops; restaurants; downtown Fort Bragg; Skunk Train
INNKEEPERS/OWNERS: Gail Brodkey and Mary Knoerdel

is a cozy under-the-eaves retreat filled with sunshine. Guests are treated to a full breakfast with freshly baked breads, egg dishes, and sausage, as well as evening hors d'oeuvres and wine from Anderson Valley. Guests also enjoy the daily *San Francisco Chronicle* and Sunday *New York Times* newspapers.

AVALON HOUSE

561 Stewart Street
Fort Bragg, CA 95437

⊗ $–$$

PHONE: (707) 964–5555
WEB SITE: www.theavalonhouse.com
FEATURES: inn; 6 rooms; fax; copier
NEARBY: Skunk Train; ocean
INNKEEPER: Jennifer Emigh
OWNERS: Raymond and Amy Neese

This 1905 Craftsman-style house, situated in a quiet residential neighborhood, is just 3 blocks from the ocean and 2 blocks from the popular Skunk Train attraction. The carefully restored home, while maintaining its antique character, has been equipped with modern luxuries and conveniences, such as soundproof walls, adequate bedside lighting, comfortable seating, and modern bathroom fixtures. The six unique guest accommodations, four with fireplaces, are furnished in an attractive mix of antique and willow furnishings. Some feature canopy beds, ocean-view decks, stained-glass windows, and in-room whirlpool baths. Bathrooms, all private, offer extra-thick towels and sparkling tile walls, and several contain whirlpool tubs, dressing tables, and stained-glass windows. A large breakfast is served in the living room and adjoining parlor; the morning fare may include such delicacies as sour-cream pancakes along with sausage, fruit, and home-baked muffins; omelettes with salsa and home-fried potatoes; or eggs, ham, fried apples, and biscuits. The inn's spacious living room is furnished with antiques, lots of paintings, and a cozy fireplace.

CLEONE GARDENS INN

26400 North Highway 1
Fort Bragg, CA 95437

♿ $–$$

Located in a rustic lumbering area, this ranch-style country inn is situated on more than five wooded acres conducive to strolling and relaxation. Guests may swim at the nearby beach and lake. Lodge

PHONE: (707) 964–2788 or (800) 400–2189 (Northern California only)
FAX: (707) 962–0446
WEB SITE: www.cleonegardensinn.com
FEATURES: inn/cottages; 10 rooms/1 cottage; limited smoking; some pets; some in-room phones; in-room televisions; spa
NEARBY: beach; lake; Skunk Train; MacKerricher State Park
INNKEEPERS/OWNERS: James and Barbara Chellberg

guest rooms and suites have private baths and antique accents; some offer fireplaces, kitchens, sitting areas, television, and decks. A separate country cottage and beach house are also available. This lodge "becomes" a B&B establishment with an optional plan of services that can include, along with the full breakfast, an outdoor spa.

This Train Ride Doesn't "Smell"

Except for the passengers' high-tech cameras, a time traveler from the nineteenth century would feel right at home on Fort Bragg's Skunk Train. The view from the restored rail cars is pretty much the same: towering trees, deer drinking from the Noyo River, cabins tucked in the forest.

The Skunk still travels the same coastal redwood route it has since 1885. Built as a logging railroad, the Skunk's original job was to move massive redwood logs to Mendocino Coast sawmills. Steam passenger service began in 1911, but steam was replaced by the gas engine that gave this train its nickname of "Skunk," from the smell originally emitted.

The vintage cars carry passengers along the scenic redwood and Pacific coastline about 40 miles from Fort Bragg on the coast to inland Willits. The halfway point, the town of Northspur, is a popular lunch spot. For reservations and information call (800) 866–1690, log on to www.skunktrain.com, or write Skunk Train, P.O. Box 907, Fort Bragg, CA 95437.

COUNTRY INN

632 North Main Street
Fort Bragg, CA 95437

♿ ⊘ $–$$

PHONE: (707) 964–3737 or (800) 831–5327
FAX: (707) 964–0289
WEB SITE: www.beourguests.com
FEATURES: inn; 8 rooms; dinner/Skunk Train packages
NEARBY: Skunk Train; beach; shops; restaurants
INNKEEPERS/OWNERS: Bruce and Cynthia Knauss

■ The early-1890s home, within walking distance to town and the Skunk Train, has been beautifully renovated. All guest rooms boast king- or queen-size brass or iron beds, private baths (one with an antique claw-foot tub), wall coverings, and colorful touches. Two guest rooms have cozy fireplaces. The redwood sundeck and skylighted sitting room with potbellied stove and art pieces are there for the guests' relaxation. A glass of complimentary wine is served each evening, and morning brings a full breakfast featuring various egg dishes, crepes, and Portuguese toast. The inn offers a special train package, including two nights' stay, dinners, and Skunk Train tickets.

GLASS BEACH INN

726 North Main Street
Fort Bragg, CA 95437

♿ $–$$$

▨ Guests at this homey, centrally located B&B can park their cars and walk to restaurants, shops, beaches, and the Skunk Train. The renovated 1920s home offers uniquely decorated guest accom-

PHONE: (707) 964–6774
WEB SITE: www.glassbeachinn.com
FEATURES: inn; 9 rooms; some in-room televisions and VCRs; computer hookups; hot tub
NEARBY: Skunk Train; beach; shops; restaurants
INNKEEPERS/OWNERS: Nancy Cardenas and Richard Fowler

modations both upstairs and down. The comfortable rooms range from a Victorian attic room to a more conventional space decorated with Asian wicker; all have private baths with shower/tub combinations, and four rooms have fireplaces. The sitting room with reading material and games is the locale of late-afternoon snacks, as well as the full breakfast, which can also be taken in the dining room or bedroom. Guests select from a wide array of breakfast entrees for their cooked-to-order meal. A private hot tub is available to guests.

THE GREY WHALE INN

615 North Main Street
Fort Bragg, CA 95437

♿ ⊗ $–$$$

▨ This stately redwood building has been a Mendocino coast landmark since 1915. The carefully renovated inn boasts beveled glass and interesting local art throughout. The spacious and airy guest rooms offer views of the town and hills or

PHONE: (707) 964–0640 or (800) 382–7244
FAX: (707) 964–4408
WEB SITE: www.greywhaleinn.com
FEATURES: inn; 13 rooms; in-room phones; some in-room televisions; some in-room VCRs; computer hookups; children welcome
NEARBY: ocean; Skunk Train; beaches; shops; restaurants
INNKEEPER/OWNER: Michael Dawson

the ocean, and they have private baths and telephones. A favorite is the Campbell Suite, with fireplace and sitting area. The Sunrise honeymoon suite has a romantic whirlpool tub for two and private deck. Guests gather in the ground-floor game room, in the television/VCR room, and in the lounge with fireplace. The delightful breakfast buffet includes juices; seasonal fruit; homemade, prize-winning coffee cakes; cereal; and a hot entree that changes daily. The inn is close to the ocean and the Skunk Train.

THE LODGE AT NOYO RIVER

500 Casa del Noyo Drive
Fort Bragg, CA 95437

♿ ⊘ $–$$$

This inn, originally built in 1868 as a residence of a lumber baron, reveals the fine woodwork and craftsmanship of the period throughout. Situated on two and a half acres of cypress trees and flower gardens, the B&B overlooks the Noyo River and village and is within walking distance of restaurants and whale-watching. Guest accommodations include spacious, carpeted guest rooms with private baths; antique furnishings; and views (several guest rooms have fireplaces). An attached carriage house contains a king-size bed, skylights, and fireplace. Suites at the inn feature such amenities as fireplaces, oversize tubs, queen-size beds, decks, and step-down sitting areas with ocean views, or sunrooms with river views. The full, American-style breakfast is served in the main lodge building, which has a dining room with a cozy fireplace.

PHONE: (707) 964–8045 or (800) 628–1126
FAX: (707) 964–9366
WEB SITE: www.noyolodge.com
FEATURES: inn/cottage; 17 rooms; some in-room televisions
NEARBY: fishing; whale-watching; river; ocean; restaurants
INNKEEPER: Robyn DeSmith

WELLER HOUSE INN

524 Stewart Street
Fort Bragg, CA 95437

⊗ $$–$$$

The Weller House Inn was built in 1886 and is Fort Bragg's most historic building. The owners have carefully restored it as a luxury bed and breakfast including sumptuous Victorian guest rooms, English gardens, and a reconstruction of the historic 40-foot-high water tower, the tallest point in Fort Bragg. Guests can ascend to the fourth floor of the water tower for whale-watching or for a commanding view of the ocean, town, and mountains. There are two unique guest rooms on the second and third floors of the water tower. The other seven rooms are located in the main house, and the home also features a 900-square-foot ballroom, paneled in rare California redwood, where guests enjoy breakfast each morning. Each guest room is individually crafted with hand-painted tiles, marble, stained glass, fluffy down comforters, and other thoughtful details. All have queen- or king-size beds, private baths, and Victorian appointments, with fireplaces, woodstoves, Jacuzzis, and claw-foot tubs in select rooms. There is a delightful hot tub located on the fourth floor of the water tower where up to six bathers can enjoy a soak. The inn also offers wine in the ballroom every evening.

PHONE: (707) 964–4415 or (877) 893–5537
FAX: (707) 961–1281
WEB SITE: www.wellerhouse.com
FEATURES: inn; water tower; 9 rooms; telephone available upon request; hot tub
NEARBY: shops; restaurants; ocean; Skunk Train
INNKEEPERS/OWNERS: Ted and Eva Kidwell

GREEN APPLE INN

520 Bohemian Highway
Freestone, CA 95472

⊗ $

 This New England–style farmhouse, built in 1862, is located on five acres in a designated historic district. The inn is furnished with some family pieces from the

PHONE: (707) 874–2526
FEATURES: inn; 5 rooms
NEARBY: Russian River; ocean; restaurants; wineries
INNKEEPER/OWNER: Rosemary Hoffman

1700s, and the cheery rooms, which have private baths, look out on the countryside. Guests enjoy a parlor with fireplace and a full breakfast. Recreation is all close by, with many fine restaurants, family wineries, biking, horseback riding, and canoeing available in this spot near the Russian River and the Pacific Ocean.

GUALALA COUNTRY INN

47955 Center Street
Gualala, CA 95445

♿ ⧂ $$

PHONE: (707) 884–4343 or (800) 564–4466
FAX: (707) 884–1018
WEB SITE: www.gualala.com
FEATURES: inn; 9 rooms; in-room telephones; in-room televisions; pets allowed
NEARBY: beaches; ocean; shops; golf; tennis; whale-watching; Fort Ross
INNKEEPERS/OWNERS: Linda and Mike Bradbrook

■ The Gualala Country Inn is situated on the Mendocino coastline, just across the Gualala River from the world-renowned Sea Ranch. The inn overlooks the Pacific Ocean, the Gualala River, and the beach. Accommodations have Pacific Ocean and/or Gualala River views. Oceanside rooms and the cozy parlor have views of crashing waves and a long sandy beach. The inn offers an excellent vantage point to watch the fall and spring migration of the California gray whales. Rooms are tastefully decorated with nostalgic oak furniture, warm comforters, and king- or queen-size beds. All rooms have a private bath and a fireplace. The Sunset Room features a queen-size brass bed, patchwork quilt, ocean and river views, a two-person whirlpool spa, and a fireplace. The Horizon Room offers exciting 180-degree ocean and river views from its hexagonal shape. It features a four-poster queen-size bed with country ginghams and floral bedding in shades of yellow and green. A fireplace and loveseat round out the ambience. Every morning, a complimentary continental breakfast is available in the parlor.

NORTH COAST COUNTRY INN

34591 South Highway 1
Gualala, CA 95445

⧂ $$$–$$$$

■ Overlooking the Pacific Ocean is this cluster of restored redwood

PHONE: (707) 884–4537 or (800) 959–4537

FAX: (707) 884–1833

WEB SITE: www.northcoastcountry inn.com

FEATURES: inn/cottage; 6 rooms; hot tub; antiques shop on premises

NEARBY: beaches; ocean; golf; tennis; whale-watching; Fort Ross

INNKEEPERS/OWNERS: Maureen Topping and Bill Shupe

buildings with rugged shake roofs nestled into a redwood and pine forest. The hillside property that houses the B&B was formerly part of a coastal sheep ranch; below the buildings is a colorful country garden with lawn, brick pathways, and fruit trees. Guest accommodations range from a private guest house with deck, fireplace, skylights, and a four-poster bed to rooms with such details as French doors, fireplaces, beam ceilings, French and European antiques, and ocean-view decks. A favorite room is the huge Southwind, with high beamed ceilings and two 7-foot picture windows for views of the south coast, and a telescope for viewing sea lions and whales. The room features a king-size brass bed and a romantic gas fireplace. All accommodations have private baths and kitchens. Guests at the inn enjoy breakfast served in the room; the full fare consists of a hot entree, fresh fruit, and freshly baked muffins, cinnamon rolls, or croissants. A freshly brewed pot of coffee is also included in the morning meal, but all guest rooms are stocked with a coffeemaker, coffee, tea, and juice. A favorite spot at the inn is the upper garden at the top of the hill, surrounded by towering pines and offering ocean vistas. Guests relax in the soothing, warm waters of a private hot tub under a towering pine.

ST. ORRES

36601 South Highway 1
P.O. Box 523
Gualala, CA 95445

♿ $–$$$$

▣ Inspired by Russian architecture and constructed of one-hundred-year-old timbers, the inn with restaurant is a coastal sanctuary and unique B&B offering. Accommodations include eight rooms in

PHONE: (707) 884–3303

FAX: (707) 884–1840

WEB SITE: www.saintorres.com

FEATURES: inn/cottages; 8 rooms, 13 cottages; hot tub; sauna; restaurant on premises

NEARBY: ocean

INNKEEPERS: Ken Call, Mary Wetterstrom, and Melissa

OWNERS: Eric and Ted Black, and Rosemary Campiformio

the inn, each with double bed and handmade quilt and some with stained-glass windows, ocean views, and balconies; these rooms share three baths (his/hers/ours) with dual shower. The inn also offers thirteen cottages. Each of the cottages offers a wet bar, refrigerator, coffeemaker, queen- and king-size beds, one or more full baths, and fireplace; they also enjoy use of the exclusive creekside spa area with hot tub, sauna, and sundeck. A full breakfast is included in the stay, and dinner is available in the restaurant.

WHALE WATCH INN

35100 Highway 1
Gualala, CA 95445

♿ ⊘ $$$–$$$$

PHONE: (707) 884–3667 or (800) 942–5342
FAX: (707) 884–4815
WEB SITE: www.whale-watch.com
FEATURES: inn; 18 rooms; private beach; spa; fax; telephones available
NEARBY: ocean; beach
INNKEEPERS/OWNERS: Jim and Kazuko Popplewell

▪ This elegant, contemporary inn is perched on a cliff 90 feet above the Pacific Ocean, with breathtaking ocean views from the deck of each guest room, all with fireplaces. A private stairway leads guests to the ½-mile-long sandy Anchor Bay beach below, where they may stroll or investigate tidal pools. Eight of the suites at Whale Watch provide two-person whirlpool tubs, some with ocean views; skylights will please stargazers. The Golden Voyage Suite includes a large living room with free-standing Swedish-style fireplace, kitchen, floor-to-ceiling windows, and a spacious deck. A full hot breakfast is delivered to the room each morning and always includes homemade breads, fresh fruit, and freshly squeezed juice. The hot entree varies, but might be mushroom phyllo turnovers or a green-chile frittata. Guests enjoy the lounge with ocean views, and wine and cheese is served on Saturday from 5:00 to 7:00 P.M.

APPLEWOOD INN & RESTAURANT

13555 Highway 116
Pocket Canyon
near Guerneville, CA 95446

♿ ⊘ $$$–$$$$

▪ The three-story, Mission Revival country home, a Sonoma County Historical Landmark, sits on six acres with redwood groves, gardens, and apple orchards; the grounds feature a large, terraced heated pool and spa. The 1922-built stucco structure with tile roof offers nineteen guest rooms with private baths, fine antique decor, and queen-size beds; ten have private patios or balconies. Special touches include freshly cut flowers, imported soaps and toiletries, down pillows and comforters, tele-

PHONE: (707) 869–9093 or (800) 555–8509

FAX: (707) 869–9170

WEB SITE: www.applewoodinn.com

FEATURES: inn; 19 rooms; swimming pool; spa; air-conditioning; in-room phones; in-room televisions; fax; computer hookups; meeting areas; restaurant on premises

NEARBY: wineries; ocean; golf; osmosis spa

INNKEEPERS/OWNERS: A. Darryl Notter and Jim Caron

vision, telephones, and evening turndown service with chocolates. The deluxe suites at the inn include such amenities as private courtyards or verandas, and sitting rooms with fireplaces. Common rooms at the inn include a solarium with bay-window views, a great room, and a large formal dining room with French doors opening to the pool and gardens. The lower level of the inn contains a sitting room and library. The full breakfast of juice, French-roast coffee, and specialties such as Grand Marnier French toast with local apple syrup, fresh peaches from the inn's two-acre garden and fruit orchard, or farm-fresh eggs Benedict on grilled ciabatta with fresh spinach and tomatoes is served in the solarium, the dining room, or by the pool. A lavish champagne brunch is served each Sunday morning. Order a specially made picnic basket or cheese board to enjoy a private picnic feast. Dinners and wine are available five nights per week by candlelight in the inn's impressive restaurant; reservations are required.

RIDENHOUR RANCH HOUSE INN

12850 River Road
Guerneville, CA 95446

⊗ $$–$$$

■ This eleven-room country house built at the turn of the twentieth century is within walking distance of the Korbel Winery's champagne cellars. The carefully restored inn offers guest rooms decorated individually in country English and American antiques with quilts, flowers, plants, and decanters of wine; all rooms feature private baths. Guests may stroll under the redwoods, soak in the hot tub, or relax in front of the comfortable living room's fireplace. The country kitchen, for-

PHONE: (707) 887–1033 or (888) 877–4466

FAX: (707) 869–2967

WEB SITE: www.ridenhourranchhouse inn.com

FEATURES: inn/cottages; 8 rooms, 2 cottages; in-room televisions; fax; catering; meeting areas; hot tub; dinners available; pet-friendly

NEARBY: Korbel Champagne Cellars; Russian River

INNKEEPERS/OWNERS: Randi and Randall Kauppi

mal dining room, and garden terrace provide settings for the full, creative breakfast that features a daily hot dish, such as stuffed French toast with mini soufflé, or sweet and gooey treats, such as blackberry cake or peach cobbler.

JENNER INN & COTTAGES

10400 Coast Highway 1
Coast Route 1, P.O. Box 69
Jenner, CA 95450

♿ ⦁ $$–$$$$

▦ This inn, offering a variety of guest rooms, suites, cottages, and vacation homes, is surrounded by 15 miles of sandy beaches and acres of state parkland. Situated at the meeting point of the Russian River and the Pacific, the B&B complex offers hiking, fishing, whale-watching, and canoeing. Guest accommodations, ten with fireplace and spa, have antique and wicker decor, plants, and private baths, and many boast handmade quilts, private entrances, view decks, and woodstoves. Suites include living rooms, six with kitchens. The turn-of-the-twentieth-century Mill Cottage, overlooking a meadow, has a full kitchen and private hot tub. The stay at Jenner Inn includes a generous vegetarian country breakfast served in the inn's Mystic Isle Cafe.

PHONE: (707) 865–2377 or (800) 732–2377
FAX: (707) 732–2377
WEB SITE: www.jennerinn.com
FEATURES: inn/cottages; 20 rooms, 5 cottages; in-room workspace; fax; copier; meeting area; in-room massage; hot tubs; weddings; boccie court; cafe on premises
NEARBY: Russian River; ocean; wineries
INNKEEPER/OWNER: Richard Murphy

AUBERGE MENDOCINO BED AND BREAKFAST (FORMERLY RACHEL'S INN)

8200 North Highway 1
Little River, CA 95456
(P.O. Box 134, Mendocino, CA 95460)

♿ ⦁ $$–$$$$

▦ Located 2 miles south of the town of Mendocino, this inn is surrounded by century-old cypress trees and informal gardens that connect with Van Damme State Park.

PHONE: (707) 937–0088 or (800) 347–9252

FAX: (707) 937–3620

WEB SITE: www.aubergemendocino.com

FEATURES: inn; 9 rooms/suites, 1 cottage; fax

NEARBY: Van Damme State Park; beach

INNKEEPERS/OWNERS: Richard and Kathy Carpenito

Beach trails leading to majestic ocean bluffs run past the inn's back door. The inn is composed of two buildings providing nine unique accommodations. The completely renovated main house was built in the 1860s and encompasses a spacious dining room with fireplace and an upstairs sitting room overlooking the park, as well as five guest rooms, all with private baths; the Parlor Room has its own sitting area with piano and ocean view. The barn building is just across the brick patio from the main house; a blend of contemporary and traditional design, it features a sitting room with fireplace and four guest rooms. The Champagne Suite stands out with its spacious sitting room, private balcony, fireplace, wet bar and refrigerator, and one king- and one queen-size bed. A full breakfast is served in the main house dining room each morning, and sherry, cookies or biscotti, and fresh fruit are offered in the sitting rooms.

GLENDEVEN INN

8205 North Highway 1
Little River, CA 95456

⊗ $$$–$$$$

▓ Unwind at a serene 1867 country estate on a headland meadow overlooking the bay at Little River, just minutes south of historic Mendocino Village. Glendeven offers gracious accommodations and restful gardens surrounded by fields, forests, and nature preserves. Guest quarters are located in the Farmhouse, nearby Stevenscroft annex, the private Carriage House Suite, and the special La Bella Vista guesthouse, all with private baths. The mood is one of casual elegance at this inn. The decor blends finely crafted antiques with well-chosen contemporary arts and crafts. Queen and king beds,

PHONE: (707) 937–0083 or (800) 822–4536

FAX: (707) 937–6108

WEB SITE: www.glendeven.com

FEATURES: inn; carriage house; guesthouse; 12 rooms; hot tub; CD players

NEARBY: Mendocino Village shops and restaurants; ocean; whale-watching

INNKEEPERS/OWNERS: Higgins and Sharon Williams

feather beds, reading areas, CD players, and robes are in every room. Most have fireplaces, private decks, and views of the ocean. The Carriage House Suite, featuring a king-size sleigh bed and two fireplaces, provides two spacious bedrooms, one and a half baths, and a living and dining room. Built in 1999, it accommodates up to five comfortably and may be used for seminars or retreats. A brick terrace and beautiful gardens tempt guests out-of-doors. The spacious sitting area in the Farmhouse, with fireplace and baby grand piano, is the locale for breakfast, or the morning meal may be enjoyed in the privacy of the room. Homemade breakfast offerings such as Colorado chile casserole, corn muffins, and fruit are delivered to your room in a basket or tray. After that, visit the art gallery on the first floor of the old barn, featuring contemporary paintings, ceramics, sculpture, jewelry, and photography by local artists. Golf, hiking, biking, canoeing, horseback riding, and tennis are available nearby. Wine and hors d'oeuvres are served each evening.

THE INN AT SCHOOLHOUSE CREEK

7051 North Highway 1
Little River, CA 95456

⊗ $$–$$$$

▨ This collection of fifteen rooms in nine cottages and an 1862 farmhouse is nestled on eight acres of gardens, meadow, and forest. The original farmhouse has paneled walls and coffered ceilings made of redwood. The inn has offered travelers lodging since the 1930s. The cottages were added from the 1930s through the 1950s. All accommodations have private baths, gas or wood-burning fireplaces, televisions and VCRs, private decks or patios, and mini- to full-size kitchens. The Whale Watch Suite features a four-poster king-size feather bed and a large whirlpool tub set under a large skylight. A full breakfast is served in the lounge when it's too cold to dine on the front porch, which overlooks the ocean. The full buffet breakfast may include scones, popovers, maple pecan granola, quiche, and fruit pudding. Wine and hors d'oeuvres are served in the evening. Guests report seeing a friendly ghost now and then.

PHONE: (707) 937–5525 or (800) 731–5525
FAX: (707) 937–2012
WEB SITE: www.schoolhousecreek.com
FEATURES: inn; 15 rooms/cottages; kitchens; in-room televisions and VCRs; in-room phones; computer hookups; fax; copier; meeting areas; hot tub; in-room spa treatments
NEARBY: village of Mendocino; ocean recreation; whale-watching
INNKEEPERS/OWNERS: Steven Musser and Maureen Gilbert

KRISTALBERG BED & BREAKFAST

715 Pearl Court
Lucerne, CA 95458

⊗ $–$$$

▧ This newer vintage Cape Cod–style house is serenely situated on a hilltop 800 feet above Clear Lake, with 30-mile panoramic vistas of the lake, mountains, and Mendocino National Forest. The interior of the house combines contemporary amenities with Victorian decor; the guest parlor features eighteenth-century Italian furnishings. The B&B

PHONE: (707) 274–8009
WEB SITE: www.kristalbergbb.com
FEATURES: home; 3 rooms; air-conditioning
NEARBY: Mendocino National Forest; Clear Lake; boating; hiking
INNKEEPER/OWNER: Merv Myers

offers three unique accommodations with televisions. The Early American–style master suite offers a balcony for morning coffee, as well as a whirlpool tub. A stay at Kristalberg includes a full breakfast, afternoon cheese and wine, and after-dinner sherry. The morning fare, served in the formal dining room, consists of fruit, granola, home-baked quiche, persimmon bread, and the owner's special muesli. The gracious host, who is fluent in German, French, and Spanish, will cook dinners by request. The surrounding area offers unlimited opportunities for boating, hiking, and horseback riding.

MCCLOUD B&B HOTEL

408 Main Street
P.O. Box 730
McCloud, CA 96057

♿ ⊗ $–$$$

▧ The McCloud Hotel was built in 1916. Through the years, it housed lumber-mill workers in this historic mill town, as well as teachers, visitors, and, in the 1960s, the town's library. The current owner has lovingly restored the hotel, which is on the National Register of Historic Places. Guests enter the hotel B&B through the lobby, which has the hotel's original registration desk and mail cubbies, pine paneling, a fireplace, and overstuffed sofas and chairs reminiscent of the 1930s; games,

PHONE: (530) 964–2822 or (800) 964–2823

FAX: (530) 964–2844

WEB SITE: www.mchotel.com

FEATURES: inn/hotel; 16 rooms/suites; fax; copier; computer hookups; catering; in-room workspace; conference/meeting areas; in-room massages

NEARBY: McCloud River Railroad; McCloud Lake and River; Pilgrim Creek Snowmobile Park; Mt. Shasta Ski Park

INNKEEPER/OWNER: Lee Ogden

books, and a piano provide entertainment. The lobby is also the site of the full gourmet breakfast each morning, many of the recipes derived from the hotel's own cookbook called . . . *with the Emphasis on Breakfast.* Juice, fresh fruit, homemade muffins and breads, and a special entree await; breakfast can be requested in the room. The sixteen guest accommodations include four spacious suites. Each of the L-shaped suites contains a luxurious whirlpool for two and a sitting area; some offer canopy beds and views from the balcony. The spacious guest rooms have private baths, antique vanities, decorator fabrics, and queen-size or twin beds; many have four-poster beds. Many of the guest room furnishings were original to the hotel and have been beautifully restored; all the antique trunks that are used as tables or benches have been gathered from the local area. The hotel provides an afternoon tea with scones for its guests on Saturday. An excursion train in McCloud offers Saturday excursion runs to the ski park and Mount Shasta City; the depot is across the street from the hotel (800–733–2141).

THE MCCLOUD GUEST HOUSE

606 West Colombero Drive
P.O. Box 1510
McCloud, CA 96057

$$–$$$

Giant oaks, pines, and lawns surround this 1907 country inn and restaurant on the lower slopes of Mount Shasta. The entire guest house has been restored to

PHONE: (530) 964–3160

FAX: (530) 964–3202

WEB SITE: www.themccloudguest house.com

FEATURES: inn; 5 rooms; air-conditioning; restaurant on premises; cedar sauna; weddings

NEARBY: Mt. Shasta Ski Park; trout fishing; Shasta Sunset Dinner Train; golf

INNKEEPER/OWNER: Debra Anderson

its turn-of-the-twentieth-century elegance with wall coverings, original chandeliers, claw-foot tubs, and pedestal sinks. Upstairs, the five spacious guest rooms are furnished with antiques, reproductions of brass and white-iron queen-size beds, and original beveled mirrors. Each accommodation has its own bath and a sitting area, which opens to the guest parlor with fireplace and antique billiards table. The full gourmet breakfast of assorted fruit, pastries, juice, and coffee or tea is served in the upstairs parlor, or on the veranda in the summer; sherry may be sipped in the parlor each evening. Four mountain bikes are available for afternoon rides; the inn is only 6 miles from Mt. Shasta Ski Park and near several golf courses and trout-fishing spots.

AGATE COVE INN

11201 North Lansing Street
P.O. Box 1150
Mendocino, CA 95460

♿ ⊗ $$–$$$$

▥ This inn is perched on a bluff above the Pacific Ocean, offering spectacular vistas of the rugged coastline. The main house, built in the 1860s, retains its Victorian flavor; scattered throughout the gardens are the various guest cottages of the B&B. Every cottage (but one) affords views of the ocean and has a fireplace and a private deck. All have private baths, some with oversize tubs or double showers. The country decor includes king- or queen-size four-poster or canopy beds and handmade quilts. In the vintage farm-house guests enjoy a living room with a large brick fireplace and antiques and a breakfast room with dramatic ocean views. The morning meal might include such entrees as croque monsieur, caramelized banana and praline pecan pancakes, French toast, or an omelette with a choice of fillings. The hot dish is accompanied by country sausage or baked ham, home-baked breads, fruit, and juice. Sherry is provided in the room, as well as a copy of the *San Francisco Chronicle*. The house specialty is choco-late walnut raspberry biscotti.

PHONE: (707) 937–0551 or (800) 527–3111
FAX: (707) 937–0550
WEB SITE: www.agatecove.com
FEATURES: inn/cottages; 10 rooms, 6 cottages; in-room televisions and VCRs; workspace; fax; in-room CD players; in-room massages
NEARBY: Mendocino Village; ocean; Skunk Train
INNKEEPERS/OWNERS: Dennis and Nancy Freeze

BREWERY GULCH INN

9401 Coast Highway 1
Mendocino, CA 95460

♿ ⊗ $$–$$$$

▪ The original 1860s-built white farm-house has been retired, and a spectacular ten-room inn now rises close by on the bluffs overlooking Smuggler's Cove. Built in 2001, the distinctive architecture captures ocean views from each individually designed room. Set on ten acres of lushly planted terrain, the inn is built with 150-year-old redwood logs discovered buried in the nearby Big River. The spacious rooms, decorated with the timeless appeal of the Arts and Crafts period, have fireplaces, queen- or king-size beds, Jacuzzis for two, and leather lounge chairs in front of the fireplace; eight have private decks. The gourmet organic breakfast includes fresh fruit, granola, and house-made breads and pastries. The hot dish highlights are croque monsieur made with croissants layered with ham, fried eggs and Mornay sauce, or rolled omelettes. Guests are served wines and hors d'oeuvres in the early evening.

PHONE: (707) 937–4752 or (800) 578–4454
FAX: (707) 937–1279
WEB SITE: www.brewerygulchinn.com
FEATURES: inn; 10 rooms; Jacuzzis; in-room televisions; in-room phones; computer hookups; concierge service; conferences; weddings
NEARBY: Mendocino Village; ocean
INNKEEPER/OWNER: Arky Ciancutti

DENNEN'S VICTORIAN FARMHOUSE

7001 North Highway 1
P.O. Box 661
Mendocino, CA 95460

⊗ $$–$$$$

▪ An apple orchard, flower gardens, School House Creek, and nearby Buckhorn Cove offer relaxation and recreation at this restored 1877 farmhouse. Guest rooms, in three buildings, all have king- or queen-size beds, private baths, and period antiques; six rooms have a fireplace. Rooms offer views of forest redwoods and ferns. A full gourmet breakfast is brought to the room each morning, with hot dishes such as quiche, strata, eggs Benedict, strudel, or frittata.

PHONE: (707) 937–0679 or (800) 264–4723
WEB SITE: www.victorianfarmhouse .com
FEATURES: inn; 12 rooms; fax; pets allowed
NEARBY: creek; ocean
INNKEEPERS/OWNERS: Jo Bradley and Fred Cox

Mendocino: California's "New England"

Nestled against the rugged California coast, Mendocino has long been known as a romantic destination. The architecture of this small community (population 1,000) reflects the New England roots of its earliest settlers. Artists flock here to "create."

The restored 1861 Kelley House is now a historical museum, containing watercolors, photographs, and histories of many of the structures in town. The museum, at 45007 Albion Street, is open to the public, but days and hours vary. Call the Kelley House Historical Museum at (707) 937–5791 for more information.

THE HEADLANDS INN

10453 Howard Street
P.O. Box 132
Mendocino, CA 95460

♿ ⊘ $$–$$$$

This popular inn, overlooking an English-style garden, with its spectacular white-water ocean views, was originally built in 1868 as the town's barbershop and then moved and expanded in later years. Restoration has preserved its charm and added present-day comforts. The seven guest accommodations each feature a queen- or king-size bed, feather beds, down comforters, fresh flowers, village or ocean views, private baths, and wood-burning fireplaces (one unit offers an old-fashioned parlor stove on a raised hearth). Guests may relax in two parlors. The full breakfast consists of fresh fruit, home-baked breads, a hot entree, and beverage served in the room on a tray along with the morning *San Francisco Chronicle*. Afternoon tea and cookies are available.

PHONE: (707) 937–4431
WEB SITE: www.headlandsinn.com
FEATURES: inn; 6 rooms, 1 cottage
NEARBY: Mendocino Village; ocean; the Headlands State Park
INNKEEPERS/OWNERS: Denise and Mitch Hokanson

THE JOHN DOUGHERTY HOUSE

571 Ukiah Street
P.O. Box 817
Mendocino, CA 95460

⊗ $$–$$$$

Nestled in the village of Mendocino, the John Dougherty House is one of the oldest houses in town. Built in 1867, the New England–style main house of the inn is decorated in country antiques and hosts impressive views of the ocean and bay. Guest rooms, each with private bath, are located in the main house as well as in the historic water tower on the grounds. The queen- or king-size bed accommodations, which include two suites, are filled with primitive and Early American antiques, fresh flowers from the abundant English garden, and dried-flower wreaths. Most rooms have television, a small refrigerator, and a wood-burning stove. One of the best views in Mendocino can be enjoyed from the Captain's Room, which features a private upstairs veranda, hand-stenciled walls, a woodstove, and a deep tub. The Water Tower suite, located in the water tower, boasts an 18-foot beamed ceiling above the four-poster bed, hand-stenciled walls, and a wood-burning stove in the cozy sitting area. Breakfast comes with a view of Mendocino Bay and the Pacific in the New England–style "keeping" room with hand-stenciled walls and crackling fireplace. The beautifully presented fare, decorated with edible flowers, includes a hot dish such as quiche, fritatta, or sausage rolls served with homemade scones, fresh fruits, almond granola with yogurt, and other cereals.

PHONE: (707) 937–5266 or (800) 486–2104

WEB SITE: www.jdhouse.com

FEATURES: inn; 8 rooms; in-room televisions (some); refrigerators (some)

NEARBY: Mendocino Village; ocean recreation; state parks

INNKEEPERS/OWNERS: David and Marion Wells

JOSHUA GRINDLE INN

44800 Little Lake Road
P.O. Box 647
Mendocino, CA 95460

⊗ $$–$$$$

■ This 1879 home, within walking distance of shops and the beach, is on two acres and offers views of the village, bay, and ocean. Guest rooms, each with private bath, are light and airy and decorated in a New England–country motif with selected antiques. In addition to the inn's accommodations, two guest rooms are located in a cottage and three are in a water-tower building. Most rooms have ocean views and fireplaces. The Watertower I room boasts a redwood beam ceiling, country pine furnishings, and a Vermont Castings fireplace. Breakfast is served each morning at the pine harvest table in the dining room; the full vegetarian fare might include quiche, muffins, and baked pears, along with cereal and fresh fruit. Each day after 4:00 P.M. guests help themselves to home-baked goodies and tea. The inn has its own cookbook for sale, *Mendocino Mornings,* which contains a selection of the inn's breakfast delights as well as local touring information.

PHONE: (707) 937–4143 or (800) 474–6353
WEB SITE: www.joshgrin.com
FEATURES: inn/cottage; 10 rooms; some in-room televisions (on request); some whirlpool tubs
NEARBY: Mendocino Village; ocean
INNKEEPERS/OWNERS: Cindy and Charles Reinhart

MENDOCINO HOTEL & GARDEN SUITES

45080 Main Street
P.O. Box 587
Mendocino, CA 95460

& $–$$$$

■ The historic hotel, established in 1878 and on the National Register of Historic Places, offers elegantly restored lodging, a restaurant, and a lounge overlooking Mendocino Bay. Four cottages, containing the garden suites, have been added in the English garden overlooking the Pacific Ocean. The guest rooms, some with shared

PHONE: (707) 937–0511 or (800) 548–0513

FAX: (707) 937–0513

WEB SITE: www.mendocinohotel.com

FEATURES: inn/hotel; 51 rooms and garden suites; limited smoking; in-room phones; some in-room televisions; fax; copier; catering; conference areas; room service; restaurant (dinner only)

NEARBY: Mendocino Village; art galleries; whale-watching; ocean

INNKEEPER/OWNER: Tom Kravis

baths, are furnished in Victorian decor with four-poster and brass beds, armoires, and assorted antiques; many rooms contain a balcony, fireplace, or marble bath. Extras at the inn include telephones and televisions. A full complimentary breakfast as well as daily lunch offerings are served in the inn's informal garden room. The inn's intimate and popular Victorian restaurant serves dinner only.

MENDOCINO VILLAGE INN

44860 Main Street
P.O. Box 626
Mendocino, CA 95460

♿ ⊘ $–$$$

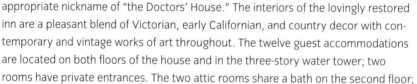

▧ Originally built as a doctor's residence in 1882, the house subsequently belonged to three more doctors and their families, thus receiving the appropriate nickname of "the Doctors' House." The interiors of the lovingly restored inn are a pleasant blend of Victorian, early Californian, and country decor with contemporary and vintage works of art throughout. The twelve guest accommodations are located on both floors of the house and in the three-story water tower; two rooms have private entrances. The two attic rooms share a bath on the second floor; all remaining rooms have private baths. Some guest rooms have ocean views, and most offer fireplaces or wood-burning stoves. The full gourmet breakfast varies each day, with specialties such as herb omelettes and Florentine tortes. Complimentary tea, wine, and hors d'oeuvres are served beginning each late afternoon.

PHONE: (707) 937–0246 or (800) 882–7029

WEB SITE: www.mendocinoinn.com

FEATURES: inn; 12 rooms; meeting area; some televisions and VCRs; pets allowed

NEARBY: Mendocino Village; ocean

INNKEEPER/OWNER: Hank McCusker

SEA GULL INN

44960 Albion Street
P.O. Box 501
Mendocino, CA 95460-0501

♿ ⊘ $–$$$

PHONE: (707) 937–5204 or (888) 937–5204
WEB SITE: www.seagullbb.com
FEATURES: inn; 9 rooms
NEARBY: Mendocino Village; ocean
INNKEEPER/OWNER: Marlene McIntyre

This circa 1878 residence, within walking distance of town, became an inn in the 1960s. A garden lush in fuchsias and featuring a century-old rosemary bush surrounds the quaint inn, which offers nine guest accommodations; a separate "barn" in the garden has a living room, bedroom, sleeping loft, and television. The neat guest rooms, all with nautical names, offer private baths and views of the headland and ocean. A generous continental breakfast, featuring hot muffins or scones, is delivered to your room or to the sunny garden.

SEA ROCK INN

11101 North Lansing Street
P.O. Box 906
Mendocino, CA 95460

⊘ $$$–$$$$

This B&B, on a 70-foot cliff with spectacular white-water views, offers individual cabins set amid a cypress grove. Along with views of the Mendocino headlands, the blue-gray cabins with white trim offer private flower gardens, fireplaces, cable television, and brewed in-room coffee. Some have antiques and kitchens; all rooms have private baths, and two feature whirlpool tubs. The buffet continental breakfast is served downstairs in the breakfast room overlooking the sea or alfresco. Guests enjoy a lawn area and an almost private beach and cove, where they may wade through tidal pools, collect shells, fish for abalone, or watch migrating whales and seals.

PHONE: (707) 937–0926 or (800) 906–0926
WEB SITE: www.searock.com
FEATURES: inn/cottages; 14 rooms; in-room televisions and VCRs; kitchens (some); telephones; fireplaces
NEARBY: ocean; beach; tidal pools
INNKEEPER: Susie Plocher
OWNERS: Susie and Andy Plocher

THE STANFORD INN AND SPA BY THE SEA

44850 Comptche-Ukiah Road
P.O. Box 487
Mendocino, CA 95460

♿ ⊘ $$$$

■ Forests and meadows surround this peaceful lodge on a hillside that overlooks both the town and ocean. The spacious guest rooms, uniquely decorated in country antiques, flowers, and art, feature televisions with VCRs, private entrances and baths, king- or queen-size four-poster or sleigh beds, sitting areas, and wood-burning fireplaces. The gourmet breakfast is served in the dining room; guests choose from items on the menu. A vintage wine awaits guests in each room. The inn, proud of its organic flower and vegetable gardens, offers regular seminars on the subject. The inn has common places for guests to enjoy and relax—dining and living rooms, and an exercise room with aerobic equipment and a weight machine. A stroll around the grounds will also bring glimpses of grazing llamas and the inn's greenhouse-enclosed swimming pool, Jacuzzi, and sauna. Canoes and mountain bikes are available at the inn, as are massages and fine dining in the Ravens, a vegetarian restaurant. The inn also has a spa with a full range of spa treatments, as well as yoga.

PHONE: (707) 937–5615 or (800) 331–8884
FAX: (707) 937–0305
WEB SITE: www.stanfordinn.com
FEATURES: inn; 33 rooms, 9 suites; in-room televisions and VCRs; pets allowed; in-room phones; fax; copier; computer hookups; audiovisual equipment; in-room workspace; catering; conference/meeting areas; swimming pool; Jacuzzi; sauna; exercise room; spa; canoes and mountain bikes available; seminars; the Ravens, a vegetarian restaurant, open daily to the public
NEARBY: Mendocino Village; ocean
INNKEEPERS/OWNERS: Joan and Jeff Stanford

STEVENSWOOD LODGE

8211 North Highway 1
P.O. Box 170
Mendocino, CA 95460

♿ Ⓢ $$–$$$$

PHONE: (707) 937–2810 or (800) 421–2810
FAX: (707) 937–1237
WEB SITE: www.stevenswood.com
FEATURES: inn; 10 rooms/suites; in-room phones with dataports; in-room televisions; in-room workspace; fax; restaurant on premises; spa; in-room massages
NEARBY: Van Damme State Park; ocean sports; whale-watching; bicycling; hiking
INNKEEPERS/OWNERS: Michael Webster and Seth Kelman

■ This award-winning contemporary lodge, built in 1988, is surrounded by the 2,400-acre Van Damme State Park on three sides, with the ocean on the other. The elegant single room and nine suites, most with distant ocean views through huge picture windows, have wood-burning fireplaces, refrigerators, queen-size beds, and modern decor. The complimentary gourmet breakfast changes daily; during your stay you may dine on breakfast tostadas with corn and avocado salsa, wild-rice pecan waffles, tarragon eggs, dried fruit and walnut scones, or quiche soufflé. Guests can enjoy the on-site art gallery, sculpture garden, and private spa in the forest. The lodge's renowned restaurant, with a focus on Mediterranean-inspired cuisine, is open to the public every day but Wednesday.

WHITEGATE INN

499 Howard Street
P.O. Box 150
Mendocino, CA 95460

Ⓢ $$$–$$$$

■ This carefully renovated 1883 house with cottage is located in the heart of the historic district. The five comfortable guest rooms in the house feature fine French and Victorian antiques, king- or queen-size feather beds, private baths, televisions, and many romantic touches; all have fireplaces, many have ocean views. Guests receive a welcome basket of fresh fruit, chocolate chip cookies, and bottled water. The Enchanted Cottage, which can accommodate three, is furnished with a king-size antique French bed and has a private bath with claw-foot tub and shower, a sitting area with daybed, and

PHONE: (707) 937–4892 or (800) 531–7282
FAX: (707) 937–1131
WEB SITE: www.whitegateinn.com
FEATURES: inn/cottage; 7 rooms; in-room televisions; in-room phones; fax; computer hookups; catering; meeting area; weddings
NEARBY: Mendocino Village; ocean
INNKEEPERS/OWNERS: Susan and Richard Strom

French doors leading to a private deck; the French Rose Room was featured in *Sunset* magazine. A full breakfast is served to guests in the dining room each morning and always includes home-baked muffins or scones and, on Sunday, the inn's special caramel-apple French toast. Light hors d'oeuvres and beverages are offered each evening at the inn. Guests relax on the deck or in the gazebo. Weddings are a specialty here.

DREAM INN Best Buy

326 Chestnut Street
Mount Shasta, CA 96067

♿ $–$$

▓ Located just 1 block from downtown Mount Shasta's shops and restaurants, Dream Inn welcomes overnight guests in its homelike setting. The 1904 two-story Victorian is surrounded by rose gardens that host a fish pond and relaxing patios. The totally renovated residence is deco-

PHONE: (530) 926–1536 or (877) 375–4744
FAX: (530) 926–1536
WEB SITE: www.dreaminnshastacity .com
FEATURES: inn; 8 rooms; pets permitted; in-room televisions and VCRs; fax; copier; in-room phones
NEARBY: downtown; Mt. Shasta Resort Golf Course; Castle Lake; Sacramento River; Mt. Shasta Ski Park
INNKEEPERS/OWNERS: Lonna Smith and David Ream

rated with many antiques, the innkeeper's doll collection, and family memorabilia and furnishings. An 1881 piano graces the front room of the inn, as does the "Dream Ship," a model ship found tucked away in an upstairs closet during renovation. Hearts and teddy bears fill the inn; a downstairs suite has a king-size bed and private bath. The four upstairs guest rooms share two baths. Two deluxe suites are located in the house next door. One has a king-size bed, family room, private bath, and a bar; the other has two bedrooms with king-size beds, private bath, living room, dining room, and a full kitchen. The innkeeper-chef provides a notable breakfast by fireside in the dining room each morning. The hearty morning fare includes cereal with fruit, juice, eggs any style or omelettes, pancakes or waffles, homemade hash browns, and toast. Recreation galore awaits in this historic town at the base of Mount Shasta; from the inn take a scenic drive halfway up the slopes of this dormant volcano.

THE INN AT OCCIDENTAL

3657 Church Street
P.O. Box 857
Occidental, CA 95465

♿ $$$–$$$$

PHONE: (707) 874–1047 or (800) 522–6324
FAX: (707) 874–1078
WEB SITE: www.innatoccidental.com
FEATURES: inn; 16 rooms/suites; in-room phones; in-room televisions on request; catering; weddings; conference/meeting areas
NEARBY: osmosis enzyme baths; wine-tasting; beach recreation; hot-air balloons
INNKEEPERS/OWNERS: Jerry and Tina Wolsborn

When the innkeepers decided to remodel this former Heart's Desire Inn in 1994 into a first-class B&B establishment, they brought their own impressive eighteenth- and nineteenth-century collection of clocks, plates, Japanese ivory, antiques, and artwork; even some of the beds are family heirlooms. The beautiful Victorian was built in 1887 as a residence and later became the site of the Occidental Water Bottling Company. Perched on a hill overlooking the quaint village of Occidental, the inn is nestled privately among redwood trees. The Victorian boasts private baths, spa tubs, fireplaces, rich fir floors, wainscoted hallways, covered porches with antique wicker seating, and exquisite decorator touches such as hand stenciling. The living room of the inn hosts a cozy fireplace; the intimate yellow dining room, with picture-window views of the ornamental grasses and herb garden, is the winter locale of breakfast. Weather permitting, the morning meal is served on the sun-dappled porch with views of the village. The full, sumptuous fare includes fresh fruit, juices, homemade granola and pastries, and a special main entree such as the inn's special creamy polenta with fruit compote, a hearty potato torta, or a frittata of the garden's fresh herbs. Wine and hors d'oeuvres are served in the late afternoon. The guest rooms at Occidental take their color themes from the original art chosen for the room; each accommodation includes antiques, down comforters, feather beds, and views of either the courtyard with English garden or the valley filled with redwoods. The inn's Sugar Suite is furnished with an antique pine king-size bed and has its own private patio overlooking the courtyard and the English cottage garden; a collection of glass made in the nineteenth century to hold the coarsely ground sugar from that era is showcased. The Marble Suite, with a distinctive watercolor of koi fish, also holds a fascinating collection of antique marbles. Dinner arrangements can be made for group functions (up to forty-eight) in the inn's private meeting facility, which has antique pine furnishings and a massive fieldstone fireplace.

PHILO POTTERY INN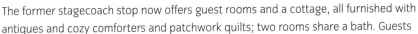

8550 Highway 128
P.O. Box 166
Philo, CA 95466

⊗ $$

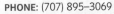 Located in the heart of Anderson Valley wine country in Mendocino County is this historic house, constructed entirely of redwood in 1888. The former stagecoach stop now offers guest rooms and a cottage, all furnished with antiques and cozy comforters and patchwork quilts; two rooms share a bath. Guests may relax in the living room, which has a woodstove and a library. A full breakfast is served in the dining room and features seasonal fresh fruit, a hearty frittata or German apple pancakes, home-baked goods, gourmet coffee, and juices. Sherry and freshly baked cookies are offered in the evening; a complimentary glass of wine is offered at arrival. From the willow furniture on the front porch, guests relax and enjoy the English garden; those with more energetic entertainment in mind can hike through the redwoods or follow one of the challenging mountain-bike trails to the coast. The inn offers cyclists a 12-mile mountain-bike trail and "chauffeur service" to local restaurants.

PHONE: (707) 895–3069
WEB SITE: www.philopotteryinn.com
FEATURES: inn/cottage; 5 rooms, 1 cottage; mountain-bike trail
NEARBY: wineries; hiking; biking
INNKEEPERS/OWNERS: Beverly Bennett and Monika Fuchs

COAST GUARD HOUSE HISTORIC INN

695 Arena Cove
P.O. Box 117
Point Arena, CA 95468

⊗ $$–$$$$

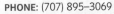 For more than fifty years, this two-story, Cape Cod–style house served as a lifesaving station for Arena Cove, housing the lifeboats and "surfmen" who rescued vessels along the rocky north coast. Today the authentically renovated 1901 house provides gracious B&B stays from its hillside perch with views of the pier and spectacular sun-

PHONE: (707) 882–2442
FAX: (707) 882–3233
WEB SITE: www.coastguardhouse.com
FEATURES: inn/cottages; 6 rooms, 2 cottages; guest phone available; spa
NEARBY: ocean; restored vaudeville house
INNKEEPERS/OWNERS: Kevin and Mia Gallagher

sets. The inn is furnished in a pleasing blend of nautical and Arts and Crafts–style decor; period and contemporary artworks are displayed throughout the house. The guest rooms and suites with private baths offer all-cotton linens and down comforters. All the rooms have themes. The Flag Room, with a nautical theme, has a built-in queen-size captain's bed, reading room, and large old-fashioned tub. The inn also offers two-story Cypress cottage with reading nook, two fireplaces, Jacuzzi, and ocean views; Boat House cottage also has a kitchenette and private patio. Breakfast is served in the dining room overlooking the pier and harbor. A full gourmet breakfast features fresh fruit, yogurt, granola, and a main course of either an egg dish, French toast, or Belgian waffles. The meal is served on authentic Navy anchorware and is garnished with herbs and flowers from the garden. Guests at the inn enjoy an ocean-view spa and the carefully maintained gardens. The nearby Arena Theatre, a renovated 1927 vaudeville house, presents theatrical productions, concerts, and films.

TIFFANY HOUSE BED & BREAKFAST

1510 Barbara Road
Redding, CA 96003

$$

PHONE: (530) 244–3225
WEB SITE: www.tiffanyhousebb.com
FEATURES: inn/cottage; 3 rooms, 1 cottage; swimming pool; local airport transportation arranged
NEARBY: hiking; fishing; swimming; boating; Mount Shasta; Mount Lassen; lakes; golf; tennis; river rafting on Sacramento River
INNKEEPERS/OWNERS: Susan and Brady Stewart

■ This two-story Victorian is nestled on a hilltop among spreading oaks with a panoramic view of the Mount Lassen range. Guests enjoy a shaded deck, a gazebo with hammock, and a refreshing swimming pool. An antiques-filled parlor, as well as the Music Room with piano, have fireplaces and make cozy indoor retreats. The three upstairs rooms have private baths, queen beds, down pillows, sitting areas, and views of Mount Lassen. The Victorian Rose offers a claw-foot tub. Lavinia's Cottage is both secluded and romantic and features a 7-foot spa tub, a laurel-wreath iron bed, and spacious sitting area. Complimentary refreshments are available all day; a gourmet breakfast is served in the dining room or outside in the gazebo.

SAMOA AIRPORT BED & BREAKFAST

900 New Navy Base Road (Eureka Municipal Airport)
Samoa, CA 95564

⊗ $–$$

▦ Lots of B&Bs can claim a beach locale, but no others can also boast residing on an original 1942-built military blimp base. The former base is now home to a small general aviation airport and Samoa's own bed-and-breakfast, which offers four guest accommodations to pilots (and nonpilots) who wing their way to this northern coastal area. The redwood-constructed structure, painted a pristine white, is close to the landing strip and housed up to sixty people during World War II. Now, totally renovated, it offers a comfortable overnight stay for recreational flyers. The four guest rooms, all nostalgically named after military base days gone by, also are decorated with flight memorabilia. The stay at Samoa includes what innkeepers call a "fighter pilot's" breakfast. The ample meal often includes Donald's "love pancakes," fresh fruit, and sausage. Even though the location is very private (a security guard is on sentry twenty-four hours a day!), there is plenty of recreation in the "neighborhood." Take a walk on the beach, eat at the Samoa Cookhouse nearby, whale-watch, ocean fish, or even take a water taxi to your destination of choice. Courtesy cars are available for a nominal fee.

PHONE: (707) 445–0765
WEB SITE: www.northcoast.com/airbb
FEATURES: inn; 4 rooms; in-room phones; airport tie-down and pick-up service; pets permitted (1 room); bicycles
NEARBY: Redwood National Forest; Old Town Eureka; Eel River Discovery Boat Ride; Ferndale; Redwood Sawmill tour; beach; fishing
INNKEEPERS/OWNERS: Shauna and Donald Burrow

SCOTIA INN

100 Main Street
Scotia, CA 95565

⊗ $$–$$$$

▦ Surrounded by redwood-forested hills and nestled along the Eel River, this historic inn has been in operation since 1888. Beautifully renovated, the B&B boasts a polished redwood lobby with comfortable seating and guest rooms, each with private

PHONE: (707) 764–5683 or (888) 764–2248
FAX: (707) 764–1707
WEB SITE: www.scotiainn.com
FEATURES: inn; 22 rooms/suites; in-room phones; in-room televisions; fax; copier; computer hookups; catering; conferences; weddings; wine and gift shop; restaurant, bar
NEARBY: redwood-mill tour; Avenue of the Giants Scenic Drive; Humboldt Bay Wildlife Refuge
OWNER: Pacific Lumber Company

bath. The spacious guest accommodations include king- and queen-size beds, antiques, European silk wall coverings, and original claw-foot tubs. The Bridal Suite features an adjoining Jacuzzi room. The homemade continental breakfast is served in the lobby each morning, and complete dining, cocktail, and banquet facilities are available. Outdoor weddings are a specialty at the inn; up to 300 persons may be accommodated.

THE LOST WHALE INN

3452 Patrick's Point Drive
Trinidad, CA 95570

⊗ $$–$$$$

■ This Cape Cod–style inn with wood-planked floors and country decor was built in 1989 as a B&B inn. The Lost Whale offers spectacular ocean views along with a private beach and 2 miles of private cove. The inn caters to families and offers lots of child-related recreation such as spacious grounds with playground. The inn also provides sleeping lofts, perfect for children (over the age of seven), in two of the suites. Guests may choose from unique suites with private baths, four with ocean views. Stays include a hearty country breakfast of casseroles and quiches, home-baked coffee cakes and scones, fresh fruit, and locally smoked salmon. Afternoon tea with wine, beverages, fresh pastries, and cookies is also served. Guests enjoy an ocean-view hot tub, a wooded-trail stroll to the inn's private cove filled with tidal pools and sea lions, and bicycling over coastal roads.

PHONE: (707) 677–3425 or (800) 677–7859
WEB SITE: www.lostwhaleinn.com
FEATURES: inn; 5 rooms; hot tub; private beach; fax; copier; meeting areas; child friendly
NEARBY: Redwood National Park; hiking; beach; tidal pools
INNKEEPERS/OWNERS: Guia and Gary Hiegert

SANFORD HOUSE

306 South Pine Street
Ukiah, CA 95482

 $$

 In the heart of the Mendocino Wine
Country is this 1904-built Queen
Anne–Victorian home that was the resi-
dence of Senator John Sanford and his
family until 1944. A rare bird's-eye-maple
fireplace warms the antiques-filled parlor of the inn. Also, the library is a popular
gathering spot with its cozy window seat. The five individually decorated guest
rooms, all named after presidents who served between 1904 and 1928, are located
upstairs and feature quaint print wall coverings, fresh flowers, antique decor, and pri-
vate baths. A chilled bottle of local wine, lemonade, iced tea, and fresh cookies greet
guests upon arrival. The complimentary full breakfast is served in the dining room on
fine china and crystal; the fare includes fresh seasonal fruit, homemade breads and
muffins, pestos and sauces, and a hot entree of farm-fresh eggs. Guests are encour-
aged to relax on the large porch, furnished with nostalgic wicker furniture, or to stroll
through the flower garden, which has a fish pond.

PHONE: (707) 462–1653
FAX: (707) 462–8987
WEB SITE: www.sanfordhouse.com
FEATURES: inn; 5 rooms; air-conditioning;
portable phones; fax; copier; small
conferences
NEARBY: Lake Mendocino; golfing; fish-
ing; wineries
INNKEEPERS/OWNERS: Bob and Dorsey
Manogue

VICHY HOT SPRINGS RESORT & INN

2605 Vichy Springs Road
Ukiah, CA 95482

♿ $$–$$$$

 A former playground for the rich and
famous, this 1850s spa resort offers historical charm with updated conveniences.
Guests may stay in one of the resort's two
original cottages built in 1854, or in one of
six new one- or two-bedroom cottages (all
eight cottages have kitchens and private
porches). The completely renovated inn
offers seventeen guest rooms with hardwood floors and Waverly floral prints, as

PHONE: (707) 462–9515
FAX: (707) 462–9516
WEB SITE: www.vichysprings.com
FEATURES: inn/cottages; 28 rooms, 8
cottages; air-conditioning; in-room
phones; spa; mineral baths; mineral
swimming pool; fax; copier; computer
hookups; in-room workspace; audiovisual equipment; catering; conferences;
massages
NEARBY: hiking; biking; all spa offerings
INNKEEPERS/OWNERS: Gilbert and Mar-
jorie Ashoff

well as private baths and phones. The buffet breakfast includes local pastries and fresh fruit. Guests can use the carbonated mineral baths and mineral swimming pool, and enjoy the 700-acre grounds for hiking, picnicking, mountain biking, and nature explorations. The resort's famous grotto, offering sparkling "champagne" baths from effervescent, 90°F mineral waters, is its special attraction. Massages are available at an additional cost.

HOWARD CREEK RANCH

40501 North Highway 1
P.O. Box 121
Westport, CA 95488

⊗ $–$$

▨ Rolling mountains, wide sandy beaches, and tranquility surround this ranch, which was first settled in 1867. The farmhouse and cottages, built in 1871, sit on forty acres of land, encompassing beach, mountain, creek, pond, lawn, and flower garden. A small herd of deer, llamas, porcupines, foxes, raccoons, and an occasional elk and bobcat frequent the property, which also hosts horses for feeding and petting; a naturalist offers tours of the grounds. The inn's antiques-furnished guest rooms and cottages are scented with homemade potpourri and offer views of the surrounding scenery; some have fireplaces. Suites and cabins have microwave ovens and refrigerators; most have private baths. Guests enjoy late-afternoon refreshments, including teas made with herbs from the garden. A hearty ranch breakfast of omelettes, bacon, sausage, and baked apples is served in the dining room; vegetarians are accommodated. This unique "health spa" has a hot tub, sauna, and pool set in the mountainside; massages are available by advance reservation.

PHONE: (707) 964–6725
FAX: (707) 964–1603
WEB SITE: www.howardcreekranch.com
FEATURES: inn/cottages; 12 rooms, 4 cottages; pets allowed; refrigerators (some); hot tub; sauna; swimming pool; massages
NEARBY: ocean; beach; Skunk Train
INNKEEPERS/OWNERS: Sally and Charles Grigg

To Ukiah To Lower Lake

Hopland

Cloverdale

Middletown

101

29

Geyserville

128

Healdsburg

Windsor Calistoga

Berryessa Lake

St. Helena

1 Rutherford

SANTA ROSA Yountville

12 12

Glen Ellen NAPA

Sonoma 29

Pacific Ocean

PETALUMA

101 37 80

N

Scale in Miles

0   5   10   15   20

1 80

To San Francisco

CALIFORNIA WINE COUNTRY

Endless fields of grapes that stretch out to picturesque mountain slopes, historic town squares, country roads dotted with quiet communities, natural hot springs, and renowned wineries all define the Wine Country of the Napa and Sonoma Valleys and the Russian River. Add the popular sport of ballooning to vineyard vistas, ideal picnic scenery, lakes, and spas, and this area becomes a natural haven for travelers. This by far is the most popular region for bed-and-breakfasts, and it is no wonder, what with the perfect settings that abound: ranches, wineries, and quiet Victorian towns. The history of the area is apparent in the town of Sonoma, with its plaza and mission, and in Yountville's unusual shopping complex reminiscent of its winery origins, vintage 1870. Calistoga still offers mud baths, mineral-spring spas, and the nearby Old Faithful geyser with its regular eruptions. Country serenity, wine picnicking, and gracious bed-and-breakfast stops throughout— Wine Country is a relaxing and most pleasurable vacation spot.

BRANNAN COTTAGE INN

109 Wapoo Avenue
P.O. Box 81
Calistoga, CA 94515

⊗ $$

▓ This 1860 Greek Revival inn with graceful arches, gingerbread, and original palm tree is the last remaining Sam Brannan–built cottage at his Calistoga Hot Springs Resort and is listed on the National Register of Historic Places. The carefully restored structure is decorated in Victorian country style with light-oak floors, pine furnishings, and white wicker. The six guest rooms and suites boast the original hand-done flower stenciling as well as private baths and entrances, queen-size beds, down comforters, ceiling fans, and central air-conditioning. The elegant parlor is furnished in rose and gray with a grapevine stencil border, etched oval window, cozy fireplace, and decanters of sherry and port. Afternoon tea is served fireside in cool weather, and wine and cheese are served in the late afternoon or early evening. The full made-to-order breakfast is served in the enclosed courtyard under the lemon trees on sunny mornings. The tranquil cottage inn is surrounded by lawns and gardens and is within walking distance of Calistoga's hot springs, restaurants, and shops.

PHONE: (707) 942–4200
WEB SITE: www.brannancottageinn .com
FEATURES: inn; 6 rooms/suites; air-conditioning; off-street parking; refrigerators; some in-room televisions
NEARBY: hot springs; shops; restaurants; wineries
INNKEEPERS/OWNERS: Doug and Judy Cook

CHELSEA GARDEN INN

1443 Second Street
Calistoga, CA 94515

⊗ $$$–$$$$

▓ Within walking distance of downtown, Chelsea Garden Inn is a unique B&B assemblage that is reminiscent of a Mediterranean villa. The corner property is quiet and private, with four buildings that center around a latticed courtyard and garden. The suites are situated in a bungalow-type arrangement around as well as in the main house. The spacious guest suites all offer sitting rooms, queen-size beds, and private

PHONE: (707) 942–0948 or (800) 942–1515
FAX: (707) 942–5102
WEB SITE: www.chelseagardeninn.com
FEATURES: inn; 5 suites; air-conditioning; swimming pool; in-room television; fireplaces (some); in-room workspace; fax; computer hookup
NEARBY: downtown Calistoga; wineries; mineral springs and spas
INNKEEPERS/OWNERS: Gary Venturi, Dave and Susan DeVries

baths and entrances; one unit has a fireplace. The Garden Room on the ground level of the main house has a private entrance, fireplace, and antique rattan furnishings. The social room, with vaulted ceiling, brick fireplace, and library, is a comfortable spot for socializing and hosting the wine and cheese hour each evening. The gardens at the inn provide beauty, relaxation, and recreation. Fruit and walnut trees, along with more than thirty rose bushes, fill the grounds, which also hold the inviting swimming pool. The full breakfast is served in the dining area with bistro-style tables for two or under umbrellas poolside.

COTTAGE GROVE INN

1711 Lincoln Avenue
Calistoga, CA 94515

♿ Ⓢ $$$$

■ If the bed-and-breakfast guest room concept is too intimate for you, or, perhaps

PHONE: (707) 942–8400 or (800) 799–2284
WEB SITE: www.cottagegrove.com
FEATURES: inn/cottage; 16 cottages; in-room televisions and VCR/DVD players; in-room phones; wet bars; refrigerators; air-conditioning; computer hookups; fax; copier; in-room workspace
NEARBY: spas; restaurants; wineries
INNKEEPERS/OWNERS: Valerie and Bob Beck, Larry Williams, Monica Bootcheck, Tom Stimpert, Georgiana Kepner

on this trip you desire some extra privacy or time to work quietly, then the cottages at Cottage Grove Inn might be your choice. Built in 1996, these romantic cottages, nestled in a century-old elm grove, are tucked away yet just a short walk from some first-class spas and restaurants. The site of the resort is the former promenade grounds for the original Brannan resort; two palms mark the site of the original Brannan cottages. The sixteen individually themed cottages—with king-size beds—offer the luxury amenities of wood-burning fireplaces, spacious bathrooms with two-person Jacuzzis, stereos, wet bars, and refrigerators. The tasteful themes, which range from the Audubon to the Architectural, are all carried out by rich textures, subtle color themes, custom-designed fabrics, overstuffed chaise lounges and reading chairs, and skylights that fill the environs with soft, filtered sunlight. The recycled wood flooring, obtained from an old whiskey distillery in Canada, lends a rich yet informal ambience. A stay at the inn includes an expanded continental breakfast, along with the morning newspaper, served in the guest lounge. The innkeepers host a hospitality hour in the late afternoon with local wines and appetizers.

FOOTHILL HOUSE

3037 Foothill Boulevard
Calistoga, CA 94515

⊗ $$$–$$$$

▓ Nestled among the western foothills north of Calistoga is this turn-of-the-twentieth-century farmhouse surrounded by trees and wildlife. The guest accommodations inside are individually decorated with country oak and pine antiques, quilts, and four-poster beds; the spacious suites offer king- and queen-size beds, private baths and entrances,

It "Rains" Hot Water in Calistoga

Calistoga, located at the head of Napa Valley, offers some of California's finest vineyards, but it is also known for being a health resort with natural hot-water geysers, mineral springs, and mud baths.

As a testimony to its underground "heat," an extinct volcano lies north of town. California's own Old Faithful geyser is located in Calistoga and is one of the few regularly erupting geysers in the world. The geyser can be found on Tubbs Lane between Highways 29 and 128.

Old Faithful is fed by an underground river with water temperatures soaring up to 350°F. The eruptions occur about every thirty minutes, for one to two minutes, with spews reaching 60 feet in the air. Self-guided tours are available. The geyser is open daily, and there is a fee for admittance. Picnicking is allowed. Call (707) 942–6463 for more information.

PHONE: (707) 942–6933 or (800) 942–6933

FAX: (707) 942–5692

WEB SITE: www.foothillhouse.com

FEATURES: inn/cottage; 4 rooms, 1 cottage; air-conditioning; in-room televisions and VCRs; in-room workspace; fax; copier; refrigerators; CD players; hot tub

NEARBY: wineries; hot-air ballooning; spas

INNKEEPER/OWNER: Darla Anderson

refrigerators, fireplaces, and air-conditioning. The 1,000-square-foot Quail's Roost cottage has a king-size four-poster, two-sided fireplace, fully equipped kitchen, washer and dryer, two-person Jacuzzi, and an oversize shower facing a waterfall, as well as a private garden. All rooms have televisions and CD players. A full gourmet breakfast, with fresh fruit and homemade breads and pastries, is served in the room, in the sunroom, or on the terrace. Guests may partake of wine and cheese each evening.

MEADOWLARK COUNTRY HOUSE & INN

601 Petrified Forest Road
Calistoga, CA 94515

⊗ $$$–$$$$

▓ Twenty acres of woods, creeks, and mountains surround this country house. Guests of the inn enjoy pastures of horses, pastoral trails, and a large non-chlorinated mineral pool (clothing optional), as well as a spacious and comfortable living room with French windows and a relaxing veranda. The two-story farmhouse, built in 1886, has been completely renovated and is decorated tastefully with country prints and a pleasing

PHONE: (707) 942–5651 or (800) 942–5651

FAX: (707) 942–5023

WEB SITE: www.meadowlarkinn.com

FEATURES: inn/guest house; 7 rooms, 1 guest house; air-conditioning; in-room televisions and VCRs; in-room telephones; pets allowed; swimming pool; fax; copier; small conferences; hot tub; sauna; massages

NEARBY: wineries; hot-air ballooning

INNKEEPER/OWNER: Kurt Stevens

combination of English country pine antiques and Early American furnishings. The guest rooms of the home offer queen-size beds, private baths, old-fashioned-print comforters, and antique touches. The guest house can accommodate up to five persons. Located next to the pool house, it has a private deck, fireplace, and a full kitchen. The inn serves a generous country breakfast of eggs, breads, fresh fruit, and juice each morning; the refrigerator is stocked with refreshments for guests' use. In-house massages are available by appointment.

THE PINK MANSION

1415 Foothill Boulevard
Calistoga, CA 94515

♿ ⊗ $$$–$$$$

▪ This meticulously restored 1875 Victorian home, painted a pale pink, belonged to Aunt Alma Simic, the mansion's last and longest resident owner. Her many and varied collections are reflected tastefully throughout the house: Collections of angels, cherubs, and Victorian and Oriental treasures adorn many of the rooms. The inn offers six guest rooms—two are suites with fireplaces—each with a private bath, king- or queen-size bed, central heating and air-conditioning, and valley or forest views. The corner Angel Room features pieces of the angel collection, a turn-of-the-twentieth-century brass bed, a bathroom with claw-foot tub, and a window seat with views of Mount St. Helens and the Palisades. Guests at the inn enjoy the use of the spacious Victorian parlor, a drawing room, dining room, and breakfast area. The stay at Pink Mansion includes a gourmet breakfast and afternoon wine tasting by the indoor heated pool and Jacuzzi.

PHONE: (707) 942–0558 or (800) 238–7465

WEB SITE: www.pinkmansion.com

FEATURES: inn; 6 rooms; air-conditioning; some pets allowed; in-room televisions and VCRs; indoor heated pool, Jacuzzi; in-room massages and facials; fax; copier; in-room workspace; all conference amenities

NEARBY: spas; wineries; restaurants

INNKEEPERS/OWNERS: Toppa and Leslie Epps

QUAIL MOUNTAIN

4455 North St. Helena Highway
Calistoga, CA 94515

⊗ $$–$$$

▪ This estate sits atop a hill on twenty-six private acres, ten acres of it planted in cabernet vineyards. The contemporary two-story house with abundant skylights and high ceilings was built as a bed-and-breakfast in 1984 and hosts a three–guest-room wing. The 350-foot climb to the gray-stained cedar inn is lined in redwood, madrona, manzanita, oak, and Douglas-fir trees. The forested acreage is also home to a variety of wildlife, including deer, raccoons, squirrels, hummingbirds, and, of course, quail. All three of the guest rooms at the inn contain brass king-size

PHONE: (707) 942–0316
FAX: (707) 942–0315
WEB SITE: www.cjasper.com/websites/quailmtn/index.htm
FEATURES: inn; 3 rooms; air-conditioning; guest fax; vineyard
NEARBY: wineries; restaurants; Calistoga baths and spas; Napa Valley Wine Train; hot-air balloon rides
INNKEEPER/OWNER: Eric Amadei

beds, private baths, and private decks granting forest and vineyard valley views; two offer private entrances. The beds are covered in handmade quilts and goose-down comforters; furnishings include some antiques. A large solarium with lots of sunlight serves both as a common area and breakfast area at the inn. Guests enjoy a full breakfast including French toast or waffles, as well as wine and appetizers each evening. More than 300 wineries and Calistoga's famous hot-water baths and spas are within a few miles' radius of the bed-and-breakfast.

SCARLETT'S COUNTRY INN

3918 Silverado Trail
Calistoga, CA 94515

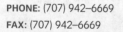 $$–$$$$

■ This intimate retreat with green lawns, woodlands, and nearby vineyards is tucked away in a quiet canyon off the road. The cottage B&B offers two suites and a garden-patio room, all with private baths and entrances. The Camellia suite, with spacious rooms, large windows, and French doors, features antiques, a wood-burning stove, and a wet bar; the Gamay suite looks out over a vineyard and seasonal creek and boasts an old-fashioned claw-foot tub, antiques, and cozy sitting area. Guests enjoy a refreshing swimming pool and a homemade, full country breakfast featuring fresh fruit and a hot entree served under the apple trees, at poolside, or in the room. This hospitable B&B welcomes children; the Gamay and Camellia suites may be combined for families or larger groups.

PHONE: (707) 942–6669
FAX: (707) 942–6669
WEB SITE: www.scarlettscountryinn.com
FEATURES: cottage; 3 rooms; air-conditioning; in-room phones; computer hookup; in-room televisions and VCRs; minirefrigerators; microwaves; swimming pool; hot tub
NEARBY: wineries; restaurants; hot springs; mud baths; hiking
INNKEEPER/OWNER: Scarlett Dwyer

SILVER ROSE INN & WINERY

351 Rosedale Road
Calistoga, CA 94515

♿ ⊘ $$$–$$$$

▪ This twenty-three-acre Wine Country estate enveloped by hills and vineyards provides a serene and hospitable escape. The grounds surrounding the contemporary-style inn are landscaped with rose gardens and flagstone paths. An irregularly shaped pool with adjoining Jacuzzi (both fed by the inn's abundant supply of hot mineral water) is carved out of the rocky hillside; a nearby gazebo, also nestled in the hillside, is a scenic spot to relax. Guests enjoy the Gathering room with huge stone fireplace, tile floors with Oriental carpets, and comfortable seating. Each afternoon inn guests gather here for a "wine and cheese experience," a gala sampling of the innkeepers' extensive wine collection and various cheeses. Guest rooms at the inn are tastefully decorated with creative themes, all with private baths and queen- or king-size beds; many feature fireplaces, balconies, and Jacuzzis for two. The Safari room offers a king-size netted-canopy bed and ceiling fan. The extended continental breakfast provides an abundant supply of fresh fruit and the innkeepers' special home-baked lemon, banana, and zucchini breads; the Hawaiian bread is a specialty. With advance notice guests may arrange for picnic lunches and group lunches or dinners at the inn. The Silver Rose spa facility contains four massage rooms, two hydrotherapy rooms, and mineral water that flows from their wells at 150°F. Spa and wedding/meeting packages are available. The inn has a fine restaurant and winery, with a barrel-tasting tour daily.

PHONE: (707) 942–9581 or (800) 995–9381
FAX: (707) 942–0841
WEB SITE: www.silverrose.com
FEATURES: inn; 20 rooms; air-conditioning; swimming pool; Jacuzzis; tennis courts; chip and putting green; exercise room; spa; in-room massages, facials; day spa; catering; weddings and meetings; picnic lunches; conference rooms; restaurant; winery
NEARBY: wineries; restaurants; hot springs and baths; hiking
INNKEEPERS/OWNERS: J-Paul, Derrick, and Sally Dumont

TRAILSIDE INN

4201 Silverado Trail
Calistoga, CA 94515

♿ ⊘ $$$

▪ This inn has three suites for guests: One attached to the two-story, 1930s

PHONE: (707) 942–4106
FAX: (707) 942–4702
WEB SITE: www.trailsideinn.com
FEATURES: inn; 3 rooms; air-conditioning; kitchens; swimming pool; hot tub
NEARBY: wineries; 3 miles from town
INNKEEPER/OWNER: Lani Gray

farmhouse, the other two within the fifty-year-old barn. All suites are decorated in a country motif with quilts and antiques and offer queen-size beds, fully equipped kitchens, and air-conditioning. Each suite features a fireplace, private entrance, and porch with views of the vineyards. The complete kitchens are stocked with a complimentary bottle of Napa Valley wine, homemade fruit bread, orange juice, butter, milk, granola, mineral water, tea, and coffee for both breakfast and refreshment time. Two units will accommodate up to four people; there is no charge for children under twelve. The inn boasts views of Sterling Winery and lovely gardens; a barbecue is available to guests.

WINE WAY INN

1019 Foothill Boulevard
Highway 29
Calistoga, CA 94515

🚫 $$–$$$

The inn, built in 1915 as a family home, is located within walking distance of shops yet offers deck views of the mountains and forests of the area. Guest rooms, all with private baths and central air-conditioning, are decorated with fine nineteenth-century American and English antiques, and most have queen-size beds. The Calistoga Room, with beamed ceiling, is furnished with a queen-size brass bed and opens to a hillside deck and flower garden. The full gourmet breakfast, featuring such specialties as French toast, omelettes, or quiche, is served in the dining room, on the back deck, or in the intimate gazebo during warmer weather. Guests also enjoy late-afternoon wine and beverages served in the beamed living room or on the back deck.

PHONE: (707) 942–0680 or (800) 572–0679

FAX: (707) 942–4657

WEB SITE: www.winewayinn.com

FEATURES: inn/cottage; 6 rooms; air-conditioning; in-room television and VCR (1 room); fax; computer hookups

NEARBY: shops; wineries; restaurants

INNKEEPERS/OWNERS: Gillian and Nick Kite

ZINFANDEL HOUSE

1253 Summit Drive
Calistoga, CA 94515

🚫 $$

🔲 This home B&B is situated on a wooded hillside overlooking vineyards and the mountains across the valley. Guests choose from three accommodations, all with comfortable beds, goose-down pillows and comforters, and handmade quilts. Two guest rooms share a bath; the private-bath accommodation features a king-size bed and private balcony with views. Fruits, melons, berries, and homemade breads and jellies highlight the morning continental fare served in the sunroom or out on the deck overlooking the valley. The outside deck and the sitting room with fireplace, reading, and music are the gathering spots here; wine and snacks are served in late afternoon. Hiking, jogging, walking, and bicycling trails are abundant. The owner, George, will be happy to put together a personalized itinerary for local winery tours.

PHONE: (707) 942–0733 or (866) 942–0733
FAX: (707) 942–4618
WEB SITE: www.zinfandelhouse.com
FEATURES: home; 3 rooms; air-conditioning; in-room workspace; fax; copier; computer hookups; spa
NEARBY: wineries; hiking
INNKEEPERS/OWNERS: Bette and George Starke

THE SHELFORD HOUSE

29955 River Road
Cloverdale, CA 95425

🚫 $$–$$$$

🔲 Bordering on acres of vineyards is this late-1800s home near the Russian River. The completely restored interiors of this intimate B&B feature king- and queen-size beds, antiques, cozy window seats, quaint wall coverings (on the ceilings, too), and several relaxing niches, including an outside wraparound porch, a game room, a parlor, an upstairs sitting room, and vineyard views from the back door. Those wanting more activity may borrow the inn's

PHONE: (707) 894–5956 or (800) 833–6479
FAX: (707) 894–8621
WEB SITE: www.shelford.com
FEATURES: inn; 7 rooms; air-conditioning; in-room massages
NEARBY: wineries; Russian River
INNKEEPERS/OWNERS: Stan and Anna Smith

"bicycle built for two." The guest rooms offer homemade quilts, antiques, and fresh flowers and plants; all guest rooms have private baths. A full homemade breakfast is included in the stay. Guests may help themselves to refreshments and old-fashioned oatmeal cookies from the kitchen. The inn offers in-room massages. Call ahead or check the Web site for special murder-mystery weekends.

THE HOPE-BOSWORTH HOUSE

21238 Geyserville Avenue
P.O. Box 42
Geyserville, CA 95441

⊗ $$–$$$

This 1904 Queen Anne–style home was earlier called the "Palms" because of the many palm trees that once lined the street. All the guest

PHONE: (707) 857–3356 or (800) 825–4233
FAX: (707) 857–4673
WEB SITE: www.hope-inns.com
FEATURES: inn; 4 rooms; swimming pool; fax; copier; computer hookups; meeting area
NEARBY: wineries; restaurants
INNKEEPERS/OWNERS: Cosette and Ron Scheiber

rooms, with private baths and queen-size beds, are decorated with silk-screened wall coverings, antique light fixtures, and period antiques. A formal dining room is the site of the full country breakfast featuring the innkeepers' prize-winning coffee cake. Beer and wine are sold at the inn. Guests at the inn enjoy a colorful, fragrant Victorian garden and use of the swimming pool.

THE HOPE-MERRILL HOUSE

21253 Geyserville Avenue
P.O. Box 42
Geyserville, CA 95441

⊗ $$–$$$

■ This 1885 Eastlake stick-style Victorian home was restored completely and carefully in 1980 with authentic wall coverings and woodwork and the original Lincrusta-Walton wainscoting. Guests may relax with a glass of wine on the wraparound porch or in the parlor. A five-course country breakfast featuring homemade breads, fresh fruit, and eggs is served in the dining room. Individually decorated guest rooms at the inn feature such varied touches as a fireplace, bay-window views, unusual antiques, Bradbury wall coverings, and antique bath fixtures in the all-private baths, which include two whirlpools. The Sterling suite, with four-poster queen-size bed, has a fireplace and two sitting areas. Guests enjoy a garden swimming pool and a gazebo in the vineyards.

PHONE: (707) 857–3356 or (800) 825–4233

FAX: (707) 857–4673

WEB SITE: www.hope-inns.com

FEATURES: inn; 7 rooms, 1 suite; in-room television (suite only); swimming pool; fax; copier; computer hookups; catering; conference/meeting areas; group dinners

NEARBY: wineries; restaurants

INNKEEPERS/OWNERS: Cosette and Ron Scheiber

ISIS SANCTUARY

20889 Geyserville Avenue
Geyserville, CA 95441

⊗ $–$$$

■ This eight-acre, twelve-room lodge (with shared baths) and cultural retreat center includes a honeymoon cottage with a private hot tub and fireplace, a two-story water tower with a guest room, and a farmhouse that accommodates a dozen guests. The grounds of the informal retreat also host a tepee, a dome, and one wine-barrel room. Guests of Isis enjoy a heated pool, a sauna, and a small zoo with birds and exotic cats, namely ocelots. Breakfast is offered each morning in the dining pavilion.

PHONE: (707) 857–4747 or (800) 679–7387

FAX: (707) 857–3544

WEB SITE: www.isisoasis.org

FEATURES: inn/cottage; 16 rooms; pets allowed; catering; conference areas; theater; swimming pool; sauna; small zoo; bird pond

NEARBY: wineries; Geyser Peak; hiking

INNKEEPER/OWNER: Loreon Vigng

BELTANE RANCH

11775 Sonoma Highway (Highway 12)
P.O. Box 395
Glen Ellen, CA 95442

🚫 $$–$$$$

This 1892 house, with graceful and airy New Orleans–style architecture, is situated on mountain-slope property, shaded by ancient oaks, with sweeping views of the Sonoma Valley vineyards. The active 1,600-acre ranch raises five varieties of wine grapes and olives, and its comfortable guest accommodations all have private baths and entrances. One guest room features a fireplace, and two suites offer separate sitting rooms and the ability to accommodate three guests. A generous breakfast of seasonal fruits and vegetables from the ranch garden; home-pressed olive oil; local eggs, meats, and cheeses; along with views; is served on the porch on warmer days. Guests enjoy a tennis court, volleyball courts, hiking trails, magnificent scenery, and excellent bird-watching and wildlife-viewing.

PHONE: (707) 996–6501

WEB SITE: www.beltaneranch.com

FEATURES: inn/cottage; 6 rooms; no credit cards; tennis courts; volleyball courts; weddings; horseback riding

NEARBY: hiking trails; bird-watching; wineries

INNKEEPER: Ann Soulier

INNKEEPER/OWNER: Alexa Wood

GAIGE HOUSE INN

13540 Arnold Drive
Glen Ellen, CA 95442

🚫 $$$–$$$$

This 1890 Queen Anne–Italianate house on one and a half acres of landscaped garden and oaks was completely renovated in 1981, but the interior of the inn lends its own interpretation of "Victorian"! The innkeeper describes its decor as Asian eclectic. The guest rooms of the inn are located in the original house and in a newer garden annex (with private entrances). All the light and airy accommodations are outfitted with Ralph Lauren linens and down comforters; some feature fireplaces and Jacuzzis. The luxurious Gaige Suite is a favorite with its 12-foot ceiling, windows on three walls, a lacy and canopied king-size bed, fireplace, Jacuzzi, and private balcony that wraps around the

PHONE: (707) 935–0237 or (800) 935–0237

FAX: (707) 935–6411

WEB SITE: www.gaige.com

FEATURES: inn/cottages; 17 rooms, 3 cottages; in-room phones; in-room televisions; computer hookups; off-street parking; swimming pool (heated May–October); whirlpool spa; conference area; air-conditioning

NEARBY: town shops and restaurants; wineries

INNKEEPER/OWNER: Kenneth Burnet

room and looks out onto the garden. In spring through fall the inn grows its own herbs in the garden; a large pool is set in the lawn in the rear garden near Calabasas Creek and is heated May through October. The bountiful breakfast at the Gaige House Inn is an event. The inn's chef, Charles Holmes, whips out such specialties as artichoke and pistachio blini with home-smoked salmon and saffron cream; and an oatmeal, banana, walnut, and raisin soufflé. The inn offers a quality wine hour with premium labels and has a twenty-four-hour cookie supply; concierge service is available. The Gaige House is conveniently situated within walking distance of restaurants on the main road that meanders through town.

GLENELLY INN & COTTAGES

5131 Warm Springs Road
Glen Ellen, CA 95442

⊗ $$$

▓ This B&B was built in 1916 as an inn and was a popular summer retreat for city

PHONE: (707) 996–6720

FAX: (707) 996–5527

WEB SITE: www.glenellyinn.com

FEATURES: inn/cottages; 8 rooms, 2 cottages; spa; fax; copier; computer; in-room televisions; in-room phones; computer hookups in common room

NEARBY: wineries; Jack London State Park; mineral springs; restaurants

INNKEEPER/OWNER: Kristi Hallamore Jeppesen

dwellers in the 1920s. The inn, restored carefully to its original glory, offers to guests once again its long verandas with wicker furniture and common room with cobblestone fireplace and French leaded-glass windows. The eight individually decorated guest rooms in the main house all boast private baths and entrances as well as iron, brass, or four-poster beds (except one trundle unit); Scandinavian down comforters; plush terry-cloth robes; and pleasantly coordinated prints. Two rooms feature fireplaces. The Valley of the Moon room features a queen-size brass bed, a couch, wood-burning stove, and romantic country decor popular with honeymooners. The cottages provide ultraprivacy and romance with fireplaces, king-size beds, and breakfast delivered to the room. The full breakfast buffet is offered each morning on the veranda under a large oak tree or, on chilly days, fireside in the common room. Breakfast specialties include corn-queso-herb soufflé and spinach-prosciutto-feta phyllo tart. Home-baked cookies, lemonade, sun tea, and hot beverages are always available. Guests enjoy a formal garden with an in-ground heated spa.

BELLE DE JOUR INN

16276 Healdsburg Avenue
Healdsburg, CA 95448

⊗ $$$–$$$$

▓ This garden B&B, built circa 1873 in the Italianate style, offers fresh white cottages nestled on six private acres with panoramic views of the countryside. The guest rooms, decorated in antiques, are situated in separate cottages and offer private baths, woodstoves and fireplaces, ceiling fans, refrigerators, and queen- or king-size beds. Special details in some of the accommodations include oversize showers and three whirlpools for two. The carriage house is a spacious second-floor suite with vaulted ceiling, fireplace, sitting area, and whirlpool for two. A sumptuous breakfast is included in the stay; winery touring in a 1925 Star vintage car can be arranged.

PHONE: (707) 431–9777
FAX: (707) 431–7412
WEB SITE: www.belledejourinn.com
FEATURES: inn/cottages; 5 rooms; air-conditioning; in-room phones; in-room workspace; computer hookups; winery tours
NEARBY: wineries; tennis; golf; fishing
INNKEEPERS/OWNERS: Tom and Brenda Hearn

CALDERWOOD INN

25 West Grant Street
Healdsburg, CA 95448

⊗ $$–$$$$

▓ This stately Queen Anne–Victorian, nestled among spruce, cedar, and redwood trees, was built in 1902 and landscaped by the original owner's friend, horticulturist Luther Burbank. The fully restored interiors of the inn are decorated throughout with fine English and American antiques and elaborate,

PHONE: (707) 431–1110 or (800) 600–5444

WEB SITE: www.calderwoodinn.com

FEATURES: inn; 6 rooms; air-conditioning; televisions (on request); fax; copier; in-room workspace; computer hookups; small conferences; weddings; no credit cards

NEARBY: wineries; restaurants

INNKEEPER/OWNER: Susan Moreno

handcrafted silk screen wall and ceiling papers, showcasing the innkeepers' collection of glass and fine art. All six guest rooms have private baths and queen-size beds and boast down comforters and romantic furnishings; one room hosts a whirlpool and another a claw-foot tub and French doors. Two rooms have new fireplaces. A full breakfast is served each morning and features fruit, freshly baked breads, egg dishes, and meat. Guests enjoy a selection of appetizers and sweets each evening. Calderwood is available for group rentals and weddings at group rates.

CAMELLIA INN

211 North Street
Healdsburg, CA 95448

♿ ⊘ $$–$$$$

■ Built in 1869, this Victorian-Italianate town house is just 2 blocks from the town plaza. The guest rooms are decorated in antiques, inlaid hardwood floors, chandeliers, and Oriental rugs. Six rooms feature private entrances, three rooms have whirlpools for two, and four have gas fireplaces. The romantic Tiffany Room features a queen-size four-poster bed, a gas fireplace, hand silk-screened wall coverings, and a whirlpool for two. Guests are encouraged to enjoy the villa-style swimming pool and the double parlors with twin marble fireplaces and ceiling medallions. The full breakfast buffet of fresh fruit, a hearty main dish, nut breads, and juice is served in the dining room. Special gift baskets with chilled champagne, locally made chocolates, and more can be arranged. The owners' award-winning Camellia Cellars Winery

PHONE: (707) 433–8182 or (800) 727–8182

FAX: (707) 433–8130

WEB SITE: www.camelliainn.com

FEATURES: inn; 9 rooms; air-conditioning; swimming pool; gift baskets; fax; catering; small conferences; audiovisual equipment; gift shop

NEARBY: wineries; town plaza; Russian River

INNKEEPERS/OWNERS: Ray, Del, and Lucy Lewand

offers wine and refreshments daily at 5:30 P.M., followed at 6:00 P.M. by wine-tasting. Every Wednesday is Chocolate-Covered Day, with a variety of chocolate surprises.

THE GEORGE ALEXANDER HOUSE

423 Mathison Street
Healdsburg, CA 95448

🚫 $$$–$$$$

▓ This impressive 1905 residence-turned-inn is most notable for its quatrefoil windows on the front and on the tower and for its interesting ornamental details. Nestled in a residential neighborhood, the inn is a short walk from the town plaza. The four guest rooms, two with fireplaces, all feature cotton bedding, queen- or king-size beds, both down and polyester pillows, down comforters, and private baths. The Back Porch room has something for everyone with a wood-burning stove, king-size bed, Jacuzzi for two, and private entrance and deck. The inn's two spacious parlors and formal dining room offer a comfortable, homey feel with period wall coverings, Oriental rugs, a mixture of antiques and contemporary furnishings, and examples of the innkeepers' vast and varied art collection. A full breakfast is offered each morning in the dining room, where guests feast on fresh fruit and juices and a special main course such as lemon ricotta pancakes. Complimentary wine is presented upon arrival; mineral water and juice are available at all times in the inn refrigerator. Guests enjoy the inn's air-conditioning and outdoor patio.

PHONE: (707) 433–1358 or (800) 310–1358

FAX: (707) 433–1367

WEB SITE: www.georgealexander house.com

FEATURES: inn; 4 rooms; air-conditioning; fax; computer hookups; sauna

NEARBY: plaza; wineries

INNKEEPERS/OWNERS: Mel and Holly Schatz

GRAPE LEAF INN

539 Johnson Street
Healdsburg, CA 95448

⊗ $$–$$$

▨ This 1900 Queen Anne–Victorian home has been completely restored and offers guest accommodations with private baths, skylights, and antiques. Five of the guest rooms and suites feature tiled whirlpools for two. The Chardonnay Suite is a spacious two-room suite with four skylight windows, an elegant bathroom with tiled whirlpool for two, a comfortable sitting room, and a separate bedroom with queen-size bed. Five luxurious rooms were added in 2000 in a Victorian-style, antiques-filled attachment; all have fireplaces. Guests read, play games, or just relax in a parlor with antiques and a living room/dining room with fireplace and comfortable seating. The two-bedroom cottage is nestled beneath giant redwoods. Relax on its wraparound deck and take in the panoramic view of the vineyards, or soak in the hot tub and enjoy the stars at night. A full breakfast featuring egg dishes and home-baked breads is served in the dining room. A wine-tasting each evening features a selection of premium Sonoma County wines and is included in the stay. The inn is just 4 blocks from downtown Healdsburg, in a quiet residential neighborhood.

PHONE: (707) 433–8140 or (866) 433–8140
FAX: (707) 433–3140
WEB SITE: www.grapeleafinn.com
FEATURES: inn/cottage; 12 rooms, 1 cottage; air-conditioning; hot tub
NEARBY: downtown shops, restaurants; wineries
INNKEEPERS/OWNERS: Richard and Kae Rosenberg

HAYDON STREET INN

321 Haydon Street
Healdsburg, CA 95448

⊗ $$–$$$

▨ A short walk from the Russian River and downtown shops takes you to this lovely Queen Anne–Victorian home in a quiet residential area. The one-time convent has been meticulously restored to its 1912 vintage, with such period detailing as picture moldings, chair rails and baseboards,

PHONE: (707) 433–5228 or (800) 528–3703

FAX: (707) 433–6637

WEB SITE: www.haydon.com

FEATURES: inn/cottage; 8 rooms; air-conditioning; fax; copier

NEARBY: Russian River; downtown shops, restaurants; wineries

INNKEEPERS/OWNERS: Dick and Pat Bertapelle

stenciling, and wall coverings. The light and airy rooms are furnished in antiques, handmade rugs, and lace curtains, in pastel colors. The cheerful guest rooms feature a favorite of honeymooners, the Turret room with skylights, and all are individually decorated with French and American antiques, dhurrie rugs, Laura Ashley prints, and custom-made down comforters. Claw-foot tubs grace several of the rooms. A bountiful breakfast featuring quiche, croissants, French toast, sourdough egg strata, or omelettes is offered in the large dining room each morning. Two accommodations are located in a separate Victorian-style cottage that boasts pine floors, whirlpools for two with skylights, and romantic lace; one has a fireplace. Complimentary wines, cheese, and other refreshments are served in the early evening.

HEALDSBURG INN ON THE PLAZA

110 Matheson Street
P.O. Box 1196
Healdsburg, CA 95448

♿ ⊘ $$$$

PHONE: (707) 433–6991 or (800) 431–8663

FAX: (707) 433–9513

WEB SITE: www.healdsburginn.com

FEATURES: inn; 12 rooms; air-conditioning; in-room phones; in-room televisions and VCRs; fax; copier; computer hookups; in-room workspace; catering; meeting areas

NEARBY: in town; wineries

INNKEEPER/OWNER: Four Sisters Inns

■ This former 1900-built Wells Fargo building in town now hosts gift shops and the inn's art gallery on the first floor and a gracious B&B upstairs. A grand staircase in the gallery leads guests to the suites of the B&B, all with private baths containing tubs-for-two, antiques, and muted peach, rose, and coral color schemes; most have fireplaces. The Early Light, decorated in creamy butternut tones, resembles a Parisian loft with large, slanted skylight; a corner fireplace; and a lace-covered French door leading to a balcony. A separate carriage house features a heart-shaped whirlpool for two and a kitchenette. All rooms have televisions, VCRs, telephones, and central air-conditioning; a video library is available. Every day guests enjoy complimentary cookies and beverages, as well as evening wine-tasting and popcorn. On weekdays, the morning fare is a generous breakfast buffet of granola, cereals, yogurt, juice, and toast, with hot entrees and fresh fruit served from 8:30 to 9:30 A.M. The weekend and holiday schedule includes dessert wine and chocolates after 8:00 P.M. and a champagne brunch from 9:00 to 10:00 A.M. Guests gather in the inn's solarium.

THE HONOR MANSION

14891 Grove Street
Healdsburg, CA 95448

♿ ⊘ $$$–$$$$

This Victorian-Italianate mansion built by "Squire" William Butcher in 1883 remained in the same family for more than one hundred years. The manor has been lovingly restored and decorated with turn-of-the-twentieth-century grace. The inviting grounds of the inn offer guests a chance to relax amid the colorful gardens with a waterfall koi pond or to take a dip in the swimming pool during summer months. Inside, the parlor fireplace is a popular spot for wine sipping. The guest rooms at the inn, decorated in soft colors, are furnished with carefully selected antiques, thick quilts, feather beds, and fine European linens. The Angel Oak room is highlighted by a hand-painted angel mural and cherub drawer pulls; the airy, spacious bathroom offers a view of a century-old oak tree. The Rose room, in shades of rose and green, has a view of the pool and is distinguished by its fireplace and hand-carved antique furniture. A full, homemade breakfast is served in the dining room each morning and includes freshly squeezed juices, seasonal fruits, home-baked pastries, and a special entree such as carameled-apple French toast or Mansion eggs Benedict. A fully automatic cappuccino machine is available to guests twenty-four hours a day. The Honor Mansion is just a stroll away from Healdsburg's antiques shops, restaurants, and boutiques around the Old Town Square.

PHONE: (707) 433–4277 or (800) 554–4667
FAX: (707) 431–7173
WEB SITE: www.honormansion.com
FEATURES: inn; 13 rooms, 1 cottage; swimming pool (summer use); in-room televisions (some); fax; computer hookups; copier; in-room workspace (some)
NEARBY: Old Town Square shops and restaurants; wineries
INNKEEPERS/OWNERS: Cathi and Steve Fowler

MADRONA MANOR

1001 Westside Road
P.O. Box 818
Healdsburg, CA 95448

♿ ⊗ $$$–$$$$

■ This lavish three-story 1881 Victorian mansion is surrounded by eight acres of wooded and landscaped grounds with a swimming pool. Today, the ornate hotel and gourmet restaurant offer guest rooms and suites decorated in antiques, Persian carpets, and hand-carved rosewood. All rooms have air-conditioning and private baths, and all but three guest rooms have fireplaces. Suite 400, an elegant offering, has French contemporary decor, a private deck, and a bathroom with Greek tiled marble and fireplace. Two elegant suites, added in 2000 in an old schoolhouse, have fireplaces and Jacuzzis for two. The acclaimed restaurant at the mansion has an extensive wine list and serves gourmet candlelit dinners using all fresh ingredients. A full breakfast is included in the stay, featuring sliced meats, imported cheeses, fresh juice, and local fruits.

PHONE: (707) 433–4231 or (800) 258–4003
FAX: (707) 433–0703
WEB SITE: www.madronamanor.com
FEATURES: inn; 23 rooms; air-conditioning; in-room phones; pets allowed; fax; copier; computer hookups; in-room workspace; catering; meeting areas; swimming pool; restaurant; weddings
NEARBY: wineries; town
INNKEEPERS: Maria and Joseph Hadley
OWNERS: Bill and Trudi Konrad

THE RAFORD HOUSE INN

10630 Wohler Road
Healdsburg, CA 95448

⊗ $$–$$$$

■ This 1880s home, formerly the Wohler Ranch, is a beautifully restored Victorian

PHONE: (707) 887–9573 or (800) 887–9503
FAX: (707) 887–9597
WEB SITE: www.rafordhouse.com
FEATURES: inn; 6 rooms
NEARBY: Healdsburg Square; wineries
INNKEEPERS/OWNERS: Diane Pitcher and Rita Wells

farmhouse surrounded by vineyards. The former summer home of Raford W. Peterson rests on a prominent knoll surrounded by palms. The six guest rooms are decorated in period pieces; three have working fireplaces, and all offer private baths. A large front porch overlooks the vineyards and orchards as well as the inn's rose bushes, which number more than one hundred. The hearty country break-fast, with items such as stuffed French toast, is personally prepared and presented by the innkeepers; a twilight sampling of Sonoma County wines and hors d'oeuvres is offered in the sunroom or on the front porch.

HOPLAND INN

13401 South Highway 101
Hopland, CA 95449

🚫 $$–$$$

■ Hopland's founder, William Thatcher, built the elegant late-Victorian manor in the Second Empire architectural style. Listed on the National Register of Historic Places, it underwent a $2 million restoration in the early 1980s. The twenty-one rooms and suites, all with private baths, have views of the surrounding vineyards and mountains. Decorations include taste-ful floral wall coverings, antiques, and

PHONE: (707) 744–1890 or (800) 266–1891
FAX: (707) 744–1219
WEB SITE: www.hoplandinn.com
FEATURES: inn; 21 rooms; in-room phones; computer hookups; air-conditioning; fax; copier; swimming pool; library; restaurant; meeting areas; weddings
NEARBY: Clear Lake; Redwood Empire; Hopland Brewery; hiking; river-rafting; wineries
INNKEEPERS: Sanchia Yonge and Sean Paul Forsha
OWNERS: Hopland Inn, LLC

period pieces; rooms on the second floor have 15-foot ceilings. The Honeymoon Suite has a king-size bed, bay window, and huge bath. The elegant Fireside Library has a marble fireplace, high-backed chairs, and rich wood bookshelves holding more than 4,000 volumes for guests to enjoy. The full gourmet breakfast can be enjoyed in the dining room or alfresco on the garden patio shaded by a 450-year-old oak tree. The inn's restaurant is open to the public for lunch and dinner.

SPIRIT LAKE BED & BREAKFAST

11865 Candy Lane
Lower Lake, CA 95457

🚫 $–$$

■ Solitude and nature surround this small bed-and-breakfast on its own ten-acre estate with a private lake. A haven for fox, deer, heron, and red-tailed hawks in this

PHONE: (707) 995–9090
WEB SITE: www.spiritlakebnb.com
FEATURES: inn; 4 rooms; hot tub; watsu and massages; private lake
NEARBY: lake; town; hiking; glider rides
INNKEEPERS/OWNERS: Elaine Marie and Peter

northern Wine Country area, the inn also offers relaxing massage and watsu tub treatments given by the innkeeper, Elaine Marie. The four spacious guest rooms all offer private baths and pleasant country decor. Downstairs holds a living room with a large library and the dining room, where the bounteous breakfast is served. Not easy to find, the inn is a relaxing escape from city life.

BIG CANYON INN Best Buy

11750 Big Canyon Road
Middletown, CA 95461
(P.O. Box 1311, Lower Lake, CA 95457)

⊗ $

PHONE: (707) 928–5631
FEATURES: inn; 2 rooms; air-conditioning; kitchenette; no credit cards
NEARBY: Clear Lake; Hoberg Airport
INNKEEPERS/OWNERS: John and Debra Wiegand

■ This secluded mountain home on twelve acres of pines and oaks is surrounded by recreational opportunities ranging from wildflower viewing in spring to wine-tasting to boating on nearby Clear Lake. Guests are accommodated in a suite with private porch, entrance, and bath as well as kitchenette, air-conditioning, and cozy woodstove. Accommodations also feature a nice front-porch view overlooking the valley. A continental breakfast of pastry and fruit is served each morning.

Next Stop: Chardonnay

Napa Valley, one of California's most famous wine-producing areas, has its own train that transports visitors through miles and miles of scenic grape- growing areas. The Napa Valley Wine Train makes the 36-mile trip through the heart of Wine Country, departing from its station at 1275 McKinstry Street in Napa.

The Pullman dining cars serve gourmet brunches, lunches, and dinners; the lounge cars are the site of wine-tasting and hors d'oeuvres. The trip is about three hours long, and the cost depends upon the meal of choice.

Reservations are required, and note that the trips are popular. For reservations and information call (707) 253–2111 or (800) 427–4124, or log on to www.napavalley.com/winetrain. For a self-guided tour of the area's many wineries, call the Napa Valley Conference and Visitors Bureau at (707) 226–7459 or e-mail communications@winetrain.com.

ARBOR GUEST HOUSE

1436 "G" Street
Napa, CA 94559

♿ ⊗ $$–$$$$

PHONE: (707) 252–8144 or (866) 627–2262
WEB SITE: www.arborguesthouse.com
FEATURES: inn; 5 rooms
NEARBY: wineries; Napa Wine Train; hot-air ballooning; horseback riding
INNKEEPERS/OWNERS: Jack and Susan Clare

▪ Trumpet vines and hanging fuchsia cover the arbor that connects this award-winning Colonial-transition home and carriage house. A garden motif is featured inside the inn with wall coverings, period antiques, and etched glass. Guest rooms in the main house and in the carriage house are beautifully appointed with antiques, private baths, and queen-size beds. Rose's Bower features a romantic fireplace faced by rose-patterned French chairs; the Winter Haven and Autumn Harvest rooms contain whirlpools for two and fireplaces. Guests are served a three- to four-course gourmet breakfast of fresh fruits, quiche or other egg dish, and baked goods in the dining room, in the carriage house, or on one of the inn's three patios surrounded by fruit and cedar trees. A complimentary glass of wine is offered to guests at check-in.

BEAZLEY HOUSE

1910 First Street
Napa, CA 94559

♿ ⊗ $$$–$$$$

▪ This chocolate-brown mansion with con-

PHONE: (707) 257–1649 or (800) 559–1649
FAX: (707) 257–1518
WEB SITE: www.beazleyhouse.com
FEATURES: inn; 10 rooms; air-conditioning; in-room phones; fax; copier; in-room workspace; catering; meeting areas; weddings
NEARBY: wineries; Napa Wine Train; hot-air ballooning
INNKEEPERS/OWNERS: Jim and Carol Beazley

verted carriage house sits on more than a half acre of landscaped grounds. Its turn-of-the-twentieth-century character is expressed throughout in stained glass, inlaid floors, and antiques-furnished rooms. Some guest rooms feature fireplaces, and the five carriage-house accommodations have private spa tubs. All guest rooms have private baths. The spacious living room is equipped with a tea cart and a refrigerator full of beverages to accompany freshly baked cookies, cheese, and crackers. A full buffet breakfast with hot gourmet treats is served in the dining room each morning.

BLUE VIOLET MANSION

443 Brown Street
Napa, CA 94559

♿ Ⓢ $$$–$$$$

▨ This award-winning B&B is housed in an elegant 1886 Queen Anne mansion, at one time the private residence of an executive of the Sawyer Tannery; his leather-tanning innovations are still evident in the embossed leather wainscoting adorning the main foyer. Nestled on one acre of gardens in a quiet residential area, the inn is within walking distance of Old Town Napa shops and restaurants. Lovingly restored with both Victorian and country ambience, the inn has gained recognition on the National Register of Historic Places. The spacious guest rooms, with queen- and king-size beds, feature fireplaces, fine antiques, and private baths with two-person showers or spas; fourteen units have whirlpools. The Camelot-themed third floor of the inn offers a private lounge, murals, and a wine/beverage bar; a special stay in the Royal suite on this floor includes a king-size bed, painted draperies, faux-painted walls, silver stars on the ceiling, a corner gas-burning fireplace, and a bathroom with a two-person whirlpool. The Duchess's Parlor room on the first floor is a welcoming guest room with fireplace, oak trim, artwork, books, and a king-size flotation bed that faces the inn's redwood trees. Guests relax in the inn's parlors; the front parlor boasts 12-foot ceilings adorned with gold-leafed moldings, a crystal chandelier, and Chinese carpet over polished wooden floors. Guests linger here for a glass of Napa wine, afternoon tea, or late-night desserts. A two-course gourmet breakfast is served each

PHONE: (707) 253–2583 or (800) 959–2583

FAX: (707) 257–8205

WEB SITE: www.bluevioletmansion.com

FEATURES: inn; 17 rooms; air-conditioning; in-room phones; in-room televisions (rental) and VCRs (rental); swimming pool; spa (May–October); fax; copier; computer hookups; catering; conference/meeting area; audiovisual equipment (rental); in-room massages; picnic baskets and dinners; bicycles (rental); weddings

NEARBY: Old Town shops and restaurants; wineries

INNKEEPERS/OWNERS: Robert and Kathleen Morris

morning, featuring juices fresh from the inn's fruit trees, quiches, omelettes, and homemade bread, muffins, and cakes. The grounds of the inn host an old-fashioned veranda, a grape arbor–shaded deck, a garden gazebo, and a swimming pool and spa. The inn prides itself on catering to guests' special needs. They offer an array of extra services that include such luxuries as private, candlelight champagne dinners; in-room massages for two; breakfast in the room with champagne; picnic baskets; flower arrangements; gift baskets; and more.

CEDAR GABLES INN

486 Coombs Street
Napa, CA 94559

Ⓢ $$$–$$$$

▪ Built in 1892 as a wedding gift by English architect Ernest Coxhead, this former home was fashioned after a sixteenth-century English country manor. The Shakespearean-like structure, which consists of more than 10,000 square feet, is framed by massive, vine-covered trees. The guest rooms of the inn are up the winding staircase; accommodations include fine antiques, queen-size beds, chandeliers, and private baths. Some of the guest rooms offer fireplaces and two-person whirlpools. The Churchill Chamber is particularly popular with its high-poster bed and Victorian-style furnishings. The airy Lady Margaret room is a mint- and rose-colored suite with French oak antiques and a wine barrel uniquely mounted as a part of the bathroom furnishings. A gourmet breakfast is served in the sunny dining nook each morning. The main entree changes daily, but the full fare also includes fresh juice and fruit as well as a variety of muffins and breads or the inn's famous French toast soufflé. Guests are invited to wine and hors d'oeuvres each evening in the publike family room that boasts an oversize fireplace and a big-screen television and VCR.

PHONE: (707) 224–7969 or (800) 309–7969

FAX: (707) 224–4838

WEB SITE: www.cedargablesinn.com

FEATURES: inn; 9 rooms; air-conditioning; fax; copier; computer hookups; some off-street parking; weddings

NEARBY: Old Town Napa; Napa Wine Train; hot-air ballooning

INNKEEPERS/OWNERS: Ken and Susie Pope

CHURCHILL MANOR BED & BREAKFAST

485 Brown Street
Napa, CA 94559

♿ ⊗ $$–$$$$

▦ This 1889 mansion built for a prominent Napa banker is now an exquisite B&B escape. The 10,000-square-foot, three-story structure, the first residence in the valley to become a National Historic Landmark, sits amid one acre of expansive lawns, rose gardens, hundred-year-old cedars and redwoods, and molded hedges. The grounds also feature a large fountain. The first floor of the mansion has four grand parlors separated by massive carved redwood pocket doors. The music parlor features a grand piano, and the cozy inner parlor contains puzzles, games, and a big-screen television with VCR and video library. Guest rooms, all with private baths, are scattered on all three floors of the mansion. Each is uniquely decorated with antiques; five of the accommodations have wood-burning fireplaces, and one has a Jacuzzi. Here pampered guests find seasonal fresh flowers, bath amenities, perfumes, and wine glasses in their rooms. Guests are tempted with late-afternoon cookies and beverages in the sunroom with its mosaic tile floor, and evening brings Napa varietal wines and an array of cheeses, fruits, and crackers in the main parlor. The breakfast, served either in the sunroom or on the veranda, begins with a buffet of freshly baked breads and muffins, fruits, and juices followed by a choice of omelettes or French toast. Among the many extra services at the inn are the complimentary use of tandem bikes and croquet in the side garden.

PHONE: (707) 253–7733 or (800) 799–7733

FAX: (707) 253–8836

WEB SITE: www.churchillmanor.com

FEATURES: inn; 10 rooms; air-conditioning; in-room phones; fax; copier; in-room workspace; catering; meeting areas; bicycles; croquet; weddings

NEARBY: wineries

INNKEEPERS/OWNERS: Joanna Guidotti and Brian Jensen

THE COTTAGES OF NAPA VALLEY

1012 Darms Lane
Napa, CA 94558

⊗ $$$–$$$$

▥ This country retreat, on two wooded acres and just a short walk from Domaine Chandon, is composed of eight casual yet luxurious cottages, all individually decorated with California contemporary furniture. Each features a living room with queen sofa bed; bedroom with king-size bed; private bath; kitchen with refrigerator, stove, and microwave; private garden and patio; and outdoor fireplace. Refrigerators in the cottages are stocked with champagne, orange juice, and fresh fruit. In addition to the food in the refrigerators,

PHONE: (707) 252–7810 or (866) 900–7810

WEB SITE: www.napacottages.com

FEATURES: cottages; 8 suites; air-conditioning; in-room televisions; fax; meeting areas; weddings; wine tours; spa services

NEARBY: wineries; bicycle rentals; restaurants; Napa Wine Train

INNKEEPERS: Mary Sandmann-Montes and Mike Smith

OWNER: Mike Smith

a basket of fresh baked goods is delivered to the cottage each morning. The Napa Valley Wine Train passes right next to the cottages, and the inn offers concierge service to arrange outings and wine tours; in-room massages can also be arranged. Rates are available for extended stays.

LA BELLE ÉPOQUE

1386 Calistoga Avenue
Napa, CA 94559

♿ ⊗ $$$$

▥ This Queen Anne–Victorian home, built in 1893, boasts impressive stained-glass windows and has been refurbished throughout with tasteful antiques, Oriental rugs, and fine linens. The rooms all have private baths, some with Jacuzzi tubs, and queen- or king-size beds; several have cozy, working fireplaces. Each evening guests are invited to taste premium vintage wines in the wine-tasting room or cellar. An "outrageous gourmet breakfast" features such items as French toast soufflé, pears poached in wine, or artichoke and cheese frittata. The eye-opening fare is served in

PHONE: (707) 257–2161 or (800) 238-8070

FAX: (707) 226-6314

WEB SITE: www.labelleepoque.com or www.napabelle.com

FEATURES: inn; 9 rooms, 3 suites; air-conditioning; in-room phones; computer hookups; in-room televisions and VCRs; in-room workspace; fax; copier; meeting areas

NEARBY: Napa Wine Train; Old Town; wineries

INNKEEPERS/OWNERS: Lynnette and Steve Sands

the sunny garden room, with its display of blooming orchids and African violets, or in the formal dining room. The full gourmet breakfast is delivered to the inn's suites in Chinese wedding baskets. The inn is located only a few blocks from historic Old Town's shops and restaurants and the Napa Wine Train depot. A twenty-four-hour hospitality bar with snacks, fruits, and beverages is available to guests. Two suites are available across the street at the refurbished Buckley House, built in 1885.

LA RESIDENCE COUNTRY INN

4066 St. Helena Highway
Napa, CA 94558

♿ ⦾ $$$$

◼ This luxurious yet comfortable inn is located on two beautifully landscaped acres and offers accommodations in two structures: the Gothic Revival–style mansion built in 1870 and Cabernet Hall, resembling a French barn. The tastefully appointed mansion rooms are decorated with American antiques and have queen-size beds and private baths; most have fireplaces and sitting rooms. Cabernet suites boast private baths, fireplaces, French and English pine antiques, queen-size beds, designer prints, and French doors leading to patios or balconies. The inn also offers a separate deluxe suite nestled in the vineyard. Included in the stay is a full breakfast, served fireside in the dining room in cool weather, and an evening wine hour with hors d'oeuvres. Guests at La Residence enjoy a heated swimming pool and a Jacuzzi.

PHONE: (707) 253–0337 or (800) 253-9203

FAX: (707) 253-0382

WEB SITE: www.laresidence.com

FEATURES: inn; 20 rooms; air-conditioning; in-room phones; in-room televisions (on request); swimming pool; Jacuzzi; fax; audiovisual equipment; meeting areas

NEARBY: wineries; restaurants

INNKEEPERS/OWNERS: David Jackson and Craig Claussen

MILLIKEN CREEK INN

1815 Silverado Trail
Napa, CA 94558

♿ ⊗ $$$$

▪ A million-dollar renovation of this nine-teenth-century coach house on the Silverado Trail has transformed the former Country Garden Inn into a showplace boutique luxury inn. Secluded behind massive wooden gates, the inn is situated on three acres of mature woodland and riverside property with rose gardens, ponds, fountains, lawns, and secluded trails meandering through the abundant maple trees. All the rooms have spa tubs, fireplaces, king-size beds, Italian linens, robes, televisions with DVD players, phones with dataports, and minibars. Decor is soothing contemporary chic. The inn now offers a separate residence to guests with accommodations for four adults, bakery basket delivered to the cottage, and full use of all inn facilities and spa. The French-style country breakfast can be enjoyed in the room or on the grounds. Guests at this hospitable inn are treated to a wine and cheese buffet in the afternoon. The inn also offers in-room massages, yoga classes, and weekend jazz concerts.

PHONE: (707) 255–1197 or (888) 622–5775
FAX: (707) 255–3112
WEB SITE: www.millikencreekinn.com
FEATURES: inn/cottage; 10 rooms; air-conditioning; fax; in-room massages; aviary; badminton; yoga deck; in-room phones; computer hookups; in-room televisions and DVDs; spa
NEARBY: wineries; restaurants; hiking; hot-air balloons
INNKEEPERS/OWNERS: David Shapiro and Lisa Holt

NAPA INN

1137 Warren Street
Napa, CA 94559

⊗ $$–$$$$

▪ This turn-of-the-twentieth-century Queen Anne–Victorian home is in a tree-lined residential section of town yet convenient to the local winery, shopping, ballooning activities, and the Napa Wine Train, a three-hour excursion on a restored antique train going from Napa to St. Helena and back again. The spacious rooms

PHONE: (707) 257–1444 or (800) 435–1144
FAX: (707) 757–0251
WEB SITE: www.napainn.com
FEATURES: inn; 7 rooms; air-conditioning; in-room phones; computer hookups; in-room televisions and VCRs (on request); fax
NEARBY: Napa Wine Train; wineries; shopping
INNKEEPERS/OWNERS: Brook and Jim Boyer

offer queen- or king-size beds, private baths, and sitting areas; some have fireplaces and whirlpool tubs. Guests enjoy afternoon refreshments in the inn's living room, furnished with antiques, as well as the inn's outstanding collection of memorabilia. A garden cottage with fireplace sleeps up to four. A full breakfast is served in the antiques-furnished dining room each morning.

THE OLD WORLD INN

1301 Jefferson Street
Napa, CA 94559

$$–$$$$

▨ This 1906 home with shady porches and beveled glass contains interior decor inspired by Swedish artist Carl Larrson. A fireside parlor has bright Scandinavian colors and offers soft classical music. The guest rooms, in shades of pale blue, pink, peach, and mint green, feature Victorian and antique furniture, queen- or king-size beds—some with canopies—private baths—most with claw-foot tubs—stenciled walls, and skylights; five guest rooms offer Jacuzzis, and most have fireplaces; one has a Franklin stove. A secluded two-bedroom cottage is in the garden. Special amenities for all guests include afternoon tea and wine in the room upon arrival, international cheeses and wine in the early evening, and a selection of homemade goodies before retiring. The generous buffet breakfast is served in the Morning Room with old-fashioned hospitality; a chocoholic's dream of a dessert buffet is set out before bedtime. Guests enjoy a soothing outdoor spa.

PHONE: (707) 257–0112 or (800) 966–6624
FAX: (707) 257–0118
WEB SITE: www.oldworldinn.com
FEATURES: inn; 9 rooms, cottage; air-conditioning; fax; computer hookups; spa
NEARBY: wineries; shopping; restaurants
INNKEEPERS/OWNERS: Sharon Fry and Russ Herschelman

CAVANAGH INN

10 Keller Street
Petaluma, CA 94952

⊗ $–$$$

▦ This 1902 mansion and adjacent 1912-built cottage compose the Cavanagh Inn; both homes were private residences in this historic downtown area until 1992. The three-story Georgian Revival mansion and the Craftsman-style cottage are nestled on one-third acre of landscaped gardens within walking distance of antiques shops, boutiques, restaurants, and the Petaluma River. The interior walls of the inn are paneled with rare heart redwood, and the decor is formal Victorian. The cottage building of the inn is decorated with a more casual cottage-garden theme, complete with a lush garden mural on the upstairs landing. The seven guest rooms are located in both the main inn and in the cottage annex; many of the beds contain fluffy feather mattresses on twin through king-size beds. The Garden room in the mansion hosts white wicker furnishings, a queen-size bed and twin bed, and a creative faux bookshelf. The innkeepers cater to guests, with bed turn-down service that includes warming the electric blankets and leaving home-baked goodies for a late-night snack. The award-winning chef-innkeeper, Jeanne, makes breakfast a highlight of the stay. Served in the mansion's dining room, the meal might include such delectables as overnight French toast and tasty cardamom pears. Sonoma County wines are poured in the early evening. The balustered back porch overlooks the garden and ancient trees, a favorite locale for special events; the carriage-house annex is available for group rentals or events.

PHONE: (707) 765–4657 or (888) 765–4658

FAX: (707) 769–0466

WEB SITE: www.cavanaghinn.com

FEATURES: inn; 7 rooms; fax; copier; in-room workspace; conference areas; Spanish spoken

NEARBY: Petaluma River; shops and restaurants

INNKEEPERS/OWNERS: Ray and Jeanne Farris

RANCHO CAYMUS INN

1140 Rutherford Road
P.O. Box 78
Rutherford, CA 94573

♿ $$$$

This unique early California–style inn with red-tile roof encircles a small, quiet central garden. The twenty-six guest rooms contain two levels and feature sitting rooms with polished oak floors, wool rugs, comfortable seating, and (in all but four rooms) hand-sculpted adobe fireplaces. Guests step up to the bedrooms, with their black-walnut queen-size beds, other handworked furnishings, and French doors that open to a private garden patio or balcony. All rooms feature hand-hewn beams, eighty-plus-year-old handmade doors, air-conditioning, televisions, telephones, refrigerators, wet bars, and luxurious bathrooms with stoneware basins and hardwood countertops. Four Getaway master suites offer kitchenettes, stained-glass windows, and Jacuzzis. A "hacienda" continental breakfast is served in chef Ken Frank's famed restaurant, La Toque, with an innovative French-California twist; also open Wednesday through Sunday for dinner.

PHONE: (707) 963–1777 or (800) 845–1777
FAX: (707) 963–5387
WEB SITE: www.ranchocaymus.com
FEATURES: inn/hotel; 26 rooms; limited smoking; refrigerators; honor bars; air-conditioning; in-room phones; in-room televisions; fax; copier; restaurant
NEARBY: wineries; biking; shopping
INNKEEPER: Otto Komes
OWNER: the Komes family

ADAGIO INN

1417 Kearney Street
St. Helena, CA 94574

⊗ $$$$

This 1904 Edwardian raised cottage offers a big front porch with mountain views in a quiet residential neighborhood. Guest rooms, furnished with queen- or king-size beds and antiques, and deco-

PHONE: (707) 963–2238 or (888) 823–2446
FAX: (707) 963–5598
WEB SITE: www.adagioinn.com
FEATURES: inn; 3 rooms; air-conditioning; in-room televisions and VCRs; in-room phones; fax; copier; computer hookups
NEARBY: wineries; town; bicycling
INNKEEPER/OWNER: Polly Keegan

rated in soft colors and tension-melting decor, have private baths, some with whirlpools, supplied with plush bathrobes. All rooms have televisions with VCRs; a downstairs room, in lavender and beige, features a separate entrance, private patio, and Jacuzzi for two. The cozy living room offers a fireplace, where each evening wine, hors d'oeuvres, and cheese are served. A full gourmet breakfast with fresh fruit, mango-orange scones, a variety of omelettes, and chicken-apple sausage is served at 9:00 A.M.; both breakfast and refreshments are offered on the large veranda, weather permitting.

AMBROSE BIERCE HOUSE

1515 Main Street
St. Helena, CA 94574

🚫 $$$$

PHONE: (707) 963–3003
FAX: (707) 963–9367
WEB SITE: www.ambrosebiercehouse
.com
FEATURES: inn; 2 rooms, 1 suite; no credit cards; air-conditioning
NEARBY: wineries
INNKEEPERS/OWNERS: John and Lisa Runnells

▓ Vines climb lazily on the 1872-built house that was once the residence of poet, essayist, and witty author Ambrose Bierce. In a residential area with well-tended gardens and lawn, this small B&B inn offers guests a spacious sitting room and bedroom suites named after late-1800s Napa Valley personalities. Each history-filled guest room contains antiques, a queen-size brass bed, an armoire, fireplace, and a decanter of port. The private bathrooms are Victorian, two with Jacuzzi tubs and one with a claw-foot tub and brass fittings. A formal, two-course gourmet breakfast greets guests in the morning with champagne and home-baked breads; complimentary sherry, wine, and cheeses are offered in the evening.

BARTELS RANCH & COUNTRY INN

1200 Conn Valley Road
St. Helena, CA 94574

♿ 🚫 $$$$

▓ This intimate country inn is set within a sixty-acre ranch with vineyard views. The ranch, surrounded by hills, pines, and oaks, offers four guest rooms with private baths, fireplaces, refrigerators, and private entrances. Terry-cloth robes, picnic baskets, and blankets are provided. The guest accommodations are decorated with

PHONE: (707) 963–4001
FAX: (707) 963–5100
WEB SITE: www.bartelsranch.com
FEATURES: inn; 4 rooms; air-conditioning; in-room phones; in-room televisions and VCRs; swimming pool; boccie; croquet; billiards; fax; copier; catering; computer hookups; bicycles
NEARBY: vineyards; town; bicycling
INNKEEPER/OWNER: Jami Bartels

antiques, wicker, and contemporary prints. All rooms have in-room coffee, satellite television and VCRs, refrigerators, and winter fireplaces. The Heart of the Valley Suite features a sunken, heart-shaped Jacuzzi for two; separate shower and sauna; stone fireplace; stereo; and private redwood deck with vineyard views. The Blue Valley room boasts a 12-by-12-foot redwood deck overlooking an oak grove and the Napa foothills. All guests enjoy a microwave, library, movie library, sundeck lounging, barbecue grill, guest refrigerator, and a recreation room with fireplace, billiards, television, and Ping-Pong. Outside there's a boccie court in an oak grove and a croquet lawn. Guests may also sip champagne under the stars by the swimming pool at this romantic retreat. A full breakfast is served until noon, and evening tea, hors d'oeuvres, and dessert are included in the stay; after-dinner popcorn is also offered. Ten-speed and tandem bicycles are available, and the hospitable innkeeper is happy to prepare personalized itineraries for guests. Honeymoon and anniversary packages are available.

ERIKA'S HILLSIDE

285 Fawn Park Road
St. Helena, CA 94574

⊗ $–$$$$

This Swiss chalet B&B on three acres of beautifully landscaped grounds enjoys views of the vineyards and

PHONE: (707) 963–2887
FAX: (707) 963–1558
WEB SITE: www.bbinv.com
FEATURES: home; 2 rooms, 2 suites; air-conditioning
NEARBY: wineries; town
INNKEEPER/OWNER: Erika Cunningham

wineries. The spacious guest accommodations include two deluxe suites, each with private entrance and views of the valley. The continental breakfast, served on the patio, deck, or in the garden room, features German specialties. Guests are welcomed with evening refreshments.

HARVEST INN

One Main Street
St. Helena, CA 94574

♿ ⊘ $$$$

■ This large Tudor-style inn was built in 1978 on the grounds of a twenty-one-acre working vineyard. Besides enjoying the grounds, guests may swim in the pools during the summer and relax in one of two spas year-round. All guest rooms have king- or queen-size beds, televisions, telephones, and antique decor; most also have fireplaces, wet bars, and refrigera-tors. A continental breakfast of pastry and rolls, fresh fruit, and juices is served in the Vineyard Room or delivered to the guest room. The hotel has been featured in *Smithsonian* magazine. Conference facilities are available.

PHONE: (707) 963–9463 or (800) 950–8466
FAX: (707) 963–4402
WEB SITE: www.harvestinn.com
FEATURES: inn/hotel; 54 rooms, suites, cottages; limited smoking; air-conditioning; in-room phones; in-room televisions and VCRs; computer hookups; pets allowed; conferences; 2 swimming pools; spas; spa services
NEARBY: wineries; town; hot-air ballooning; bicycling; mud baths
INNKEEPER: Meredith Wood
OWNER: Rick Swig

HILLTOP HOUSE B&B

9550 St. Helena Road
P.O. Box 726
St. Helena, CA 94574

⊘ $$–$$$$

■ This contemporary ranch house, on 135 acres of unspoiled wilderness, is located on top of a high ridge overlooking the historic Mayacamas Mountains. The house offers panoramic views of the peaceful surroundings and spectacular sunrises and sunsets from its large deck outside the guest rooms. The B&B is decorated throughout with beautiful antiques. Guests enjoy a spacious common room with stereo, television, woodstove, guest refrigerator, and library. The Sunrise suite offers a private deck, skylights, queen-size bed, and private bath. Hilltop House serves a generous full breakfast on the outside deck or in the dining room, provides afternoon refreshments, and serves evening sherry and port in your room. Guests also enjoy numerous hiking trails, picnic areas, and use of a hot tub under the stars.

PHONE: (707) 944–0880
WEB SITE: www.hilltophousebed &breakfast.com
FEATURES: home; 4 rooms; air-conditioning; in-room television (suite only); hot tub; fax; copier; in-room workspace; small conferences
NEARBY: mountains; hiking trails; town
INNKEEPER/OWNER: Annette Gevarter Keefe

HOTEL ST. HELENA

1309 Main Street
St. Helena, CA 94574

⊘ $–$$$$

▓ The 1881 hotel on the town's Main
Street has been completely renovated
and carefully restored to full Victorian
glory. Today, the hotel offers guest rooms
upstairs decorated in antiques, teddy
bears and dolls, authentic wall coverings, quilted spreads, armoires, and carpeting;
some have shared baths. A suite with sitting room can accommodate four people.
The downstairs is devoted to shops and a comfortable sitting area with fireplace
where the inn serves a continental breakfast buffet of muffins and assorted baked
goods and fresh fruit cocktail. The inn hosts group functions.

PHONE: (707) 963–4388 or (888)
478–4355
FAX: (707) 963–5402
WEB SITE: www.hotelsthelena.com
FEATURES: inn/hotel; 17 rooms, 1 suite;
air-conditioning; in-room phones; in-
room televisions; fax; copier; computer
hookups; conferences; weddings
NEARBY: wineries; town
INNKEEPER/OWNER: Mary Haney

THE INK HOUSE

1575 St. Helena Highway
St. Helena, CA 94574

⊘ $$–$$$$

▓ This 1884 Victorian-Italianate home
listed on the National Register of Historic
Places has been restored to its original
colors, a cheerful yellow and white with
sky blue accents. The inn features 12-foot-high ceilings, oak floors, and English,
American, Italian, and French antiques throughout. Guests enjoy three common parlors, one with a fireplace and an antique pump organ, another with a concert grand
piano, and a third-floor glass-enclosed observatory with panoramic vistas of the surrounding hills and vineyards. The guest rooms offer queen-size beds and private
baths. A full-size pool table, eighteen-speed bicycles, a video library, and VCR-
equipped televisions are available to guests. A full gourmet breakfast is served daily
in the dining room or by the fireplace. Complimentary mineral water, sherry, and
brandy are offered during the day; wine and an extensive selection of appetizers are
served each evening in the parlor.

PHONE: (707) 963–3890
FAX: (707) 968–0739
WEB SITE: www.inkhouse.com
FEATURES: inn; 7 rooms; air-conditioning;
bicycles; antique pool table
NEARBY: wineries; town
INNKEEPER/OWNER: Hilary Lamie

JUDY'S BED & BREAKFAST   Best Buy

2036 Madrona Avenue
St. Helena, CA 94574

⊘ $$

Vineyards surround this ranch-style B&B on three sides. The one suite consists of a bedroom, sitting room, and private bath and entrance. The quarters are decorated in antiques with a queen-size brass bed, air-conditioning, wood-burning stove, and television. In addition to a full breakfast served in-room, freshly baked goodies are served in the room or by the pool. The suite is supplied with beverages, fruit, and candies.

PHONE: (707) 963–3081
FAX: (707) 963–3081
FEATURES: home; 1 room; air-conditioning; in-room television; swimming pool
NEARBY: town; vineyards
INNKEEPERS/OWNERS: Judy and Bob Sculatti

PRAGER WINERY B&B

1281 Lewelling Lane
St. Helena, CA 94574

♿ $$$$

This home B&B with two three-room suites is located right on the winery premises. The Winery suite is situated above the barrel-aging cellar and offers a private entrance, bath, bedroom, living room, fireplace, and a veranda with views of the vineyard and mountains. The Vineyard suite, attached to the house, offers a private entrance, fireplace, garden, and bath as well as a comfortable living room with piano. The full home-cooked breakfast is served in the suite, and guests enjoy a personal wine-tasting and tour of the winery.

PHONE: (707) 963–3720 or (800) 969–PORT
FAX: (707) 963–7679
WEB SITE: www.pragerport.com
FEATURES: home; 2 suites; air-conditioning; fax; copier; in-room television and VCR (some)
NEARBY: wineries; town
INNKEEPERS/OWNERS: Imogene and Jim Prager

SPANISH VILLA

474 Glass Mountain Road
St. Helena, CA 94574

⊗ $$$–$$$$

■ The two-story Spanish-style villa is surrounded by country roads and woods. The Mediterranean design features rose gardens, a green lawn fed by artesian-well water, and a central patio with European fountain and canopied swing. The La Galleria lounge with arched windows looks out on the patio and garden and is the site of the morning gourmet breakfast, featuring a hot egg dish (the patio is also a choice on sunny days). The library at the inn features books from the seventeenth century; the main sitting room offers a television, VCR, and large Spanish-style fireplace. Each of the spacious guest rooms offers a private entrance, king-size bed with hand-carved Spanish headboard, private bath, and Tiffany lamp replicas. Suites also have separate sitting areas. The inn can accommodate small groups for meetings or banquets.

PHONE: (707) 963–7483
FAX: (707) 967–9401
WEB SITE: www.napavalleyspanish villa.com
FEATURES: inn; 8 rooms/suites; air-conditioning; meetings for small groups; weddings
NEARBY: wineries; town
INNKEEPERS/OWNERS: Roy and Barbara Bissember

THE WINE COUNTRY INN

1152 Lodi Lane
St. Helena, CA 94574

♿ ⊗ $$$–$$$$

■ This small country hotel, opened in 1975, is located off a busy highway in a peaceful setting. Most of the guest accommodations boast rural views, and some have patios, balconies, or fireplaces usable fall through spring. All rooms have private baths and telephones and are decorated uniquely in country antiques and fresh colors. A buffet-style full breakfast, featuring a variety of egg casseroles, is served each morning. An afternoon wine-tasting social offers a spectacular spread of appetizers. Guests relax in a beautiful pool and spa. The innkeeper has prepared maps for eight special tours and will make necessary reservations.

PHONE: (707) 963–7077 or (888) 465–4608
FAX: (707) 963–9018
WEB SITE: www.winecountryinn.com
FEATURES: inn/hotel/cottages; 24 rooms, 5 cottages; air-conditioning; in-room phones; swimming pool; spa; fax; copier
NEARBY: wineries; town
INNKEEPER/OWNER: Jim Smith

ZINFANDEL INN

800 Zinfandel Lane
St. Helena, CA 94574

🚳 $$–$$$$

🔲 A "castle in the vineyards" is this 1984-
built English Tudor–style B&B fronted by a
fountain and boasting enviable vineyard
views. Situated on two acres of land-
scaped grounds with gazebo, patios, fish
pond, lagoon, and aviary, the inn offers just three special suites. The Chardonnay
Room has a massive stone fireplace as its focal point, a king-size brass bed, oversize
Jacuzzi tub, and a private garden entrance through sunny French doors. The Zinfan-
del Suite, in shades of blue and beige and decorated with oak furnishings, king-size
four-poster bed, wood-burning stove, and 6-foot stained-glass window, offers a
Jacuzzi tub and a private balcony overlooking the garden. The Chablis Room, with a
beveled-glass fireplace, is aptly named with its panoramic views of the vineyards.
Champagne and truffles greet guests upon arrival, and the inn serves a full breakfast
each morning, featuring pesto eggs, caramelized French toast, or Gringo Rancheros
served in the formal dining room. Evening sherry and lemonade are offered.

PHONE: (707) 963–3512
FAX: (707) 942–4618
WEB SITE: www.zinfandelinn.com
FEATURES: inn; 3 rooms; in-room
phones; air-conditioning; in-room
televisions; in-room VCR; fax; copier
NEARBY: wineries
INNKEEPERS/OWNERS: Diane and Jerry
Payton

THE GABLES WINE COUNTRY INN

4257 Petaluma Hill Road
Santa Rosa, CA 95404

♿ 🚳 $$$–$$$$

🔲 Fifteen gables crown the unusual keyhole-shaped
windows of this High Victorian Gothic Revival inn nes-
tled on three and a half acres of former dairy pasture
land. The elegant 1877-built home with 12-foot-high
ceilings, three Italian marble fireplaces, and a
mahogany spiral staircase offers guests accommodations with comfortable antique
furnishings, brass beds, and private baths. The William and Mary cottage, next to
Taylor Creek, which traverses the grounds, is a private country retreat with wood-
stove, kitchenette, and sleeping loft. Breakfast at the Gables is a three-course coun-
try feast served in the spacious dining room with a warm sunny-rose and light-green

PHONE: (707) 585–7777 or (800) 422–5376
FAX: (707) 584–5634
WEB SITE: www.thegablesinn.com
FEATURES: inn/cottage; 7 rooms, 1 cottage; air-conditioning
NEARBY: wineries; antiques shopping; Luther Burbank Center for Performing Arts
INNKEEPERS/OWNERS: Mike and Judy Ogne

decor; the meal begins with freshly squeezed juices and a fresh-fruit dish. Entrees might include a specialty dish such as vegetable frittata topped with sour cream and tomatoes, served with just-baked pastries, muffins, and breads. Home-baked cookies and tea are offered each afternoon. Guests at the inn enjoy a formal sitting room as well as a deck with views stretching across the valley.

MELITTA STATION INN

5850 Melita Road
Santa Rosa, CA 95409

$$–$$$

In the late 1880s the railroad station was a stagecoach stop, then went on to be a freight station, general store, boardinghouse, and antiques shop. Carefully converted to a B&B inn and home, the inn's interior reflects a country feel with antiques and hand stencilings. The comfortably furnished guest rooms have private baths. A sitting room features a wood-burning stove and French-door views of the countryside. The full buffet breakfast, including homemade scones, muffins, fruit, and various hot dishes, is served by candlelight; an evening glass of wine is enjoyed on the outside deck. Guests enjoy the inn's beautiful setting, which is surrounded by parks offering hiking and other forms of recreation.

PHONE: (707) 538–7712 or (800) 504–3099
WEB SITE: www.melittastationinn.com
FEATURES: inn; 6 rooms; air-conditioning; computer hookups
NEARBY: hiking; wineries
INNKEEPERS/OWNERS: Jackie and Jim Thresh

PYGMALION HOUSE

331 Orange Street
Santa Rosa, CA 95401

⊗ $–$$

▓ This lovely Victorian home with 12-foot-high ceilings is nestled right in downtown Santa Rosa, just 3 blocks from Railroad Square. The six guest rooms offer queen- or king-size beds, private baths with showers and claw-foot tubs, and an interesting selection of antique furnishings. The B&B's antiques collection includes pieces that once belonged to burlesque star Gypsy Rose Lee and the famous madam and former Sausalito mayor Sally Stanford. Guests congregate in the inn's main room, or double parlor, which contains an inviting fireplace and a sitting area nestled around the distinctive octagon-shaped windows. The breakfast includes fresh fruit, freshly squeezed orange juice, home-baked muffins and croissants, a popular crustless quiche with either bacon or sausage, and a special blend of coffee.

PHONE: (707) 526–3407
FAX: (707) 526–3407
WEB SITE: www.bedandbreakfast.com
FEATURES: inn; 6 rooms; air-conditioning; some in-room televisions; fax; copier
NEARBY: Old Town; Railroad Square
INNKEEPER/OWNER: Caroline Berry

VINTNERS INN

4350 Barnes Road
Santa Rosa, CA 95403

♿ ⊗ $$$–$$$$

▓ A small French "village," with a central plaza and fountain surrounded by four separate stucco and red-tile-roof buildings with arched windows, has been created in the middle of a forty-acre working vineyard as a unique B&B. The inn offers forty-four individually decorated, spacious guest rooms furnished in a country French motif with antique pine furnishings, custom-made pine beds, and brass appointments; some have wood-burning fireplaces, beamed ceilings, televisions, refrigerators, telephones, voice mail and dataports, private baths, and balcony or patio views of the plaza or vineyards. A common building contains a library and breakfast area, where the complimentary full breakfast fare of waffles, cereals, homemade pastries, fruit, and juices is served. The inn can accommodate executive conferences, with separate conference and dining rooms also available. Guests enjoy a large sundeck with spa, as well as the nationally renowned John Ash & Co. restaurant, specializing in Sonoma regional cuisine.

PHONE: (707) 575–7350 or (800) 421–2584
FAX: (707) 575–1426
WEB SITE: www.vintnersinn.com
FEATURES: inn/hotel; 44 rooms; air-conditioning; in-room phones; computer hookups; in-room televisions; all business/conference services; spa; restaurant on premises
NEARBY: vineyards; plaza; bicycling
INNKEEPER: Percy Brandon

THE COTTAGE INN AND SPA

302 First Street East
Sonoma, CA 95476

♿ ⊗ $$–$$$$

Located just 1 block north of the Sonoma Mission and Plaza is this exclusive duo of cottage-type accommodations found within an award-winning courtyard building with 7-foot-high white stucco walls embracing the exterior. The designers/innkeepers carefully remodeled the 1947 home with a Southwestern and Mediterranean feel, as well as four rooms in the adjoining cottage with spa. The rooms feature queen- and king-size beds, private baths, and two-person Jacuzzis. The studio in the cottage unit offers a dramatic living room with cathedral ceiling, skylight, arched fireplace, and warm, Mexican tile floors. The cottage suite has French doors in the bedroom that open to a small private garden. The dining area offers views of the mountains through its French doors; the European kitchen grants views of the hills. The kitchens are equipped for preparing a Sonoma-style meal, with garden produce, local wineries, and award-winning cheese available a short walk away. The Studio at the B&B has a private courtyard and is reminiscent of a carriage house, with huge redwood doors and fireplace. It also is punctuated with cathedral ceilings and skylights. An accommodation not located in the cot-

PHONE: (707) 996–0719 or (800) 944–1490
FAX: (707) 939–7913
WEB SITE: www.cottageinnandspa.com
FEATURES: inn; 8 rooms; in-room phones; in-room televisions; kitchens; in-room workspace; health club services; spa
NEARBY: mission; Sonoma Plaza; wineries; shops and restaurants
INNKEEPERS/OWNERS: Marga Friberg and Robert Behrens

tage, the Courtyard room, is also available. The accommodations are outfitted with coffeemakers and supplied with coffee, fresh fruit, granola, butter, milk, and juice; each morning a basket of freshly baked rolls and muffins is hung on the door. Before guests arrive, the in-room breakfast tables are set with fine china and fresh flowers. Innkeepers will arrange facials, massages, and the use of a fitness club upon request.

THE HIDDEN OAK

214 East Napa Street
Sonoma, CA 95476

⊗ $$–$$$

 Situated just 1½ blocks from Sonoma's historic Plaza is this 1914-built California Craftsman–style bungalow. Now totally redecorated, the brown-shingled structure was originally used as a refectory. The three spacious and airy guest rooms feature private baths and queen-size beds. Room decor is a blend of wicker and antiques with floral prints and fluffy comforters. Guests enjoy the parlor with early-morning newspaper and coffee, as well as fireside reading in the library. A full breakfast, served in the dining room on weekends, consists of fresh fruit and juice, pastries, and an egg dish with breakfast meat. An extended continental breakfast is served on weekday mornings. Afternoon refreshments are also offered. Guests may use the inn's bicycles for touring nearby wineries.

PHONE: (707) 996–9863 or (877) 996–9863
WEB SITE: www.hiddenoakinn.com
FEATURES: inn; 3 rooms; bicycles
NEARBY: plaza; wineries
INNKEEPERS/OWNERS: Don and Valerie Patterson

MAGLIULO'S ROSE GARDEN INN

691 Broadway
Sonoma, CA 95476

♿ ⊗ $$

 This late-1800s Victorian residence, with restaurant of the same name next door, is within walking distance of Sonoma Plaza and boasts beautifully landscaped yards. The guest rooms at the inn, in shades of rose, offer fresh flowers, fine antiques, quilts, ceiling fans, iron and brass beds, and both private and shared baths. Guests

PHONE: (707) 996–1031
E-MAIL: magliulo@comcast.net
FEATURES: inn; 4 rooms
NEARBY: Sonoma Plaza; wineries
INNKEEPER/OWNER: Marilyn Magliulo

enjoy an outdoor cabana and a cozy parlor with glowing fireplace. A generous continental breakfast is served in the inn's dining room each morning; wine and cookies are offered in the evening.

SONOMA CHALET BED & BREAKFAST

18935 Fifth Street West
Sonoma, CA 95476

⊗ $$–$$$$

 This Swiss-style farmhouse with three cottages was built in 1940 and is situated on three acres within an easy walk of downtown Sonoma. In the main house the two upstairs guest rooms have private baths and balconies; the two downstairs rooms share a bath and a common sitting room. The cottages offer private baths and cozy wood-burning stoves; two feature lofts. An expanded continental breakfast of juice, fruit, pastries, and cereals is included in the stay, as is use of the hot tub. Guests enjoy strolls around the peaceful farm grounds.

PHONE: (707) 938–3129 or (800) 938-3129
FAX: (707) 996–0190
WEB SITE: www.sonomachalet.com
FEATURES: inn/cottages; 7 rooms, 3 cottages; air-conditioning; hot tub
NEARBY: town; wineries
INNKEEPER/OWNER: Joe Leese

SONOMA HOTEL

110 West Spain Street
Sonoma, CA 95476

♿ ⊗ $–$$$$

 The exact age of this old hotel is unknown, but records show it to be at least of 1870s vintage. The hotel was completely restored in 1999; remodeled and updated rooms feature private baths and French country furniture.

PHONE: (707) 996–2996 or (800) 468–6016
FAX: (707) 996–7014
WEB SITE: www.sonomahotel.com
FEATURES: inn/hotel; 16 rooms; fax; copier; air-conditioning; in-room televisions; in-room phones; computer hookups; restaurant on premises
NEARBY: plaza; wineries
INNKEEPERS/OWNERS: Craig Miller and Tim Farfan

The overnight stay at Sonoma Hotel includes a continental breakfast, complimentary bottle of wine upon arrival, and wine-tasting daily from 5:00 to 6:00 P.M. Lunch and dinner are available in the hotel's restaurant, the Girl and the Fig.

THISTLE DEW INN

171 West Spain Street
Sonoma, CA 95476

♿ ⊘ $$$–$$$$

▪ The inn is located in a quiet residential neighborhood just three doors off the main plaza. It consists of two one-story Victorian houses surrounded by lawns and gardens and decorated with collector's pieces of Arts and Crafts–style furniture. The guest rooms, all with private baths and queen-size beds, have washstands, ceiling fans, telephones, and air-conditioning; three rooms have fireplaces, whirlpools for two, and decks surrounded by gardens. A full gourmet breakfast, served in the dining room, may include lemon poppy-seed pancakes with honey butter, fresh herb omelettes or blintzes, or popular "Dutch baby" pastry. Appetizers and beverages are offered on the deck each evening, weather permitting. Bicycles and picnic baskets are available for guests' use; a relaxing heated spa is nestled between the two buildings.

PHONE: (707) 938–2909 or (800) 382–7895
FAX: (707) 996–8413
WEB SITE: www.thistledew.com
FEATURES: inn; 5 rooms; air-conditioning; in-room phones; voice mail; spa; bicycles; picnic baskets
NEARBY: plaza; wineries
INNKEEPERS/OWNERS: Larry and Norma Barnett

TROJAN HORSE INN

19455 Sonoma Highway
Sonoma, CA 95476

♿ ⊘ $$–$$$

▪ This 1887 Victorian farmhouse-style home sits on the banks of Sonoma Creek. The inn, painted white and trimmed in Williamsburg blue, has been completely renovated. Outside features include two levels of well-kept gardens and patios, beautiful old trees, and a spa. The inn is furnished in English and French antiques, and guest rooms offer queen-size beds, plush

PHONE: (707) 996–2430 or (800) 899–1925
FAX: (707) 996–9185
WEB SITE: www.trojanhorseinn.com
FEATURES: inn; 6 rooms; air-conditioning; spa; fax; copier; computer hookups
NEARBY: Sonoma Creek; town; wineries
INNKEEPERS/OWNERS: Joe and Sandy Miccio

linens and bedspreads, ceiling fans, air-conditioning, and private baths. One guest room offers a fireplace, and another boasts a whirlpool for two. A full breakfast with home-baked goodies and a hot dish is served graciously in the dining room each morning; hors d'oeuvres and wine are offered in the early evening.

VICTORIAN GARDEN INN

316 East Napa Street
Sonoma, CA 95476

🚫 $$–$$$$

 This 1880s farmhouse with water tower features a secluded acre with meandering walks through creekside Victorian gardens. Guest rooms are individually furnished in antiques and have quaint wall coverings; all but one have private baths. The Woodcutter's Cottage has a fireplace, private entrance, and claw-foot tub. A generous California breakfast may be

PHONE: (707) 996–5339 or (800) 543–5339
FAX: (707) 996–1689
WEB SITE: www.victoriangardeninn.com
FEATURES: inn; 4 rooms; air-conditioning; swimming pool; spa
NEARBY: plaza; wineries
INNKEEPER/OWNER: Donna Lewis

enjoyed in the dining room or garden or carried on a wicker tray to the room. During the day guests may swim in the garden-set pool, walk to shops, or relax in the therapeutic spa. Afternoon and evening refreshments are available. The inn is 1½ blocks from local wineries.

COUNTRY MEADOW INN

11360 Old Redwood Highway
Windsor, CA 95492

♿ 🚫 $$–$$$$

 This Queen Anne–style Victorian farmhouse sits on a knoll within its six-acre country setting, lush with trees and informal flower gardens. The common areas of the inn

are pleasantly and comfortably decorated with country antiques, plants and
fresh flowers, old-fashioned radios, rocking chairs, and an abundance of pillows.
The five guest rooms, all with private
baths, have down comforters and some
fireplaces. The forest green and white
Garden suite offers a romantic escape
with king-size canopy bed, whirlpool for
two, fireplace, wet bar, refrigerator,

PHONE: (707) 431–1276 or (800) 238–1728
FAX: (707) 431–2776
WEB SITE: www.countrymeadowinn.com
FEATURES: inn; 5 rooms; air-conditioning; in-room workspace; tennis court; swimming pool
NEARBY: wineries; Russian River
INNKEEPER/OWNER: Susan Hardesty

atrium, and a sitting area. A variety of egg casseroles or crustless quiche, homemade
preserves, juice, fresh breads, muffins, and pastries greet guests each morning. In the
late afternoon and evening, guests partake of a variety of beverages and appetizers.

BURGUNDY HOUSE COUNTRY INN

6711 Washington Street
P.O. Box 3156
Yountville, CA 94599

⊗ $$–$$$

PHONE: (707) 944–0889
WEB SITE: www.burgundyhouseinn.com
FEATURES: inn; 5 rooms; air-conditioning
NEARBY: wineries; hiking trails; bicycling
INNKEEPER: Cindy Jeanty

▦ This French country–style stone structure, built in the early 1890s of local fieldstone
and river rock, is on the National Register of Historic Places. Starting out as a brandy
distillery, the structure went on to house a winery, a hotel, and an antiques warehouse
until its present function as a fine bed-and-breakfast inn. Antique country furnishings
accent the unique 22-inch-thick walls and hand-hewn beams of the inn. The five guest
rooms all offer private baths, and quilted bedspreads. The inn serves a continental
breakfast in the "distillery," or guests may dine in the intimate garden surrounded by
hedges, roses, and trees. Guests gather in the evening for a glass of wine.

MAISON FLEURIE

6529 Yount Street
Yountville, CA 94599

♿ ⊗ $$–$$$$

▦ This French country inn consists of three vine-covered brick buildings. The one-
hundred-year-old lobby boasts 2-foot-thick walls, terra-cotta tile, paned windows, and,

in season, a crackling fire. The upstairs guest rooms view the surrounding vineyards. Other guest accommodations are found in the Old Bakery and carriage house buildings situated within the colorful gardens. These charming structures house six additional romantic rooms, all with fireplaces, king-size beds, spa tubs, and patios. The country inn offers a pool for summer swims and a hot tub for cool nights; bicycles are available for exploring nearby vineyards. This Four Sisters Inn provides all the amenities, from a full country breakfast along with the morning paper to evening wine, hors d'oeuvres, turndown service, and home-baked cookies.

PHONE: (707) 944–2056 or (800) 788–0369
FAX: (707) 944–9342
WEB SITE: www.maisonfleurienapa.com
FEATURES: inn/hotel/cottage; 13 rooms; air-conditioning; in-room phones; in-room televisions; fax; copier; swimming pool; hot tub; bicycles
NEARBY: wineries; shops; restaurants
INNKEEPERS/OWNERS: Four Sisters Inns, Roger Post

OLEANDER HOUSE

7433 St. Helena Highway
P.O. Box 2937
Yountville, CA 94599

⊗ $$–$$$

This gracious French country–style home is located in the heart of Napa Valley, about 100 yards from the acclaimed Mustard's Grill restaurant. Guests enjoy the B&B's patio, relaxing spa, and upstairs common room with a wet bar stocked with a wide assortment of beverages. Each of the five accommodations features high ceilings, queen-size brass bed, antiques, private bath, balcony, and fireplace; all guest rooms are uniquely decorated in Laura Ashley wall coverings and prints. A full gourmet breakfast is offered in the dining room each morning and features a hot entree, such as apple-cranberry-pecan bread pudding with vanilla custard sauce or oatmeal brûlée, freshly roasted coffee, fruit, and freshly squeezed orange juice. Complimentary beverages are offered in the lounge.

PHONE: (707) 944–8315 or (800) 788–0357
FAX: (707) 944–0980
WEB SITE: www.oleander.com
FEATURES: inn; 5 rooms; air-conditioning; fax; copier; computer hookups; small conferences; spa
NEARBY: wineries; restaurants
INNKEEPER: Kathleen Matthews
OWNERS: Barbara and Jack Kasten

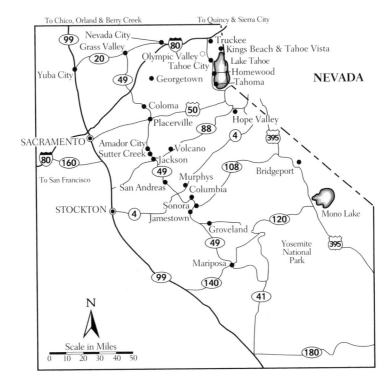

To Chico, Orland & Berry Creek   To Quincy & Sierra City

99   Nevada City   80   Truckee
Grass Valley   Kings Beach & Tahoe Vista
20   Olympic Valley   Lake Tahoe
Tahoe City   Homewood
Yuba City   49   Georgetown   Tahoma

NEVADA

Coloma   50
Placerville   Hope Valley
SACRAMENTO   88   4   395
Amador City   Volcano
Sutter Creek   Jackson
80   160   49   108   Bridgeport
To San Francisco   Murphys
San Andreas   Columbia
STOCKTON   4   Sonora   120   Mono Lake
Jamestown
Groveland   Yosemite   395
49   National
Mariposa   Park
99   140
41

N

Scale in Miles
0   10   20   30   40   50

180

CALIFORNIA GOLD COUNTRY

Communities born of the gold-rush days, which feature old mines, vineyards, rolling hills with oaks, lakes, museums, the Sierra Nevada's grandeur, unlimited recreation, and the cornucopian fields of the great Central Valley, make up this region's diverse character. The traveler may still pan gold here; or tour the state's preserved gold-rush town, Columbia; or a thriving historic town, such as Sutter Creek, Amador City, Jackson, or Nevada City—all steeped in the history of the "golden days." Nestled high in the Sierra Nevada are the communities of Tahoe City, Kings Beach, and Olympic Valley, which, still rich in history, are better known for their nearby casinos, skiing, and lake sports and beaches. The state's capital, Sacramento, offers history in the making as well as its Old Town to explore. History, the lure of gold-rush days, recreation, and scenic paradise—Gold Country's generous offerings are waiting.

IMPERIAL HOTEL

14202 Highway 49
P.O. Box 195
Amador City, CA 95601

⊗ $–$$

 B. Saguinetti originally built this brick structure as a mercantile store, but the city already had a lot of stores and not enough lodging. As a result, plans were changed and walls moved, and the Imperial Hotel was opened in 1879. In 1988 the impressive brick Gothic hostelry was restored—with white balcony, herb garden, and secluded patio with flowers and fountains—to once again lodge visitors. It also offers a delightful restaurant and full bar. The six charming, unique guest rooms (all with private baths) are filled with antique, wicker, and Art Deco appointments. Sunny Room #1 has a romantic queen-size canopy bed, a sitting area, balcony, and views overlooking Main Street. Another room (#6) offers a hand-painted queen-size bed and Art Deco furnishings designed by Moreno Larose. Some of the guest rooms adjoin; hair dryers and heated towel bars are in all the guest baths. A full breakfast is included in the stay at the hotel and is served on the balcony, in the restaurant, on the native-stone patio, or in the individual guest rooms. The hotel's restaurant, with attractive decor, artwork, and Victorian ambience, serves dinner nightly; group lunches can be arranged. Special-order desserts are a specialty of the restaurant's pastry chef. B&B guests can wander down Main Street or along Amador Creek to browse through antiques shops and boutiques.

PHONE: (209) 267–9172 or (800) 242–5594

FAX: (209) 267–9249

WEB SITE: www.imperialamador.com

FEATURES: inn/hotel; 6 rooms; air-conditioning; fax; copier; catering; conference/meeting areas; picnic baskets; restaurant/bar on premises

NEARBY: town shops and restaurants; wineries

INNKEEPER/OWNER: Rhonda Uhlmann

MINE HOUSE INN

14125 Highway 49
P.O. Box 245
Amador City, CA 95601

⊘ $–$$$

PHONE: (209) 267–5900 or (800) 646–3473

FAX: (209) 267–5900

WEB SITE: www.minehouseinn.com

FEATURES: inn/cottage; 13 rooms; air-conditioning; swimming pool; spa; small meetings; weddings

NEARBY: shops; restaurants

INNKEEPERS/OWNERS: Allen and Rose Mendy

■ This very unusual 1870 hostelry is the former Keystone Consolidated Mining Office Building. Each guest room is named after its original use: the Mill Grinding Room, with remnants of the grind-wheel-shaft supports; the Vault Room, with the walk-in bullion safe; and so on. All rooms are decorated with original nineteenth-century antiques and have private baths and air-conditioning; several have fireplaces. Three rooms have spas. An adjacent Victorian House has three luxury suites—two with fireplaces, refrigerators, and Jacuzzis for two. Guests enjoy a heated swimming pool from spring through fall. A hearty breakfast, which typically includes home-baked muffins and breads, and such specialties as spinach-sausage, apple-cheddar quiche, or baked crepes stuffed with egg, sausage, and cheese, is served in the guest room or on the outdoor patios.

LAKE OROVILLE BED AND BREAKFAST

240 Sunday Drive
Berry Creek, CA 95916

♿ ⊘ $$–$$$

■ Perched high on a hill overlooking the state's second-largest lake is this secluded bed-and-breakfast offering spectacular valley and lake views. Owners Ron and Cheryl Damberger built the inn in 1991, giving special consideration to capturing the vistas from every room and from the covered porches that wrap around the structure. The inn is immersed in forty acres worthy of strolling and filled with native trees, wildflowers, rabbits, deer, and gently rolling hills. The guest rooms, with queen- or king-size beds, feature Victorian decor, granting a feeling of yesteryear; all accommodations offer private entrances with porches and seating, as well as private bathrooms, five with whirlpools. Televisions and VCRs are available upon request; the inn offers a video library of more than sixty film selections. The Rose Petal Room is a

PHONE: (530) 589–0700 or (800) 455–5253

FAX: (530) 589–3800

WEB SITE: www.lakeoroville.com/lake oroville

FEATURES: inn; 6 units; air-conditioning; in-room phones; in-room televisions and VCRs (on request); children welcome upon arrangement; billiards; fax; copier; meeting areas; catering for small meetings/receptions; wedding services; boat and RV parking

NEARBY: Lake Oroville and lake and marina activities; Oroville Dam; Feather Falls; Feather River; horseback riding; hiking; antiques shops; golfing; Oroville Chinese Temple & Garden

INNKEEPERS/OWNERS: Ron and Cheryl Damberger

romantic choice with rose wall coverings and white Battenburg accents; it has a lake view. The Monet Room features French period decor, French Impressionist prints, and a country/wooded view. The common areas include a parlor with sunny bay windows, television, and large fireplace; billiard room with pool table and games; and a sunroom that makes a quiet spot for reading or just relaxing over the view. A full gourmet breakfast featuring quiches or other egg dishes and waffles or French toast is served each morning. Picnic suppers are encouraged at the inn, which has a barbecue available for guests.

THE CAIN HOUSE

340 Main Street
P.O. Box 454
Bridgeport, CA 93517

⊗ $–$$

▦ The Cain family was a wealthy mining, banking, and real estate family in the town of Bodie; later generations brought the Cain legacy to Bridgeport. This former residence was a classic western-style 1920s home that the current owners totally remodeled with warm cedar siding, white picket fence, and modern comforts. A highlight of the stay at Cain House is the evening glass of fine California wine and cheeses on the front porch, as the sun sets, with the eastern Sierra Nevada as a backdrop. A gourmet country breakfast awaits guests each morning in the din-

PHONE: (760) 932–7040 or (800) 433–CAIN

FAX: (760) 932–7419

WEB SITE: www.cainhouse.com

FEATURES: inn; 7 rooms; air-conditioning; in-room phones; in-room televisions; fax; copier; closed winters

NEARBY: hiking; boating; fishing; hunting; cross-country skiing

INNKEEPERS/OWNERS: Christopher and Marachal Gohlich

ing room at "couple tables" for ultimate privacy; a light breakfast is also available. Start the day with such country delights as French toast stuffed with boysenberries and cream cheese, along with Tennessee sausage and rosemary-and-thyme potatoes. All the guest rooms, decorated in comfortable elegance, have private baths, queen- or king-size beds, and televisions. The deluxe J. S. Cain Room downstairs features a private entrance, a refrigerator, and a mahogany four-poster bed. The upstairs Aurora Room is a spacious and romantic choice awash in pink, peach, and whitewashed pine. Downhill skiing and Nevada gaming are within an hour's drive of the inn.

JOHNSON'S COUNTRY INN

3935 Moreheap Avenue
Chico, CA 95928

♿ ⊘ $–$$

This "new" Victorian farmhouse-style inn is situated on ten acres of almond trees and surrounded by flowering gardens and bushes. A gazebo, a wraparound veranda, fragrant garden paths, and country walks make this B&B a good choice for a relaxing getaway. A tray of juices, coffee, and tea are delivered to the room each morning; breakfast, served overlooking the orchard, is a full gourmet affair with such delectables as zucchini waffles or raspberry pancakes with freshly packed apple sausage. Guests also enjoy evening wine and afternoon cookies and juices or soft drinks. The guest rooms are supplied with fresh flowers from the garden, robes, and bath amenities. The Harrison Room makes a great honeymoon retreat with an 1860s Victorian double bed, Eastlake antiques, fireplace, and Jacuzzi. The upstairs Jarrett Room features classic waterfall-designed furniture of the 1930s and paintings by artist Charles Dixie Jarrett. The traditional parlor, with bay-window seating overlooking the garden, a cozy fireplace, and a piano, is a popular indoor retreat.

PHONE: (530) 345–7829

FAX: (530) 345–7829

WEB SITE: www.chico.com/johnsons inn or www.northvalley.net/johnsons inn

FEATURES: inn; 4 rooms; air-conditioning; in-room phones; fax; copier; computer hookups; catering; conference/meeting area

NEARBY: downtown Chico; Chico State University

INNKEEPERS/OWNERS: Joan and David Johnson

L'ABRI BED & BREAKFAST

14350 Highway 99
Chico, CA 95973

🚫 $–$$

PHONE: (530) 893–0824 or (800) 489–3319
FAX: (530) 895–0735
WEB SITE: www.northvalley.net/labri
FEATURES: inn; 3 rooms; air-conditioning; in-room phones; airport pick-up; in-room computer hookups
NEARBY: Bidwell Park; California State University at Chico; Lassen Volcanic National Park; Oroville Dam; Feather River Fish Hatchery; hiking; bicycling; golfing
INNKEEPERS/OWNERS: Stephen and Lauree Janak

▓ *L'abri* is the French word for "shelter," making it a most appropriate name for this ranch-style home on two and a half acres away from it all. A seasonal creek passes through the acreage, which also hosts a small barnyard of animals to pet (mainly sheep and chickens), patios, and lawns. The house was built in 1972 and remodeled in 1995 for use as a bed-and-breakfast by the current owners. The decor is comfortable with a country feel. Katey's room has a Mary Emmerling motif in red, white, and blue. It offers sunset views from its own sitting area. Teddi's room is abundant with teddy bears, dolls, and quilts, featuring sliding glass doors facing the creek. All guest rooms offer queen-size beds and have outside entrances. Two rooms are detached from the main house. Breakfast at the inn is an extended continental fare midweek and expands to a full meal on weekends. The weekend offering includes various egg dishes; breakfast may be enjoyed in the room. The great room at the bed-and-breakfast is the spot for gathering with other guests or enjoying a hot beverage.

MUSIC EXPRESS INN

1091 El Monte Avenue
Chico, CA 95928–9153

♿ 🚫 $–$$

PHONE: (530) 345–8376
FAX: (530) 893–8521
WEB SITE: www.northvalley.net/music express
FEATURES: inn; 9 rooms; in-room phones; air-conditioning; ceiling fans; in-room televisions and VCRs; fax; copier; computer hookups
NEARBY: town; college; antiquing; fishing
INNKEEPERS/OWNERS: Barney and Irene Cobeen

▓ A big draw for this elegant country inn, built in 1977, is the spotlight on music. Guests are welcome to try their own musical talents on the Steinway grand piano in the living room. Irene, a music teacher, plays mandolin in the local Chico band, coincidentally called the Music Express. The country comfort of the inn, with twin through king-size beds, is due to the antiques-filled decor and the spacious rooms, which also have refrigerators and microwave ovens. All have private baths and Jacuzzis, and one has a roll-in, wheelchair-accessible shower. The full breakfast is highlighted by homemade breads and rolls. The inn, with its many office conveniences, is popular with business travelers.

THE COLOMA COUNTRY INN

345 High Street
P.O. Box 502
Coloma, CA 95613

⊘ $$–$$$$

■ Surrounded on all sides by history is this quiet house built in the 1850s on five private acres in the midst of a 300-acre state park. Sutter's Mill and pioneer churches sit alongside the inn, and many attractions, including the Marshall Gold Discovery Park and white-water rafting, are within walking distance of the gold-rush-era home. The inn has been carefully renovated, and guest rooms and suites are decorated in a pleasing combination of American and English antiques, primitives, quilts, and stenciling. The Rose room features its own private brick courtyard and rose garden, and the upstairs Eastlake room offers a reading nook and private balcony beyond the French doors. The 1898 carriage house at the inn features a one-bedroom suite that can accommodate four, with private brick courtyard and garden, and a kitchenette. The full homemade breakfast, which includes muffins, seasonal fruits, juice, and scrambled eggs, frittatas, or casseroles with fresh vegetables from the garden, is served in the rooms or in the formal dining room overlooking the pond. The inn offers special hot-air-ballooning tours with champagne over the American River Valley; gourmet picnics and wine-tasting tours may also be arranged with advance notice. The charming garden at the inn serves as an excellent locale for weddings and teas.

PHONE: (530) 622–6919

FAX: (530) 626–4959

WEB SITE: www.colomacountry inn.com

FEATURES: inn/cottage; 4 rooms, 1 cottage; air-conditioning; in-room workspace; fax; catering; meeting areas; wine/ballooning tours; kitchenettes; weddings; teas; no credit cards

NEARBY: Sutter's Mill; Marshall Gold Discovery Park; white-water rafting; wineries

INNKEEPERS/OWNERS: Kerry and Candie Bliss

COLUMBIA CITY HOTEL

P.O. Box 1870
Columbia, CA 95310

 $$

■ A part of the Columbia Historic State Park, a historic 1800s town, this Victorian hotel and its sister, the Fallon Hotel, is a combined living museum, training center for hotel management, restaurant, and B&B establishment. Each luxuriously appointed guest room, with balcony or sitting area, has a private half-bath and authentic antiques. Shower baskets are provided for the down-the-hall shower. Overnight lodging includes a buffet breakfast each morning with homemade granola, quiche, fruit, and freshly baked rolls or muffins. Other meals are available in the restaurant, which offers a mouthwatering assortment of entrees, such as rack of lamb or grilled beef tenderloin with leek and Roquefort cheese confit and red wine demiglaze. Visitors and guests frequent the hotel's historic What Cheer Saloon to sample from the award-winning wine list. The hotel offers some fun lodging packages that might include a three-course meal, dessert, a theater production, and drinks in the saloon. Afternoon sherry is served at 5:00 P.M.

PHONE: (209) 532–1479 or (800) 532–1479
FAX: (209) 532–7027
WEB SITE: www.cityhotel.com
FEATURES: inn/hotel; 10 rooms; air-conditioning; fax; copier; catering; conference/meeting areas; restaurant; bar
NEARBY: in Columbia Historic State Park
OWNER: Columbia Historic State Park

FALLON HOTEL

P.O. Box 1870
Columbia, CA 95310

 $-$$

■ The state of California finished restoration of the 1857-built Fallon Hotel in the historic park of Columbia in 1986. The lodging establishment with brick facade and wooden balcony is a "living museum,"

PHONE: (209) 532–1479 or (800) 532–1479
FAX: (209) 532–7027
WEB SITE: www.cityhotel.com
FEATURES: inn/hotel; 14 rooms; air-conditioning; dinner/theater packages; closed Monday, June 1 through Labor Day; open Thursday through Sunday rest of the year
NEARBY: in Columbia Historic State Park
OWNER: Columbia Historic State Park

Gold-Rush Fever Alive in Columbia

From 1850 to 1870 Columbia mines yielded more than $87 million in gold. Columbia, in the foothills of the Sierra Nevada, was one of the largest and most important mining towns along the Mother Lode. Columbia Historical State Park covers 12 square blocks in the old business district of Columbia, having been restored to its gold-rush days. It is almost eerie to wander streets pretty much as they were during this exciting period of California's history.

Visit the old schoolhouse, the bank, the newspaper building, the barbershop, saloons, the Wells Fargo Building, and the City Hotel—a wonderful bed-and-breakfast inn you can call "home" during your visit. Park admission is free, but there are charges for stagecoach rides, goldpanning, and gold mine and horseback tours. Call the state park at (209) 532–0150 or log on to www.parks.ca.gov for general information.

boasting many of its original furnishings and other antiques as well as authentic wall-covering reproductions that return it to its Victorian grandeur. Most of the guest rooms offer half-baths and share showers, and accommodations range from the intimate hall rooms to the elaborate Balcony Suite. Five rooms open to the balcony for a bird's-eye view of the charming town. The complimentary continental breakfast includes fresh breads, sweet rolls, juices, and coffee or tea and is served to guests only in the parlor on the first floor. The hotel participates in a number of special events year-round and offers special lodging, dinner, and theater packages. The Fallon is partially staffed by hospitality-management students from Columbia College. Check for hours of operation when visiting in nonsummer months.

THE AMERICAN RIVER INN

6600 Main at Orleans Street
P.O. Box 43
Georgetown, CA 95634

♿ $–$$

■ This restored 1853 miners' boarding-house and the 1907 Queen Anne home is a former stagecoach stop nestled in the Sierra Nevada foothills. It offers guests strolls through Victorian

PHONE: (530) 333–4499 or (800) 245–6566
FAX: (530) 333–9253
WEB SITE: www.americanriverinn.com
FEATURES: inn; 13 rooms; swimming pool; Jacuzzi; games; bicycles; business/ meeting services; small pets allowed; picnic lunches
NEARBY: white-water rafting
INNKEEPERS/OWNERS: Will and Maria Collin

gardens, a dove aviary, and a unique antiques shop. Guests enjoy local wines and hors d'oeuvres in the parlor each evening and may relax in a refreshing mountain-stream pool or the Jacuzzi. Bicycles are provided, as are picnic lunches by prior arrangement. Guests may stay in one of three honeymoon suites. The guest rooms at the inn feature turn-of-the-twentieth-century decor, feather beds, down comforters, and private as well as shared bath accommodations; some have fireplaces and/or balconies. A full breakfast is served in the dining room or on the patio. Games in the garden—where you'll find a putting green and a mini–driving range—include croquet, badminton, Ping-Pong, and horseshoes. The inn is only ten minutes from white-water rafting, which the inn will arrange.

COMEBACK KELLY'S

304 South Church Street
Grass Valley, CA 95945

⊗ $$–$$$

▨ Vivid imagination is revealed in the restoration of this 1850s Victorian home set amid shading redwoods. Some of the rooms and suites are named after colorful, if not infamous, women: Lola Montez, Sally Stanford, Marilyn Monroe, and Madam's Quarters. The rooms, which feature tasteful, although slightly risqué, artwork, have queen- and king-size beds, private baths, and one- or two-person Jacuzzis. The opulent Sally Stanford Suite (named for the fabled San Francisco madam) features a bay window seat, fireplace, adjoining bedroom, Victorian bath with claw-foot tub, and a private patio. Guests can enjoy the huge swimming pool and ten-person spa. The inn, with on-site parking, is only 1 block from the historic town.

PHONE: (530) 477–8181
FAX: (530) 477–1976
WEB SITE: www.comebackkellys.com
FEATURES: inn; 4 rooms; air-conditioning; computer hookups; swimming pool; spa; horseshoe pit; one- or two-person Jacuzzis
NEARBY: historical town; Empire Mine State Park; restaurants; wine-tasting; white-water rafting; gold-panning
INNKEEPER/OWNER: Fran Fields

SWAN-LEVINE HOUSE

328 South Church Street
Grass Valley, CA 95945

Ⓧ $–$$

PHONE: (530) 272–1873
FAX: (530) 272–3939
WEB SITE: www.swanlevinehouse.com
FEATURES: inn; 4 rooms; pets permitted; art studio; swimming pool; badminton court; family oriented
NEARBY: restaurants; shops; historic landmarks; recreation
INNKEEPERS/OWNERS: Howard Levine and Margaret Warner Swan

 This pre-1880 Victorian mansion, filled with prints by the innkeepers and other artists, has been restored by the artist owners. The main house features upstairs guest rooms, all with private baths, including one suite with private parlor, others with oak bedsteads and wicker, queen- or king-size beds, and suites with extra beds for families. The renovated carriage house is used as a printmaking studio. Reservations are required. Guests enjoy a full breakfast, an outdoor pool surrounded by redwood decks, a badminton court, and a tree-shaded yard at this family-oriented inn.

THE GROVELAND HOTEL

18767 Main Street
P.O. Box 289
Groveland, CA 95321

♿ Ⓧ $$–$$$$

▓ Along historic Highway 120, a little more than 20 miles from the main entrance to Yosemite National Park, is the gold-rush town of Groveland. In this one-time mecca for gold miners is the Groveland Hotel, its original 1849-built adobe features still intact, along with its central staircase, wraparound verandas, and roof. The second building of the inn, built in 1914 during the Hetch-Hetchy Dam Project, is a Queen Anne–style wooden structure with bay windows and six rooms. The hotel was approved as a historic property by the state in 1994 and is included on the National Register of Historic Places. The Groveland now features seventeen rooms for guests, including three suites, each distinctively designed and decorated and boasting European antiques, down comforters, and private baths. The suites contain Jacuzzis and fireplaces. The elegant Hetch Hetchy suite at the hotel features an antique French bed and sitting area with

PHONE: (209) 962–4000 or (800) 273–3314

FAX: (209) 962–6674

WEB SITE: www.groveland.com

FEATURES: inn/hotel; 17 rooms; air-conditioning; in-room phones; pets allowed; children welcome; airport pick-up; fax; copier; in-room computer hookups; audiovisual services; meeting areas; catering for groups or receptions; wedding services; restaurant on premises

NEARBY: Yosemite National Park; Pine Mountain Lake; white-water rafting; golf; tennis; horseback riding

INNKEEPERS/OWNERS: Peggy and Grover Mosely

floral sofa facing the fireplace. Treat yourself to a relaxing escape with in-room extras such as a wine, cheese, and fruit tray; champagne and chocolates; or a bubble-bath basket with champagne. The hotel has chosen to limit television to the common lounge area in the main building, where classic videotapes are available. Breakfast at the inn is buffet style. Guests help themselves to juices, cereals, freshly baked muffins and breads, and seasonal fresh fruits; complimentary wines are served in the evenings. A gourmet restaurant at the hotel offers an award-winning wine list and entrees that range from the imaginative to a "down home" variety. The hotel's conference room holds up to twenty-five persons and is equipped for multimedia presentations; in-house catering is available for all functions, ranging from weddings to business conferences. The hotel is the site of many special events during the year, including Winemaker dinners from local wineries and the renowned Mark Twain Sierra Living History Dinner Shows.

ROCKWOOD LODGE

5295 West Lake Boulevard
P.O. Box 226
Homewood, CA 96141-0226

⊗ $$–$$$

■ Hand-hewn beams, restored golden-pine paneling, and local rock exteriors are featured in this former "summer home" built in the 1930s. Located among tall pines near the west shore of Lake Tahoe, the B&B offers rooms decorated in a pleasing mixture of European and American antiques and Laura Ashley fabrics. Guest rooms feature large feather beds, down comforters and pillows, sitting areas, pedestal sinks, and private, tiled baths. The full breakfast, featuring juice, muffins, croissants, and special entrees such as fruit

PHONE: (530) 525–5273 or (800) 538–2463

FAX: (530) 525–5949

WEB SITE: www.rockwoodlodge.com

FEATURES: inn; 5 rooms; in-room workspace; fax; copier; computer hookups; weddings; no credit cards

NEARBY: Lake Tahoe; all lake and mountain activities

INNKEEPERS/OWNERS: Louis Reinkens and Constance Stevens

crepes, or pancakelike pastries known as Dutch babies, is served in the dining room or on the terrace in summer. Guests also enjoy a large stone patio with outside fireplace in front of the inn.

SORENSEN'S RESORT

14255 Highway 88
Hope Valley, CA 96120

♿ ⊗ $–$$$$

This 165-acre resort in the High Sierra meadowland was homesteaded by Danish shepherders in 1876 and opened in 1926. The guest cabins are nestled in a grove of aspens, and each cabin is uniquely appointed with such details as freestanding, wood-burning stoves; cathedral ceilings; lofts; and kitchenettes. Three units at the resort offer a complimentary breakfast; in the thirty-three cabins, with up to three bedrooms, the generous breakfast can be ordered from a reasonably priced cafe menu at an additional charge. This bed-and-hospitality establishment provides a complimentary glass of wine as well as coffee, tea, or hot cocoa throughout the day. Unlimited recreation at the resort includes barbecues, a kids' "catch-and-release" fishing pond, and river rafting as well as trail-walking tours that include meals, lodging, and tour guides. The resort also offers cross-country skiing with its own trails, rentals, and lessons. Fly fishing, astronomy, and watercolor classes are also offered at the resort.

PHONE: (530) 694–2203 or (800) 423–9949

WEB SITE: www.sorensensresort.com

FEATURES: inn/cottages; 30 rooms, 33 cabins; pets allowed; copier; catering; conferences; fishing pond; classes; walking tours; computer hookups; audiovisual equipment; fax; weddings

NEARBY: trails; cross-country skiing; fishing; llama tours; rafting

INNKEEPERS/OWNERS: Michael and Jennifer Carmago

COURT STREET INN

215 Court Street
Jackson, CA 95642

♿ ⊗ $$–$$$

This fully restored 1870 Mother Lode home and Indian House cottage is listed on the National Register of Historic Places. Fine antiques, lace curtains, fluffy down comforters, and abundant fresh flowers are some of the special touches here. Guest accommodations in the house include three rooms downstairs with private baths and a suite upstairs complete with private

PHONE: (209) 223–0416

FAX: (209) 223–5429

WEB SITE: www.courtstreetinn.com

FEATURES: inn/cottage; 6 rooms, 1 cottage; air-conditioning; in-room television (suite); fax; audiovisual equipment; meeting areas; weddings

NEARBY: wineries; lakes; hiking; forests; historical park

INNKEEPERS/OWNERS: Dave and Nancy Butow

whirlpool. Two guest rooms have fireplaces. The Indian House cottage, originally built as a museum to house Native American artifacts, offers two bedrooms and a spacious living room with a fireplace, a 61-inch television, and a VCR. The inn offers complimentary refreshments in the evening. The generous morning fare, which is served in the dining room, usually consists of fresh fruit, the inn's own version of Orange Julius, and a special entree, such as croissants with orange marmalade and Black Forest ham or egg soufflés with apple cinnamon sausages.

THE GATE HOUSE INN

1330 Jackson Gate Road
Jackson, CA 95642

⊗ $$–$$$

▨ This country Victorian, recently painted in its original color scheme and registered as a National Historic Landmark, has a separate summerhouse that provides a special romantic retreat. Decorated with Early American,

PHONE: (209) 223–3500 or (800) 841–1072

FAX: (209) 223–1299

WEB SITE: www.gatehouseinn.com

FEATURES: inn/cottage; 4 rooms; air-conditioning; swimming pool; gift shop; weddings; free airport pick-up service

NEARBY: lakes; golf; hiking; historic parks; downtown shops and restaurants

INNKEEPERS/OWNERS: Jamie and Dave Ciardella

oak, and Irish pine furnishings, as well as elegant French pieces, the inn is a step into the past. Guest rooms in the main house all have private baths and brass or Victorian-era queen-size beds; some have fireplaces. The summerhouse's two-room suite offers a wood-burning stove and whirlpool for two. Guests are invited to relax on the porches, play Ping-Pong, and use the inn's swimming pool. A hearty country breakfast, featuring baked French toast, chicken-turkey sausage, quiches, or casseroles, may be enjoyed with other guests or in the privacy of the room; complimentary tea and baked goods are available in the afternoon. This country retreat provides an easy stroll to several fine restaurants. An angel-theme gift shop featuring handmade articles is located at the Gate House; angels decorate the inn.

THE WEDGEWOOD INN

11941 Narcissus Road
Jackson, CA 95642

⊗ $$–$$$$

█ This turn-of-the-twentieth-century-designed inn, built in 1987 as a B&B, is situated on five private acres dotted with pines and oaks. The main "Victorian" house with colorful flower boxes boasts a wraparound porch with a swing and a balcony off the two upstairs guest rooms. Inside the nostalgic house, which is furnished with European and American antiques, including stained-glass and Victorian lace lamps, guests also enjoy a sitting parlor with grand piano and cozy wood-burning stove; the dining room has an interesting tapestry collection. Guest rooms in the house all have private baths (some with antique claw-foot tubs) and are decorated individually with fine antiques; four guest rooms have wood-burning stoves. The carriage house, the largest accommodation at the inn, is decorated in a country theme with four generations of family heirlooms; it has a carved, queen-size, canopied bed, as well as a television and VCR, private patio, Jacuzzi for two, and wood-burning stove. Coffee is available for early risers, and a full gourmet breakfast is graciously served on fine bone china in the formal dining room. Upon arrival guests are served a cheese-and-beverage snack. Outdoor pleasures include the inn's terraced garden areas with rose arbor, fountains, and gazebo. The lawn is set up for croquet, and guests can nap or read in the hammocks at this quiet, secluded retreat.

PHONE: (209) 296–4300 or (800) 933–4393

WEB SITE: www.wedgewoodinn.com

FEATURES: inn/cottage; 5 rooms, 1 cottage; air-conditioning; fax; copier; in-room televisions; croquet

NEARBY: wineries; antiques; golf; fishing; skiing; restaurants

INNKEEPERS/OWNERS: Vic and Jeannine Beltz

1859 HISTORIC NATIONAL HOTEL—A COUNTRY INN

18183 Main Street
P.O. Box 502
Jamestown, CA 95327

⊗ $$–$$$

▧ Nestled in the Gold Country between Lake Tahoe and Yosemite National Park, this gold-rush hotel is one of California's ten oldest continuously operating hostelries. Built in 1859, the authentically restored two-story hotel features many of the original furnishings, including brass beds and reproductions of typical period lace curtains and quilts. The inn's original redwood bar is retained, where one can imagine miners trading gold dust for drinks. A bountiful continental breakfast buffet is served in the hotel's renowned restaurant, which has been featured in *Gourmet* and *Bon Appétit* magazines. Oh, yes, and you just might get a sighting of "Flo," the playful resident ghost.

PHONE: (209) 984–3446 or (800) 894–3446

FAX: (209) 984–5620

WEB SITE: www.national-hotel.com

FEATURES: hotel; 9 rooms; air-conditioning; in-room phones with computer hookups; in-room televisions; fax; copier; restaurant and bar; weddings; meeting room; pets allowed (extra cost)

NEARBY: historic town; Rail Town 1897 State Historic Park; gold-panning; antiquing; skiing; water sports; live theater

INNKEEPER/OWNER: Stephen Willey

Mark Twain's "Jimtown"

The first gold discovery in Tuolumne County was made in the burg known affectionately as "Jimtown" in 1848. Many of Jamestown's buildings may be familiar to you since the circa-1870 buildings have served filmmakers through the years. In Jamestown be sure to visit the Jimtown 1849 Gold Mining Camp at 18170 Main Street. The camp, with restored buildings, is a real re-creation effort. The cabin was purportedly inhabited at one time by Mark Twain. Allow an hour for exploring the camp, which is open daily from 10:00 A.M. to 5:00 P.M. Admission is free, but there is a fee for gold-panning. For more information call (209) 984–4653 or (800) 596–0009 or log on to www.goldprospecting.com.

JAMESTOWN HOTEL— A COUNTRY INN

18153 Main Street
P.O. Box 539
Jamestown, CA 95327

♿ ⊗ $$

■ The historic Jamestown Hotel, with adjoining restaurant and
pub, is located on the main street of town, where miners and
budding tycoons once strolled. At present, the refurbished
buildings of the 1800s town hold quaint antiques shops and boutiques. The antiques-
filled rooms of the inn are named after the era's famous women; all rooms have private baths (most with antique claw-foot tubs and pull-chain toilets), and some have whirlpools and sitting rooms. The Diamond Lil, which sleeps two to four persons, is complete with ornate daybed in the sitting area surrounded by flowered wall coverings and a queen-size antique wrought-iron bed. Guests enjoy an expanded continental breakfast of fresh fruit, juice, two varieties of cereal, and rolls each morning in the restaurant dining room. The Cafe on the Patio features California cuisine.

PHONE: (209) 984–3902 or (800) 205–4901
FAX: (209) 984–4149
WEB SITE: www.jamestownhotel.com
FEATURES: inn/hotel; 8 rooms; air-conditioning; in-room phones; in-room televisions and VCRs; fax; copier; computer hookups; catering; in-room workspace; restaurant and pub
NEARBY: Main Street shops; Sierra Railroad Museum; Columbia State Park; gold-panning; river rafting
INNKEEPERS/OWNERS: Brian and Dawn Solomon

ROYAL CARRIAGE INN

18239 Main Street
P.O. Box 219
Jamestown, CA 95327

♿ ⊗ $–$$

■ This hotel nestled in historic Jamestown was actually built in 1922 but has undergone a major renovation to give it a late-1880s feel. The inn, with quaint garden cottages, offers Victorian charm and warmth and lots of personal touches. The very reasonable rooms all have private baths, although some are located across the hall. Guests are greeted each morning with a continental breakfast consisting of juices, fresh fruit, bagels, and pastries, as well as coffee that you grind fresh in your room. Guests find relaxation in the parlor or on the balcony that looks out on the gold-mining Main Street in town.

PHONE: (209) 984–5271

FAX: (209) 984–1675

WEB SITE: www.royalcarriageinn.com

FEATURES: inn/cottages; 14 rooms, 10 cottages; pets allowed

NEARBY: town shops and cafes; historic railroad park; gold-panning; river rafting

INNKEEPER/OWNER: Pamela Hatch

BOULDER CREEK BED & BREAKFAST

4572 Ben Hur Road
Mariposa, CA 95338

 $

This cozy B&B submerged in nature backs on picturesque Boulder Creek and scenic meadowland, where guests can view roaming deer, waterfalls, wildflowers, and abundant trees with foliage that changes seasonally. The chalet-style home with lots of picture windows to capture the views offers three guest rooms, all with private baths. Guests choose from accommodations with twin, queen-, or king-size beds.

PHONE: (209) 742–7729 or (800) 768–4752

FAX: (209) 742–5885

WEB SITE: http://mariposa.yosemite .net/boulder_creek

FEATURES: inn; 3 rooms; air-conditioning; fax; computer hookups; hot tub

NEARBY: Yosemite National Park; gold-rush town

INNKEEPERS/OWNERS: Michael and Nancy Habermann

Rooms are comfortably furnished with such details as down pillows, comforters, antiques, and antique collectibles. Breakfast is a treat at Boulder Creek, presented on fine china and German crystal by the inn's gourmet chef/innkeeper (a former restaurateur from Hamburg, Germany). The full meal may include such delights as Michael's farmer's omelette filled with farm-fresh vegetables and bacon, soufflé, quiche, and Nancy's special cheesecake. Guests enjoy a hot tub nestled in a romantic gazebo as well as a living room with wood-burning stove and comfortable seating where evening refreshments are served. Boulder Creek is located near the year-round entrance to Yosemite National Park and just 2 miles from town.

MEADOW CREEK RANCH

2669 Triangle Road, Highway 49 South
Mariposa, CA 95338

 $–$$

 This original 1858 overnight stagecoach stop on seven acres of land contains the main two-story ranch house and
a country cottage. Innkeepers greet
guests with refreshments and encourage them to take a relaxing stroll around the
grounds, which feature an old waterwheel. The two comfortable guest rooms have
European and country antiques, original art, and lots of plants. The Country Cottage
room offers a private bath with a two-person, claw-foot tub; gas fireplace; and queen-
size canopy bed. The full breakfast is served family-style in the dining room.

PHONE: (209) 966–3843 or (800) 853–2037
WEB SITE: www.meadowcreek ranchbnb.com
FEATURES: inn; 2 rooms
NEARBY: Yosemite National Park; fishing; hiking; town
INNKEEPERS/OWNERS: Willie and Diana Wilcoxen

THE PELENNOR

3871 Highway 49 South
Mariposa, CA 95338

 $

 This hospitable B&B with a Scottish theme offers a two-story B&B building with
two baths and a common room with kitch-
enette. The fifteen-acre country setting
offers serenity and pretty gardens. The
decor is basic but features some tartan
touches; the innkeepers will play a few
tunes on the bagpipes upon request. A
continental breakfast includes muffins,
juice, cereal, and fruits. Guests enjoy the
home's country quiet, lap pool, and spa.

PHONE: (209) 966–2832
FEATURES: home; 4 rooms; pets allowed; lap pool; spa; no credit cards
NEARBY: Yosemite National Park; town; lake
INNKEEPERS/OWNERS: Dick and Gwen Foster

POPPY HILL BED & BREAKFAST

5218 Crystal Aire Drive
Mariposa, CA 95338

♿ ⊝ $$

About a thirty-minute drive from the entrance of Yosemite National Park is this restored country home B&B. The home, surrounded by bright-orange poppies, is furnished in pleasant European and American antiques. The second-story guest rooms, all with queen-size beds, down comforters, private baths, and sitting areas, are spacious. Pampered guests may dine in their room, outdoors, at the sunny bay-window seating, or in the family-style dining room. The full morning meal is hearty country fare. Later in the day guests enjoy complimentary beverages and hors d'oeuvres. A hot tub and an above-ground pool at Poppy Hill are for guests' use; local recreation abounds with the Yosemite, Sierra, and Stanislaus national forests nearby.

PHONE: (209) 742–6273 or (800) 587–6779
FAX: (209) 742–6273
WEB SITE: www.poppyhill.com
FEATURES: home; 3 rooms; air-conditioning; a TV/VCR (on request); fax; copier; hot tub; above-ground pool
NEARBY: Yosemite, Sierra, and Stanislaus national forests
INNKEEPERS/OWNERS: Tom and Mary Ellen Kim

RESTFUL NEST RESORT B&B

4274 Buckeye Creek Road
Mariposa, CA 95338

⊝ $–$$

Nestled in the foothills of the Sierra Nevadas on eleven acres, this bed and breakfast's sylvan setting re-creates the flavor of Provence. This relaxing rural resort offers a variety of secluded spots, barbecue and picnic areas, and a large catch-and-release fishing pond. The inn's thoughtfully decorated guest

PHONE: (209) 742–7127 or (800) 664–7127
FAX: (209) 742–7127
WEB SITE: http://mariposa.yosemite.net/restful
FEATURES: inn; 3 rooms; air-conditioning; computer hookups; in-room televisions and VCRs; in-room workspace; swimming pool; spa; fax; copier; catch-and-release fishing pond
NEARBY: Yosemite National Park; Gold Country
INNKEEPER/OWNER: Lois Moroni

rooms have queen-size beds, private baths and entrances, and magnificent views. The guesthouse includes a living room, bedroom, minikitchen, and wood-burning stove. The gourmet breakfast, featuring Lois's homemade sausages, brioche, and other breads, is highly praised by visitors.

DUNBAR HOUSE, 1880

271 Jones Street
P.O. Box 1375
Murphys, CA 95247

⊗ $$$–$$$$

■ This restored 1880 Italianate-style home was Calaveras County's first B&B and offers an elegant yet comfortable stay. Decorated in light and cheery color schemes, guest rooms at the Dunbar House, 1880 are furnished with antiques, art, lace, pillows, and down comforters and provide air-conditioning, central heating, private baths, and romantic wood-burning stoves. A personal refrigerator in each room is stocked with ice, an appetizer plate, and a complimentary bottle of wine; a television and VCR with classic video library offers in-room entertainment. On the garden level of the inn is the Cedar suite, featuring a bath with whirlpool for two and electric towel warmers, as well as a private sunporch that extends into the garden, where suite guests can sip a complimentary bottle of champagne while sunning. An old-fashioned country breakfast, by candlelight, with home-baked goodies and special entrees such as lemon-cheese–stuffed French toast or cheese soufflé, is served fireside in the dining room, in the century-old gardens, or in the privacy of the guest room. Other refreshments at the inn include lemonade and cookies on the porch, and an afternoon appetizer plate is served in the room with local wines and assorted beverages.

PHONE: (209) 728–2897 or (800) 692–6006
FAX: (209) 728–1451
WEB SITE: www.dunbarhouse.com
FEATURES: inn; 5 rooms; air-conditioning; in-room televisions and VCRs; in-room refrigerators; fax; copier; in-room workspace; in-room phones
NEARBY: wineries; shopping; skiing; golf
INNKEEPERS/OWNERS: Arline and Rich Taborek

DEER CREEK INN

116 Nevada Street
Nevada City, CA 95959

⊗ $$–$$$

■ This warm and friendly inn is nestled alongside beautiful Deer Creek, which grants both fishing and gold-panning opportunities, as well as picturesque views. This Queen Anne Victorian was built in 1860 and was, for most of its existence, occupied by the Colley family, local pioneers and business owners. Deer Creek itself was a lucrative gold-panning locale in gold-rush days, referred to as a "pound-a-day" creek for the amount of gold you could pan there. The house has been carefully restored, offering six guest rooms, named after former owners of the house, each with a private bath, queen- or king-size bed, private veranda with town or creek views, antiques, marble bath, claw-foot tub, and four-poster or canopy bed with down comforters. The formal dining room of the inn or the creek-side deck is the locale of the morning breakfast. The hearty meal normally includes an egg casserole, a potato dish, a sweet dish such as apple-crisp pancakes, granola, and juices. The inn offers wine each evening. This parklike setting has made the inn a popular spot for weddings and group gatherings.

PHONE: (530) 265–0363 or (800) 655–0363

FAX: (530) 265–0980

WEB SITE: www.deercreekinn.com

FEATURES: inn; 6 units; air-conditioning; fax; copier; telephone (on request); computer hookups; meeting areas; catering for receptions/small meetings; wedding services

NEARBY: hiking; boating; fishing; gold-panning; Empire Mine; horse-drawn carriage rides; art galleries; Malakoff Diggins State Historic Park; theater playhouse

INNKEEPERS/OWNERS: Eileen and Ken Strangfeld

THE EMMA NEVADA HOUSE

528 East Broad Street
Nevada City, CA 95959

⊗ $$–$$$

This charming pre-Victorian house with rose-covered white picket fence, built in 1856, was possibly the childhood home of nineteenth-century opera star Emma Nevada. The completely restored home hosts some of the refurbished antiques, as well as gaslit chandeliers, claw-foot tubs, and rare original glass windows throughout. The muted peach-colored, two-story B&B inn is located in a quiet residential neighborhood near the historic district. Outside, guests relax on the wraparound front porch and on two large back decks; the back garden, filled with daffodils and ancient trees, provides strolls down to a small creek. All six suites at the inn offer queen beds, private baths, down comforters, and fine linens; the most popular rooms boast Jacuzzis and wood-burning stoves. Nightingale's Bower, formerly the house's parlor, is an elegant main-floor accommodation with rich Italian bedding, bay windows, antique stove, and Jacuzzi; Emma's Hideaway is just that, with its cozy, connecting hideaway rooms in the former attic. The very romantic Empress' Chamber, in burgundy and ivory, hosts a French antique bed and armoire, a wall of windows, sitting area, and Jacuzzi with shower. Around check-in time at the inn, tea and home-baked cookies are available; guests lounge in the fireplace-warmed living room or enjoy the inn's game room with antique slot machines. The Sun Room, with six walls of floor-to-ceiling antique windows, offers stunning views of the local Sierra scenery. The full breakfast is served in the Sun Room overlooking the garden or in the dining room; fresh fruit, juices, mini muffins or scones, and a special entree such as pumpkin waffles or Emma's special cobbler await each morning.

PHONE: (530) 265–4415 or (800) 916–EMMA

FAX: (530) 265–4416

WEB SITE: www.emmanevadahouse.com

FEATURES: inn; 6 rooms; air-conditioning; in-room phones (some); in-room televisions (some); fax; computer hookups

NEARBY: historic district; galleries, museums; buggy ride; Tahoe National Forest; shops and restaurants

INNKEEPERS/OWNERS: Andrew and Susan Howard

FLUME'S END BED & BREAKFAST INN

317 South Pine Street
Nevada City, CA 95959

⊗ $$–$$$

◼ The historic flume beside this 1863-built Victorian inn brought Sierra mountain waters of good fortune rushing to gold miners in the 1800s. Flume's End rests on a picturesque hillside, sloping down to the natural waterfalls of a 3-mile-long winding creek. The restored home offers comfortable accommodations, including two rooms with Jacuzzis and the Garden and Creekside rooms, which boast private decks over the waterfalls and share a sitting room with television, wet bar, and refrigerator. The romantic cottage offers a four-poster bed, fireplace, and kitchenette, as well as a deck overlooking the waterfalls. Guests relax in the inn's large common rooms with piano and fireplaces. Stays at the inn include a generous buffet breakfast, early-morning coffee or tea, and afternoon refreshments. The inn specializes in weddings and retreats.

PHONE: (530) 265–9665
WEB SITE: www.flumesend.com
FEATURES: inn/cottage; 5 rooms, 1 cottage; air-conditioning; kitchenette (cottage); computer hookups; weddings and retreats
NEARBY: historic district; shops; restaurants
INNKEEPERS/OWNERS: Carol Wyrick and Mary Anne Kelly

THE PARSONAGE BED AND BREAKFAST

427 Broad Street
Nevada City, CA 95959

⊗ $$–$$$

◼ Built in the 1860s, this distinctive blue home is listed on the National Register of Historic Places. Guests will enjoy a progressive time warp back to those times. The owners have carefully and lovingly restored the home and have made a special effort to retain the original look of the Victorian era, right down to the historically correct raised wall coverings and period furniture in each room. All rooms, most with queen-size beds, have private baths; one has a fireplace and balcony. The Parsonage Bed and Breakfast serves a full breakfast, and each morning, fresh eggs are brought in from a local ranch. During the

PHONE: (530) 265–9478
FAX: (530) 265–8147
WEB SITE: www.theparsonage.net
FEATURES: inn/cottage; 6 rooms; air-conditioning; in-room televisions; fax; copier; computer hookups; library; restaurant; weddings
NEARBY: Gold Country; historic Nevada City; live theater; skiing; water sports; golf; fishing
INNKEEPERS/OWNERS: Chuck and Susan Shea

summer months, fresh strawberries and blueberries are also on the menu, along with special signature dishes such as peach French toast. Guests enjoy a complimentary beverage bar day and night.

PIETY HILL COTTAGES

523 Sacramento Street
Nevada City, CA 95959

⊗ $–$$

▨ One of the area's oldest continuously operating hostelries, the inn was originally built in 1933 as an auto court. At present, the nine charming cottages surround a grassy, tree-shaded courtyard and garden with picnic tables, barbecues, comfortable chairs, and a gazebo-covered spa. Each of the one-, two-, and three-room cottages, done in fresh country decor, has a kitchenette stocked with complimentary hot and cold beverages, king- or queen-size bed, private bath, television, and air conditioner. The two-room Apple Blossom Cottage is done in country French, with cheery French blue and golden yellow colors that set off the white wicker furnishings. The three-room White Birch Cottage with sitting area is nestled in its own garden for optimum privacy. A breakfast basket is delivered to the cottage each morning, filled with fresh fruits, juice, homemade breads, and a main dish such as quiche or orange sourdough French toast with homemade applesauce. The inn is a popular romantic retreat, but it is also well suited for families and business gatherings.

PHONE: (530) 265–2245 or (800) 443–2245

FAX: (530) 265–6528

WEB SITE: www.pietyhillcottages.com

FEATURES: inn/cottages; 9 cottages; air-conditioning; in-room phones; in-room televisions; in-room workspace; computer hookups; conference/meeting area; kitchenettes; spa

NEARBY: historic district; shops; restaurants; state parks; fishing

INNKEEPERS/OWNERS: Steve and Joan Oas

RED CASTLE INN

109 Prospect Street
Nevada City, CA 95959

⊗ $–$$$

▧ Atop a heavily forested hill overlooking pic-
turesque Nevada City sits this four-story Gothic
Revival structure resembling a castle. The
impressive, 1859-built brick mansion is a well-
photographed historical landmark and has been an inn since 1963. It offers lush ter-
raced gardens, verandas, and interiors filled with period antiques. The uniquely
furnished guest rooms showcase many historical treasures; antique books; fresh
flowers; private, newly updated baths; and sweets. The entire top floor of the inn
comprises the Garret suite, featuring two guest rooms that share a sitting room and
bath; the suite is ideal for families or two couples. The candlelight, five-course buffet
breakfast, featuring a dish from the gold-
rush days, an egg specialty, home-baked
cereals and breads, fruit, and juice, is
served in the elegant parlor; afternoon
Victorian refreshments of sweets and bev-
erages are also served in the parlor, with
its 1880s pump organ. The parlor is also
the site of tea and "conversations with
Mark Twain" on occasional Sunday after-
noons. On Christmas Day the inn serves a
Victorian ten-course dinner to guests.

PHONE: (530) 265–5135 or (800)
761–4766

WEB SITE: www.redcastleinn.com

FEATURES: inn; 7 rooms; air-conditioning;
special dinners; special teas

NEARBY: historic district; shops;
restaurants; state parks; gold-mine
tours; theater

INNKEEPERS/OWNERS: Mary Louise and
Conley Weaver

INN AT SHALLOW CREEK FARM

4712 Road DD
Orland, CA 95963

⊗ $

▧ This two-story farmhouse surrounded by a white picket fence is a real country
getaway serenely nestled in the Sacramento Valley. On its three acres are well-
established citrus orchards; walnut, plum, fig, and pomegranate trees; and roaming

PHONE: (530) 865–4093 or (800) 865–4093

FAX: (530) 865–4093

WEB SITE: www.bbonline.com/ca/shallow creek

FEATURES: inn/cottage; 3 rooms, 1 cottage; air-conditioning; in-room phones; in-room workspace; computer hookups

NEARBY: Sacramento River; Black Butte Lake

INNKEEPERS/OWNERS: Mary and Kurt Glaeseman

chickens, geese, and ducks. The 1900-built farmhouse has been renovated to accommodate B&B visitors in both the main house and the former caretaker's cottage, which includes a complete kitchen; an old-fashioned, enclosed sitting porch; and a wood-burning stove. The Brookdale Room is a spacious upstairs accommodation overlooking the creek and flower garden; it has twin beds and shares a bath with the Heritage Room. The light and airy Penfield Suite downstairs has a private bath, a queen-size bed, and Americana touches. Farm-fresh breakfasts are included in the stay at Shallow Creek, featuring local fresh fruit and farm produce. A special breakfast offering is old-fashioned egg custard served with an assortment of fresh berries. Home-baked breads and muffins complete the extended continental fare that is served in the family-style dining room or on the sunporch overlooking the orchard. The old red barn on the property formerly served as a livery stable on the route between the Sacramento River and Newville, which is now a ghost town. The country retreat is about 90 miles from Sacramento.

THE CHICHESTER-MCKEE HOUSE

800 Spring Street
Placerville, CA 95667

⊗ $$

▦ A gold mine is hidden under the dining area of this lovingly restored 1892 Victorian home located on a hillside. California oaks, flower gardens, and a 60-foot tulip tree surround the inn and its carriage house. (The main house is thought to have been the first house in the city with plumbing!) The interior of the home features antique furnishings and a storybook doll collection, and the library and parlor offer fireplaces and cozy reading nooks. The guest rooms are fur-

PHONE: (530) 626–1882 or (800) 831–4008
FAX: (530) 626–7801
WEB SITE: www.innlover.com
FEATURES: home; 4 rooms; air-conditioning, in-room phones; computer hookups
NEARBY: Apple Hill; white-water rafting; Marshall Gold Discovery Park
INNKEEPERS/OWNERS: Doreen and Bill Thornhill

nished in period pieces, and each has its own bath; the Chichester suite has a fireplace. A full gourmet breakfast awaits guests each morning and features goodies such as eggs Benedict, German apple pancakes, crepes, and quiche.

THE FEATHER BED

542 Jackson Street
P.O. Box 3200
Quincy, CA 95971

♿ ⊗ $–$$

Situated near downtown Quincy and surrounded by the trees and meadows of a national forest is this 1893 Queen Anne home with 1905 Greek Revival touches. The B&B, with a cozy cottage honeymoon suite, has a large turn-of-the-twentieth-century parlor with wood columns and a formal dining room, where winter breakfast is served. The antiques-filled guest rooms all have private baths with brass fixtures and claw-foot tubs as well as showers. The unique accommodations range from Edward's Suite, with sitting room and fireplace, to the Guest House, featuring a gas fireplace and a private front porch. A generous full breakfast featuring homegrown berry smoothies, baked-apple crisp, cheese puffs, and almond muffins is served on the front porch and in the dining room year-round. The inn offers bicycles for guests' use.

PHONE: (530) 283–0102 or (800) 696–8624
FAX: (530) 283–0102
WEB SITE: www.featherbed-inn.com
FEATURES: inn/cottage; 7 rooms; air-conditioning; in-room phones; in-room televisions; bicycles; fax; copier; computer hookups; in-room workspace
NEARBY: theater; shops; restaurants; county museum; fishing; mountain and lake recreation
INNKEEPER/OWNER: Bob Janowski

AMBER HOUSE

1315 Twenty-second Street
Sacramento, CA 95816

⊗ $$$–$$$$

▦ This inn offers deluxe accommodations in two meticulously restored vintage structures. The inn's Poets' Refuge is a Craftsman-style home touched with period elegance, such as beveled glass, boxed-beam ceilings, a clinker-brick fireplace, and hardwood floors. Its five guest rooms feature wall coverings, antiques, and stained-glass or French windows; all have private baths, one with a large antique tub and others with Jacuzzis for two (some heart-shaped tubs). The Musician's Manor is an 1895-built colonial restoration that houses five deluxe guest rooms with marble-tiled baths; the Mozart features a fireplace and heart-shaped Jacuzzi. All guest accommodations at the inn include hidden televisions and VCRs, clock radios, telephones, and central air-conditioning. A full gourmet breakfast, including fresh fruit, a special entree, and homemade pastries, is served in the formal dining room, in one's room, on the veranda, or in the garden. Bikes are available; a meeting or reception facility for small groups may be reserved, as well as the garden for outdoor weddings and events. The inn, located in a residential neighborhood, is just a few blocks from shops, restaurants, the state capitol, and the convention center.

PHONE: (916) 444–8085 or (800) 755–6526
FAX: (916) 552–6529
WEB SITE: www.amberhouse.com
FEATURES: inn; 10 rooms; air-conditioning; in-room phones; in-room televisions and VCRs; in-room workspace; fax; copier; computer hookups; conferences/weddings; bicycles
NEARBY: state capitol; convention center; shops; restaurants
INNKEEPERS/OWNERS: Judith Bommer and Kevin Cartmill

THE INN AND SPA AT PARKSIDE

2116 Sixth Street
Sacramento, CA 95818

♿ ⊗ $$–$$$$

▦ Designated a Significant Historical Building by the city of Sacramento, the Inn and Spa at Parkside was also one of four finalists for an award for commercial historic renovation by Old Town Sacramento. The impressive grand mansion, built in 1936, was

PHONE: (916) 658–1818 or (800) 995–7275

FAX: (916) 658–1809

WEB SITE: www.innatparkside.com

FEATURES: inn; 7 rooms; in-room phones; in-room televisions and VCRs; guest kitchenette; spa; conference/meeting area; weddings; audiovisual equipment; dance floor/ballroom

NEARBY: Southside Park; state capitol; Old Town Sacramento

INNKEEPERS/OWNERS: Bill Swenson and Will Sawyer

the official U.S. residence for the North American ambassador to Nationalist China and overlooks the scenic Southside Park in the heart of Sacramento. The luxurious accommodations with museum-quality antiques include one suite, the Olympus, that boasts original artwork, a king-size bed, fireplace, kitchenette, and marble bath with tub and shower for two. The Pretty in Pink is a large, airy room with a view of treetops; amenities include a walk-in closet, antique lamps, a queen-size four-poster bed with mirrored canopy, and a spa tub-for-two. Two additional rooms feature fireplaces. Award-winning breakfasts greet guests in the inn's elegant dining room each morning. The library at the inn offers a deck and records that go with an antique phonograph, but, if you wish to dance, head for the inn's Art Deco ballroom, which hosts a 500-square-foot, spring-loaded maple dance floor. A guest kitchenette is available at all hours. Have an in-room massage or visit the spa for a facial, massage, or herbal wrap. Packages are available. Southside Park, adjacent to the inn, offers tennis courts and trails for walking and jogging.

Sacramento the Way It Used to Be

With a population of more than 360,000, Sacramento is a large city, full of cultural diversity, museums, gold-rush history, and fine restaurants and theaters. The state capital brings tourists from all over the world to partake of its many offerings and events.

Near the Capitol Mall is Old Town Sacramento, a must-see locale. The 4-block section bordered partially by the Sacramento River was the commercial district of the city during the gold rush. Redeveloped with museums, restaurants, and shops, it lives today as a tribute to the city's heritage.

One of the area's most popular museums is the California State Railroad Museum, located at Second and First Streets. The steel, brick, and glass three-story structure houses twenty-one restored locomotives and train cars and offers exhibits and films describing the state's railroad history. Allow a few hours to take it all in. Call (916) 324–0539 for information.

VIZCAYA

2019 Twenty-first Street
Sacramento, CA 95818

♿ ⊗ $$–$$$$

▪ A lot of care has gone into preserving this 1899 family mansion with corner tower in the heart of downtown Sacramento. A sweeping staircase and stately entry lead to the parlor and dining room with leaded glass and fireplaces. The guest rooms, spacious and beautifully appointed in unusual walnut and mahogany furniture, original art, and rare Victorian lighting, have private marble-tiled baths with Victorian fixtures. All guest rooms feature such modern touches as wall-to-wall carpeting, private phones, and central air-conditioning and heat. There are also deluxe master suites and spas and a restored carriage house boasting fireplaces and Jacuzzis. The stay includes a full breakfast. Guests enjoy the landscaped gardens with Victorian gazebo, as well as proximity to city entertainment and the capitol. Vizcaya is a popular wedding locale, offering its gardens with fountain and Pavilion with stained-glass chandeliers and dome; gatherings for up to 400 may be accommodated.

PHONE: (916) 455–5243 or (800) 456–2019
FAX: (916) 455–6102
WEB SITE: www.sterlinghotel.com
FEATURES: inn; 9 rooms, 3 cottages; air-conditioning; in-room phones; in-room televisions; fax; copier; computer hookups; in-room workspace; catering; meeting areas; weddings
NEARBY: state capitol; restaurants; shops
INNKEEPER/OWNER: Sandi Wasserman

THE ROBIN'S NEST BED AND BREAKFAST

247 West St. Charles Street
San Andreas, CA 95249

♿ ⊗ $$

▪ This relaxed country estate consists of an 1895 Queen Anne–Victorian home with views of the Sierra foothills and charming gardens with many fruit trees. The spacious inn, within walking distance of shops and restaurants, features two large, light-filled parlors; a sitting room; and a dining

PHONE: (209) 754–1076 or (888) 214–9202

FAX: (209) 754–3975

WEB SITE: www.robinest.com

FEATURES: inn; 9 rooms; air-conditioning; in-room phones; computer hookups; in-room televisions; fax; copier; hot tub; catering; conferences; weddings; badminton; croquet

NEARBY: shops; restaurants

INNKEEPERS/OWNERS: Karen and Bill Konietzny

room. An extensive library is available. The inn's guest rooms feature turn-of-the-twentieth-century antiques and private baths, except for two that share one bath. The Carousel is a gabled suite in maroon and pink shades with a 17-foot-high ceiling and views of the countryside. The inn's major attraction is its gourmet, four- or five-course breakfast offered each morning. The bountiful fare consists of a cold fruit soup such as kiwi soup, home-baked goods, a main course with such delights as ham and cheese strudel or eggs Benedict, and dessert. Treats and beverages are always available. The inn hosts weddings and seminars; corporate rates are available. Guests relax in the garden hot tub.

HIGH COUNTRY INN

Highway 49 at Gold Lake Road
HCR 2, Box 7
100 Green Road
Sierra City, CA 96125

⊗ $–$$

▨ Spacious decks surround this mountain home, granting spectacular views of the majestic Sierra Buttes and the aspen- and pine-filled acreage of the estate. The Yuba River is a mere 45 feet from the house; Howard Creek borders the other side of the house. Guests also enjoy the inn's private pond, stocked by the innkeepers, and a double hammock under the aspens. Guests congregate in the 30-foot-long living room with cathedral ceiling and stone fireplace. The spacious guest rooms, decorated with interesting antiques, art, and collectibles, all boast mountain views as well as both private and shared baths. The Sierra Buttes suite offers tall windows, a private bath with antique tub and

PHONE: (530) 862–1530 or (800) 862–1530

WEB SITE: www.hicountryinn.com

FEATURES: inn; 4 rooms; pond

NEARBY: Yuba River; fishing; cross-country skiing; golfing; hiking; horseback riding; snowmobiling; museums; biking

INNKEEPERS/OWNERS: Bette and Bob Latta

modern shower, a dressing room, fireplace, and king-size bed. A full gourmet break-fast featuring homemade muffins and breads, egg dishes, fresh fruit and juices, and breakfast meats is served on the deck in summer, or at the dining table with fabulous views of the Sierra Buttes. Coffee and tea carafes are delivered outside each room early in the morning. In addition to fishing, guests enjoy cross-country skiing, snow-mobiling, hiking, golfing, biking, museums, horseback riding, summer concerts, and fine dining within a few miles of the inn. The inn has been featured in *Bon Appétit*.

BARRETTA GARDENS INN

700 South Barretta Street
Sonora, CA 95370

$-$$$$

This turn-of-the-twentieth-century Victorian inn has been completely restored and now offers five individually decorated one- and two-bedroom accommodations. All have private baths, antique furnishings, some stained glass, queen- or king-size beds, and air-conditioning. The elegant Cabernet Sauvignon Suite boasts the original crys-tal chandelier, an ornate floor-to-ceiling mirror, an adjoining solarium, sitting room, television, and VCR. The Tempranillo Room on the first floor offers a whirlpool for two and picture-window views of the Sonora Hills. Two rooms can be made into a two-bedroom suite. Complimentary beverages are served on the three porches, in the parlors, or in front of the living room fire-place. The inn is situated on more than an acre of colorful gardens and lawns over-looking town. A full breakfast, including fresh fruit, freshly baked breads, and a special entree, is offered on the screened porch or in the formal dining room with its crystal chandelier. The inn is within an easy drive of Yosemite National Park, local wineries, river rafting, and golf.

PHONE: (209) 532–6039 or (800) 206–3333

FAX: (209) 532–8257

WEB SITE: www.barrettagardens.com

FEATURES: inn; 4 rooms, 1 suite; air-conditioning; in-room televisions (some); fax; meeting areas

NEARBY: restaurants; antiques shop-ping; theater; gold-panning; golfing; skiing; wineries

INNKEEPERS/OWNERS: Daniel Stone and Astrid Wasserman

BRADFORD PLACE INN & GARDENS

56 West Bradford Street
Sonora, CA 95370

⊗ $–$$$

▓ Known as the historic Keil-Burgson
house, this imposing Victorian built in
1889 became a bed-and-breakfast in the
late 1980s and offers views of historic
downtown Sonora. All spacious rooms
have queen-size beds and private baths.
The imposing Bradford suite, filled with
antiques, has a 9-foot window seat, fire-
place, microwave, refrigerator, and an
enclosed sunporch. For the sumptuous breakfast, served until 11:30 A.M., guests
have a choice of several hot entrees, such as Mother Lode omelettes, filled with
every goodie imaginable; sizzling skillets; Hawaiian French toast; or a combination of
all. The repast can be enjoyed in the elegant dining room, on the veranda, or in the
verdant garden. Refreshments are available throughout the day and evening.

PHONE: (209) 536–6075 or (800)
209–2315
FAX: (209) 532–0420
WEB SITE: www.bradfordplaceinn.com
FEATURES: inn; 4 rooms; air-conditioning;
in-room phones; computer hookups;
in-room televisions and VCRs; fax
NEARBY: art galleries; theater; caverns;
Yosemite National Park
INNKEEPER/OWNER: Dottie Musser

GUNN HOUSE

286 South Washington Street
Sonora, CA 95370

$

▓ This 1850 residence was the first two-
story adobe built in Sonora. The original
adobe makes up the core of the restored
hotel. All the guest rooms are decorated
in priceless antiques but have the modern
conveniences of air-conditioning, electric
heat, and television. Guests enjoy a pleas-
ant patio area and a swimming pool. A
continental breakfast is served each morning, and cocktails are available in the
Josephine room (the inn's restaurant).

PHONE: (209) 532–3421
WEB SITE: www.gunnhousehotel.com
FEATURES: inn/hotel; 19 rooms; air-
conditioning; in-room televisions;
swimming pool; restaurant
NEARBY: Columbia State Park;
Yosemite; lakes; rivers
INNKEEPERS/OWNERS: Mike and Shirley
Sarno

THE FOXES IN SUTTER CREEK

77 Main Street
P.O. Box 159
Sutter Creek, CA 95685

⊗ $$$

■ This popular inn, formerly known as the Brinn House, was built in 1857 during the gold-rush days. Accommodations include suites that are furnished in specially selected antiques and have dining and sitting areas, private baths, queen-size beds, and air-conditioning. The downstairs suite boasts a fireplace and large bath with crystal chandelier and claw-foot tub as well as private entrance and porch. Four accommodations at the inn have fireplaces. The bountiful country breakfast, which features dishes such as chiles rellenos de las Zorras, Swiss eggs, and Swedish pancakes, is cooked to order and served on a silver service, along with the morning newspaper, in the suite or on the tree-roofed gazebo surrounded by colorful azaleas. Guests enjoy covered parking and courtesy pick-up at the airport with prior notification.

PHONE: (209) 267–5882 or (800) 987–3344
FAX: (209) 267–0712
WEB SITE: www.foxesinn.com
FEATURES: inn; 7 rooms; air-conditioning; in-room televisions (some); airport pick-up; fax; copier; computer hookups
NEARBY: in town; shops; restaurants; Amador County Museum; El Dorado National Forest; theater; wineries
INNKEEPERS/OWNERS: Jim Travnikan and Bob Van Alstine

GREY GABLES INN

161 Hanford Street
P.O. Box 1687
Sutter Creek, CA 95685

♿ ⊗ $$–$$$

■ This English country manor house brings a touch of "England" to the Gold Country area with its terraced garden abloom with flowers and hosting vine-clung arbors and redbrick pathways. In true English tradition guests enjoy an afternoon tea with cakes or scones served in the parlor; wine from local wineries and hors d'oeuvres are served each evening. The eight guest rooms at the inn are each fully carpeted and have their own fireplaces with marble tile; rooms also boast armoires, fine antique furnishings, colorful wall coverings in floral prints, and tiled bathrooms with showers,

PHONE: (209) 267–1039 or (800) 473–9422

FAX: (209) 267–0998

WEB SITE: www.greygables.com

FEATURES: inn; 8 rooms; air-conditioning; fax; copier; computer hookups

NEARBY: antiques and gift shops; wineries; Chaw Se Indian Grinding Rock State Park; Amador County Museum; golf; fishing; hiking

INNKEEPERS/OWNERS: Roger and Sue Garlick

many with claw-foot tubs. The Victorian suite on the upstairs level of the inn has dark green carpeting, soft pink walls, and a king-size four-poster bed; it overlooks the garden and the historic churchyard. The Byron on the main floor of the inn is decorated in dark rose and forest greens and contains an impressive Renaissance Revival four-poster, canopied king-size bed; claw-foot tub; and garden view. Breakfast may be served in the privacy of the guest room or in the dining room on fine bone china. The morning fare includes fruits and juices followed by a special gourmet entree such as quiche, frittatas, or stuffed baked French toast. Located in the town of Sutter Creek, the inn is an easy stroll to antique and gift shops.

THE HANFORD HOUSE B&B INN

61 Hanford Street, Highway 49
P.O. Box 1450
Sutter Creek, CA 95685

& ⊗ $$–$$$

▓ This classic redbrick inn, covered in ivy, is nestled on a quiet corner of Main Street in downtown Sutter Creek. The 6,200-square-foot inn offers nine spacious guest rooms furnished in gold-rush antiques; all have private baths, and many feature such extras as Jacuzzis and marble fireplaces. Each room contains a diary for guests' comments; the Rooftop suite also has a "secret box," where guests will discover (if they can find it) handwritten notes penned by former guests. A rooftop deck provides sunbathing and country views. The full gourmet breakfast at the inn might include, in addition to the innkeepers' homemade granola, an entree such as Amish French toast, crepes with

PHONE: (209) 267–0747 or (800) 871–5839

FAX: (209) 267–1825

WEB SITE: www.hanfordhouse.com

FEATURES: inn; 9 rooms; air-conditioning; in-room televisions (some); conference center; all business services; weddings; retreats

NEARBY: downtown; restaurants; shopping; wineries; gold-panning

INNKEEPERS/OWNERS: Bob and Karen Tierno

scrambled eggs, or smoky bacon. Sunday breakfasts add a "gentle wake-up" to the menu with a glass of orange juice, a cranberry juice ice cube, and a dash of champagne. Home-baked goodies, light appetizers, and a glass of wine are served in the afternoon. The inn is a popular site for weddings and corporate retreats.

SUTTER CREEK INN

75 Main Street
P.O. Box 385
Sutter Creek, CA 95685

🚫 $–$$$

▦ The 1859-built inn, the biggest house in town, offers accommodations upstairs and in several outbuildings in the rear of the house that have been totally refurbished. The unusual colors and eclectic decorating schemes include swinging beds (which can be stabilized), fireplaces, Franklin stoves, canopies, and brightly colored wicker. Guests may relax in the living room or on outside hammocks. An imaginative full country breakfast, featuring egg, meat, and potato dishes, is prepared and served buffet-style in the spacious old kitchen; coffee and tea are served each afternoon. Handwriting analysis is done upon request at this hospitable inn, as are professional massages or reflexology.

PHONE: (209) 267–5606
FAX: (209) 267–9287
WEB SITE: www.suttercreekinn.com
FEATURES: inn/cottages; 17 rooms; air-conditioning; in-room televisions (some); fax; airport pick-up; massages, reflexology, and handwriting analysis by appointment
NEARBY: shops; restaurants; Amador County Museum; wineries; golf
INNKEEPERS/OWNERS: the Way family

CHANEY HOUSE

4725 West Lake Boulevard
P.O. Box 7852
Tahoe City, CA 96145

🚫 $$–$$$

▦ This historic stone lakefront home was built in the 1920s by Italian stonemasons.

PHONE: (530) 525–7333
FAX: (530) 525–4413
WEB SITE: www.chaneyhouse.com
FEATURES: inn; 4 rooms; in-room television (1 unit); fax; copier; in-room workspace; private beach and pier
NEARBY: Lake Tahoe; golf; ski areas
INNKEEPERS/OWNERS: Gary and Lori Chaney

The distinct European-style construction boasts 18-inch-thick stone walls throughout the house, a massive fireplace extending to the cathedral ceilings, and Gothic stone arches and walls outlining the paths around the three patios. The guest accommodations all have down comforters, warm wood paneling, private baths, and some family antiques. The Honeymoon Hideaway has a sitting area with wet bar, fireplace, television/ VCR, and a "duo" granite whirlpool. A full breakfast is served on the lake-view patio or in the formal dining room; the house specialty is Grand Marnier oven French toast served with homemade hot blackberry sauce and crème fraîche. Evening refreshments are offered by fireside. Guests at the Chaney House enjoy a private beach and pier and abundant recreational opportunities year-round.

THE COTTAGE INN

1690 West Lake Boulevard, Highway 89
P.O. Box 66
Tahoe City, CA 96145

♿ $$–$$$$

 Knotty-pine-paneled cottages on two acres of pine trees provide twenty-one lodging accommodations at this B&B on the west shore of Lake Tahoe. The cottages cluster around a central garden that contains a path leading to a private beach. Each

PHONE: (530) 581–4073 or (800) 581–4073
FAX: (530) 581–0226
WEB SITE: www.thecottageinn.com
FEATURES: inn/cottages; 21 rooms; in-room televisions and VCRs; fax; computer hookup in lodge; copier; conference/meeting areas; private beach; sauna
NEARBY: Lake Tahoe; golf; ski areas; restaurants
INNKEEPER/OWNER: Suzie Muhr

uniquely themed cottage has a private bath, fireplace, and television with VCR. Guests may choose from an array of guest rooms and suites, some of them featuring a rock Jacuzzi, a balcony with a view, a kitchenette, or a loft bedroom. The lodge with its stone fireplace is for guests' enjoyment. A hearty country breakfast is served in the dining room or on the outdoor deck. Beverages and fresh popcorn are offered fireside each afternoon, and homemade cookies are always available.

MAYFIELD HOUSE B&B AT LAKE TAHOE

236 Grove Street
P.O. Box 8529
Tahoe City, CA 96145

⊗ $$–$$$

■ This remodeled wood-and-stone inn with pretty gardens and patios offers a living room with cozy fireplace, individually decorated guest rooms, and a mountain-decor private cottage. The guest rooms have private baths and queen- and king-size beds covered with down comforters and pillows and fine linens. A full gourmet breakfast, served in the room, on the patio, or in the breakfast area, includes such delectables as apple-walnut pancakes or cinnamon French toast with bananas. The menu changes daily, and all meals are served on fine china with fresh flowers. Evening snacks are served, and complimentary beverages are available any time of the day. The B&B is ½ block from the lake and convenient to major ski resorts.

PHONE: (530) 583–1001 or (888) 518–8898
FAX: (530) 581–4107
WEB SITE: www.mayfieldhouse.com
FEATURES: inn/cottage; 6 rooms, 1 cottage; in-room televisions and VCRs (some); fax; computer hookup
NEARBY: lake; skiing; hiking; restaurants
INNKEEPER/OWNER: Kristin Beddard

THE SHORE HOUSE AT LAKE TAHOE

7170 North Lake Boulevard
P.O. Box 499
Tahoe Vista, CA 96148

⊗ $$$–$$$$

■ This former resort was built in the 1950s to lodge the 1960 Olympics at Squaw Valley and then went on to be a vacation home. The current owners of the Shore House purchased the property in 1994, totally remodeling it as a romantic B&B getaway on the North Shore of Lake Tahoe. The inn hosts gardens filled with blooms, lawns stretching out to the lake, a pier, and an adjoining sandy beach. The mountain-lodge architecture with redwood siding boasts decks surrounding the entire structure on two levels with abundant views of the lake. The guest accommodations at the inn all have private outdoor entrances, bathrooms, minirefrigerators, gas/log fireplaces, custom log furnishings, knotty-pine-covered walls, down comforters, and feather beds. The Tree House guest

PHONE: (530) 546–7270 or (800) 207–5160

FAX: (530) 546-7130

WEB SITE: www.shorehouselaketahoe .com

FEATURES: inn/cottages; 8 rooms, 1 cottage; fax; copier; in-room work-space; conference/meeting areas; wedding services; hot tub

NEARBY: Lake Tahoe and mountain recreation

INNKEEPERS/OWNERS: Barb and Marty Cohen

room on the upper floor is framed by two towering ponderosa pine trees; guests sleep in a queen-size log bed, and the decor carries a Native American motif. The separate Honeymoon cottage on the inn's waterfront offers a spectacular view of the lake and a two-person whirlpool in the bedroom. Aspen trees frame the lake-front garden of the inn, where the full breakfast is served. The meal begins with a fruit dish such as Granola Parfait or baked apples and is followed by a main entree that varies from such delights as stuffed French toast with chicken-apple sausage to their award-winning Tomato-Potato Surprise. On chilly days breakfast is offered at individual tables in the lakefront dining room by the large river-rock fireplace. Wine and appetizers are served each evening at sunset; freshly baked cookies are placed in the room each day and choco-lates at night. Weddings (accommodating up to twenty-six people) are a specialty at the inn.

NORFOLK WOODS INN

6941 West Lake Boulevard
P.O. Box 262
Tahoma, CA 96142

⊗ $$–$$$$

PHONE: (530) 525–5000

FAX: (530) 525-5266

WEB SITE: www.norfolkwoods.com

FEATURES: inn/cottages; 11 rooms, 6 cottages; in-room phones; in-room tel-evisions (cottages); pets allowed (cot-tages); kitchens (cottages); swimming pool; spa; restaurant; bar; fax; copier

NEARBY: lake; skiing

INNKEEPERS/OWNERS: Patty and Al Multon

▦ This completely renovated log inn with a fine European-style restaurant and cozy bar boasts an Alpine decor and a swim-ming pool and spa surrounded by trees and gardens. The interior of the inn, built in the 1940s, features warm pine walls, Bavarian and Swiss imports, and bell-shaped lantern light fixtures. The inn offers six cottages (including a one-hundred-year-old log cabin) with kitchens and fireplaces, guest rooms, and a two-bedroom suite with full kitchen. The guest rooms all have private baths, hand-painted pine headboards, cozy comforters, pine closets, and country wall coverings. Guests may enjoy a comfort-able lounge with a small bar and rock fireplace. The full breakfast (not served to guests in the cottages) changes daily but might include omelettes, blueberry muffins, juice, and fresh fruit. The restaurant/dining room, featuring fresh California cuisine, is open for breakfast, lunch, and dinner. Pets are allowed in cottages.

RICHARDSON HOUSE

10154 High Street
P.O. Box 2011
Truckee, CA 96160

♿ ⊘ $$–$$$

PHONE: (530) 587–5388 or (888) 229–0365
FAX: (530) 587–0927
WEB SITE: www.richardsonhouse.com
FEATURES: inn; 8 rooms; air-conditioning; hot tub; fax; copier; catering; weddings; receptions
NEARBY: Lake Tahoe; ski areas; shopping; restaurants; golf
INNKEEPERS/OWNERS: Jim and Sandi Beck

Perched atop a hill overlooking historic downtown Truckee, the restored, 1880s-built inn was at one time the private home of the Warren Richardson family. Gingerbread accents punctuate the detailing of the house, which offers eight guest rooms, some with fireplaces; six rooms have private baths, and two adjoining suites have a shared bath. A romantic choice is the Tamsen & George room with queen-size bed and claw-foot tub-for-two; Maggie's Garden room overlooks the inn's Victorian garden with gazebo. A full buffet breakfast, featuring Florentine quiche and black bean cakes with *pasilla* chile sauce or honey-glazed pecan French toast, is served in the dining room each morning, and guests have twenty-four-hour access to the refreshment center. A player piano, television with VCR, and CD player await guests' enjoyment in the parlor; a relaxing Jacuzzi is located on the outside deck. Richardson House has a wedding consultant available to create packages for weddings and receptions that may be held both inside the inn and in the Victorian garden.

THE TRUCKEE HOTEL

10007 Bridge Street
P.O. Box 884
Truckee, CA 96161

⊘ $–$$

This 1873 hotel nestled in the picturesque Sierra Nevadas is just a minute's walk from Amtrak; the town's historic district is right outside the door. The guest rooms, eight with private baths, are each uniquely decorated and furnished with antiques;

PHONE: (530) 587–4444 or (800) 659–6921

FAX: (530) 587–1599

WEB SITE: www.truckeehotel.com

FEATURES: inn/hotel; 37 rooms; fax; conference/meeting areas; restaurant; gift shop

NEARBY: Lake Tahoe; ski areas; downtown shopping

INNKEEPER: Jenelle Potvin

OWNERS: Jeff and Karen Winter

some baths have claw-foot tubs. Twenty-nine rooms are European-style with a sink in each room and a shared bath down the hall. The hotel will combine four rooms to form two suites for families or groups. The Victorian parlor is a pleasant spot to relax fireside. The lobby level of the hotel offers a fine restaurant and a gift shop. Hotel guests enjoy an expanded continental breakfast with their stay; weekend guests also receive complimentary coffee, tea, and cookies from 5:00 to 8:00 P.M.

ST. GEORGE HOTEL

16104 Main Street
P.O. Box 9
Volcano, CA 95689

♿ ⊘ $–$$

B. F. George built this Greek Revival hotel in 1867 with brick walls 14 inches thick. It was named the St. George to "thwart the demonic fire dragon," which had destroyed two previous hotels on the site. The three-story structure, with double-tiered wraparound verandas, is a showplace in the tiny gold-rush hamlet of

PHONE: (209) 296–4458

FAX: (209) 296–4457

WEB SITE: www.stgeorgehotel.com

FEATURES: hotel/cottage; 18 rooms, 1 cottage; ceiling fans in hotel rooms; air-conditioning (annex room); fax; copier; volleyball; weddings; conference room; hotel open Wednesday through Sunday; restaurant open Thursday through Sunday

NEARBY: Gold Country; swimming hole; antiquing; fishing; live theater; skiing

INNKEEPERS/OWNERS: Nick and Niki Nickerson

Volcano. The slanting floors, period parlor, and dining room with 15-foot ceiling add character to the hotel, which is listed on the National Register of Historic Places. The rooms in the hotel share the bath at the end of each floor. An annex added in 1960 offers rooms with private baths and air-conditioning. The Garden Cottage is the most private and romantic room the hotel has to offer. With its private deck, king-size bed, fireplace, double Jacuzzi tub, shower, television, and DVD player, it is truly a getaway. A continental breakfast is served in the main parlor.

THE HARKEY HOUSE

212 "C" Street
Yuba City, CA 95991

⊗ $–$$$

▨ This 1874 Victorian Gothic, formerly the residence of William Harkey, sheriff of Sutter County, is situated along the Feather River. The B&B offers a comfortable living room with marble fireplace and antique piano, a library, and art gallery. Outside, guests enjoy a spa, a trellis-shaded brick patio, rose garden, and hammock. Guest rooms, all with private baths and queen-size beds, are supplied with fresh flowers and bathrobes. The Harkey Suite, with antique furnishings and rich burgundy paisley prints, is complete with a remote television and VCR, adjoining library room, and cozy stove. A full breakfast, featuring French toast with date-nut butter sauce, is served in the glass-paned French country dining room each morning; popcorn is offered during the day. The romantic Harkey House is a popular spot for weddings and receptions.

PHONE: (530) 674–1942
FAX: (530) 674–1942
WEB SITE: www.harkeyhouse.com
FEATURES: home; 4 rooms; air-conditioning; in-room phones; in-room televisions and VCRs; spa; weddings
NEARBY: Gray Lodge Wildlife Area; golf; fishing; airport
INNKEEPERS/OWNERS: Bob and Lee Jones

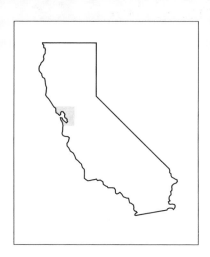

SAN FRANCISCO BAY AREA

Synonymous with Fisherman's Wharf, cable cars, and Chinatown, the city also offers numerous cultural activities, fine restaurants, and splendid examples of Victorian architecture blended with the ultramodern edifices. The communities that surround San Francisco, all just minutes away, bring suburban and country settings. Nearby Berkeley reflects the University of California campus with small coffeehouses and boutiques, as well as stately homes. The suburban communities of Sunnyvale, Pleasanton, Palo Alto, and Los Gatos are home to commuters, but each has retained its own identity. Just over the Golden Gate Bridge lies Sausalito with its hillside homes perched over the bay and its many tourist shops and art galleries. Over by the coast, but still within a modest drive, are communities such as Muir Beach, Moss Beach, Marshall, Half Moon Bay, Tomales Bay, Point Reyes, and Inverness. They offer forests with hiking, seafood stops, beautiful beaches, and wilderness areas.

WEBSTER HOUSE

1238 Versailles Avenue
Alameda, CA 94501

⊘ $–$$

▮ This historic Gothic Revival home was designed by Andrew Jackson Downing, known as the "Father of American Architecture." The home was precut in New York, then shipped around Cape Horn to be assembled in Alameda in 1854. This is the oldest house in Alameda and is listed on the National Register of Historic Places. Restoration in the 1980s included providing private bathrooms for the four rooms and furnishing them with antiques as well as modern double and queen-size beds; one room has a fireplace. Breakfast, a full gourmet affair often featuring creamy French scrambled eggs and omelettes to order, is served in the inn's popular English Tearoom or alfresco in the garden. Guests may request vegetarian or heart-smart dishes. Afternoon tea is served to guests in addition to an evening snack. An extra-cost high tea includes diminutive sandwiches, scones, Devonshire cream, English bangers, and specialty desserts. Dinner is served daily by reservation only. Entrees include beef Wellington, Norwegian poached salmon, and chicken Cordon Bleu, just to name a few. The inn is popular for weddings and small group meetings and parties.

PHONE: (510) 523–9697
FAX: (510) 523–9697
WEB SITE: www.lanierbb.com
FEATURES: inn; 4 rooms; meeting/banquet facilities; restaurant; weddings
NEARBY: beach; ferry terminal; historic homes; Berkeley; Napa Wine Country
INNKEEPERS/OWNERS: Andrew and Susan McCormack

THE INN AT BENICIA BAY

145 East "D" Street
Benicia, CA 94510

♿ ⊘ $$–$$$$

▮ A sample of gold-rush architecture circa 1854, the Victorian inn is located in Benicia's Old Town near the marina, noted for its specialty shops, cozy restaurants, and crafts and glass-blowing studios. The rooms, each with a specific period theme,

PHONE: (707) 746–1055
FAX: (707) 745–8361
WEB SITE: www.theinnatbeniciabay.com
FEATURES: inn; 9 rooms; in-room phones; in-room televisions; fax; copier; computer hookups; meetings; weddings
NEARBY: historic homes; Berkeley; San Francisco; Napa Wine Country
INNKEEPER/OWNER: Jim Harris

have original paintings and sculpture, Persian rugs, and private baths with Jacuzzis. The Jack London room, with a 1930s theme in deep cranberry and cream, has antique bird's-eye maple furniture and two queen-size beds; the Orient Express has a tall, six-panel Chinese screen as a headboard. The extended continental breakfast is served in the elegant dining room; afternoon wine, cheeses, and other snacks are served in the sitting room. The inn's gazebo/courtyard garden setting is popular for weddings with up to 175 guests.

BANCROFT HOTEL

2680 Bancroft Way
Berkeley, CA 94704

⊗ $$

■ Directly across the street from the University of California, Berkeley campus, the Bancroft Hotel building was constructed in 1928 as a private clubhouse by the College Women's Club, a group of Panhellenic women. The building, designed by Julia Morgan associate Walter T. Steilberg, is a distinguished example of the Arts and Crafts movement with Asian and Mediterranean influences. The inn, listed on the National Register of Historic Places, was carefully restored, refurbished, and upgraded and now offers twenty-two airy guest rooms and a 4,000-square-foot great hall for conferences and special events. Guest rooms at the inn offer views of the San Francisco Bay and the Berkeley Hills and are pleasantly appointed with original antiques or reproductions; many offer large balconies or decks. A complimentary continental breakfast is served each morning, or guests may visit Berkeley's most popular outdoor cafe, Caffe Strada, next door. Besides the great hall with its coffered ceilings, two large fireplaces, and historic stained-glass windows, the B&B offers a rooftop garden with panoramic views, and the Steilberg Board Room for small meetings or lectures.

PHONE: (510) 549–1000 or (800) 549–1002
FAX: (510) 549–1070
WEB SITE: www.bancrofthotel.com
FEATURES: inn/hotel; 22 rooms; in-room televisions; in-room phones; computer hookups; conference/meeting areas; fax; audiovisual equipment
NEARBY: University of California, Berkeley; cafes; shops; theater
INNKEEPER: Barry Stade

Fly a Kite over Berkeley

The hometown of one of the nation's leading universities, UC Berkeley, this Bay Area city offers a lively, artistic side. The university area is brimming with coffeehouses, boutique restaurants, and quaint shops. The surrounding area is marked by unusual museums and impressive gardens.

The Charles Lee Tilden Regional Park on the northeast edge of the city grants panoramic views of the surrounding city and features a golf course, botanical garden, picnic grounds, and camping, as well as hiking, biking, and horse trails. Swimming and fishing are allowed at Lake Anza here; there is also a merry-go-round, miniature train, and pony rides. The park is open daily; park admission is free. Call (510) 562–7275 for park information.

ROSE GARDEN INN Best Buy

2740 Telegraph Avenue
Berkeley, CA 94705

♿ ⊗ $$–$$$$

▓ Two side-by-side, turn-of-the-twentieth-century homes with gardens, a carriage house, a garden house, and a cottage house built in 1991 form this B&B not far from the University of California campus. The Queen Anne original B&B structure offers two parlors, a fireplace, ornate moldings, inlaid floors, and chintz fabrics and antiques. The adjacent Fay House has marble fireplaces, hand-painted ceilings, stained-glass windows, and Oriental rugs. The unique, enlarged guest accommodations with private baths offer such amenities as antiques, fireplaces, private decks, armoires, and stained-glass windows. A continental breakfast is served in the dining room, the garden, or the greenhouse. Coffee, tea, and cookies are offered every evening.

PHONE: (510) 549–2145 or (800) 992–9005
FAX: (510) 549–1085
WEB SITE: www.rosegardeninn.com
FEATURES: inn/cottage; 40 rooms; in-room phones; computer hookups; in-room televisions; fax; copier; conferences
NEARBY: University of California, Berkeley; cafes; shops
INNKEEPER: Kevin Allen
OWNER: Anand Goekel

NEW DAVENPORT BED & BREAKFAST INN

31 Davenport Avenue
P.O. Box J
Davenport, CA 95017

⊗ $$–$$$

■ Housed in a restored turn-of-the-twentieth-century bathhouse (one of the town's original buildings) is this inn, with additional B&B accommodations above the owner's Cash Store Restaurant next door. The restaurant, serving homemade fare for breakfast, lunch, and dinner, also has a gift shop displaying a wide variety of pottery, rugs, jewelry, and folk art. The guest rooms, all with private baths, are furnished with antique beds, oak dressers, colorful rugs, and art. Accommodations above the restaurant feature outside decks with views of the dramatic coast; bathhouse rooms have patios and sitting rooms. A hearty continental breakfast is served in the sitting room each morning. The inn is within walking distance of local craft studios and is close to a popular beach and whale-watching spot.

PHONE: (831) 425–1818 or (800) 870–1817
FAX: (831) 423–1160
WEB SITE: www.davenportinn.com
FEATURES: inn; 12 rooms; in-room phones; in-room televisions and VCRs (some); restaurant; gift shop
NEARBY: beach; whale-watching
INNKEEPERS/OWNERS: Bruce and Marcia McDougal

CYPRESS INN ON MIRAMAR BEACH

407 Mirada Road
Half Moon Bay, CA 94019

♿ ⊗ $$–$$$$

■ This 1989-built contemporary beach house, situated directly on a 5-mile-long sandy beach, offers spectacular ocean views from every guest room, as well as four luxurious accommodations in the adjacent beach house, and six rooms in the Lighthouse building, most of which offer fireplaces and Jacuzzis. The pole-structure inn is decorated with colorful folk art and boasts terra-cotta tile floors covered with brightly colored rugs throughout. The luxurious guest accommodations feature king- and queen-size beds with comforters, fireplaces, private baths and decks, nat-

PHONE: (650) 726–6002 or (800) 832–3224

FAX: (650) 712–0380

WEB SITE: www.innsbythesea.com/cypress or www.cypressinn.com

FEATURES: inn; 18 rooms; in-room phones; computer hookups; in-room televisions and VCRs (some); in-room massages; all conference/meeting services

NEARBY: beach; horseback riding; bike trails; whale-watching; golfing; fishing; sailing

INNKEEPER: Mark Coleman

OWNER: Inns by the Sea

ural pine and wicker furnishings, skylights, and shuttered windows. Guests awake to a full breakfast of freshly squeezed orange juice, just-baked croissants, and a gourmet entree such as peaches-and-cream French toast, served in the main room. A continental breakfast is available in the room. Guests enjoy wine, hors d'oeuvres, and homemade desserts each evening. The Cypress Inn offers massages by its own in-house massage therapist. Within ten minutes of the inn, guests may enjoy sailing, fishing, whale-watching, horseback riding, biking, golfing, and wine tasting.

LANDIS SHORES OCEANFRONT INN

211 Mirada Road
Half Moon Bay, CA 94019

♿ ⦻ $$$$

▦ Spectacular, unobstructed views of the ocean are among the highlights of this impressive, luxurious inn, literally just a stone's throw from the beach. Built in 1999, this contemporary inn features rooms with queen- or king-size beds; antiques; fireplaces; private balconies; natural stone floors with radiant heat; and baths with extra-deep whirlpools, separate showers, and luxurious robes; many have refrigerators. The full breakfast is served in the room or the inn's dining area. Complimentary wine and hors d'oeuvres are served in the afternoon. Guests often catch glimpses of the famous elephant seals of nearby Año Nuevo.

PHONE: (650) 726–6642

FAX: (650) 726–6644

WEB SITE: www.landisshores.com

FEATURES: inn; 8 rooms; in-room phones; computer hookups; in-room televisions and VCRs; in-room workspace; weddings; in-room massages

NEARBY: beach; historic town; golf; horseback riding; bicycling

INNKEEPER: Diane Landis

OWNERS: Ellen and Ken Landis

THE MILL ROSE INN

615 Mill Street
Half Moon Bay, CA 94019

⊗ $$–$$$$

▨ This graceful Victorian, built in the early 1900s, was restored by the owners in 1982 to become an award-winning country inn in the classic old-world tradition. All rooms have private entrances and baths, feather queen- or king-size beds, antiques, wet bars, and well-stocked refrigerators; five have fireplaces. The Bordeaux Rose suite, a favorite with honeymooners, is decorated in shades of crimson, ivory, and peach. A ceiling-to-floor lace canopy covers the carved wooden bed, and the sitting room has a fireplace; the bath has a whirlpool for two. The gourmet breakfast, which might include artichoke frittatas or apple-cranberry crunch, can be taken in the room or the dining room. Guests are offered afternoon tea, wine, cheese, and homemade desserts. Historic Old Town is just a short walk away, as is the beach.

PHONE: (650) 726–8750 or (800) 900–7673
FAX: (650) 726–3031
WEB SITE: www.millroseinn.com
FEATURES: inn; 6 rooms; in-room phones; computer hookups; in-room televisions and VCRs; refrigerators; spa
NEARBY: beach; Old Town; horseback riding; bicycling; theater
INNKEEPERS/OWNERS: Terry and Eve Baldwin

OLD THYME INN

779 Main Street
Half Moon Bay, CA 94019

⊗ $$–$$$$

▨ Located in Main Street's historic district, this 1899-built B&B is within walking distance of quaint boutiques and restaurants. In the rear of the redwood-constructed Victorian is an herb garden with more than fifty varieties of sweet-smelling herbs. Guests may explore the garden, which provides garnishes and breakfast ingredients. The many return guests to this B&B may choose from seven individual accommodations ranging from the cozy Chamomile room, with antique American decor, to the plush Thyme room, with double-size whirlpool, a fireplace, and a Louis XVI–style queen-size bed. All the guest rooms feature private baths. The inn offers a suite with its own private entrance through the herb garden; the suite boasts a four-poster bed,

PHONE: (650) 726–1616 or (800) 720–4277

FAX: (650) 726–6394

WEB SITE: www.oldthymeinn.com

FEATURES: inn; 7 rooms; in-room televisions and VCRs; fax; copier; computer hookups; meeting areas

NEARBY: historic district; shops; restaurants

INNKEEPERS/OWNERS: Rick and Kathy Ellis

a fireplace, a whirlpool for two, and a refrigerator stocked with beverages. The gourmet morning fare typically includes such specialties as fresh juice, coffee, homemade cakes and muffins, and entrees such as Belgian waffles, scrambled eggs, and cheese tortillas with salsa. Both breakfast and evening wine and sherry are served with local cheese, grapes, and crackers in the lounge by a cozy fire.

SAN BENITO HOUSE

356 Main Street
Half Moon Bay, CA 94019

♿ $–$$$

■ This upstairs historic hostelry, built around 1900, is filled with European antiques and fresh flowers from the inn's English garden. Guest rooms bordering the garden boast more elaborate decor. Nine rooms have private baths. The continental breakfast is served in the room or on the sunny redwood deck, which is dressed with flower boxes and a massive fire pit for the evening cognac. A "nonhistoric" sauna is available, as well as lunch and dinner in the hotel's Garden Deli and highly acclaimed San Benito House Restaurant; chef/owner Greg Regan provides imaginative cuisine using fresh local produce and seafood.

PHONE: (650) 726–3425

FAX: (650) 726–9507

WEB SITE: www.sanbenitohouse.com

FEATURES: inn/hotel; 12 rooms; limited smoking; in-room phones; fax; catering; conference areas; restaurant on premises (lunch, dinner); sauna; weddings

NEARBY: shopping; ocean

INNKEEPER/OWNER: Greg Regan

Take Me to the Seashore

The Point Reyes National Seashore lies on a scenic stretch of Highway 1 that extends from Tomales south to Bolinas. More than 65,000 acres of protected beaches, tidal pools, and forests make up this national treasure. More than 350 species of birds and more than 70 species of mammals also inhabit this area, rich in both history and recreation.

The park's headquarters is located in Bear Valley, just west of Olema on Bear Valley Road. The visitor center is open daily, imparts information on nature trails, and offers interesting exhibits. Popular activities within the National Seashore include bird-watching, hiking, searching for tidal pools, swimming, and observing sea lions and migrating whales. For additional information or camping permits, call (415) 464–5100 or log on to www.nps.gov/pore.

ZABALLA HOUSE

324 Main Street
Half Moon Bay, CA 94019

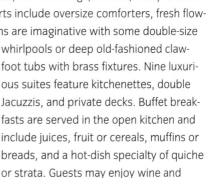

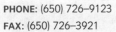 $–$$$

■ This historic structure at the entrance to Main Street is described as the "oldest building still standing in Half Moon Bay." Constructed by early city planner Estanislao Zaballa around 1863, the renovated bright and cheery inn now welcomes guests with period comfort. All guest accommodations are decorated individually with antiques, wall coverings, and art; many feature 10-foot-high ceilings and fireplaces. Comforts include oversize comforters, fresh flowers, and fluffy towels. The private bathrooms are imaginative with some double-size whirlpools or deep old-fashioned claw-foot tubs with brass fixtures. Nine luxurious suites feature kitchenettes, double Jacuzzis, and private decks. Buffet breakfasts are served in the open kitchen and include juices, fruit or cereals, muffins or breads, and a hot-dish specialty of quiche or strata. Guests may enjoy wine and cheese in the parlor each evening. Fine restaurants and shops are all within walking distance of the Zaballa House.

PHONE: (650) 726–9123
FAX: (650) 726–3921
WEB SITE: www.zaballahouse.net
FEATURES: inn; 21 rooms; well-behaved pets allowed; fax; conference/meeting areas; kitchenettes (suites); in-room televisions and VCRs (some).
NEARBY: bay; shops; restaurants
INNKEEPER/OWNER: David Cresson Jr.

THE ARK

180 Highland Way
P.O. Box 273
Inverness, CA 94937

♿ $$$

▪ Tucked away up the ridge from Inverness, this two-room cozy retreat is nestled in the forest. It was built by architecture students from UC Berkeley in the 1970s of mostly recycled materials. The main room, which used to be an artist's studio, has a cozy queen-size bed beneath a soaring cathedral ceiling with a large skylight and a large bank of windows looking into the forest. A woodstove warms the room, and up a ladder is a sleeping loft with a double futon and picture-window views of a lush meadow frequented by a resident buck. The other room has two twin beds and also has the feel of a study with its desk, bookshelves supplied with classic and contemporary works, stereo, and games. The full kitchen is stocked with breakfast fare of fresh fruit, granola, juice, organic eggs, pastries or muffins, home-baked bread, jam, and coffee and tea. Guests enjoy a picnic, barbecue, and sunning area a few steps outside the cottage.

PHONE: (415) 663–9338 or (800) 808–9338
WEB SITE: www.rosemarybb.com
FEATURES: cottage; sleeps 6; in-room phone; pets allowed by arrangement; kitchen; in-room workspace
NEARBY: forest; ocean; whale-watching
INNKEEPER: Suzanne Storch
OWNER: Sim Van der Ryn

BLACKTHORNE INN

266 Vallejo Avenue
P.O. Box 712
Inverness, CA 94937

⊘ $$$–$$$$

▪ The multilevel wood-and-glass inn, described as a "carpenter's fantasy," resembles a tree house nestled in a rustic, tree-filled canyon. Guest rooms, with private baths, perched from top floor to bottom yield views as well as added privacy and lead to a deck offering spectacular views and a hot tub for guests' use. For a memorable stay try the Eagle's Nest, perched high at the top of the spiral staircase; octagonally shaped and enclosed by glass, this tower room has a private sundeck and spectacular views of the stars. An A-frame living room with a stone hearth is for guests' enjoyment, as is a 3,500-square-foot sun-

PHONE: (415) 663–8621
FAX: (415) 663–8635
WEB SITE: www.blackthorneinn.com
FEATURES: inn; 5 rooms; fax; hot tub
NEARBY: Point Reyes National Seashore; golf; horseback riding
INNKEEPERS/OWNERS: Susan and Bill Wigert

deck. A buffet breakfast consisting of quiche, coffee cakes, juice, and fresh fruit salad with toppings is served at 9:30 A.M.; coffee, tea, and desserts are served in the afternoon. November through April the inn offers special whale-watching packages.

FAIRWINDS FARM BED AND BREAKFAST

P.O. Box 581
Inverness, CA 94937

⊗ $$

High atop Inverness Ridge amid towering pines and ocean views sits this wilderness farm reminiscent of the Scottish Highlands. Guests enjoy the privacy of what was once the children's wing of the farmhouse. Dan's Room boasts a private entrance with Dutch doors and a wraparound deck to take in all the views. Guests awaken to the freshness of the country dawn as the pet barnyard animals, including goats, chickens, donkeys, horses, and a potbellied pig, venture out to enjoy the day. To start your day, step out the door to your private deck and into a romantic redwood and stained-glass window–enclosed outdoor bath with a large shower and separate claw foot tub. Fresh coffee and homemade jams and baked goodies are served on the deck, or visit your kitchenette to cook your own meal. Spend a few quiet moments in the garden, enjoy the ponds and waterfalls, or open the gate to directly access the 75,000 acres of Point Reyes National Seashore. For spectacular bird-watching and a chance meeting with elk or deer, hike Bayview trail to Muddy Hollow and Limantour Beach. In the opposite direction, a quiet stroll on forest and meadow trails will acquaint you with the early-morning fauna that abound. The trail joins others so that you may enjoy the breathtaking views from Sky Camp and Mount Wittenberg, where you often catch a glimpse of deer, elk, fox, bobcat, possum, squirrel, raccoon, and chipmunk. Before you turn in, enjoy a soak in your private hot tub beneath the stars, watching the fishing boats out at sea.

PHONE: (415) 663–9454
FAX: (415) 663–1787
WEB SITE: www.fairwindsfarm inverness.com
FEATURES: home; 2 rooms; hot tub
NEARBY: Point Reyes National seashore; hiking; golf; bird-watching; whale-watching
INNKEEPER/OWNER: Joyce Goldfield

THE FIR TREE

75 Balboa Avenue
P.O. Box 273
Inverness, CA 94937

$$$–$$$$

■ This rustic haven overlooks the fir trees adjacent to the Point Reyes National Seashore. The quiet forest setting of the cottage makes it a great base for exploring the surrounding abundant nature. The living room of the cottage features a cathedral ceiling of aged pine and old beams recycled from a San Francisco dock; handcrafted windows overlook a grove of 200-foot-tall firs. A woodstove warms the room; antiques and Oriental rugs complete the decor. The cottage contains a fully equipped kitchen with a deck. A curved stairway leads to two bedrooms, one with a king-size bed and the other with a queen and a twin. The garden hosts a hot tub for secluded soaks. A full breakfast is included in the stay. Families are welcome.

PHONE: (415) 663–9338 or (800) 808–9338
WEB SITE: www.rosemarybb.com
FEATURES: 1 cottage; in-room phone; in-room workspace; pets allowed (by arrangement); kitchen; hot tub; no credit cards
NEARBY: Point Reyes National Seashore; Tomales Bay; hiking; bird-watching
INNKEEPER/OWNER: Suzanne Storch

ROSEMARY COTTAGE

75 Balboa Avenue
P.O. Box 273
Inverness, CA 94937

$$$$

■ Located on Inverness Ridge is this French country cottage with panoramic, picture-window views of the forest. The B&B offers a large bedroom with queen-size bed; a main room with high ceilings, wood-burning stove, and additional sleeping areas; a full kitchen; and a bath with tub and shower. A full breakfast of juice, seasonal fruit, granola, fresh eggs (guests cook their own), pastries or muffins, and homemade breads is offered each morning. A large deck nestled under an old oak overlooks the herb and flower garden at this secluded getaway near Point Reyes National Seashore and Tomales Bay.

PHONE: (415) 663–9338 or (800) 808–9338
FAX: (415) 663–9057
WEB SITE: www.rosemarybb.com
FEATURES: 1 cottage; in-room phone; in-room workspace; spa; pets allowed (by arrangement); kitchen; no credit cards
NEARBY: Point Reyes National Seashore; horseback-riding; shops; restaurants
INNKEEPER/OWNER: Suzanne Storch

TEN INVERNESS WAY

10 Inverness Way
P.O. Box 63
Inverness, CA 94937

 $$–$$$

This inn is designed for avid readers and hikers and is ideal for anyone who appreciates colorful gardens and seclusion near the Point Reyes National Seashore. A flagstone path leads to a wisteria-covered arbor and the sweet smells of blooms and fruit trees. The comfortable rooms of this 1904 guesthouse boast the original Douglas-fir floors and paneling; the guest rooms have white wainscoting, sloped ceilings, and an abundance of windows. All the accommodations offer queen-size beds, and all rooms have private baths, handmade quilts, and, of course, flowers from the garden. The Garden Suite has sitting and dining areas and a private patio. Breakfast, served in the sunroom or delivered to the room, includes specialties such as pancakes with chicken-apple sausage or a variety of egg dishes. A mug of tea or other refreshments can be enjoyed by the stone fireplace in the living room. Guests may soak in a private hot tub in the garden cottage; bathrobes are provided. Picnics are lovingly packed, and personalized hiking tours are available.

PHONE: (415) 669–1648
FAX: (415) 669–7403
WEB SITE: www.teninvernessway.com
FEATURES: inn; 5 rooms; fax; hot tub; picnics; hiking tours
NEARBY: Point Reyes National Seashore; hiking; beach
INNKEEPERS/OWNERS: Teri Mattson and Brett Poirier

THE GOOSE AND TURRETS B&B

835 George Street
P.O. Box 370937
Montara, CA 94037

$$–$$$

Built circa 1908, the Italian villa–style B&B surrounded by rose, herb, and vegetable gardens is a haven for nature lovers, readers, and pilots who may fly into Half Moon Bay Airport. The five-guest-room inn offers a comfortable

PHONE: (650) 728–5451
FAX: (650) 728–0141
WEB SITE: www.goose.montara.com
FEATURES: inn; 5 rooms
NEARBY: Montara Mountain; Montara State Beach; hiking; whale-watching; seal preserve
INNKEEPERS/OWNERS: Raymond and Emily Hoche-Mong

decor with a common lounge area outfitted with woodstove, piano, game table, and library of books for every taste. Guest rooms enjoy individual motifs; the Goose room and the Lascaux room both boast beds that once belonged to the Teddy Roosevelt family. The Hummingbird room offers a sitting area with wood-burning stove. All rooms are furnished with a German down comforter and an English towel warmer. All rooms have private baths; three have fireplaces. Guests enjoy a four-course breakfast in the dining room with such homemade delicacies as Dutch baby, Southwest corn-pepper pancakes, eggs Einhover, or Black Forest ham. Afternoon tea is special at the inn, with varying delights such as homemade Scottish shortbread or Italian squares topped with melted Gorgonzola; salmon, cream cheese, and dill open-face sandwiches; and dense chocolate cake. Both English and French are spoken at the inn.

SEAL COVE INN

221 Cypress Avenue
Moss Beach, CA 94038

♿ ⊗ $$$–$$$$

PHONE: (650) 728–4114 or (800) 995–9987
FAX: (650) 728–4116
WEB SITE: www.sealcoveinn.com
FEATURES: inn; 10 rooms; in-room phones; in-room televisions and VCRs; video library; fax; copier; computer hookups; audiovisual equipment; conference/meeting areas
NEARBY: Half Moon Bay; ocean recreation; Fitzgerald Marine Reserve; horseback riding
INNKEEPERS/OWNERS: Rick and Karen Brown-Herbert

▧ Common sense will tell you that a world-renowned travel writer who is constantly in search of the most charming of country inns would own a top-notch award-winning "charmer" herself! The European-style Seal Cove Inn, nestled between spectacular ocean views and dazzling wildflowers, offers secluded, pampered stays. The English country home was constructed in 1991 on a scenic hillside bordered by cypress trees and overlooking acres of county parkland reaching out to the ocean, making the inn an ideal base for exploring tidal pools, whale-watching, and salmon fishing; a tree-lined path leads guests along the ocean bluffs for seal-gazing and romantic strolls. Country antiques and prints, original watercolors, and rich fabrics fill the environs of the country inn. The living room beckons guests on foggy days with its inviting fireplace and after-dinner sherry or brandy. Each guest room or suite is designed for privacy with cozy sitting areas that front a wood-burning fireplace, and French doors that reveal a private patio with ocean views. The Fitzgerald room has a high, vaulted ceiling; a dramatic king-size canopy bed; Jacuzzi; and unobstructed ocean views off the balcony. Pink and green floral prints punctuate the Garden room decor, and wicker chairs with fluffy down pillows front the cozy fireplace; this downstairs accommodation is just steps from a path leading to the park area. A tempting full breakfast awaits guests each morning in the dining room and includes fresh fruit, freshly squeezed juice, and a hot entree such as Grand Marnier French toast or strawberry waffles. Those wishing breakfast in the room are served an extended continental fare with fruit, juice, yogurt, granola, and croissants or muffins. A buffet of hors d'oeuvres and wine is presented each evening in the dining room. The inn easily accommodates small groups with a handsome conference room for fifteen. The small village of Moss Beach is just 30 miles south of San Francisco and 6 miles north of Half Moon Bay.

THE PELICAN INN

10 Pacific Way
Muir Beach, CA 94965-9729

♿ ⊘ $$$$

This Tudor-style country inn with pub and restaurant captures the spirit of sixteenth-century England. The English theme is maintained throughout with English antiques, full- or half-canopied queen- or king-size beds, a hearty English breakfast, and British ales; all rooms have private baths. The Pelican Inn is nestled near the magnificent redwood trees of Muir Woods and the Pacific Ocean; it is surrounded by open countryside with miles of cycling and hiking trails, bird-watching, and beachcombing. The inn's "snug" is well suited for relaxing. Its restaurant and pub, which are wheelchair accessible, are open to the public for lunch and dinner Monday through Saturday and for buffet lunch on Sunday; they are closed on most Mondays November through March.

PHONE: (415) 383–6000
FAX: (415) 383–3424
WEB SITE: www.pelicaninn.com
FEATURES: inn; 7 rooms; fax; copier; restaurant; pub
NEARBY: Muir Woods; ocean; hiking and bicycling trails; bird-watching
INNKEEPERS/OWNERS: Ed and Susan Cunningham

ROUNDSTONE FARM BED & BREAKFAST INN

9940 Sir Francis Drake Boulevard
P.O. Box 217
Olema, CA 94950

⊗ $$–$$$

This rambling cedar farmhouse was built to be a bed-and-breakfast inn in 1986. Situated on a ten-acre Arabian and Connemara horse farm that is actually within the Golden Gate National Recreation Area, the inn offers some incredible vistas of the Point Reyes National Seashore. Each of the five guest rooms has been oriented to take advantage of the changing views of nature; every room has a view of Mount Wittenberg, Olema Valley, Inverness Ridge, or Tomales Bay. Each guest room offers total privacy, with each accommodation on its own level. All five rooms have fireplaces, European armoires, custom headboards, down comforters, pleasant contemporary artwork, and fresh flowers. All rooms have baths with shower and tub. Afternoon refreshments are served in the common room, with comfortable seating and highlighted by 16-foot ceilings and skylights, or on the deck overlooking the pond and horse pasture. A full "California-country gourmet" breakfast is served in the dining room, which opens to the patio garden; highlights include apple puff pancakes and red-pepper quiche.

PHONE: (415) 663–1020 or (800) 881–9874
FAX: (415) 663–8056
WEB SITE: www.roundstonefarm.com
FEATURES: inn; 5 rooms; pond; hot tub; gazebo; fax; computer hookup
NEARBY: Point Reyes National Seashore; Golden Gate National Recreation Area; hiking; bird-watching; beaches; horseback riding; kayaking; bicycling
INNKEEPERS/OWNERS: Karen Anderson and Frank Borodic

COWPER INN

705 Cowper Street
Palo Alto, CA 94301

⊗ $–$$

This inn, on tree-lined Cowper Street, is just a five-minute walk from downtown Palo Alto's charming shops, galleries, and restaurants, and the Stanford University campus is less than a mile away. The B&B is actually composed of two vintage

PHONE: (650) 327–4475
FAX: (650) 329–1703
WEB SITE: www.cowperinn.com
FEATURES: inn; 14 rooms; in-room phones; in-room televisions; air-conditioning (some); in-room workspace; computer hookups; fax; copier; meeting area; on-site parking; public transportation
NEARBY: downtown; Stanford University
INNKEEPERS/OWNERS: Peggy and John Woodworth

houses: a Victorian and a Craftsman-style bungalow. The rooms are furnished comfortably; the parlor offers a fireplace and piano. The fourteen guest rooms, some with unusual shapes, are decorated with antiques and have televisions and telephones; only two accommodations share a bath. Breakfast is served in the paneled dining room and includes freshly baked breads and fruit. Outside relaxation is provided on the inn's two wicker-furnished porches or in the garden.

THE VICTORIAN ON LYTTON

555 Lytton Avenue
Palo Alto, CA 94301

♿ Ⓢ $$$–$$$$

■ This historic inn, built in 1895 as a private residence, also provides accommodations in an addition in the rear; the grounds are graced by a fragrant English country garden. The ten unique guest rooms are named after Queen Victoria and her nine children and offer such "royal" touches as separate sitting parlors, private baths, canopy or four-poster queen- or king-size beds, romantic laces, down comforters, claw-foot tubs, and fine antiques. The Queen's room features a unique step-down bathroom. An extended continental breakfast is served in the room between 7:00 and 9:00 A.M. Guests may relax in the tastefully decorated parlor with classical music; coffee, tea, and biscuits are available throughout the day and evening.

PHONE: (650) 322–8555
FAX: (650) 322–7141
WEB SITE: www.victorianonlytton.com
FEATURES: inn; 10 rooms; air-conditioning; in-room phones; in-room televisions; fax; computer hookups
NEARBY: Stanford University; shops; restaurants; golf
INNKEEPERS/OWNERS: Maxwell and Susan Hall

EVERGREEN

9104 Longview Drive
Pleasanton, CA 94588

Ⓢ $$–$$$$

■ This custom, contemporary home is perched high in the hills, surrounded by oak

PHONE: (925) 426–0901

FAX: (925) 426–9568

WEB SITE: www.evergreen-inn.com

FEATURES: home; 5 rooms; air-conditioning; in-room phones; in-room televisions; fax; copier; computer hookups; hot tub; exercise room; in-room refrigerators

NEARBY: downtown Pleasanton; Augustin Bernal Park

INNKEEPERS/OWNERS: Jane and Clay Cameron

trees. Hiking trails greet guests at this secluded location and lead through adjacent Augustin Bernal Park to hiking trails on the Pleasanton Ridge, yet the B&B is only five minutes away from downtown Pleasanton. The lower level of the two-story family home was converted to a B&B in 1995, providing five spacious suites with many amenities. Guests may choose from the Grand View, with antique king-size sleigh bed, a fireplace, a private deck, and bathroom with Jacuzzi; the Hideaway room, which boasts a king-size canopy bed, is aptly named with its private entrance and deck. All the guest rooms contain telephones with separate phone numbers, in-room refrigerators stocked with complimentary sodas and candy bars, and carefully concealed televisions. Breakfast, enjoyed in the skylight-illuminated dining area or on the outside deck, includes fresh juices, fresh fruit, homemade baked goods and granola, a variety of eggs, omelettes, or French toast. Chocolate chip cookies, fruit, and cheese keep guests content all day. A relaxing hot tub under the stars adds to the tranquility of the spot; a private exercise room helps guests gear up for local hiking and biking.

CARRIAGE HOUSE BED AND BREAKFAST

P.O. Box 1239
Point Reyes Station, CA 94956

⊗ $$–$$$

▨ Just minutes from the Point Reyes National Seashore, this sophisticated private retreat—built in 1938 in California-country style—offers stunning views of Inverness Ridge, Black Mountain, and the pristine countryside. The large suites have bedrooms with queen-size beds, living rooms with a fireplace and queen hide-a-bed, full or minikitchens, private baths, and in-room televisions and VCRs. In-room

PHONE: (415) 663–8627 or (800) 613–8351

FAX: (415) 663–8707

WEB SITE: www.carriagehousebb.com

FEATURES: inn; 3 rooms; in-room phones; in-room televisions and VCRs; in-room workspace; computer hookup; in-room massage; fax

NEARBY: Point Reyes National Seashore; horseback riding; village

INNKEEPER/OWNER: Felicity Kirsch

refrigerators are stocked with goodies for guests to prepare a hefty continental breakfast. Guests are within easy walking distance of the beaches, Tomales Bay, and the village of Point Reyes Station with restaurants, galleries, and shops.

HOLLY TREE INN AND COTTAGES

3 Silverhills Road
P.O. Box 642
Point Reyes Station, CA 94956

Ⓢ $$–$$$$

This B&B inn, located on nineteen acres of land, is surrounded by fir, bay, and oak trees; fragrant gardens; lilacs in the spring; and festive holly trees just in time for Christmas. The 4,000-square-foot inn with beamed ceilings and fireplaces offers four guest rooms (two with king-size four-poster beds), a living room with fireplace and comfortable seating, and a dining room, as well as a back deck that joins a hillside draped in heather. Inn and cottage guests may reserve the garden-set spa as well as arrange for therapeutic massages. The guest accommodations

PHONE: (415) 663–1554 or (800) 286–4655
FAX: (415) 663–8566
WEB SITE: www.hollytreeinn.com
FEATURES: inn/cottages; 4 rooms, 3 cottages; conference areas; spa; massages
NEARBY: Point Reyes National Seashore; Tomales Bay; beaches; whale-watching; hiking; shops; restaurants
INNKEEPER: Adeline Davis
OWNER: Tom Balogh

offer plush carpeting, antique furnishings, Laura Ashley prints, garden views, and private baths. The generous country breakfast of farm-fresh eggs, homemade scones, juice, and fruit is served by the cozy curved hearth in the dining room; cottages receive a breakfast basket. Tea is served in the afternoon. The inn also offers three contemporary cottages with privacy and views of the gardens, creek, and forest or sea. One cottage boasts a sitting room/library, wood-burning stove, king-size bed, kitchenette (for self-serve breakfast), bath with claw-foot tub, and patio. The inn's Sea Star Cottage is an intimate rustic house, about 4 miles away, built out over the tidal waters of Tomales Bay with unobstructed views in all directions. The cottage features a 75-foot-long dock leading to the front door, a cozy living room with fireplace, a four-poster queen-size bed, a full kitchen, bath, and solarium with hot tub. The Vision Cottage is ideal for families traveling together; the two-bedroom unit boasts a country-cottage decor, a wood-burning fireplace, and floor-to-ceiling windows that take in views of the surrounding bishop pines.

INN ON TOMALES BAY

22555 Highway 1
Point Reyes (Marshall), CA 94940

⊗ $$

■ The wood-sided, two-story home, orig-
inally built in the 1940s, was renovated in
1992 to provide three private suites and
large bay and picture windows that take in
views of Tomales Bay just 100 feet away. The home B&B is situated on a knoll and
framed by pine and cypress trees. The guest suites are furnished with queen-size
beds, fireplaces, and comfortable reading chairs, and all three suites enjoy spectacu-
lar views of the bay and have private entrances and large, private bathrooms. The full
hot breakfast is served either in the dining area with wood-burning fireplace or in the
guest room. The breakfasts vary each day but may include such delicacies as sea-
sonal fruit crepes with chicken-apple sausage, buttermilk pancakes with Sonoma Val-
ley bacon, or home-cured lox and bagels. Caffè latte is a specialty at the B&B. The
nearby Point Reyes National Seashore provides miles of walking and hiking trails; a
boat ramp nearby provides easy access to the bay.

PHONE: (415) 663–9002
WEB SITE: www.tomalesbay.com
FEATURES: home; 3 suites; no credit
cards; in-room refrigerators
NEARBY: bay; Point Reyes National
Seashore; hiking; bird-watching
INNKEEPERS/OWNERS: Bob and Lyn-
nette Kahn

JASMINE COTTAGE & GRAY'S RETREAT

P.O. Box 56
Point Reyes Station, CA 94956

♿ ⊗ $$–$$$$

■ This compound is surrounded by a
country garden at the top of a hill north of
Point Reyes Station. The cottage, a former
1878 schoolhouse, is a pleasant five-
minute walk from town and a five-minute
drive from the National Seashore. The
romantic hideaway is situated among aro-
matic blooms, a vegetable garden, an
herb garden, fruit trees, and chickens
(they provide eggs for breakfast). The cottage offers a fully equipped kitchen, sleep-

PHONE: (415) 663–1166
FAX: (415) 662–9300
WEB SITE: www.jasminecottage.com
FEATURES: 1 main cottage, 3 smaller
cottages; in-room phones; pets
allowed (by arrangement); in-room tel-
evisions, VCRs (by request); kitchens;
in-room workspace; hot tub; laundry;
picnic baskets; jogger strollers
NEARBY: Point Reyes National
Seashore; town; bicycling
INNKEEPER/OWNER: Karen Gray

ing arrangements for up to six adults and a baby, a garden room with deck and library, and a woodshed well stocked for the cottage's cozy woodstove; a Barn Loft offers a kitchen and great views. The stay includes a full breakfast basket laid out in the kitchen before guests arrive. The bountiful offering consists of eggs, muffins, homemade jams, fruit, coffees, teas, and cereals. The owners also rent a larger unit, Gray's Retreat; the units share a hot tub, outdoor fireplace, hammock, and laundry. The innkeeper is the author of *Family Guide to Point Reyes,* a rich resource for families visiting the area.

MARSH COTTAGE

P.O. Box 1121
Point Reyes Station, CA 94956

⊗ $$–$$$

PHONE: (415) 669–7168
WEB SITE: www.marshcottage.com
FEATURES: 1 cottage; kitchen; portable crib; in-room workspace; no credit cards
NEARBY: Point Reyes National Seashore; Tomales Bay; wetlands; bird-watching
INNKEEPER/OWNER: Wendy Schwartz

▧ Built in the 1930s and restored in 1985, this cottage sits amid untamed wild roses, grasses, fir trees, mint, and blackberry brambles. A relaxing deck overlooks marsh wetlands dotted with cattails, a pier, the bay, and hills. An ideal retreat for bird-watchers, this B&B, with its own driveway and entrance, offers complete privacy. The one main room of the gray wooden cottage boasts a freestanding fireplace, sitting area, queen-size bed and futon, and full kitchen. The hallway leads to an adjoining shower, tub bathroom, and closet. The sunny room with white wooden walls is decorated in beige, teal, and terra-cotta shades with coordinating country print fabrics. The kitchen is stocked at all times with tea, coffee, and sherry; breakfast in the cottage consists of fresh orange juice, home-baked breads and muffins, fresh fruits, granola, a basket of fresh eggs, cheeses, and French-roast coffee. Families are welcome; a portable crib is available.

POINT REYES STATION

P.O. Box 824
Point Reyes Station, CA 94956

⊗ $$–$$$

▧ This inn is a contemporary version of an old Cape Cod. The spacious rooms have 13-foot vaulted ceilings and large expanses of windows to take advantage of the spectacular views of the surrounding hills. Each antiques-filled room has a queen- or king-size bed, private bath, fireplace, whirlpool, and balcony. The continental breakfast is served in the great room overlooking the garden. Homemade cookies, tea, and coffee are available all day.

PHONE: (415) 663–9372

WEB SITE: www.pointreyesstationinn.com

FEATURES: inn; 3 rooms; in-room phones; in-room televisions and VCRs; computer hookups; spa

NEARBY: Point Reyes National Seashore; Tomales Bay; town; restaurants

INNKEEPER/OWNER: Renee Giacomini

EAST BROTHER LIGHT STATION

117 Park Place
Point Richmond, CA 94801

⊗ $$$$

▓ The historic East Brother Light Station has been functioning as a lighthouse since 1874 and is perched atop an island in San Francisco Bay. It has been serving as a bed and breakfast, off and on, for more than twenty years. An "island" experience, the stay requires a ten-minute boat trip to reach the inn and includes hors d'oeuvres and champagne on arrival, along with a tour of the island. A breakfast featuring popovers and specialties such as Lighthouse French toast soufflé and a four-course gourmet dinner are also included. Each of the rooms is unique and has a queen bed; Walter's Quarters, a little smaller and more rustic, is located in the fog signal building, far enough from the main building to provide optimum privacy. The multicourse gourmet dinner, with accompanying wines, is the highlight on the "island" and features such favorites as salmon Wellington and citrus-glazed rock Cornish game hen. The entire station serves as a living museum of American maritime history, and income from the bed and breakfast is partially allocated to the preservation of the island and lighthouse.

PHONE: (510) 233–2385

WEB SITE: www.ebls.org

FEATURES: inn; 5 rooms; four-course dinner included; accessible by boat only

NEARBY: 30 minutes from downtown San Francisco

INNKEEPERS: Elan and Katy Stewart

OWNER: East Brother Light Station, Inc.

THE PILLAR POINT INN

380 Capistrano Road
Princeton-by-the-Sea, CA 94018
(P.O. Box 388, El Granada, CA 94018)

♿ ⊘ $$–$$$$

▪ Located on the only harbor between San Francisco and Santa Cruz is this Cape Cod–style B&B that proves a haven for homesick New Englanders. The inn was built to blend with the architecture of the quaint fishing village and offers eleven luxurious guest accommodations, all with views of the harbor, Half Moon Bay, and the Pacific Ocean. Each room offers a fireplace, private bath, European-style feather mattress, and bay or window seat, as well as VCR, concealed television, radio, and refrigerator. A dining room and living room, which share an open fireplace, are furnished in country pine and maple; a separate conference room accommodates up to fourteen people. The full and varied complimentary morning fare, which is served in the dining room, includes eggs, meat, bread, fruit dishes, and creative quiches and frittatas or Belgian waffles. Guests enjoy a harbor-view terrace as well as afternoon tea.

PHONE: (650) 728–7377 or (800) 400–8281
FAX: (650) 728–8345
WEB SITE: www.pillarpointinn.com
FEATURES: inn; 11 rooms; in-room phones; in-room televisions and VCRs; in-room refrigerators; fax; copier; conference areas; one computer hookup
NEARBY: ocean; Half Moon Bay; harbor; golf; whale-watching
INNKEEPER: Marny Shuster
OWNERS: Dr. James and Kazuko Popplewell

ALBION HOUSE

135 Gough Street
San Francisco, CA 94102

⊘ $–$$

▪ Built after the great earthquake of 1906, the inn near Symphony Hall has gone through many periods of decor, including extensive renovation in 2000. The three-story building hosts a restaurant on the bottom floor and the B&B inn on the two upper levels. Each guest room offers a combination of Victorian, Oriental, and Californian decor and features many carved wooden antiques and brass beds with lots of pillows. All guest rooms have private baths, telephones, televisions, and VCRs; some have fireplaces. Floral pastels

PHONE: (415) 621–0896 or (800) 400–8295
FAX: (415) 621–3811
WEB SITE: www.albionhouseinn.com
FEATURES: inn; 9 rooms; in-room phones; in-room televisions and VCRs; fax; copier; computer hookups; restaurant on premises
NEARBY: Symphony Hall; Chinatown
INNKEEPER: Jean Yees
OWNERS: Carol and Alexander Sachal

decorate the Joplin room, with its charming canopy bed, pine armoire, and cozy roof deck for soaking up the sun. This room takes its name after Janis Joplin, who stayed here in the 1960s when she performed at the Carousel Ballroom around the corner. Wine is served fireside in the spacious living room, with a piano, and the three-course breakfast is served in the dining room. Wine and cheese are served in the evening; refreshments are available all day.

THE ANDREWS HOTEL

624 Post Street
San Francisco, CA 94109

⊗ $–$$$

◾ This neat and cheerful B&B is simply yet comfortably furnished with white wrought-iron beds, desks, European lace curtains, fresh flowers, and upholstered armchairs. This gracious European-style hotel also offers in-room televisions and telephones and private baths. Fresh fruit, baked goods, and coffee or tea are served on each floor in the morning. The hotel is within walking distance of restaurants,

PHONE: (415) 563–6877 or (800) 926–3739
FAX: (415) 928–6919
WEB SITE: www.andrewshotel.com
FEATURES: inn/hotel; 48 rooms; in-room phones; in-room televisions; fax; copier; computer hookups; catering; restaurant
NEARBY: Union Square; Chinatown; theaters
INNKEEPER: Barbara Vogler
OWNER: Harry Andrews

stores, and theaters and is 2 blocks from Union Square. Complimentary wine is offered in the hotel's Italian restaurant. Parking is available for an additional charge.

Your Pass to San Francisco

If you plan to visit several of San Francisco's sights, you might want to purchase a CityPass to save a little cash for perhaps a special dinner in one of the city's renowned restaurants. The pass will admit you to seven of the city's most popular destinations, including a San Francisco Bay cruise, the Exploratorium, the San Francisco Zoo, and more.

The passes may be purchased from one of the attractions or from visitor information centers. The CityPass is valid for seven days after first used. For more information call the San Francisco Visitor Information Center at (415) 391–2000, or log on to www.sfvisitor.com.

THE ARCHBISHOP'S MANSION

1000 Fulton Street
San Francisco, CA 94117

⊗ $$–$$$$

Built for the archbishop of San Francisco in 1904, this elegantly restored mansion with open, carved mahogany staircase, stained-glass dome, and spacious country-manor guest suites is a luxurious B&B offering. The guest rooms, all with carved queen-size beds, private baths (some with two-person Jacuzzis), sitting areas, and fireplaces, are filled with Oriental carpets, museum-quality French antiques, canopies, oil paintings, period chandeliers, and many pieces of Americana, including Noel Coward's piano, a mirror belonging to Mary Todd Lincoln's family, and an original crystal chandelier from the movie set of *Gone with the Wind*. As a salute to the nearby opera house, each guest room is named after a nineteenth-century opera. Guests gather for wine tastings in the late afternoon, and gourmet baked goods, jams, juice, and beverages are delivered to the room at guests' specified time each morning.

PHONE: (415) 563–7872 or (800) 543–5820
FAX: (415) 885–3193
WEB SITE: www.thearchbishops mansion.com
FEATURES: inn; 15 rooms; in-room phones; computer hookups; in-room televisions and VCRs; fax; copier; catering; conference areas
NEARBY: opera
INNKEEPER: Jennifer P. Huggins
OWNER: Joie de Vivre Hospitality

THE CHATEAU TIVOLI

1057 Steiner Street
San Francisco, CA 94115

⊗ $–$$$$

This 1892 Victorian town house has won many awards for the complete restoration to its original splendor, with hardwood floors, a grand oak staircase, stately columns, and double parlors. The historic building, located in the Alamo Square Historic District of the city, stands out with its more than twenty-color paint scheme highlighted by 23-karat gold-leaf trim. The interior of the inn is abundant with impressive, original antiques, including a $10,000 French canopy bed. The guest rooms and suites feature such amenities as

PHONE: (415) 776–5462 or (800) 228–1647

FAX: (415) 776–0505

WEB SITE: www.chateautivoli.com

FEATURES: inn; 9 rooms; in-room phones; computer hookups; pets allowed (by arrangement); fax; copier; catering; conferences; weddings

NEARBY: Alamo Square Historic District

INNKEEPERS/OWNERS: Steven and Geraldine Shohet

marble baths, balconies, city views, stained glass, towers, and turrets; four accommodations share two baths. The Luisa Tetrazzini suite features an eighteenth-century canopy bed, marble bath, balcony, and private parlor with fireplace. The elegant inn offers a generous continental breakfast each morning, which includes fresh fruit salad, cereal, yogurt, juice, and croissants, served in the dining room; weekend guests enjoy a full champagne brunch. Complimentary beverages, wine, and cheeses are served in the afternoon; the inn will make arrangements for champagne, desserts, or roses on request. The Chateau also provides a romantic setting for small weddings, parties, meetings, or receptions.

A COUNTRY COTTAGE

5 Dolores Terrace
San Francisco, CA 94110

⊗ $

 This 1906 cottage-style home in the heart of San Francisco offers four guest rooms comfortably furnished in country antiques with big brass beds. There are two shared baths. The house is located at the end of a quiet street 1 block from Dolores Park, so it's like being in the country with all of the amenities of the big city. Enjoy a full breakfast of scrambled eggs, cheese omelettes, sausage, and juice in the sunny kitchen, then relax on the patio and take in the serenity of the birds and trees. Or hop on the nearest streetcar to visit downtown, Union Square, or Moscone Center only three to four stops away. Complimentary wine is always available to guests.

PHONE: (415) 899–0600

FAX: (415) 899–9923

WEB SITE: www.bedandbreakfast
.com/california/a-country-cottage.html

FEATURES: inn; 4 rooms

NEARBY: shops; aquarium; beach; museums; Chinatown

INNKEEPERS/OWNERS: Susan and Richard Kreibich

EDWARD II INN

3155 Scott Street
San Francisco, CA 94123

♿ Ⓧ $–$$$$

▨ Located in the marina district, this
three-story 1915-vintage hotel offers
proximity to the shopping areas of Chest-
nut and Union Streets. Decorated
throughout in an English-country mood,
the inn offers accommodations from the
quaint to the deluxe. Six luxurious suites in the hotel and in a nearby carriage house
are offered with canopy beds and wet bars; kitchens and Jacuzzis are offered in some
suites. Nineteen guest rooms boast private baths. The continental breakfast is served
in the hotel's breakfast area; its Bloomer's Pub (which does not serve dinner, but
serves pastries, cheese and crackers, fresh fruit, and beverages from 6:00 to 9:00
P.M.) is popular. Parking is available in the surrounding neighborhood, and there is lim-
ited parking in the hotel lot for an additional fee.

PHONE: (415) 922–3000 or (800) 473–2846
FAX: (415) 931–5784
WEB SITE: www.edwardii.com
FEATURES: inn/hotel; 32 rooms; in-room phones; in-room televisions; kitchens (some); computer hookups (some); in-room workspace (some)
NEARBY: marina district; shopping
INNKEEPERS/OWNERS: Bob and Denise Holland

INN ON CASTRO

321 Castro Street
San Francisco, CA 94114

♿ Ⓧ $–$$$

▨ This Edwardian B&B offers a surprise of contemporary furnishings splashed with
bright colors, vibrant paintings, and an abundance of exotic plants and fresh flowers.
This friendly inn that caters to the gay community offers tasteful and inviting guest rooms and suites with views and private baths. Guests are served a full breakfast in the upstairs dining room, also decorated in a contemporary yet hospitable motif with cozy fireplace. The inn is situated on a hill with views of the city and bay and with village shops and bistros a stroll away.

PHONE: (415) 861–0321
FAX: (415) 861–0321
WEB SITE: www.innoncastro2.com
FEATURES: inn; 4 rooms; in-room phones; computer hookups; in-room televisions; in-room VCRs (on request)
NEARBY: Castro district; shops; restaurants
INNKEEPER/OWNER: Jan R. de Gier

THE INN SAN FRANCISCO

943 South Van Ness Avenue
San Francisco, CA 94110

$–$$$$

■ This charming 1872 Italianate mansion and its adjacent garden cottage have been restored to their original grandeur and feature period decor. Each guest room has been individually decorated with antique furnishings, fresh flowers, marble sinks, and polished-brass fixtures. Cozy rooms have double or queen-size beds, and most include private baths. The more spacious accommodations feature queen feather beds and private baths; luxury suites also offer spa tubs and some fireplaces. One special suite has its own redwood hot tub! Guests may stay in the large garden-cottage apartment with kitchen, which can sleep up to six. Guests may wander in the inn's charming English garden with redwood hot tub in a tropical gazebo. The sundeck offers 360-degree views of the city. Complimentary beverages are always available at the inn; a generous buffet breakfast is served each morning, including quiches, cheeses, eggs, and cold cuts. Limited reserved parking is available.

PHONE: (415) 641–0188 or (800) 359–0913
FAX: (415) 641–1701
WEB SITE: www.innsf.com
FEATURES: inn/cottage; 21 rooms; limited smoking; in-room phones; computer hookups; in-room televisions; fax; kitchen (cottage); hot tubs (suite and garden); limited on-site parking
NEARBY: shops; restaurants; theater
INNKEEPERS/OWNERS: Marty Neely and Connie Wu

MARINA INN B&B

3110 Octavia Street
San Francisco, CA 94123

♿ 🚭 $–$$

PHONE: (415) 928–1000 or (800) 274–1420
FAX: (415) 928–5909
WEB SITE: www.marinainn.com
FEATURES: inn/hotel; 40 rooms; in-room phones; in-room televisions; computer hookups; in-room workspace; fax; copier
NEARBY: marina district; Fisherman's Wharf; Ghirardelli Square
INNKEEPER: Kelly Wuthrich
OWNER: Four Sisters Inns

■ This four-story Victorian hotel on the corner of Octavia and Lombard Streets was built in 1924 and welcomes guests with its elegant marble lobby and country furnishings. The extensively renovated and redecorated inn with bay windows offers a second-floor sitting room, which is the locale of the morning continental breakfast and afternoon sherry; a microwave is provided here as well. Each of the forty rooms boasts pastel-flowered wall coverings, forest green carpet, pine furnishings, poster beds, and a full bath with marble sink. Televisions and telephones are also available in each guest room.

MOFFATT HOUSE

1401 Seventh Avenue
San Francisco, CA 94122

$–$$

■ These two early-1900s homes near Golden Gate Park and the University of California Medical Center offer a casual, friendly retreat with light interiors and flowering plants. Guests gather in the cheery kitchen for tourist information and a self-catered, generous continental-plus breakfast of neighborhood produce-market fruit, juice, home-baked muffins, toast, Danish, cheeses, and boiled eggs. Six guest rooms share baths. Queen-size, twin, and double beds are offered, and a crib is available for a one-time nominal charge at this reasonable B&B.

PHONE: (415) 661–6210
WEB SITE: www.moffatthouse.com
FEATURES: inn; 8 rooms; in-room televisions; in-room phones (some); fax
NEARBY: Golden Gate Park; University of California Medical Center
INNKEEPER/OWNER: Ruth Moffatt

THE MONTE CRISTO

600 Presidio Avenue
San Francisco, CA 94115

⊗ $–$$

■ The 1875-vintage inn was originally built as a saloon and hotel. Its colorful history includes serving as a bordello, a refuge after the 1906 earthquake, and a speakeasy. It is listed on the National Register of Historic Places and is located just 2 convenient blocks from the elegantly restored shops, restaurants, and antiques stores on Sacramento Street. The spacious rooms are pleasantly furnished in authentic period pieces of early American and English antiques, wall coverings, down comforters, and fragrant potpourri; three rooms

PHONE: (415) 931–1875
FAX: (415) 931–6005
WEB SITE: www.bedandbreakfast .com/california/monte-cristo.html
FEATURES: inn/hotel; 14 rooms; some in-room phones; in-room televisions; in-room VCRs (on request); fax; computer hookup
NEARBY: shops; restaurants; theater; art galleries
INNKEEPER/OWNER: George Yuan

share baths. A popular guest accommodation is the Oriental room, with a Chinese wedding bed and sunken tub. The continental breakfast buffet includes fresh juice, fresh fruit, muffins, and cereals.

PETITE AUBERGE

863 Bush Street
San Francisco, CA 94108

🚫 $$–$$$$

This romantic French country inn in the heart of downtown is a finely restored mansion offering an ornate, Baroque exterior design and warm, burnished woods on the interior. An antique carousel horse and fresh flowers greet guests, and an antiques-filled lounge with fireplace is a cozy retreat. The twenty-six guest rooms all feature private baths, French wall coverings, antiques, handmade pillows, and quilted bedspreads; eighteen rooms boast fireplaces. A garden-view dining area offers a buffet-style full breakfast including a hot entree, cereals, homemade breads and muffins, fruit, and juice. Guests are pampered at this inn with a special afternoon tea, complimentary cookies and beverages, early-morning coffee service with the morning newspaper, and nighttime turndown service. Valet parking and breakfast in bed are available for a small charge.

PHONE: (415) 928–6000 or (800) 365–3004
FAX: (415) 673–7214
WEB SITE: www.jdvhospitality.com
FEATURES: inn/hotel; 26 rooms; in-room phones; computer hookups; in-room televisions; fax; copier; hot tub
NEARBY: downtown; shops; restaurants
INNKEEPER: Chip Connelly
OWNER: Joie de Vivre Hospitality

THE QUEEN ANNE

1590 Sutter Street
San Francisco, CA 94109

♿ $–$$$$

In the heart of the Civic Center area, this nineteenth-century refurbished guesthouse is a classic Queen Anne example with a cascading staircase, glass skylights, and window settees. Room furnishings blend the old and new with newly renovated

PHONE: (415) 441–2828 or (800) 227–3970
FAX: (415) 775–5212
WEB SITE: www.queenanne.com
FEATURES: inn/hotel; 48 rooms; limited smoking; in-room phones; computer hookups; in-room televisions and VCRs; all business services; limo service; laundry service; conference area
NEARBY: Civic Center
INNKEEPER: Michael Wade
OWNER: Franklin Cabuyadao

bathrooms, marble sinks, brick fireplaces, and antiques. The expanded continental breakfast, along with the morning newspaper, is served in the salon; afternoon tea and sherry are offered in the parlor. Laundry and business services (such as a conference facility, fax machine, and special corporate rates) are available. Complimentary limo service is available to downtown areas on weekends.

THE RED VICTORIAN

1665 Haight Street
San Francisco, CA 94117

⊗ $$–$$$$

■ This small upstairs hotel is as colorful as the well-known Haight-Ashbury neighborhood in which it resides. Teddy bears, red rugs, and lace curtains grace the inn and its uniquely decorated shared- and private-bath guest rooms. A vegan and

PHONE: (415) 864–1978
FAX: (415) 863–3293
WEB SITE: www.redvic.com
FEATURES: inn/hotel; 18 rooms; in-room phones; computer hookups; fax; audiovisual equipment; conferences; gift shop; art gallery
NEARBY: Haight-Ashbury neighborhood
INNKEEPER/OWNER: Sami Sunchild

vegetarian continental breakfast of croissants, muffins, and coffee is served in the bay-windowed "peace gallery." The bed-and-breakfast accommodations are a part of a complex that includes a human-relationship center and staff-training program. Downstairs, a global-family-network center promotes planetary consciousness with an art gallery and a gift shop.

STANYAN PARK HOTEL

750 Stanyan Street
San Francisco, CA 94117

♿ ⊗ $$–$$$$

■ This hotel of the early 1900s, listed on the National Register of Historic Places, has

PHONE: (415) 751–1000

FAX: (415) 668–5454

WEB SITE: www.stanyanpark.com

FEATURES: inn/hotel; 36 rooms; in-room phones; computer hookups; in-room televisions; in-room workspace; fax; copier; kitchens (suites)

NEARBY: Golden Gate Park; University of San Francisco; University of California Medical Center

INNKEEPER: John K. Brocklehurst

been meticulously restored to its early glory, including the reconstruction of its rare cupola and roof balustrade. The thirty-six guest rooms and suites are individually decorated in Victorian furnishings, four-poster beds, brass chandeliers, and patterned wall coverings and have the modern amenities of phones, televisions, and private tiled bathrooms with pedestal sinks. Suites at the inn also offer full kitchens, dining rooms, and living rooms. Many of the guest accommodations overlook Golden Gate Park, and guests may park across the street from the B&B in an attended lot. Coffee, juice, fresh fruit, croissants, and sweet rolls are served in the hotel dining room each morning; guests enjoy tea and cookies in the evening.

UNION STREET INN

2229 Union Street

San Francisco, CA 94123

⊗ $$$–$$$$

▓ This turn-of-the-twentieth-century Edwardian house-turned-inn has a garden setting within the city's downtown. The European-style decor includes canopy and brass beds, armoires, bay windows, and private baths. The spacious Wild Rose room in soft, rose-colored hues offers warm antiques, a king-size bed, artwork, a garden view, and a tiled bath with Jacuzzi. A carriage house is separated from the inn by a garden and has a Jacuzzi reserved for carriage-house guests. The expanded continental breakfast featuring home-baked muffins is served in the parlor, the garden, or the room.

PHONE: (415) 346–0424

FAX: (415) 922–8046

WEB SITE: www.unionstreetinn.com

FEATURES: inn/cottage; 6 rooms; in-room phones; in-room televisions, in-room VCRs (some); fax; in-room workspace; Jacuzzi (carriage house)

NEARBY: downtown San Francisco; shops; restaurants

INNKEEPERS/OWNERS: Jane Bertorelli and David Coyle

THE WASHINGTON SQUARE INN

1660 Stockton Street
San Francisco, CA 94133

♿ ⊘ $$–$$$$

■ This intimate B&B hotel is located in the heart of North Beach, the city's Italian district, on historic Washington Square. The guest rooms, individually decorated with an elegant country flavor, boast English and French antiques, coordinated fabrics, telephones, terry-cloth robes, down pillows and comforters, and fresh flowers; all have private baths. Two spacious guest rooms feature cozy bay-window seating overlooking the square, where tai chi is performed every morning. A complimentary continental breakfast of croissants, fresh juice, fruit, and coffee is served in bed or by the hearth in the spacious lobby. Guests enjoy a delightful afternoon tea with cakes; evening wine and hors d'oeuvres are also offered for guests and their visitors. Guests are further pampered at the inn with a local newspaper and valet parking.

PHONE: (415) 981–4220 or (800) 388–0220
FAX: (415) 397–7242
WEB SITE: www.wsisf.com
FEATURES: inn/hotel; 15 rooms; in-room phones; computer hookups; in-room televisions; in-room VCRs (on request); fax; copier; valet parking
NEARBY: North Beach; Washington Square; Fisherman's Wharf; Ghirardelli Square
INNKEEPERS/OWNERS: Daniel and Maria Levin

WHITE SWAN INN

845 Bush Street
San Francisco, CA 94108

⊘ $$–$$$$

■ One of San Francisco's first inns, the White Swan has been resurrected with new ownership and offers a European-style bed and breakfast stay in the heart of the city. The English-inspired inn features rich floral carpets, comfortable furniture, and English art and collectibles. The twenty-six guest rooms all offer fireplaces and private baths. The stay includes a gourmet breakfast buffet, afternoon cookies, and evening wine and hors

PHONE: (415) 775–1755 or (800) 999–9570
FAX: (415) 775–5717
WEB SITE: www.whiteswaninnsf.com
FEATURES: inn; 26 rooms and suites; fireplaces; in-room VCRs (some); wet bar; wireless Internet access; voice mail; dataports; fitness room; valet parking (fee); newspaper
NEARBY: walking distance to restaurants, theaters, cable cars; Union Square; Chinatown
INNKEEPER: Pamela Flank
OWNER: Joie de Vivre Hospitality

d'oeuvres served in the newly renovated parlor. Special guest room amenities include a wet bar stocked with complimentary beverages, a sitting area, bathrobes, and phones with voice mail and data port. For an additional cost, breakfast is served in the room.

THE WILLOWS INN

710 Fourteenth Street
San Francisco, CA 94114

$-$$

■ Convenient to downtown and Union Square, the inn, housed in a 1903 Edwardian, also provides parking for guests. Rooms are individually furnished in "gypsy willow" furniture designed for the inn, antiques, armoires (with robes), Laura Ashley prints, and private phones; all have in-room sinks and shared baths. The expanded continental breakfast, served in bed or in the sitting room, arrives with a morning newspaper; complimentary cocktails are served in the evening. The Willows has a gay and lesbian clientele.

PHONE: (415) 431–4770 or (800) 431–0277
FAX: (415) 431–5295
WEB SITE: www.willowssf.com
FEATURES: inn/hotel; 12 rooms; in-room phones; in-room televisions and VCRs (some); in-room refrigerators (some); fax; computer hookups
NEARBY: downtown San Francisco; Union Square
INNKEEPER/OWNER: Brad Goessler

COXHEAD HOUSE

37 East Santa Ynez Avenue
San Mateo, CA 94401

$$-$$$

■ San Mateo's first bed-and-breakfast, this Tudor Revival inn is a survivor of the town's century-old past. Ernest Coxhead, a noted English architect, built the home around 1891 to be his family's country retreat from the rapidly growing city of San Francisco nearby. He gave it a rural feel to resemble an English cottage with a double-gabled roof and leaded windows throughout. The inn is a walk away from shops and restaurants in downtown San Mateo. The front room and dining rooms are accented by redwood paneling, and bay windows bring in a soft light in both the rear and front of the inn. Antiques decorate throughout the bed-and-breakfast, and hand-painted murals complete a theme in each guest room, as

PHONE: (650) 685–1600

FAX: (650) 685–1684

WEB SITE: www.coxhead.com

FEATURES: inn; 5 rooms; in-room phones; in-room televisions; airport pick-up service; fax; copier; in-room computer hookups; in-room workspace

NEARBY: downtown San Mateo; Filoli Centre; Bay Meadows Race Course; Stanford University; *Sunset* magazine; tennis; golf

INNKEEPERS/OWNERS: Pat Osborn and Steve Cabreru

do historical books and notes. Four rooms have queen-size beds and one has a double; two rooms share a bath. The Bernard Maybeck room features interesting nooks, including sitting and dressing room areas. The private bathroom has an oversize whirlpool. The intimate Julia Morgan room is named after one of Coxhead's famous architect friends of the period, Julia Morgan, of Hearst Castle fame. This accommodation has a wraparound fireplace and a cozy window seat. The Angel Porch room might be your choice, with the house's original stone fireplace and vaulted ceiling. Its name comes from the Gothic angel sculpture that highlights the room. Breakfast is served in the formal dining room or in the garden courtyard. The dining room version boasts a formal place setting; breakfast includes fruits, egg dishes, sausages, and assorted rolls and breads. A complimentary evening fare, which includes soft drinks, juices, and snacks, is offered. The inn's carriage house hosts the fax and computer for business travelers.

GERSTLE PARK INN

34 Grove Street
San Rafael, CA 94901

♿ Ⓢ $$$–$$$$

■ This century-old estate borders on the woods of Marin County Open Space in the foothills overlooking town. The secluded property contains one and a half acres of oak, cedar, fruit, and redwood trees but is a short walk from downtown San Rafael's shops and restaurants. The home's history spans its beginnings as the Lewis Sloan Estate to a boardinghouse in later years. The present owners renovated the estate in 1995, including its main house with 6,800 square feet and a carriage house that now houses two one-bedroom suites. A sweeping veranda fronts the inn and welcomes guests with its wicker rocking chairs. The living room of the inn features a 16-foot arched ceiling, rich antiques, and a cozy fireplace. Each guest suite has its own parlor area and deck or patio; two suites have kitchen facili-

PHONE: (415) 721–7611 or (800) 726–7611

FAX: (415) 721–7600

WEB SITE: www.gerstleparkinn.com

FEATURES: inn; 2 cottage suites and 10 suites; in-room phones; voice mail; in-room televisions and VCRs; fax; copier; computer hookups; in-room workspace; audiovisual equipment; catering; meeting areas

NEARBY: parkland; downtown San Rafael

INNKEEPERS/OWNERS: Jim and Judy Dowling

ties. The spacious guest suites are decorated in dramatic color themes, rich fabrics, and European or Oriental antiques. The Oak suite on the second floor has a balcony overlooking a large oak tree and gardens, a king-size bed, and a private parlor; the Victorian-style decor features a Jacuzzi and a dramatic black, deep rose, and dark green color scheme. The full breakfast is served in the dining room, on the veranda, or in the room. Guests relax over a glass of wine in the evening; beverages and snacks such as cookies and popcorn are available all day.

THE PANAMA HOTEL, RESTAURANT, AND INN

4 Bayview Street
San Rafael, CA 94901

⊗ $–$$

▓ This urban inn, situated in the central shopping area of town, comprises two 1910 Victorian homes connected by a rambling garden patio. Accommodations include cozy rooms, many with balconies. Most rooms have televisions and direct-dial telephones; eleven units have private baths. Six of the guest rooms have kitchenettes, but all rooms at this B&B/ restaurant have access to a guest kitchen. The locally renowned restaurant at the inn serves lunch, Sunday brunch, and dinner. The continental breakfast is offered for free to B&B guests each morning, either in the restaurant or on the patio.

PHONE: (415) 457–3993 or (800) 899–3993

FAX: (415) 457–6240

WEB SITE: www.panamahotel.com

FEATURES: inn/hotel; 16 rooms; in-room phones (most); in-room televisions (most); in-room workspace; computer hookups; fax; copier; catering; conference areas; kitchenettes (some); guest kitchen; restaurant on premises (lunch, dinner); weddings; banquets

NEARBY: in town; shops; restaurants

INNKEEPER/OWNER: Daniel T. Miller

THE MADISON STREET INN

1390 Madison Street
Santa Clara, CA 95050

⦻ $–$$

▪ This restored Queen Anne home in grays and blues is situated in a quiet residential area and has a pretty yard with redbrick pool, redwood deck, and hot tub. Guests enjoy a parlor, decorated in Oriental rugs and comfortable antiques, and its fireplace. The antiques-filled guest rooms with high ceilings have wall coverings and plush peach carpeting. Three of the guest rooms have private baths, and the two rooms that share a bath have sink/vanity areas; one of the rooms is a family suite with queen-size bed and sofa bed. Breakfast treats at the inn may include Belgian waffles, eggs Benedict, and orange chocolate muffins; the repast may be enjoyed in your room, on the patio, or in the dining room. A television, VCR, and movies are available, as are bicycles. Complimentary sherry is offered at all times. The inn offers package stays for room, dinner, and tickets to the Winchester Mystery House.

PHONE: (408) 249–5541, (408) 249–6058, or (800) 491–5541

FAX: (408) 249–6676

WEB SITE: www.madisonstreetinn.com

FEATURES: inn; 6 rooms; in-room phones; televisions and VCRs (some); pets allowed; fax; computer hookups; in-room workspace (some); catering; meeting areas; bicycles; pool and spa; weddings; murder-mystery weekends

NEARBY: Winchester Mystery House; Paramount's Great America

INNKEEPERS/OWNERS: Theresa and Ralph Wigginton

CASA MADRONA HOTEL & SPA

801 Bridgeway
Sausalito, CA 94965

⦻ $$$$

▪ San Francisco Bay is out the front door of this inn, and out the back door are the national and state parks of Muir Woods, Point Reyes, and the Golden Gate National Recreation Area. Strolling the small shops and bistros of Sausalito, participating in a favorite water sport, hiking, and picnicking are all close by at Casa Madrona. Casa Madrona has been a hotel since 1885; the hostelry, which added thirty-one rooms/suites, a spa, and a second restaurant in January 2002, includes the Victorian house, decorated in tasteful antiques; surrounding cottages; and hillside casitas. Nestled high in the hills above Sausalito, the rooms cascade down the hillside, offering views of the harbor. Individually decorated in themes that range from Oriental to Southwest, the guest rooms, cottages, and casitas offer such amenities as some

PHONE: (415) 332–0502 or (800) 567–9524

FAX: (415) 332–2537

WEB SITE: www.casamadrona.com

FEATURES: inn/hotel/cottages; 63 rooms; in-room televisions and VCRs; all business/meeting services; restaurant on premises; laundry; massages; Jacuzzi

NEARBY: Muir Woods; Point Reyes; Golden Gate National Recreation Area; shops; restaurants; beaches; bay

INNKEEPER: Erick Halliday

OWNER: Rockresorts

bathtubs for two, antique fireplaces, some kitchens, and some private gardens and decks. The Bridgeway to Hollywood guest room offers a classic film library; the Katmandu is a regal room, filled with cushions for lounging and tiny secret alcoves. Extras at the inn include a private outdoor Jacuzzi, massage and body treatments, room service, laundry and dry cleaning, and an award-winning restaurant. Guests enjoy a complimentary continental breakfast each morning, as well as a wine-and-cheese social hour in the evening.

HOTEL SAUSALITO

16 El Portal
Sausalito, CA 94965

♿ ⊘ $$–$$$$

The Hotel Sausalito has been around for nearly a century, but its most recent reincarnation makes it worth a special stay. Reminiscent of a French boutique hotel that might be found along the Riviera, this Mission Revival inn/hotel grants the luxury and convenience of a larger hotel with the intimacy of a small inn. The

PHONE: (415) 332–0700 or (888) 442–0700

FAX: (415) 332–8788

WEB SITE: www.hotelsausalito.com

FEATURES: inn/hotel; 16 rooms; air-conditioning; in-room phones; voice mail; computer hookups; in-room televisions; in-room fax (on request); copier; in-room workspace

NEARBY: town shops and restaurants; Vina del Mar Park; harbor; ferry; Golden Gate Bridge; San Francisco

INNKEEPER/OWNER: William Purdie

sixteen guest accommodations include two suites. Many items in the hotel are handmade; colors are warm, vibrant, and restful all at once. Faux finishes, stained cement, shattered glass mosaic mirrors, and hand-forged wrought iron are a few of the design elements used throughout. The hotel still retains its original stained-glass windows, a leftover of its heritage, which ranges from its use as a bordello to beatnik hang-out. Walking down the hallway of the hotel is like a trip through an Impressionist art gallery. Guest room luxuries include generous showers and lush linens; rooms offer harbor or park views. Guests may choose from rooms with twin, queen-, or king-size beds; each has cable television hidden in a custom-designed and hand-built armoire.

Guests at Hotel Sausalito enjoy a rooftop garden for lounging over the complimentary morning newspaper or partaking of the breakfast meal that can also be enjoyed in the room, on the patio, or in the cafe next door. (Vouchers are given to guests for coffee and pastry.)

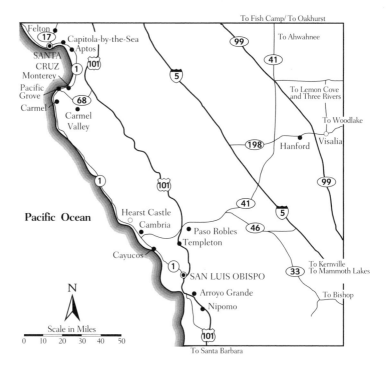

Felton
Capitola-by-the-Sea
17
Aptos
SANTA
CRUZ
1   101
Monterey
Pacific
Grove   68
Carmel
Carmel
Valley

Pacific Ocean

To Fish Camp/ To Oakhurst
99   To Ahwahnee
41
5
To Lemon Cove
and Three Rivers
To Woodlake
198   Visalia
Hanford
99
101
41
5
Hearst Castle
Cambria   46
Paso Robles
Templeton
Cayucos
1   SAN LUIS OBISPO
33   To Kernville
To Mammoth Lakes
Arroyo Grande
Nipomo   To Bishop

N

Scale in Miles
0   10   20   30   40   50

101
To Santa Barbara

CENTRAL CALIFORNIA

Central Coast

California's Central Coast offers an array of small communities that dot the dramatic Pacific Coast with unparalleled "Mediterranean" sunbathing beaches plus rich historical offerings. Original California missions can be found in several towns, such as San Juan Bautista, San Miguel, Carmel, and San Luis Obispo, and along with them stately examples of turn-of-the-century architecture, tree-lined streets, and coastal beauty. This region may be best known for the Hearst Castle in San Simeon, the state's most popular tourist attraction after Disneyland. But this region is becoming known for its grape-growing industry, as wineries and vineyards are beginning to compete with Wine Country as the state's "Little Napa." Travelers may stroll the boardwalk in Santa Cruz, observe the butterfly migration in Pacific Grove, and enjoy the quaint shops of Carmel, the "living Mission" and annual Mozart Festival in San Luis Obispo, and the unending, peaceful country drives through the rolling hills and wildflowers of the inland valleys.

APPLE LANE INN

6265 Soquel Drive
Aptos, CA 95003

♿ ⊗ $$–$$$

▧ This restored Victorian farmhouse was
built in the 1870s among apple orchards
and meadows. Before walking to the
nearby beach about a mile away or visiting the local wineries, guests are invited
to partake in a game of darts in the Cider
room or meet the various farm animals on the grounds. The five antiques-decorated
guest rooms have private baths. The Blossom room, in mauve and white, features a
queen-size lace canopy bed and a spacious private bath with skylight, a wicker chaise
lounge, and claw-foot tub. The Attic suite with sitting room and refrigerator, on the
top floor, makes an ideal family suite. The farmhouse inn, set on two and a half acres
of gardens, vineyards, and fields, serves a full country breakfast featuring such specialties as Eggs Christy or Morning Monte Cristo.

PHONE: (831) 475–6868 or (800)
649–8988
FAX: (831) 464–5790
WEB SITE: www.applelaneinn.com
FEATURES: inn; 5 rooms; in-room tele-
visions; pets allowed; small meetings;
weddings; children welcome; horse
and buggy charters
NEARBY: wineries; beach; Santa Cruz
INNKEEPERS/OWNERS: Diana and Doug
Groom

BAYVIEW HOTEL BED & BREAKFAST

8041 Soquel Drive
Aptos, CA 95003

⊗ $$–$$$$

PHONE: (831) 688–8654 or (800)
422–9843
FAX: (831) 688–5128
WEB SITE: www.bayviewhotel.com
FEATURES: inn; 12 rooms; in-room tele-
visions; in-room workspace; in-room
phones; fax; copier; catering; audiovi-
sual equipment; restaurant; weddings;
conferences
NEARBY: beaches; town
INNKEEPERS/OWNERS: Sandra and
Roland Held

▧ This Victorian hotel with restaurant,
built in 1878, is a local architectural land-
mark and is on the National Register of
Historic Places. The three-story structure
has been extensively restored with new
decor, plumbing, and electrical systems,
but the original marble fireplaces and
many original furnishings still grace the
rooms. Guest rooms feature private
baths, some with soaking tubs-for-two,

and antique furnishings, with the more luxurious accommodations on the third floor; a two-room suite is also available. The morning continental breakfast, consisting of juices, fruits, cereals, and pastries, is delivered to the room or served in the Victorian Garden, which features the second-oldest known magnolia tree in the world.

HISTORIC SAND ROCK FARM BED AND BREAKFAST

6901 Freedom Boulevard
Aptos, CA 95003

$$$–$$$$

This 1880s Arts and Crafts–style country estate, originally a 1,000-acre ranch and winery, sits on ten acres of meadows, twisting oaks, and towering redwoods on Monterey Bay. Owned by only two families in 112 years, Historic Sand Rock Farm has been restored to its original glory, replete with vintage lighting, lustrous redwood milled on-site, and hand-printed wall coverings. Each room at Sand Rock Farm has a private bath and unique features. The three upstairs rooms each have romantic two-person Jacuzzi tubs. The Honeycomb Suite features an en-suite Jacuzzi in a secluded "grotto" and a sitting area with antique French furnishings. The room displays a portion of the home's original wall covering and antique fleur-de-lis wall sconces. The picturesque windows on three walls overlook the gardens and hills. The two downstairs rooms share access to a large and private outdoor hot tub. The Hidden Garden Suite, the former great room of the original ranch house built in 1888, features a queen-size pine sleigh bed decorated with vine metal scrollwork. The room also features high ceilings and an extra-large sitting area with a wall of windows overlooking lush greenery. A private entrance to an outdoor seating area overlooks Eva's Rose Garden. Chef Lynn's breakfast menu changes daily, with offerings such as sunrise citrus salad, golden goat cheese soufflé on asparagus, seasonal vegetable frittata, and rosemary potatoes. The inn offers guests exclusive local wine tastings, herb walks, and cooking classes by Lynn.

PHONE: (831) 688–8005
WEB SITE: www.sandrockfarm.com
FEATURES: inn; 5 rooms; massages; cooking classes; limited smoking
NEARBY: state beaches and parks; town
INNKEEPERS/OWNERS: Lynn Sheehan and Kris Sheehan

ABELLA GARDEN INN

210 Oak Street
Arroyo Grande, CA 93420

🚫 $$–$$$$

Built in 1984, the inn is styled to
look like a Victorian–English country
home and tastefully blends the
charm of yesterday with the comfort
and convenience of today. Each of the seven guest accommodations has a private
bath; four offer queen-size beds, and three have kings and sitting areas. The suites
are furnished in a variety of Laura Ashley prints with garden themes: Forget-Me-Not,
Night Blooming Jasmine, Spring Bouquet,
and more. Guest accommodations feature
such special touches as country wreaths,
rockers, baskets, antiques, window seats,
balconies, and skylights; some feature
fireplaces or spas. The full gourmet break-
fast might include such specialties as frit-
tatas, Mexican quiche, or Dutch apple
pancakes. The comfortable parlor is the
site of fireside refreshments, including
tea, wine, and cordials all day.

PHONE: (805) 489–5926 or (800)
563–7762
WEB SITE: www.abellagardeninn.com
FEATURES: inn; 7 rooms; air-conditioning;
meeting area; in-room phones (on
request); in-room televisions and VCRs
(on request)
NEARBY: village; beach; wineries; golf
INNKEEPER/OWNER: Gina Glass

THE BLUE WHALE INN

6736 Moonstone Beach Drive
Cambria, CA 93428

♿ 🚫 $$$$

This newer gray Cape Cod–style inn on the bluffs overlooks the Pacific Ocean and
offers six individually designed minisuites. Each guest suite in this award-winning inn
features a king- or queen-size canopy bed draped in French and English country fab-
rics that coordinate with the designer wall coverings. The luxurious accommodations
with vaulted ceilings each contain an armoire with television, a writing desk, and a
telephone; further amenities include an oversize dressing room with small refrigera-
tor, ceramic-tiled bath, gas fireplace, picture window, and love seat. A complete

PHONE: (805) 927–4647 or (800) 753–9000

FAX: (805) 927–4647

WEB SITE: www.bluewhaleinn.com

FEATURES: inn; 6 rooms; in-room phones; computer hookups; in-room televisions; in-room workspace; in-room refrigerators; fax; copier

NEARBY: beach; ocean; village; Hearst Castle

INNKEEPERS: Jay and Karen Peavler

OWNERS: the Crowther and McGill families

country breakfast is served each morning in the dining room, which boasts six picture windows overlooking the ocean. The sitting room/library of the inn is the locale of afternoon wine and cheese or cookies and tea, and it also offers picture-window views of the Pacific. It also has a romantic woodstove, lots of reading material, and an entertainment center concealed in a French country armoire. Guests enjoy the inn's garden area, complete with benches and a waterfall pond.

THE J. PATRICK HOUSE

2990 Burton Drive
Cambria, CA 93428

⊗ $$–$$$$

■ Just above the village of Cambria is this log main house with annex building overlooking a forest of tall Monterey pines. Seven of the inn's eight guest accommodations are located in the carriage house annex, reached through a blooming garden and arbor stroll from the main house; one attractive and spacious minisuite is situated in the log house. This suite boasts a king-size bed, large wood-burning fireplace, and the privacy of the whole home after the evening's wine and hors d'oeuvres! The carriage house rooms host queen-size beds, private baths, antiques, hand-stitched quilts, feather-filled duvet covers, wood-burning fireplaces, and lots of country touches. The full breakfast, served in the garden room, includes fresh orange juice, a hearty bowl of fresh fruit with toppings (choose from nonfat yogurt, fresh raisins, and homemade granola), home-baked breads and muffins with spreads, and hot

PHONE: (805) 927–3812 or (800) 341–5258

FAX: (805) 927–6759

WEB SITE: www.jpatrickhouse.com

FEATURES: inn; 8 rooms; children welcome

NEARBY: beach; ocean; village; wineries; Hearst Castle

INNKEEPERS/OWNERS: Ann O'Connor and John Arnott

beverages. At 5:30 P.M. the innkeepers host a fireside feast of homemade vegetarian hors d'oeuvres and wines; later in the evening, a plate of their "killer" chocolate chip cookies and ice-cold milk are served as a before-bed snack. J. Patrick House is just minutes from both the ocean and the village, with its quaint shops and restaurants.

Be a "Guest" in William's Castle

Near Cambria is the town of San Simeon, home to one of the state's most impressive homes: the Hearst San Simeon State Historical Monument. More commonly referred to as Hearst Castle, this incredible "vacation home" of the Hearst family draws more than one million visitors annually. A wide range of tours is offered, but none as unique as the evening "Living History" tours.

The evening tour, which lasts more than two hours, takes in highlights of the day tours but is really a step back into the glamorous 1930s, a chance to experience firsthand the opulent lifestyles of the celebrated guests and occupants of the "Enchanted Hill." While guests tour the softly lit grounds and environs of the estate, docents in authentic 1930s costumes assume a variety of guest and staff roles. The evening is not over until you've viewed a "movie" in the castle's theater—a Hearst Metrotone newsreel recounting some of the important events of 1933.

Evening tours are available most Fridays and Saturdays from March through May and from September through December as well as certain holiday periods. For information and reservations (highly recommended), call (800) 444–4445.

OLALLIEBERRY INN

2476 Main Street
Cambria, CA 93428

♿ ⊘ $$–$$$$

This small historic inn at the far end of Cambria's East Village, within easy strolling distance of restaurants and shops, takes its name from the scrumptious dark-red berry that grows in the area. Framed by beautiful gardens and Santa Rosa Creek, the two-story, cream-colored Greek Revival–style home with delicate pinkish-red trim was

PHONE: (805) 927–3222 or (888) 927–3222
FAX: (805) 927–0202
WEB SITE: www.olallieberry.com
FEATURES: inn; 9 rooms, 1 cottage; fax; massage
NEARBY: village; beach; ocean; Hearst Castle; wineries
INNKEEPERS/OWNERS: Marilyn and Larry Draper

built in 1873 and is registered with the Historic House Association of America. The inn's nine romantic and tastefully appointed guest rooms feature charming wall coverings and fabrics and private baths (some outside of the room) with some oversize tubs; eight guest rooms have fireplaces. The Cambria room, a honeymoon favorite, offers a raised fireplace, a queen-size bed with moire and lace headboard, and a spacious bath with sunken tub and shower. The innkeeper's cottage offers a downstairs suite and two upstairs guest rooms, all with fireplaces and private baths. The inn serves a full gourmet breakfast as well as afternoon wine, sparkling water, and hot and cold hors d'oeuvres.

PICKFORD HOUSE B&B

2555 MacLeod Way
Cambria, CA 93428

⊗ $$–$$$

▨ This newer vintage inn with a turn-of-the-twentieth-century flavor offers interesting antiques, a spacious 1860s pub area, and views of the Santa Lucia Mountains. The guest rooms, all with televisions, king- or queen-size beds, and private baths featuring claw-foot tubs with showers, are named after silent-movie stars, with the decor to match. Three rooms offer fireplaces with antique mantels. The full breakfast is served downstairs in the parlor, decorated with antiques and floral carpeting, and features the innkeeper's homemade abelskivers (Danish pancakes); evening wine and fruit bread are offered in the parlor with its antique walnut bar.

PHONE: (805) 927–8619 or (888) 270–8470
WEB SITE: www.thepickfordhouse.com
FEATURES: inn; 8 rooms; in-room televisions; computer hookups
NEARBY: village; ocean; beach
INNKEEPER/OWNER: Patricia Moore

INN AT DEPOT HILL

250 Monterey Avenue
Capitola-by-the-Sea, CA 95010

♿ ⊘ $$$–$$$$

It is hard to believe that this multiaward-winning inn was at one time a railroad depot, yet the romance of the grand days of rail adventure is alive in every room. Situated on a bluff 2 blocks from the bay is this stately turn-of-the-twentieth-century railroad-station-turned-inn. Built in 1901, the building's original white columns, round ticket window, 12-foot door, and 16-foot ceilings still remain. The meticulous design and renovation of the structure has included the addition of 5,000 square feet and imaginative and tasteful decor that is reminiscent of a fine European hostelry. Each of the guest rooms and suites of the inn evokes a unique romantic "destination"; all feature fireplaces, private entrances and gardens, and amenities such as bathrobes and hair dryers. The spacious Paris suite is a romantic hideaway offering a fireplace between the bedroom and living room and double French doors that open to the garden; the suite's walls are upholstered in French toile, and the windows are covered with French lace. The Delft is a departure to "Holland," beautifully obtained through hand-worked lace and a private tulip garden; guests here sink into a huge feather bed and soak in a Jacuzzi for two. The Library is a three-level suite with separate reading and sitting area, loft, gas fireplace, and two-person marble shower. The inn's garden is a classic delight, with roses, azaleas, ferns, and trumpet vines that embrace a reflecting pond and brick patio. The full breakfast is served in the dining room, on the garden patio, or brought to the room. Depot Hill's dining room features a clever trompe l'oeil, a scene that creates the illusion of the dining car of a train, complete with vista of the countryside out the windows. The main hot dish varies daily, depending upon the chef's inspiration, and is accompanied by juice, a choice of pastries, and cereal. Guests relax each afternoon with wine and hors d'oeuvres, and a special dessert is offered each evening. The parlor of the inn is a popular gathering spot, with its antique piano and furnishings designed for comfort and beauty.

PHONE: (831) 462–3376 or (800) 572–2632
FAX: (831) 462–3697
WEB SITE: www.innatdepothill.com
FEATURES: inn; 12 rooms; in-room phones; computer hookups; in-room televisions and VCRs; fax; copier; in-room workspace; audiovisual equipment rentals; conference/meeting areas; off-site catering; off-street parking
NEARBY: village; beach; bay
INNKEEPER: Tom Cole
OWNER: Coastal Inns of Distinction

THE BRIARWOOD INN

San Carlos Street at Fourth and Fifth
P.O. Box 5245
Carmel, CA 93921

⊗ $–$$$$

■ Nestled in the heart of quaint Carmel-by-the-Sea, a few steps from shops and restaurants, is this B&B spread over six separate buildings on three downtown lots. The structures, all remodeled, are of different vintages but carry an English Tudor feel. Some of the guest rooms have verandas or patios; the casual and comfortable decor features designer fabrics. The spacious guest accommodations include fireplaces, tiled baths predominantly, and refrigerators. Briarwood serves an extended continental fare each morning that may be enjoyed in the lobby or in the room. Port and sherry are served each evening by the fireplace or on the outside patio.

PHONE: (831) 626–9056 or (800) 999–8788
FAX: (831) 626–8900
WEB SITE: www.briarwood-inn-carmel.com
FEATURES: inn; 12 rooms; in-room phones; computer hookups; in-room televisions and VCRs; on-site parking
NEARBY: village; ocean
INNKEEPER: George Costa
OWNER: Clyde Sturges

CARMEL COUNTRY INN

Third and Dolores Streets
P.O. Box 3756
Carmel, CA 93921

⊗ $$–$$$$

PHONE: (831) 625–3263 or (800) 215–6343
FAX: (831) 625–2945
WEB SITE: www.carmelcountryinn.com
FEATURES: inn; 12 suites; in-room phones; computer hookups; in-room televisions; pets welcome; fax; copier; on-site parking
NEARBY: village; ocean; Pebble Beach
INNKEEPER/OWNER: Amy Johnson

■ This quaint inn is situated just 3 blocks from the center of Carmel's charming village area, within walking distance to shops and restaurants, yet in a quiet residential area. The inn is surrounded by pretty blooms from the garden, and freshly cut buds often fill the rooms. The one- and two-bedroom suites of the inn offer spacious sitting rooms with fireplaces, wet bars with refrigerators, and tasteful traditional and contemporary furnishings. The country kitchen of the inn is the site of the morning continental breakfast. An assortment of muffins, sweet rolls, cereals, granola, juices, and seasonal fruit make up the extended fare.

CYPRESS INN

Seventh Avenue and Lincoln
P.O. Box Y
Carmel, CA 93921

♿ $$–$$$$

Originally opened in 1929, this land-
mark Spanish-Moorish-Mediterranean inn was carefully renovated in 1986 and claims
a celebrity owner, Doris Day. Located in the heart of Carmel Village, the inn features a
spacious living room with fireplace and an
intimate library overlooking a private garden/
courtyard. A variety of rooms, including
six luxury suites, are offered to guests,
most with oversize beds and all with pri-
vate baths, phones, and cable televisions;
some units boast fireplaces, sitting areas,
wet bars, verandas, and ocean views. A
continental breakfast is offered each
morning; the inn has a full-service cocktail
lounge and restaurant. Guests enjoy tea
and sherry each afternoon and a fruit bas-
ket in the room. Guests' pets are welcome
at Cypress Inn (there is an additional
charge) but are not allowed to be left in
the room unattended.

PHONE: (831) 624–3871 or (800) 443–7443

FAX: (831) 624–8216

WEB SITE: www.cypress-inn.com

FEATURES: inn/hotel; 45 rooms; limited smoking; pets allowed; in-room phones; computer hookups; voice mail; in-room televisions; fax; copier; cocktail lounge and restaurant; work-out facility; weddings

NEARBY: in village; beach; ocean; Monterey Bay Aquarium

INNKEEPER/GENERAL MANAGER: Hollace Thompson

OWNERS: Doris Day and Dennis LeVett

GREEN LANTERN INN

Casanova and Seventh Avenue
P.O. Box 1114
Carmel, CA 93921

⊘ $–$$$$

This collection of six quaint and inviting
cabins, divided into eighteen rooms in the
country style, is secreted in this coastal com-
munity. Only 4 blocks from the beach in one
direction and 3 blocks from the village in the

PHONE: (831) 624–4392 or (888) 414–4392

FAX: (831) 624–9591

WEB SITE: www.greenlanterninn .com

FEATURES: inn; 18 rooms; in-room phones; computer hookups; in-room televisions; in-room refriger-ators; fax; copier

NEARBY: town; beach; restaurants; art galleries; wine tasting; 17-mile drive; golf; Big Sur; Cannery Row

INNKEEPER/OWNER: Bill Fowler

other direction, this inn is nestled among verdant gardens surrounded by pine and oak trees. The rooms have queen- or king-size beds, private baths, refrigerators, televisions, and private entrances; four have fireplaces. The expanded continental breakfast is served either in the breakfast dining area overlooking the manicured garden or in the garden itself. Wine and cheese are offered to guests in the afternoon.

HAPPY LANDING INN

Monte Verde and Fifth Streets
P.O. Box 2619
Carmel, CA 93921

♿ ⊗ $–$$$

This 1925-built, Comstock-designed inn features guest rooms furnished with antiques, some fireplaces, and cathedral ceilings; accommodations surround an award-winning central garden with pond and gazebo. The two suites feature a living room with fireplace and wet bar, and bedroom with king-size bed. Centrally located, the inn is just 4 blocks from the beach and less than 2 blocks from the center of town. The continental-plus breakfast is served in the room each morning and features homemade breads and muffins, quiche, fresh fruit, and juice. A spacious lounge with cathedral ceilings and a stone fireplace offers daytime refreshments and relaxation.

PHONE: (831) 624–7917
FAX: (831) 624–4844
WEB SITE: www.virtualcities.com/ons/ca/c/cac8051.htm
FEATURES: inn; 7 rooms; in-room televisions
NEARBY: beaches; village
INNKEEPER: Robert Ballard
OWNER: Richard Stewart

L'AUBERGE CARMEL

Monte Verde between Ocean and Seventh Avenues
Carmel, CA 93921

⊗ $$$–$$$$

L'Auberge Carmel is a new landmark for dining, accommodations, and classic architecture in the heart of Carmel. Built in 1929, the European-style inn is located just 4 blocks from the beach. Recent renovations of the inn, formerly the Sundial

PHONE: (831) 624–8578
FAX: (831) 626–1018
WEB SITE: www.laubergecarmel.com
FEATURES: inn/hotel; 20 rooms; in-room phones with dataports; televisions; CD players; minibars; fax; copier; restaurant; room service
NEARBY: village; beach
INNKEEPERS/OWNERS: David and Kathleen Fink

Lodge, have transformed the guest rooms, entrance, and landscaping into a luxuriously romantic venue. Warm jewel tones accent the quaint charm of the architecture, and the decor of the guest rooms is rich and pleasing, featuring fine fabrics, linens, and down bedding. The owners have strived to present old-world ambience, such as plaster-covered walls, French windows, and antique doorknobs. Each guest room also has a large private bath, some with soaking tubs, and all with heated floors. Accommodations include a sumptuous continental breakfast. Lunch and dinner are also available at the Restaurant at L'Auberge, which many consider to be the highlight of the inn. Executive chef Walter Manzke prepares a special menu reflecting contemporary California cuisine with European influences daily, using ingredients fresh from the garden and farm.

PINE INN

Ocean Avenue and Monte Verde
P.O. Box 250
Carmel, CA 93921

♿ ⊗ $$–$$$$

This building, Carmel's first hotel, was constructed in 1889 and moved to its present location four years later. It was host to artists and writers who populated the scenic town in its early years. Situated in the heart of Carmel's village, the hotel B&B continues to be a charming overnight

PHONE: (831) 624–3851 or (800) 228–3851
FAX: (831) 624–3030
WEB SITE: www.pine-inn.com
FEATURES: inn/hotel; 49 rooms; in-room phones; in-room televisions; fax; copier; in-room workspace; catering; conference areas; weddings; restaurant
NEARBY: village; ocean/beaches
INNKEEPER: John Wilson
OWNER: Richard Gunner

retreat for honeymooners, travelers, and generations of visitors. The lobby of the inn is comfortable yet elegant, with rich wood paneling, antiques, and padded wall panels. Guests also relax in the inn's intimate library with a good book and brandy. Each of the inn's guest rooms and suites is unique and furnished with European or Far Eastern touches. Guests will find some ocean views, feather beds, armoires, and antiques. Rooms enjoy an interior, flowered courtyard. Award-winning Il Fornaio is the inn's own Italian restaurant with bar and bakery. It serves the complimentary breakfast (weekdays only) as well as Italian cuisine for lunch and dinner. The restaurant is available for parties and business meetings. Four blocks down from Pine Inn is one of the town's scenic, sandy beaches.

SAN ANTONIO HOUSE

San Antonio between Ocean and Seventh Avenues
P.O. Box 6226
Carmel, CA 93921

⊗ $$$–$$$$

■ Each of the guest rooms at the inn has its own entrance, telephone, refrigerator, television, fireplace, and private bath, plus lots of antiques and paintings. The two-story turn-of-the-twentieth-century house is surrounded by trees, gardens, lawns, and stone terraces and is close to shops, golfing, and the beach. Breakfast is served in the room, but guests may also dine in the courtyard. The continental fare includes fresh fruit, juices, cereal, and freshly baked pastries.

PHONE: (831) 624–6926 or (800) 313–7770
FAX: (831) 624–4935
WEB SITE: www.carmelgarden courtinn.com
FEATURES: inn; 5 rooms; in-room phones; in-room televisions; in-room workspace; refrigerators; fax; computer hookups
NEARBY: village; beach
INNKEEPERS/OWNERS: Ross and Lynette Farley

SANDPIPER INN

2408 Bay View Avenue
Carmel, CA 93923

⊗ $$–$$$$

■ Just 100 yards from Carmel's white, sandy beaches is the Sandpiper Inn, which offers ocean

PHONE: (831) 624–6433 or (800) 590–6433
FAX: (831) 624–5964
WEB SITE: www.sandpiper-inn.com
FEATURES: inn/cottage; 17 rooms; fax; weddings
NEARBY: beach; village
INNKEEPER: Bill Lee
OWNERS: Andrew and Beth Lewis

views across the bay to Pebble Beach. The guest rooms, which also include three cottage accommodations, all with private baths, are individually decorated with country antiques, fresh flowers, and paintings. Guests may choose from rooms with fireplaces or ocean or garden views. Continental buffet breakfast and afternoon sherry are served in the fireplace lounge.

SEA VIEW INN

Camino Real between Eleventh and Twelfth Streets
P.O. Box 4138
Carmel, CA 93921

⊗ $–$$

This 1906 three-story guesthouse is furnished with both antiques and contemporary pieces and has been redecorated throughout. Located just 3 blocks from the ocean and 5 blocks from town, it is situated centrally. Guest rooms, six with private baths, feature bay-window seats and queen- or king-size beds; one room features an intricate canopy bed with coordinated fabrics and wall covering. The homemade continental buffet breakfast, consisting of fruit, juice, cereals, yogurt, and muffins or coffee cake, is served fireside in the parlor, the site of afternoon coffee and tea and evening sherry, wine,

PHONE: (831) 624–8778
FAX: (831) 625–5901
WEB SITE: www.seaviewinncarmel.com
FEATURES: inn; 8 rooms; fax; meeting area (if whole inn is reserved)
NEARBY: beaches; village
INNKEEPER: Margo Thomas
OWNERS: Marshall and Diane Hydorn

and light hors d'oeuvres as well. Even guests wanting to get away from it all can connect with civilization at the inn via a telephone located in the hall; there is no television in the inn. The lounge provides a perfect retreat for reading the morning newspaper or looking at the view.

THE STONEHOUSE INN

Eighth Avenue below Monte Verde
P.O. Box 2517
Carmel, CA 93921

♿ ⊗ $$–$$$

PHONE: (831) 624–4569 or (800) 748–6618
FAX: (831) 624–8209
WEB SITE: www.carmelstone house.com
FEATURES: inn; 7 rooms
NEARBY: beaches; village
INNKEEPER: Terri Navaille
OWNER: Addie Shapiro

This turn-of-the-twentieth-century home is most notable for its stone exterior, hand shaped by Indians around 1906, and is listed on the National Register of Historic Places. The guest rooms, named after famous artists/guests from earlier days, feature airy colors, antiques, cozy quilts, and fresh flowers; four rooms share two baths. The George

Sterling room features a king-size bed with a billowing canopy, an ocean view, a reading area, and a walk-in closet. The full Southern-style breakfast is offered in the dining room or garden or by the large stone fireplace. Cheese and wine are offered each afternoon. Located in a quiet residential area, the inn is only 2 blocks from town, and the beach is just 3 blocks away.

SUNSET HOUSE BED AND BREAKFAST

Camino Real between Ocean and Seventh Avenues
P.O. Box 1925
Carmel, CA 93921

⊗ $$–$$$

■ This bed-and-breakfast, just a two-minute stroll from the village or to the beach, began in 1960 but was totally upgraded and renovated in 1992 by its present owners. The Sunset House is a quaint stucco structure highlighted by used-brick fireplaces and a wooden shake roof; all rooms have fireplaces, private baths, and sitting areas. The central cobblestone courtyard with flower-filled window boxes and fountain is an inviting spot; off of this area is the Porpoise Suite with romantic canopy bed, love seat, wood-burning fireplace, and bathroom with Jacuzzi and shower. The Sea Otter Suite features lovely antiques, including the "Hans Christian Andersen" king-size bed from the Grand Hotel in Denmark. A unique stay at the inn would be in the Sea Lion Suite, nestled in the treetops and granting incredible views of the Pacific Ocean and, of course, the sunset. Each of the secluded accommodations also hosts a private balcony, a wood-burning fireplace, and a kitchenette with refrigerator, wet bar, and microwave. A special breakfast featuring juice, fresh fruit, coffee cakes or freshly baked breads, and granola is delivered to the room. The hospitable inn is "dog friendly" and located in a quiet residential neighborhood.

PHONE: (831) 624–4884 or (877) 966–9100

FAX: (831) 899–9500

WEB SITE: www.sunset-carmel.com

FEATURES: inn; 4 rooms; in-room phones; in-room televisions; pets allowed; children welcome; fax; computer hookups; in-room workspace; catering for small receptions; on-site parking

NEARBY: Carmel village shops, restaurants, and art galleries; Carmel Beach; golf; wineries

INNKEEPERS: Mike and Lynn Shields, Teri Hardy

OWNERS: Ray and Diane Roedel

TALLY HO INN

Monte Verde at Sixth Street
P.O. Box 3726
Carmel, CA 93921

 $$–$$$$

Only ½ block from Carmel's village is this secluded inn reminiscent of an English country retreat. Flower-filled decks, patios, and views create a relaxing setting. The inn, a traditional Comstock adobe-design building, was the former residence of Jimmy Hatlo, the nationally syndicated cartoonist of "Little Iodine" and "They'll Do It Every Time." The dining room of the inn is named for Mr. Hatlo and overlooks beautiful Carmel Bay. Breakfast may be enjoyed here, on the peaceful deck by the outdoor fireplace, or on your own private deck. The expanded continental buffet includes oatmeal, homemade granola, muffins, croissants, fruit, and juice. Many of the guest rooms and suites have a patio or sundeck that takes in sweeping views of the bay and Point Lobos; all the unique guest accommodations, with traditional furnishings, are sunny and spacious. Rooms and suites feature many fireplaces and Jacuzzis; the marble bathrooms with fluffy towels are luxurious. Guests may walk to the beach, just 4 blocks away.

PHONE: (831) 624–2232 or (800) 652–2632
FAX: (831) 624–2661
WEB SITE: www.tallyho-inn.com
FEATURES: inn; 14 rooms; in-room phones; computer hookups; in-room televisions; fax; copier; on-site parking
NEARBY: village; ocean/beaches
INNKEEPER: John Wilson
OWNER: Richard Gunner

VAGABOND'S HOUSE INN

Fourth and Dolores Streets
P.O. Box 2747
Carmel, CA 93921

 $$–$$$$

This English Tudor country inn, a cluster of several cottages, features wood-burning fireplaces and refrigera-

tors or kitchens in each antiques-decorated guest room. All rooms, some with "tree-top" views, look out onto the flagstone courtyard filled with oaks, ferns, flowers, and

PHONE: (831) 624–7738 or (800) 262–1262

FAX: (831) 626–1243

WEB SITE: www.vagabondshouseinn.com

FEATURES: inn; 11 rooms, cottages; in-room phones; in-room televisions; computer hookups; pets allowed; refrigerators or kitchens; fax; copier; weddings

NEARBY: village; beach

INNKEEPER: Dawn Dull

OWNER: Dennis LeVett

assorted hanging plants. Each room has a queen- or king-size bed; its own coffeepot, complete with freshly ground coffee; and a decanter of sherry. A continental breakfast is served each morning in the room. Afternoon wine and cheese are served in the parlor; either may be enjoyed in the garden.

THE CARMEL VALLEY LODGE

Carmel Valley and Ford Roads
P.O. Box 93
Carmel Valley, CA 93924

♿ $$$–$$$$

■ This country inn with conference center is nestled in sunny Carmel Valley. Accommodations include garden/patio rooms, fireplace suites with wet bars and decks, and one- and two-bedroom cottages with fireplaces and kitchens. All guest rooms, with private baths, are individually decorated in a blend of Shaker reproductions and comfortable country pieces and have beamed ceilings and rustic-looking wood trim. Fresh coffee and tea, cable television, and flowers fresh from the garden are special touches for the guests' enjoyment. Guests may enjoy the pool, a hot spa and sauna, an exercise room, and a game area. Pets are welcome; on-site pet sitting is available. The inn is a short walk from village shops and restaurants. A complimentary breakfast is served in the conference-center dining room or in the room. Groups of up to thirty may be accommodated in the conference facilities.

PHONE: (831) 659–2261 or (800) 641–4646

FAX: (831) 659–4558

WEB SITE: www.valleylodge.com

FEATURES: inn/cottages; 31 rooms, 12 cottages; limited smoking; air-conditioning; pets allowed (fee); in-room phones; computer hookups; in-room televisions and VCRs; swimming pool; spa; exercise room; all business/conference services

NEARBY: shops; restaurants; horseback riding; hiking; golf

INNKEEPER/OWNER: Peter Coakley

CAYUCOS SUNSET INN BED & BREAKFAST

95 South Ocean Avenue
Cayucos, CA 93430

♿ Ⓢ $$–$$$$

▪ A perfect place for a romantic getaway, the inn's nine guest rooms include five luxurious suites; each is equipped with European linens, custom-made furniture, private patio or balcony (many with sunset views), in-room refrigerator and minibar, two-person Jacuzzi, television with DVD player and DVD library, antique armoire, robes, private entrance, and fireplace. The second-floor suites boast separate bedrooms and setting-sun views over the Pacific. The stay includes a full gourmet breakfast and evening hors d'oeuvres, wine, and sparkling water. Swedish, shiatsu, and sports massage, as well as salt glow treatments, are offered at the inn. Ask about the inn's "romance package" and "guest chef nights" for an extra-special stay.

PHONE: (805) 995–2500 or (877) 805–1076

FAX: (805) 995–2999

WEB SITE: www.cayucossunsetinn.com

FEATURES: inn; 9 rooms; refrigerators; private entrances; massage and spa treatments

NEARBY: beach; pier; antiques stores; coffee shops; tennis courts; Morro Bay; San Simeon

INNKEEPERS/OWNERS: John and Lisa Mankins

THE INN AT FELTON CREST

780 El Solyo Heights Drive
Felton, CA 95018

♿ Ⓢ $$$–$$$$

▪ This romantic hideaway is situated on an acre in the Santa Cruz Mountains overlooking San Lorenzo Valley. Guests enjoy a living room with large fireplace and French doors leading to the three-story home's decks, which grant impressive forest views. Each guest accommodation also grants inspiring redwood views. A main-floor suite has a sitting room, and the Treetop Penthouse offers a fireplace, big-screen television, and private deck. An extended breakfast is served in the dining room or may be requested in bed. Other amenities include in-room iced champagne, bowls of fresh fruit, and cold drinks and ice. Restaurants are close by, as are wineries and some antiques stores. Felton Crest is about a twenty-minute drive from Santa Cruz and its many attractions.

PHONE/FAX: (831) 335–4011 or (800) 474–4011

WEB SITE: www.feltoncrest.com

FEATURES: inn; 4 rooms; in-room televisions and VCRs

NEARBY: Santa Cruz Mountains; Santa Cruz; wineries; restaurants; shops

INNKEEPER/OWNER: Hanna Peters

THE JABBERWOCK

598 Laine Street
Monterey, CA 93940

⊗ $$–$$$$

■ Goose-down pillows, romantic Victorian beds, eyelet-lace linens, and fresh flowers await guests who visit this converted convent that is only 4 blocks from Cannery Row and the Monterey Bay Aquarium and near the scenic 17-mile drive. Guests enjoy the living-room sunporch that overlooks fern falls or the estate gardens, the site of evening hors d'oeuvres and aperitifs. The breakfasts, which include "razzleberry flabjous," are served fireside in the elegant dining room or in the room; the innkeepers "tuck" guests into bed with cookies and milk. The guest rooms feature a second-floor suite with an oversize king-size bed, a fireplace, private bath, dressing room, and spectacular views of the bay. The third floor of the inn, the Garrett floor, has two guest rooms that share a sitting room and bath.

PHONE: (831) 372–4777 or (888) 428–7253
FAX: (831) 655–2946
WEB SITE: www.jabberwockinn.com
FEATURES: inn; 7 rooms; in-room massage; fax; copier
NEARBY: Cannery Row; Monterey Bay Aquarium
INNKEEPERS/OWNERS: Joan and John Kiliany

OLD MONTEREY INN

500 Martin Street
Monterey, CA 93940

⊗ $$$$

■ Surrounded by an acre of landscaped grounds with gardens and old oak trees, this 1920s English country home is within walking distance of the historic sites of Monterey. The living room tempts guests with a warming fireplace and a sampling of wines and cheeses. Rooms feature wicker and English antiques; skylights; fireplaces; private baths, many with whirlpools; and garden views. The Ashford suite offers a

PHONE: (831) 375–8284 or (800) 350–2344

FAX: (831) 375–6730

WEB SITE: www.oldmontereyinn.com

FEATURES: inn/cottage; 10 rooms, 1 cottage; in-room phones (some); computer hookps; in-room televisions and VCRs (on request)

NEARBY: Cannery Row; Monterey Bay Aquarium; golf

INNKEEPER: Patti Kreider

OWNERS: Ann and Gene Swett

bedroom with king-size bed, a private bath, a dressing room, and a wisteria-draped sitting room with wood-burning fireplace, bay window, and antique pine furnishings. A separate cottage has stained glass and a bay-window seat. The full breakfast is served in the dining room or in the room at this award-winning inn. Wine and hors d'oeuvres are served in the afternoon.

THE SPINDRIFT INN

652 Cannery Row
Monterey, CA 93940

♿ $$$$

▧ The tastefully appointed four-story inn has a New Orleans look and boasts colorful flower boxes. Its superb location is just 1½ blocks from the aquarium, directly on the beach in Cannery Row. Guest rooms are distinctly decorated and furnished with canopies, imported fabrics, feather beds, Oriental carpets, window seats, fireplaces, and comforters; some rooms have Swedish dry saunas. Guest rooms offer such extras as remote-control televisions in armoires, nightly turndown service, refrigerators, bathrobes, and Swiss chocolates, and all rooms have private marble-and-brass baths with a second telephone and hair dryers. The continental breakfast arrives with the morning newspaper on a silver tray and is enjoyed in the room. Afternoon tea, wine, and cheese are offered, and guests may relax on the roof garden with ocean vistas. Lunch and dinner room service is available at the hotel.

PHONE: (831) 646–8900 or (800) 841–1879

FAX: (831) 646–5342

WEB SITE: www.spindriftinn.com

FEATURES: inn/hotel; 42 rooms; in-room phones; in-room televisions and VCRs; fax; copier; in-room workspace (some); in-room refrigerators; CD players; video rentals; lunches, dinners available

NEARBY: on Cannery Row; Monterey Bay Aquarium

MANAGER: Randy Vernard

OWNER: Coastal Hotel Properties

THE KALEIDOSCOPE INN

130 East Dana Street
P.O. Box 1297
Nipomo, CA 93444

⊗ $$

■ This gingerbread-trimmed Victorian was built by a retired rancher in 1887 and then sold to the historic Dana family, who were pioneers in this region. Multicolored stained glass frames the windows, which inspired the inn's descriptive name, "Kaleidoscope." The grounds, nearly an acre, contain beautiful gardens and a romantic gazebo that is the setting for numerous weddings. The inn's antique furnishings and accessories all lend a late-1800s ambience. Guests may enjoy the downstairs parlor or the library with fireplace and a decanter of sherry. The individually decorated guest rooms are upstairs; the spacious baths, fully equipped with two sinks, Jacuzzi, and shower, are just down the hall (bathrobes are provided in each room). Guests may choose from king or queen accommodations; the Lover's Nest features four large picture windows draped with romantic lace. A full gourmet breakfast, served in the antiques-filled dining room, varies daily but always includes juice, fresh fruit, muffins, and breakfast cakes. Guests may opt to eat in the garden or in their rooms.

PHONE: (805) 929–5444 or (866) 504–5444
FAX: (805) 929–5440
WEB SITE: www.kaleidoscopeinn.com
FEATURES: inn/cottage; 4 rooms, 1 cottage; weddings
NEARBY: ocean; wineries; Lopez Lake; golf
INNKEEPERS/OWNERS: Kevin Beauchamp and Carolayne Holley

CENTRELLA INN

612 Central Avenue
P.O. Box 51157
Pacific Grove, CA 93950

♿ ⊗ $$–$$$$

■ Located at the tip of the Monterey Peninsula, this century-old Victorian hotel, founded in 1875 as a Methodist resort, invites guests to enjoy its brick walk-

PHONE: (831) 372–3372 or (800) 233–3372

FAX: (831) 372–2036

WEB SITE: www.centrellainn.com

FEATURES: inn/hotel/cottages; 26 rooms; in-room phones; in-room televisions (some); in-room VCRs (some); fax; copier; in-room workspace; computer hookups; refrigerators (some); small conferences

NEARBY: town; ocean; Cannery Row; Monterey Bay Aquarium

INNKEEPER/ OWNER: Marion Taylor

THE GOSBY HOUSE

643 Lighthouse Avenue
Pacific Grove, CA 93950

♿ ⧂ $$–$$$

▪ In the heart of historic Pacific Grove, this tastefully restored Queen Anne mansion with rounded corner tower and bay windows has two parlors, one offering late-

PHONE: (831) 375–1287 or (800) 527–8828

FAX: (831) 655–9621

WEB SITE: www.gosbyhouseinn.com

FEATURES: inn; 22 rooms; in-room phones; in-room televisions (some); computer hookups; fax; copier; small meetings

NEARBY: town; ocean; Cannery Row

INNKEEPER: Kalena Mittleman

OWNER: Four Sisters Inns

ways and surrounding gardens. All accommodations are appointed with hand-selected antiques and private baths with claw-foot tubs or showers. All suites feature skylights, wet bars, and televisions, while cottages contain fireplaces, televisions, refrigerators, and wet bars. Both the complimentary continental breakfast and afternoon tea are served buffet style before a cheery fire.

afternoon tea by the fire and one that hosts the generous buffet breakfast, which may be taken to the garden or to the room on a tray. The guest rooms feature polished natural woods, comforters, delicate wall covering prints, ruffled curtains, armoires, fireplaces, and fresh fruit, and all but two accommodations have private baths with antique claw-foot tubs or modern tubs. Two suites offer fireplaces, balconies, and luxury bathrooms with Jacuzzis for two. Sherry, wine, and tea are offered each evening.

GRAND VIEW INN

557 Ocean View Boulevard
Pacific Grove, CA 93950

♿ ⊗ $$–$$$$

■ This imposing Edwardian-style inn,
built in 1910 by noted marine biologist Dr.
Julia Pratt, sits on a Monterey Bay bluff
overlooking Lover's Point beach. All ten
guest rooms, which offer queen-size beds, private baths, and unobstructed views of
the bay, are filled with antiques or reproductions to provide a re-creation of an elegant and graceful era. The full breakfast and afternoon tea are served in the inviting
dining room overlooking the sea. Guests enjoy strolling through the inn's gardens or
along the seashore.

PHONE: (831) 372–4341
WEB SITE: www.pginns.com
FEATURES: inn; 10 rooms; computer hookups
NEARBY: town; restaurants; beach; 17-mile drive; Cannery Row; Monterey Bay; Fisherman's Wharf
INNKEEPERS/OWNERS: the Flatley family

GREEN GABLES INN

104 Fifth Street
Pacific Grove, CA 93950

⊗ $$–$$$$

■ This half-timbered, step-gabled,
Queen Anne–Victorian mansion, built
in 1888 on the edge of the Pacific
Grove shoreline, offers a panoramic

PHONE: (831) 375–2095 or (800) 722–1774
FAX: (831) 375–5437
WEB SITE: www.greengablesinnpg.com
FEATURES: inn; 11 units; in-room phones; in-room televisions; fax; copier; bicycles
NEARBY: town; ocean; Cannery Row; Monterey Bay Aquarium
INNKEEPER: Lucia Root
OWNER: Four Sisters Inns

view of Monterey Bay. The living room,
with antiques and a stained-glass-adorned
fireplace, is the locale of afternoon tea.
Each morning a generous breakfast is
served in the dining room or in the cozy
living-room alcoves. The guest accommodations include upstairs rooms and guest
rooms in the carriage house across the
courtyard. Rooms feature soft colors,
views, flowers, fruit, cozy quilts, and
antiques. Suites at the inn have sitting
rooms or areas with fireplaces, bedrooms,
and private baths.

THE MARTINE INN

255 Oceanview Boulevard
Pacific Grove, CA 93950

♿ ⊘ $$$–$$$$

▪ Just 4 blocks from the Monterey Bay Aquarium and Cannery Row sits this gracious mansion, high on the cliffs overlooking picturesque Pacific Grove. Built in 1899, it was soon the home of Laura and James Parke of Parke Davis Pharmaceuticals; the Victorian home with cupolas and dormers became a Mediterranean-style house after extensive remodeling and expansion by the family through the years. The present owner renovated the grand mansion once again in the early 1970s to carefully bring back the home's Victorian beauty, and, at present, it retains much of its authentic opulence, such as original fixtures and claw-foot tubs, as well as modern amenities such as individual-room-control heat. Each of the guest accommodations at the inn has a private bath, authentic museum-quality antiques, a fresh rose, and a silver Victorian bridal basket filled with fruit. Some of the rooms offer spectacular ocean views and/or wood-burning fireplaces. For a luxurious stay reserve the Parke room, offering three walls of view windows that take in crashing waves, a corner fireplace, a four-poster bed with canopy and side curtains, and a sitting area. Guests at the Martine Inn awake to a newspaper outside the door and a full gourmet breakfast served with old Sheffield silver, Victorian-style china, crystal, and lace. Breakfast recipes from the old 1880s White House cookbooks are prepared. Hot and cold hors d'oeuvres and a vegetable tray with dip are served in the parlor, furnished with a baby grand piano, at twilight; beverages are Monterey County white and red wines as well as sparkling cider. The game room at the inn includes a 1917 nickelodeon, an 1890 white oak pool table, and stained-glass windows. A spa room contains a six-person hot tub for guests' relaxation. Be sure to check out the inn's vintage auto display!

PHONE: (831) 373–3388 or (800) 852–5588

FAX: (831) 373–3896

WEB SITE: www.martineinn.com

FEATURES: inn; 20 rooms; in-room phones; fax; copier; computer hookups; in-room workspace; audiovisual equipment; catering; meeting areas; off-street parking; spa; lunch baskets upon request; weddings; special dinners

NEARBY: Monterey Bay Aquarium; Cannery Row

GENERAL MANAGER: Lori Anderson

OWNER: Don Martine

OLD ST. ANGELA INN

321 Central Avenue
Pacific Grove, CA 93950

♿ ⊗ $$–$$$$

▦ Just ½ block from the ocean and within walking distance of Cannery Row is this 1910-built country home. Converted to a rectory and then to a convent in 1920, the Cape Cod–style inn has returned to its origins with country pine furnishings, soft quilts, fresh flowers, and fine linens. Guests relax with afternoon wine, tea, or sherry by the living-room fireplace and, outside, enjoy the peaceful garden patio. Some rooms at the inn offer such amenities as private sitting areas, canopy beds, and handmade country pine furniture; accommodations include both private and shared baths. The generous full breakfast buffet is served in the remodeled glass-and-redwood solarium.

PHONE: (831) 372–3246 or (800) 748–6306

FAX: (831) 372–8560

WEB SITE: www.sueandlewinns.com or www.oldstangelainn.com

FEATURES: inn; 9 rooms; fax; in-room phones; computer hookups; spa

NEARBY: ocean; Cannery Row; Monterey Bay Aquarium

INNKEEPER: Honey Spence

OWNERS: Lewis Shaefer and Susan Kuslis

PACIFIC GROVE INN

581 Pine Avenue
Pacific Grove, CA 93950

♿ ⊗ $–$$$

▦ This four-story 1904 Queen Anne–Victorian mansion is on the National Register of Historic Places. Situated just 2 blocks from Main Street and 5 blocks from the beach, the inn overlooks picturesque Monterey Bay. Popular city hiking and biking trails nearby lead to Cannery Row. Rose gardens bloom around the inn, which has been completely renovated yet hosts its original woodwork and fretwork. Cherrywood antique furnishings and some Belgian wool paisley carpets decorate throughout. The elegant guest rooms and suites, in both the main house and rear Victorian house annex, boast private baths, brass beds, roman blinds, and George Washington Bates bedspreads, as well as enclosed remote-control televisions and VCRs, heated towel

PHONE: (831) 375–2825 or (800) 732–2825
FAX: (831) 375–0752
WEB SITE: www.pacificgrove-inn.com
FEATURES: inn; 17 rooms; in-room phones; in-room televisions and VCRs; minibars
NEARBY: Monterey Bay; Cannery Row; Monterey Bay Aquarium
INNKEEPER: Donna Braden
OWNER: Herb Johnson

racks, and gas-jet fireplaces. Some rooms offer views of the bay. The complimentary continental breakfast consists of juice, fresh fruit, muffins, assorted breads, homemade granola, cereal, and yogurt. The inn offers all-day coffee and tea service and afternoon wine and hors d'oeuvres.

SEVEN GABLES INN

555 Ocean View Boulevard
Pacific Grove, CA 93950

🚫 $$$–$$$$

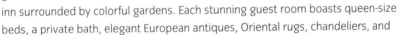

🖼 Spectacular ocean views are enjoyed from each of the sunny and cheerful guest rooms at this 1886-built Victorian inn surrounded by colorful gardens. Each stunning guest room boasts queen-size beds, a private bath, elegant European antiques, Oriental rugs, chandeliers, and antique stained-glass windows. A generous full breakfast is served in the stately dining room with chandelier; high tea is offered each day at 4:00 P.M., featuring homemade treats, sandwiches, and imported cakes. The award-winning inn is conveniently located near all the Monterey Peninsula attractions.

PHONE: (831) 372–4341
WEB SITE: www.pginns.com
FEATURES: inn; 14 rooms, 2 cottages
NEARBY: ocean; town; Cannery Row
INNKEEPERS/OWNERS: the Flatley family

VILLA TOSCANA BED & BREAKFAST

4230 Buena Vista
Paso Robles, CA 93447

♿ 🚫 $$$$

🖼 This extraordinary villa bathed in yellows, reminiscent of Tuscany, is nestled on the vineyards of the Martin & Weyrich Vineyards in the heart of the lush Paso Robles

PHONE: (805) 238–5600
FAX: (805) 238–5605
WEB SITE: www.myvillatoscana.com
FEATURES: inn/hotel; 8 rooms; dinners
available; complimentary minibar;
weddings and special occasions
NEARBY: wineries; town; hot springs
spa
INNKEEPER: Patricia Korberl
OWNER: Martin & Weyrich

wine country. A perfect getaway from stress and for a special occasion, the villa offers eight opulent suites and one separate winemaker's residence with two bedrooms, private courtyard, and absolute privacy. The villa is set within a "village" onto itself, with an intimate bistro open to guests only. The bistro is the site of a very special morning feast and afternoon local wines and appetizers by fireside or on the deck overlooking the vineyards and rolling hills. The oversize suites include a great room with bed area, sitting area with fireplace, and a spacious bathroom with Jacuzzi. Guests receive a complimentary bottle of wine on arrival.

BRIDGE CREEK INN

5300 Righetti Road
San Luis Obispo, CA 93401

⊗ $$–$$$

▥ This inviting Craftsman-style, multilevel inn, built in 1975, commands a hilltop on ten acres in Edna Valley. A seasonal creek runs through the rural property, which features foot and bridle paths to explore.

Guests may choose to relax on the inn's redwood deck or in the outdoor spa. The Golden Gate room includes a king-size bed, whirlpool, and sauna; the Arroyo Seco room features a queen-size bed and claw-foot tub with reading rack. Both rooms have private decks. The bountiful breakfast may include goat cheese and rosemary omelettes, or orange-stuffed French toast and lots of fresh fruit. Evening refreshments include local wines and gourmet appetizers.

PHONE: (805) 544–3003
FAX: (805) 544–2002
WEB SITE: www.bridgecreekinn.com
FEATURES: inn; 2 rooms; ceiling fans;
in-room phones; computer hookups;
in-room televisions and DVDs; spa
NEARBY: town; wineries; California
Polytechnic State University; Mission
Plaza
INNKEEPERS/OWNERS: Eugene and
Sally Kruger

GARDEN STREET INN

1212 Garden Street
San Luis Obispo, CA 93401

♿ ⊘ $$–$$$

▦ This 1887 Queen Anne–Italianate residence boasts an interesting history: It evolved from a single-story home to a vintage two-story boardinghouse; the house was lovingly renovated in 1989. The inn is conveniently located on a quiet street, just a stroll from downtown shops, restaurants, and Mission Plaza. The nine guest rooms and four suites of the inn, some with fireplaces, are located both upstairs and down, and all feature unique, tasteful decor with pleasing fabrics and wall coverings, private baths with oversize tub/showers, and reproduction radios with tape decks and cassette libraries to match the theme of the room. Room themes, reflecting the histories of the innkeepers and of the area, range from the Dollie McKeen (named after a former owner), with a restored marble fireplace, original stained-glass windows, and a Jacuzzi tub/shower, to the Lovers suite, with its spacious sitting room and romantic half-canopy bed. The McCaffrey Morning Room, with rich woodwork and local art, is the locale of evening wine and cheese, as well as the family-style breakfast. Accompanied by piped-in music, breakfast includes fresh juice and fruit, an egg entree, and homemade breads. Guests enjoy a library with fireplace, a spacious outside upper deck, and a private, cleverly designed telephone booth.

PHONE: (805) 545–9802 or (800) 488–2045
FAX: (805) 545–9403
WEB SITE: www.gardenstreetinn.com
FEATURES: inn; 9 rooms, 4 suites; air-conditioning; in-room phones; in-room workspace; fax; copier; computer hookups; meeting area
NEARBY: in town; Mission Plaza
INNKEEPER/OWNER: Sheila Gow

Enjoy an "Ancient" Soak

Just south of San Luis Obispo, venture toward the Pacific Ocean on San Luis Bay Drive and follow it to the area's original 1897 hot mineral springs resort.

Sycamore Mineral Springs Resort, at 1215 Avila Drive, is nestled among oaks and sycamore trees off the winding road and offers a soothing end to a day in the sun. The totally renovated resort boasts twenty redwood tubs situated privately along paths under the trees and filled with natural soothing mineral water. Tub sizes vary from tubs for one or two to Oasis, which can hold up to forty people.

The recreational offerings of Sycamore include sand volleyball courts, a heated swimming pool, and a body-care center specializing in massages and herbal facials. Guests also enjoy a gourmet restaurant, the Gardens of Avila. For information and reservations call the springs at (805) 595–7302 or (800) 234–5831, e-mail info@smsr.com, or log on to www.sycamoresprings.com.

HERITAGE INN

978 Olive Street
San Luis Obispo, CA 93405

♿ 🚭 $–$$

 Yielding creekside and mountain views a short distance from downtown is this turn-of-the-twentieth-century inn with its old-fashioned porch draped in wisteria and adjacent "cobblestone" parking. The common areas of the comfortable and warm B&B are decorated in pastel peaches and burgundy; the inn offers a cozy parlor with fireplace and window seat, where wine and cheese is served in the evening and plates of fresh cookies are offered during the day. The redecorated inn features guest rooms with warm antiques, cheerful color themes, and interesting family mementos; each guest room hosts either a cozy window seat, fireplace, or walk-out terrace with views. Both shared- and private-bath accommodations are available; all shared-bath

PHONE: (805) 544–7440

WEB SITE: www.heritageinnslo.com

FEATURES: inn; 7 rooms; pets allowed (by arrangement)

NEARBY: town; California Polytechnic State University; Mission Plaza; wineries

INNKEEPER/OWNER: Georgia Adrian

guest rooms have in-room vanity areas, and the shared baths have authentic claw-foot tubs and pull-chain toilets. The White Lace and Promises room upstairs is decorated around a bridal theme, with lots of white lace, the innkeeper's family wedding photos dating from the 1800s, and a private bath with shower. The full breakfast, featuring fresh fruit, juice, cereals, a delicious egg entree, and home-baked breads and muffins, is served fireside in the dining room.

PETIT SOLEIL

1473 Monterey Street
San Luis Obispo, CA 93401

$$–$$$$

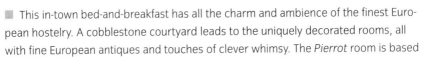

This in-town bed-and-breakfast has all the charm and ambience of the finest European hostelry. A cobblestone courtyard leads to the uniquely decorated rooms, all with fine European antiques and touches of clever whimsy. The *Pierrot* room is based on the French children's book, complete with murals and children's antique mementos; the *Chocolat* room will have you craving chocolate from the mural on the wall of dripping chocolate. The Provence-inspired breakfast room is the site of the morning gourmet offering, as is the sun-filled rear patio with fountain. Every evening guests experience a wine-tasting adventure, complete with local and French wines paired with delectable appetizers.

PHONE: (805) 549–0321 or (800) 676–1588
FAX: (805) 549–0383
WEB SITE: www.petitsoleilslo.com
FEATURES: inn; 15 rooms; in-room televisions; CD players
NEARBY: town (5 blocks); restaurants; university; park
INNKEEPERS/OWNERS: John and Dianne Conner

THE ADOBE ON GREEN STREET

103 Green Street
Santa Cruz, CA 95060

$$–$$$

Created in a historic adobe home on a hill in the Historic District of Santa Cruz, the rooms of this bed-and-breakfast offer distinctly different decor. One may offer Shaker, another Mission; one has a blend of Mexican and Native American, while the earth-toned Ohlone has a canopied four-poster queen-size bed, gas fireplace, whirlpool, and sacred art, all destined to create a peaceful sanctuary. One room has a private patio, but there are multiple courtyards for guests to enjoy the outdoors. The substantial full vegetarian breakfast is served in the dining room. An in-house steam room is available on request. Hosts can arrange for guests to be picked up at the inn for a horse-drawn carriage ride through the town.

PHONE: (831) 469–9866
FAX: (831) 469–9493
WEB SITE: www.adobeongreen.com
FEATURES: inn; 4 rooms; in-room phones; computer hookups; in-room televisions and VCRs; movie library; in-room massages; steam room
NEARBY: Pacific Garden Mall; beaches; Mission Plaza; restaurants; art galleries
INNKEEPERS/OWNERS: Arnie Leff and Judith Hutchinson

THE BABBLING BROOK INN

1025 Laurel Street
Santa Cruz, CA 95060

♿ Ⓢ $$–$$$$

▨ Cascading waterfalls, a meandering creek, and an acre of gardens, pines, and redwoods surround this secluded inn built on the foundation of an 1870s tannery and an Ohlone Indian village. Just recently the historic 1796 waterwheel that once powered the state's first gristmill came home to the inn to spill and splash once again. The thirteen guest accommodations offer country French decor, private baths, telephones, televisions, fireplaces, private decks, and outside entrances; four rooms feature deep-soaking whirlpools for two. The Contessa room has stained glass, a fireplace, library, and antiques. A country buffet breakfast and afternoon wine, cheese, and tea are included in the stay. The inn is within walking distance of the beach, wharf, shopping, and tennis.

PHONE: (831) 427–2437 or (800) 866–1131
FAX: (831) 427–2457
WEB SITE: www.babblingbrookinn.com
FEATURES: inn; 13 rooms; in-room phones; in-room televisions and VCRs; fax; copier; in-room workspace; audio-visual equipment; computer hookups
NEARBY: beach; shops; tennis
INNKEEPER/OWNER: Inns by the Sea

CHATEAU VICTORIAN

118 First Street
Santa Cruz, CA 95060

🚫 $$–$$$

▧ This turn-of-the-twentieth-century home
was converted to a B&B in 1983 and is situated
just a block from the beach near the boardwalk
and wharf. The guest rooms all feature queen-size beds, private tiled baths, fireplaces, individually controlled heating systems, and Victorian decor; most accommodations overlook the gardens or the patio.
An expanded continental breakfast of fruit
juice, fruit, croissants, and muffins may be
enjoyed in the dining room or on several
areas surrounding the outside of the inn.
Late-afternoon snacks and refreshments
are also included in the stay.

PHONE: (831) 458–9458
WEB SITE: www.chateauvictorian.com
FEATURES: inn; 7 rooms
NEARBY: beach; boardwalk; pier
INNKEEPER/OWNER: Alice June

CLIFF CREST

407 Cliff Street
Santa Cruz, CA 95060

🚫 $–$$$$

▧ This 1887 estate is a historical landmark noted for
its gardens and proximity to the ocean, about 2 blocks
away. Each guest room has its own bath, antique fur-
nishings, and
fresh flowers;
the Rose room offers views of the Pacific and
has a king-size bed and cozy fireplace. The
smallest unit, the Pineapple room, boasts a
pineapple-carved four-poster bed and an
1887 stained-glass window, and the Empire
room offers a king-size four-poster bed and
fireplace. Guests relax on a second-story cov-
ered porch with peaceful views of the garden

PHONE: (831) 427–2609
FAX: (831) 427–2710
WEB SITE: www.cliffcrestinn.com
FEATURES: inn; 5 rooms; in-room
phones; in-room televisions (on
request); computer hookups; fax
NEARBY: beach
INNKEEPERS/OWNERS: Adriana and
Constantin Gehriger

and the bay. The healthy, full breakfast, featuring juice, fresh fruit, muffins or coffee cake, and a main entree, which Adriana can adjust to your dietary needs, is served in the room or in the downstairs solarium.

THE DARLING HOUSE

314 West Cliff Drive
Santa Cruz, CA 95060

♿ ⊗ $–$$$$

◼ The sweeping verandas of this pre-served Mission Revival home that was built in 1910 overlook the Pacific Ocean and Monterey Bay. The oceanside grounds of the residence are filled with citrus trees, roses, palms, and blossoms. The interior of the house has eight different inlaid hardwoods—found on walls, floors, and doors—as well as beveled glass, stenciled borders, and open-hearth fireplaces. The guest rooms and separate cottage are decorated in period pieces with Tiffany lamps, matching antique bedroom suites, and cozy down comforters and pillows. The cottage sleeps a family of four. Breakfast consists of goodies made from scratch and is served in the ocean-view dining room. Guests enjoy a Jacuzzi located behind the inn, and the innkeepers can arrange horse-drawn carriage rides along the ocean.

PHONE: (831) 458–1958 or (800) 458–1958
FAX: (831) 458–0320
WEB SITE: www.darlinghouse.com
FEATURES: inn/cottage; 8 rooms; hot tub; small meetings; carriage rides
NEARBY: beach; boardwalk
INNKEEPERS/OWNERS: Darrell and Karen Darling

PLEASURE POINT INN BED & BREAKFAST

2-3665 East Cliff Drive
Santa Cruz, CA 95062

♿ ⊗ $$$–$$$$

◼ This inviting beachhouse, extensively renovated in 2001, overlooks Monterey Bay and offers spectacular ocean views from most of its rooms. The cozy home-style inn offers four guest rooms, each with private bath (two with Jacuzzis), fireplaces, and unique beach decor. All rooms have private patios, custom furniture, refrigerators, microwaves, and coffeemakers. The Pleasure Point Suite boasts a sitting room with

PHONE: (831) 469–6161 or (877) 557–2567
FAX: (831) 464–3045
WEB SITE: www.pleasurepointinn.com
FEATURES: home; 4 rooms; in-room phones; in-room televisions and VCRs; in-room workspace; computer hookups; fax; small conferences; hot tub
NEARBY: beach; shops; golf; tennis
INNKEEPER/OWNER: Tom Perry

fireplace and breathtaking ocean views from its private deck. A continental breakfast is served in the dining room, at a more intimate table by the wine bar with views of the bay, or on the rooftop deck, weather permitting; the morning fare includes juice, fresh fruit, croissants, muffins, and breads. The inn is within walking distance of shops and excellent surfing beaches.

COUNTRY HOUSE INN

91 Main Street
Templeton, CA 93465

 $$

■ This 1886 Victorian, a designated historic landmark, is located on Main Street in Templeton, a turn-of-the-twentieth-century town with a Western flair in the heart of the area's wine country. Guest rooms and suites are in the main house and in the adjacent restored carriage house. Accommodations boast king- or queen-size beds, private baths, and interesting antique furnishings; one has a fireplace. The spacious Garden View room was once a formal parlor and now offers a king-size bed; window seat; private bath with claw-foot tub, shower, and pedestal sink; and French doors that open onto a private porch with views of the back garden and grape arbor. The common areas of the inn feature two fireplaces for relaxing; a full breakfast is served in the formal dining room and consists of home-baked breads, a special hot

PHONE: (805) 434–1598 or (800) 362–6032
WEB SITE: www.thecountryhouseinn .com
FEATURES: inn/cottage; 5 rooms
NEARBY: village; wineries
INNKEEPER/OWNER: Diane Garth

entree, fresh fruit, and juice. Afternoon refreshments are also offered. The inn occasionally hosts English high teas in its tearoom; these special events are open to the public as well, and an additional fee is charged. Guests enjoy the surrounding lawns and flower gardens. The inn is just a country stroll from the town's quaint shops and restaurants and an easy drive to numerous area wineries.

CENTRAL CALIFORNIA

Central Valley

California's Central Valley offers a wide spectrum of scenery, from agricultural fields to snow-capped mountains, from deserts with creeks to nature's intriguing Devil's Postpile, and from Death Valley to Mount Whitney. Visitors delight in ghost towns, ski resorts, and unlimited recreation. The Central Valley is so wide that you can't see from one side to the other, and it boasts one of the richest agricultural areas in the world, an area growing everything from dry crops, such as cotton, to intensive crops, such as table grapes, wine grapes, fruits, nuts, and vegetables. The southern portions of the valley are known for their oil production. The area is notable for its extreme weather variations, which range from hot temperatures in the summer months to tule fog conditions and colder weather in the wintertime. Bishop lies on the edge of the Sierra Nevada in the Owens Valley. The valley is flanked by the spectacular rise of these mountains and also boasts desertlike conditions. It is noted for its winter skiing and the Mammoth Mountain and June Lake recreational offerings. The Owens Valley is not noted, however, for its agricultural production due to the diversion of its water supply to Los Angeles.

HOMESTEAD COTTAGES

41110 Road 600
Ahwahnee, CA 93601

♿ ⦸ $$–$$$

▪ "Private, quiet, and romantic" best describe the ambience of this inn built in 1992 on 160 acres near Yosemite National Park. Careful thought has gone into the construction and decoration of the four cottages and Star Gazing loft by the creative owners. The cottages feature private baths, queen-size beds in the separate bedrooms, living rooms with fireplaces, private outdoor sitting areas, and kitchens with refrigerators stocked with supplies for guests to create their own continental breakfasts. There is also a large luxury loft in the barn with queen-size bed, sitting area, and private bath. A unique feature is the stabling area for up to five guest horses.

PHONE: (559) 683–0495 or (800) 483–0495
FAX: (550) 683–8165
WEB SITE: www.homesteadcottages.com
FEATURES: inn/cottages; 4 cottages; in-room satellite television; fax; computer hookups; kitchens; in-room massages; stabling area
NEARBY: Yosemite National Park; gold-panning; bicycling; hiking; golf
INNKEEPERS/OWNERS: Larry Ends and Cindy Brooks

1898 CHALFANT HOUSE

213 Academy
Bishop, CA 93514

⦸ $–$$

▪ P. A. Chalfant, the editor and publisher of the valley's first newspaper, built this home in 1898. The beautifully restored house, in the center of the Western-style town, offers tastefully furnished guest rooms, all with comfortable beds, antiques, handmade quilts and comforters, private baths, ceiling fans, and central air-conditioning. The suite offers a private parlor and television. Guests may relax in the parlor with fireplace, the site of afternoon and evening refreshments, which might include hot-fudge sundaes. A full breakfast is served by the fireplace in the dining room and includes juice, fresh fruit, homemade jams and bread, and a special entree. The inn is within walking distance of shops, restaurants, the park, and a movie theater.

PHONE: (760) 872–1790 or (800) 641–2996
WEB SITE: www.chalfanthouse.com
FEATURES: inn; 7 rooms; air-conditioning; in-room television (suite)
NEARBY: town; mountain recreation; Law's Railroad Museum; tennis; horseback riding
INNKEEPERS/OWNERS: Patty LePera and Nancy Gilliland

YOSEMITE FISH CAMP B&B INN

1164 Railroad Avenue
P.O. Box 25
Fish Camp, CA 93623

⊗ $

▓ This two-story mountain home 2 miles from Yosemite's south entrance is surrounded by silver-tipped Christmas trees and meadows and overlooks a mountain

PHONE: (559) 683–7426
WEB SITE: www.sierratel.com/bazhawley
FEATURES: home; 3 rooms
NEARBY: Yosemite National Park; Sugarpine Railroad; water sports; horseback riding; golf
INNKEEPER/OWNER: Baz Hawley

pond and river. The homey guest rooms are decorated uniquely in country style with antiques, oak and brass double and queen-size beds, and original Yosemite art pieces; the common sitting room hosts a cozy antique wood-burning stove. For breakfast, guests help themselves to coffee, tea, and juice on the table before being served the generous fare of fresh fruits and such home-cooked delicacies as fruit pancakes, French toast, and eggs. The inn is conveniently situated for winter skiing, golfing, horseback riding, and summer water sports, and it's close to the historic Yosemite Sugarpine Railroad.

THE IRWIN STREET INN

522 North Irwin Street
Hanford, CA 93230

⊗ $–$$

▓ This charming Victorian inn with popular restaurant is a few steps from Hanford's enchanting downtown area, rich in historic buildings and small-town activities. The Irwin Street Inn hosts a profusion of leaded-glass windows and antiques throughout its guest rooms and intimate restaurant, which serves breakfast and lunch daily and a three-course gourmet dinner on Tuesday through Saturday

PHONE: (559) 583–8000 or (866) 583–7378
FAX: (559) 583–8793
WEB SITE: www.irwinstreetinn.com
FEATURES: inn/hotel; 27 rooms; air-conditioning; in-room phones; in-room televisions; in-room workspace; all meeting and business services; swimming pool; restaurant; weddings/conferences
NEARBY: historic downtown shops, restaurants
INNKEEPER: Cindy Vidaurri
OWNER: American Inns, Inc.

nights. Guest accommodations, scattered throughout the three adjacent turn-of-the-twentieth-century structures, all feature private baths and such detailing as oak-rimmed tubs, pull-chain toilets, king- and queen-size four-poster beds, armoires, and Oriental rugs, as well as cable television, radios, and telephones. The continental breakfast of homemade goodies is offered in the main-house dining area, on the Victorian brick-lined garden patio, or in the privacy of the guest room. Hanford is about one hour's drive from Sequoia National Park. Guests enjoy the inn's swimming pool; banquet facilities and tree-shaded grounds of the inn are popular locales for weddings, private parties, and conferences.

KERN RIVER INN BED & BREAKFAST

119 Kern River Drive
P.O. Box 1725
Kernville, CA 93238

♿ ⊗ $$

▮ This recent-vintage, two-story farmhouse with wraparound porch is practically on the banks of scenic Kern River, providing views of the river from every room. There are yards graced by rosebushes, berry vines, and fruit trees. The inn's guest rooms, all with private baths, are uniquely and tastefully decorated to reflect Kern River Valley themes and offer either queen- or king-size beds; three rooms feature fireplaces made of Kern River rock, and two accommodations include whirlpools. The

Small-Town America Thrives in Hanford

A late-summer street fair in the Central Valley community of Hanford rivals a Hollywood movie set: a clear, balmy night; stars shining brightly; the charmingly restored 1877 downtown draped in hundreds of twinkling lights; the quaint town square with old-fashioned carousel awhirl. Even in the midday sun Hanford stands as the epitome of small-town America, or, as the local visitors agency calls it, "one of California's hidden treasures."

Most of the sights are within walking distance of the town square, at the heart of which is the one-hundred-year-old former courthouse, which now houses shops and restaurants and is surrounded by flowing lawns. Also near here is the Hanford Fox Theatre, one of the state's "fantasy palaces," built in 1929 by William Fox. Don't miss a special showing here, then stop by the 1929-founded Superior Dairy for a scoop (or two) of the best ice cream in these parts. Call Hanford's visitor hot line for information on all the best Hanford has to offer at (800) 722–1114, or log on to www.hanfordca.com.

PHONE: (760) 376–6750 or (800) 986–4382
FAX: (760) 376–6643
WEB SITE: www.kernriverinn.com
FEATURES: inn; 5 rooms; air-conditioning; fax; copier; computer hookup; meeting area
NEARBY: river and lake sports; winter skiing; town
INNKEEPERS/OWNERS: Jack and Carita Prestwich

Movie Street room, in rust and dark blue shades, is filled with pictures of movie stars who made movies in Old Kernville and has a French door leading to the side porch. The full, country breakfast is served family-style in the dining room and features inn specialties such as giant home-baked cinnamon rolls, stuffed French toast, chilled strawberry soup, and crunchy granola. Afternoon refreshments, served in the parlor or on the porches, include cheese, crackers, and fruit or tea and cookies; root-beer floats are an evening treat. The Kern River Inn is conveniently located for local recreation with fishing right in front of the inn; several antiques and craft stores are within walking distance.

PLANTATION BED & BREAKFAST

33038 Sierra Highway 198
Lemon Cove, CA 93244

⊗ $$$–$$$$

PHONE: (559) 597–2555 or (800) 240–1466
FAX: (559) 597–2551
WEB SITE: www.plantationbnb.com
FEATURES: inn; 8 rooms; air-conditioning; in-room televisions; in-room VCRs (some); computer hookups (some); fax; swimming pool; hot tub
NEARBY: Sequoia National Park; Lake Kaweah
INNKEEPERS/OWNERS: Scott and Marie Munger

▩ Nestled in the foothills of the Sierra Nevada, among acres of orange groves, is this former citrus plantation from the late 1800s. The plantation theme is carried throughout the inn, with each room named after a character from *Gone with the Wind* and decorated accordingly. Many of the accommodations offer fireplaces, televisions, VCRs, claw-foot tubs or whirlpools (thick terry-cloth robes are provided), a nice selection of antiques, and verandas; two rooms share a bath. A full gourmet breakfast is served in the formal dining room or in the 5,000-square-foot brick courtyard, complemented by fine linens and china. Oranges are picked from the orchard each morning for a freshly squeezed juice to accompany the morning fare. Guests enjoy the heated swimming pool year-round and also a hot tub, nestled for privacy among the orange blossoms in the orchard. The Plantation is about 16 miles from Sequoia National Park and only 2 miles from Lake Kaweah.

CINNAMON BEAR INN

113 Center Street
Mammoth Lakes, CA 93546

⊗ $–$$$

■ This quaint inn nestled among the
pines was built in the 1960s and
expanded in the 1970s. All rooms, in New
England colonial-style decor, have queen-
size beds and private baths; suites have romantic, four-poster canopy beds, fire-
places, and kitchens. One-bedroom units are also available. The inn offers a full
breakfast, with such items as stuffed French toast, omelettes, and specialty pan-
cakes. Wine and cheese are available in the afternoon and early evening. Adjacent to
downtown, the inn is across the street from a free shuttle to ski areas.

PHONE: (805) 381–1367 or (800) 845–2873
WEB SITE: www.cinnamonbearinn.com
FEATURES: inn; 22 rooms; in-room tele-
visions; in-room phones; computer
hookups; kitchens (some); spa
NEARBY: town; skiing; mountain and
lake recreation; horseback riding
INNKEEPER/OWNER: Russ Harrison

CHÂTEAU DU SUREAU

48688 Victoria Lane
P.O. Box 577
Oakhurst, CA 93644

♿ ⊗ $$$$

■ This elegant French country estate on the
way to Yosemite National Park offers a combination of fine dining and accommoda-
tions that might otherwise be found only in the European countryside. Though it was
constructed in 1991, the 9,000-square-foot award-winning inn is reminiscent of a
nineteenth-century French castle. Complete with stone turret, arched windows, and
"weathered" wooden doors, this structure also features imported building materials
from France, such as marble, stone, red-clay floor tiles, and wrought-iron balconies.
Each guest room honors an herb in color, decor, and mood; design details range from
hand-printed Provençal fabrics to antique French furnishings. All rooms feature sitting
areas with tile and stucco fireplaces, CD players, eiderdown comforters, fresh flowers,
limestone floors, balconies with expansive views, and luxurious bathrooms with vanity-
dressing areas, hand-painted tile and marble, gigantic sunken tubs, plush bathrobes,
and French-milled soaps. The Romarin (rosemary) room is done in soft rosemary-like
greens with a forest green drape around the king-size bed. The chateau offers a
Parisian-themed villa nestled on two acres. On the grounds of the hillside estate are
several fountains, a swimming pool, and walking paths. The elegantly appointed Grand

Salon and the Music Tower, with its soaring frescoed ceiling and 1870 Erard grand piano, offer quiet relaxation. The chateau's breakfast room is the site of the morning gourmet feast, which may also be enjoyed alfresco on the adjoining terrace. Guests enjoy fresh fruit and such delicacies as crusty dark bread from Los Angeles chef Wolf-

PHONE: (559) 683–6860
FAX: (559) 683–0800
WEB SITE: www.chateaudusureau.com
FEATURES: inn; 10 rooms; air-conditioning; in-room phones; fax; CD players; swimming pool; gourmet restaurant; weddings
NEARBY: Yosemite National Park
INNKEEPER/OWNER: Erna Kubin-Clanin

gang Puck, Black Forest ham, Brie, smoked salmon, chicken sausage, and softly boiled quail eggs. Like the chateau, Erna's adjacent Elderberry House restaurant is a French retreat and boasts award-winning gourmet cuisine available for lunch and dinner.

THE CORT COTTAGE

P.O. Box 245
Three Rivers, CA 93271

 $$

PHONE: (559) 561–4671
WEB SITE: www.cortcottage.com
FEATURES: cottage; air-conditioning; in-room television; fax; hot tub
NEARBY: Sequoia National Park; town
INNKEEPER/OWNER: Elsah Cort

▓ Overlooking mountains and a meadow of spring wildflowers is this B&B cottage nestled in a hillside near the main house. The contemporary wooden cottage, not far from the entrance to Sequoia National Park, was built in 1985 and offers a full kitchen and bath, a queen-size bed, and double futon sofa. The B&B boasts a large half-circle window in the living room and a unique, relaxing deck constructed from the bottom of a wine barrel. Coffee and tea are stocked in the kitchen of the cottage, and the gracious innkeeper delivers the morning breakfast of juice, fruit, muffins or fruit bread, and cereal as well as fresh eggs for the guest to cook as desired. In season, guests enjoy a hot tub for two, located directly under the Milky Way! A two-night minimum stay is required.

BEN MADDOX HOUSE Best Buy

601 North Encina Street
Visalia, CA 93291

$-$$

▓ Ben Maddox was the president and manager of the Mount Whitney Power Company, the first electric serv-

PHONE: (559) 739–0721 or (800) 401–9800
FAX: (559) 625–0420
WEB SITE: www.benmaddoxhouse.com
FEATURES: inn; 5 rooms; air-conditioning; in-room phones; in-room televisions; fax; copier; computer hookups; in-room work-space; meeting area; spa; swimming pool; off-street parking; weddings
NEARBY: downtown Visalia; Sequoia National Park
INNKEEPERS/OWNERS: Diane and Al Muro

ice company in the Central Valley, as well as the first publisher of the *Visalia Daily Times*. This inn, his former home, was built in 1876 and con-structed of redwood from the nearby sequoias. Listed on the National Regis-ter of Historic Places, the home is situ-ated on one-half acre on a quiet residential street lined with more his-toric homes in Visalia's historic dis-trict. A wrought-iron fence encloses the inn's garden and century-old trees, and four 1927 antique post lights illuminate the grounds. The parlor, guest rooms, and dining room of the inn have been restored to their original state with dark pine trim, 14-foot ceilings, and varnished white-oak floors; the entire inn has been furnished with late-eighteenth- and nineteenth-century antiques. The inn's guest rooms all boast sitting areas, private baths, fine antiques, and queen- or king-size beds. The Rose room is often used as a honeymoon suite; the romantic interiors fea-ture a shuttered and windowed alcove, wicker and oak furnishings, rose designs, and the scent of rose petals everywhere. Guests at Ben Maddox are given a breakfast menu for the following morning that allows for a custom dining experience; guests choose from at least three main entrees, such as blueberry pancakes or poached

Explore a Cave or Two

The Sequoia and Kings Canyon National Parks together make up more than 80,000 acres of wilderness with a minimum of roads. The opportu-nity to create your own wilderness adventure among these 200-foot giant sequoias awaits, or the parks will provide you with films, displays, ranger-led or pamphlet-led explorations, and more.

The list of natural wonders to take in is quite long at these parks, but one visit that more than hints at uniqueness is the ranger-led tour of Crystal Cave, just below Giant Forest. Discovered by two fishermen in 1918, the cave is now open to the public from late May to the end of September. The hike to the cave is scenic, but inside the cave, visitors are treated to a fifty-minute tour of exciting crystalline marble forma-tions, dramatic stalactites and stalagmites, and gurgling rivers. Tours run on the hour or half-hour; there is a small fee. Call (559) 565–3134 or log on to www.nps.gov/seki for park information.

eggs with lemon-butter sauce and chives, a breakfast meat, and a variety of breads, cereals, fruit, and juice. Allergies or special diets are accommodated when possible. Guests dine by candlelight in the dining room or on the patio. The delightful inn is available for small groups and weddings.

WICKY-UP RANCH BED & BREAKFAST

22702 Avenue 344
Woodlake, CA 93286

♿ 🚭 $–$$

PHONE: (559) 564–8898
FAX: (559) 564–3981
WEB SITE: www.wickyup.com
FEATURES: inn; 2 rooms, 1 cottage; air-conditioning; airport pick-up service; fax; copier; meeting area
NEARBY: Sequoia National Park; Kings Canyon National Park; Mineral King; Lake Kaweah; rafting; miniature golf; horseback riding
INNKEEPERS/OWNERS: Monica and Jack Pizura

When President Warren G. Harding's cousin, Fred E. Harding, arrived in this rural territory near the Sierra Nevada foothills to check out the citrus ranching potential, he was taken with its beauty. The former senator from Illinois purchased many acres, built this charming two-story California Craftsman-style ranch house, and began his citrus growing ranch, which he named "Wicky-Up." Today, Wicky-Up is still a full-time working orange ranch, and guests at the bed-and-breakfast are welcome to walk through the groves, inhaling the scent of orange blossoms and selecting their own oranges for morning juice! The hosts of the bed-and-breakfast are fourth-generation descendants of Senator Harding, and they have full intentions of keeping the ranch in the family for generations to come. Their 1902-built home features one-of-a-kind Port Orford cedar woodwork throughout; the antiques, paintings, and Oriental rugs have been passed down through the family. Guests may choose the Harding suite with antique queen-size bed, private bath, and television/VCR; or the Calico room cottage has a full-size feather bed and a twin-bed loft, private bath, and private patio entrance. The antiques-furnished guest rooms are pleasantly supplied with down comforters and fresh flowers. An early-evening social hour includes beverages in the inviting living room with fireplace or on the veranda. The generous gourmet breakfast is served in either the garden (in the summer) or the dining room as classical music plays in the background. The meal, with varying entrees, is elegantly presented on collectible china and is enjoyed by candlelight. Recreation abounds at Wicky-Up, with its locale only twenty minutes from the entrance to Sequoia National Park and nearby Lake Kaweah for water sports. If you visit the ranch in the spring, check out the Springtime Blossom Trail.

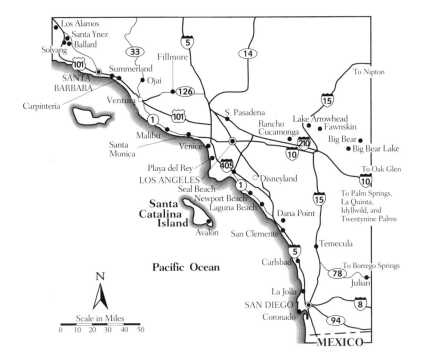

Los Alamos
Santa Ynez
Ballard
Solvang
101
SANTA
BARBARA
Carpinteria

33
Summerland
Ojai
Ventura

Fillmore
5
126

14

To Nipton
15

Pacific Ocean

N

Scale in Miles
0   10   20   30   40   50

1
101
Malibu
Santa
Monica
Venice
Playa del Rey
LOS ANGELES
Seal Beach
Newport Beach
Laguna Beach

Santa
Catalina
Island
Avalon

S. Pasadena
Rancho
Cucamonga
210
405
10
Disneyland
1
15

San Clemente
Dana Point

Temecula
5
Carlsbad
78

La Jolla
SAN DIEGO
Coronado
94

Lake Arrowhead
Fawnskin
Big Bear
Big Bear Lake
To Oak Glen
10
To Palm Springs,
La Quinta,
Idyllwild, and
Twentynine Palms

To Borrego Springs
Julian
8

MEXICO

SOUTHERN CALIFORNIA

Known best as the home of Disneyland and the Hollywood stars, the "southland" also boasts spectacular swimming, surfing, and yachting from Santa Barbara to San Diego, mountain retreats, and desert playgrounds. It even offers its own island (Catalina) with inviting beaches and rolling hills dotted with buffalo. Within this varied expanse may be found serene country settings such as citrus-filled Ojai, the vineyard and horse-ranch areas of Los Olivos and Ballard, and the Danish community of Solvang. Artistic communities such as Laguna and Santa Barbara abound, as do several respected art museums, including the Norton Simon and Getty Museums. The urban areas offer lots of people and cars, as well as theater, fine restaurants, shopping, and history. A trip through downtown Los Angeles and Olvera Street will give a glimpse of the area's rich past, as do the many historic communities with original missions and adobes, such as San Juan Capistrano and San Diego (with zoo and animal park as well). Late-1880s California can be relived through the towns of Los Alamos and Julian. Southern California's desert offerings range from sandy expanses abloom with wildflowers and cacti to resort playgrounds with golf, tennis, spas, and gambling.

"Submerge" Yourself in Wonder

If the submarine ride at Disneyland has always been a favorite of yours, then Catalina's *Starlight,* Avalon's semisubmersible submarine, will keep you mesmerized. It feels like the Disneyland version, complete with tiny seats aimed at viewing portholes and bubble clouds as the action begins. The 60-foot-long, fifty-ton vessel makes its way from Avalon's main pier to Lover's Cove, a protected underwater preserve. The preserve is home to fascinating kelp beds with some eerie inhabitants, such as bat rays. Fish of all sorts congregate in such plentitude that the forty-minute tour is hardly enough time to take it all in.

Sub tours leave on the hour daily; night tours are available. Call (310) 510–2000, ext. 6, for more information or reservations.

THE INN ON MT. ADA

398 Wrigley Road
P.O. Box 2560
Avalon, CA 90704

⊗ $$$$

 The inn was built in 1921 as a summer home for William Wrigley Jr., the philanthropic owner of Santa Catalina Island; in 1978 the home was given to the University of Southern California, which now leases the house for the purpose of maintaining a high-quality lodging establishment on the island. Located on five and a half acres atop Mount Ada, the old Georgian colonial house with shutters, moldings, and trim in grays, whites, and greens is surrounded by native trees and gardens and grants awesome views of the ocean. A traditionally furnished den, card lounge, and sunroom form the west wing of the first floor, while a spacious living room with vistas and an exquisite dining room make up the remaining common areas.

PHONE: (310) 510–2030 or (800) 608–7669

FAX: (310) 510–2237

WEB SITE: www.catalina.com/mtada

FEATURES: inn; 6 rooms; in-room televisions; fax; copier; catering; meeting areas; golf carts; lunch included in stay

NEARBY: bay and town; Catalina Museum

INNKEEPERS/OWNERS: Susie Griffin and Marlene McAdam

The second floor of the mansion offers the four guest rooms and two suites of the inn. Such details as fireplaced sitting areas, walk-in closets, full bathrooms, and eclectic decor are found in these special accommodations. A full and hearty breakfast, deli-style lunch, and complimentary afternoon refreshments, including appetizers, wine, and champagne, are included in the stay at this elite inn. The inn provides guests with golf carts for the perfect transportation around Avalon.

THE OLD TURNER INN

232 Catalina Avenue
P.O. Box 97
Avalon, CA 90704

$$–$$$$

This 1927 guesthouse, 1 block from the beach, has been given a new life as a cozy B&B with five guest rooms and suites. The quaintly decorated rooms feature antiques, brass beds, wall coverings, and private baths, and four accommodations offer romantic wood-burning fireplaces. The King and Queen suites have private sitting porches. Guests enjoy a living room and dining room with massive brick fireplace and country decor as well as a glassed-in porch and colorful flower garden. Each morning an extended continental breakfast featuring muffins and pastries, yogurt, fresh fruit, juice, homemade granola, and freshly baked and prepared dishes is served on the antique buffet; wine, beverages, and light appetizers are served each late afternoon. Bicycles are complimentary for one hour.

PHONE: (310) 510–2236 or (800) 410–2236
FAX: (310) 510–8504
WEB SITE: www.catalina.com/old_turner_inn
FEATURES: inn; 5 rooms; in-room televisions
NEARBY: town; bay; Catalina Museum; Wrigley Memorial and Botanical Garden
INNKEEPER: Christa Foster
OWNERS: Jeanne and Bill Hill

THE BALLARD INN

2436 Baseline Avenue
Ballard, CA 93463

♿ ⊘ $$$–$$$$

![] This B&B inn, nestled in the historic town of Ballard within the lush Santa Ynez Valley, offers guests a blend of the old and new. The gabled inn, built in 1984 in a nostalgic design with a multitude of fireplaces, offers four common rooms and fifteen guest rooms, each decorated in a theme consistent with the area's history yet containing the most modern conveniences. Three common rooms offer relaxation, wine, and a library, and the William Ballard dining room is the locale of a full breakfast with hot entree. Guests also may dine on the veranda, and a wine tasting of quality local wines along with specialty hors d'oeuvres is held each day at 4:30 P.M. Each guest room at the inn features a private bath and individual touches that include balconies, American antiques, quilts, Chumash Indian designs, and unique circular windows; several rooms have fireplaces. Business and group rates are available. Guests will enjoy the on-site restaurant, Cafe Chardonnay.

PHONE: (805) 688–7770 or (800) 638–2466
FAX: (805) 688–9560
WEB SITE: www.ballardinn.com
FEATURES: inn; 15 rooms; televisions (on request); phones (on request); copier; in-room workspace; computer hookups; conference/meeting areas; restaurant
NEARBY: town; wineries; Solvang; art galleries; restaurants
INNKEEPER: Christine Forsyth
OWNERS: Larry Stone and Steve Hyslop

GOLD MOUNTAIN MANOR HISTORIC B&B

1117 Anita
P.O. Box 2027
Big Bear, CA 92314

⊘ $$–$$$$

![] This beautiful 6,000-square-foot mansion with bird's-eye maple floors and beamed ceilings was built in 1928 as a weekend lodge for a wealthy Hollywood industrialist. The log inn, on an acre of towering pine trees, has been

meticulously restored and recently remodeled. It offers guests seven unique accommodations—all with wood-burning fireplaces, one with a spa, and two with private access to the veranda—a pool table, and a player piano. The guest rooms, all with private baths and queen-size beds, range from a rustic decor with stone-hearth fireplace and pine floors to the Clark Gable room, with an antique French walnut bed and old Franklin stove that honeymooned with Gable and Lombard. As a special treat, baths are stocked with the innkeeper's homemade bath products. A homemade breakfast with such delights as breakfast pizza, fresh fruit bruschetta, ginger Belgian waffles, and baked apples is served on the veranda or in the dining room; gourmet afternoon hors d'oeuvres are offered. The inn is ½ block from the national forest and less than ten minutes from Big Bear Lake and ski slopes.

PHONE: (909) 585–6997 or (800) 509–2604

FAX: (909) 585–0327

WEB SITE: www.goldmountainmanor.com

FEATURES: inn; 7 rooms; fax; in-room workspace; audiovisual equipment; computer hookups; meeting areas; billiard table; weddings; homemade bath products

NEARBY: skiing; Big Bear Lake; hiking; fishing

INNKEEPERS/OWNERS: Trish and Jim Gordon

ALPENHORN BED AND BREAKFAST

601 Knight Avenue
P.O. Box 2912
Big Bear Lake, CA 92315

⊗ $$$–$$$$

■ This fine European-style inn is nestled on two professionally landscaped acres of land midway between the village and Snow Summit ski resort. The gardens surrounding the inn are filled with an abundance of wildflowers, two mountain streams, aspens, and pines. The eight guest rooms all have private baths with spa tubs-for-two, balconies, phones, VCRs (and a large collection of videos), king- or queen-size feather beds, and fireplaces. No one goes to the ski slopes hungry at Alpenhorn. The four-course breakfast consists of fresh breads, seasonal fruit, homemade granola, fresh hot oatmeal

PHONE: (909) 866–5700 or (888) 829–6600

FAX: (909) 878–3209

WEB SITE: www.alpenhorn.com

FEATURES: inn; 8 rooms; computer hookups; concierge service; shuttle to ski resorts; massages; snowboard lessons; guided hikes; tours of the area

NEARBY: ski resorts; village; lake; hiking

INNKEEPERS/OWNERS: Chuck and Robbie Slemaker

banana brûlée, and a hot dish such as cheese strata or apple pancakes. Hot and cold beverages as well as freshly baked cookies are available all day; complimentary hors d'oeuvres and wine are offered early evening, and guests are treated to after-dinner liqueurs and chocolates.

APPLES BED & BREAKFAST INN

42430 Moonridge Road

P.O. Box 7172

Big Bear Lake, CA 92315

♿ 🚭 $$–$$$

▨ This 9,000-square-foot Victorian-style hostelry was built to be a first-class bed-and-breakfast and opened in 1993. The hospitable innkeepers, Jim and Barbara McLean, have thought of all the needs of their guests. The thirteen guest rooms are located upstairs in the main house and in the annex that overlooks the "bridal garden." The romantic rooms (named after different apples) are all outfitted with fireplaces, comfortable king-size beds, down comforters and pillows, matching recliners, and private baths. Four of the guest rooms have oversize Jacuzzis; all of the rooms are decorated with warm country touches, wall coverings, and stuffed bears. The Snow room in the annex features a pink iron four-poster bed with crocheted cover and potted "flowers" over the fireplace. The rear yard of the inn contains a relaxing spa, lots of grassy areas, a paddle tennis court, and two gazebos. The yard is private and lined with majestic pines. The main house of the inn is just as inviting, with a large common area with overstuffed seating, game table, and baby grand piano. Snacks are plentiful all day; you can help yourself to popcorn for popping in the microwave, fudge, cookies, and all beverages. Before-dinner cheese and crackers are offered in the common area; an after-dinner home-made dessert is also available here, making it a popular spot for inn-goers to visit before retiring. The lounge hosts an impressive video library for use in the rooms.

PHONE: (909) 866–0903
FAX: (909) 866–6524
WEB SITE: www.applesbedandbreak
fast.com
FEATURES: inn; 13 rooms; in-room tele-
visions and VCRs; spa; paddle tennis;
fax; conference center; computer
hookups; catering for small meetings;
wedding services; gazebos
NEARBY: Bear Mountain and Snow
Summit ski resorts; village shops and
restaurants; lake; forest trails
INNKEEPERS/OWNERS: Jim and Barbara
McLean

Upstairs from the lounge is a landing-perched library with comfortable seating and reading material. Breakfast at Apples is served at 9:00 A.M. in the inn's dining room and is an extravaganza. The dining room holds a long table to seat all twenty-four guests in a very convivial atmosphere. The breakfast is a country affair with such delicacies as honey-apple sausages, thick and crunchy French toast with apple cider syrup, homemade granola, home-baked muffins, and incredible hot porridge with cream. Apples hosts a number of weddings in its bridal garden, which can accommodate up to 125 people. The village shops and restaurants and lake activities are close by, as are the two main ski resorts.

KNICKERBOCKER MANSION COUNTRY INN

869 Knickerbocker Road
P.O. Box 1907
Big Bear Lake, CA 92315

⊗ $$–$$$$

This historic Big Bear landmark was originally built by the first dam keeper of the Big Bear Lake Dam in 1920. The carefully restored private log home and carriage house carries with it a charming rustic elegance in a quiet, forested area near the village. The two log structures are set on two and a half acres that back up to the national forest, yet are walking distance to the village shops and bistros. The inn hosts nine standard rooms and two suites—all with full private baths, tel-

PHONE: (909) 878–9190 or (877)
423–1180
FAX: (909) 878–4248
WEB SITE: www.knickerbocker
mansion.com
FEATURES: inn; 11 rooms; in-room
phones; in-room televisions and VCRs
NEARBY: village shops and restaurants;
the forest; lake; ski resorts
INNKEEPERS/OWNERS: Thomas Bicanic
and Stanley Miller

evisions, VCRs, and phones; the two suites feature spa tubs, massive fireplaces, and coffee service areas. The stay includes a full gourmet breakfast and wine and appetizers each evening.

STARGAZERS INN & OBSERVATORY

717 Jeffries Road
P.O. Box 2819
Big Bear Lake, CA 92315

♿ ⊗ $$–$$$

This B&B offering is perfectly situated near the village and lake and offers some unique touches normally found at large resorts. The inn's theme is astronomy and features a spectacular gallery of space photography throughout, as well as an evening astronomy program that utilizes the inn's computerized telescope. In addition to the entry-level living room and library with fireplaces, the bottom level of the inn hosts a game room with billiards and an adjoining indoor heated pool and sauna for year-round swimming. Each of the five guest rooms is equipped with queen-size feather bed covered in down comforter and television with VCR and DVD; some rooms boast private spa tubs and fireplaces. The stay includes a full breakfast with homemade specialties, and wine and hors d'oeuvres are served each evening. Shuttle service is provided to guests to and from ski resorts and the Big Bear Airport.

PHONE: (909) 878–4496 or (866) 482–7827
FAX: (909) 878–4067
WEB SITE: www.stargazersinn.com
FEATURES: inn; 5 rooms; in-room televisions and VCRs/DVDs; in-room fireplaces (some); heated indoor swimming pool; sauna; astronomy program; shuttle service
NEARBY: ski and snowboarding resorts; golf; village shopping; lake
INNKEEPER/OWNER: Doreen Wiggins

BORREGO VALLEY INN

405 Palm Canyon Drive
P.O. Box 2038
Borrego Springs, CA 92004

♿ ⊗ $$–$$$$

Gracious hosts Allisen Wolever and Grant Rogers built their casita-style bed-and-breakfast to blend harmoniously with nature on this ten-acre site near the entrance to the Anza-Borrego Desert State Park Visitor Center. The fourteen casitas, with kitchenettes and private patios, are arranged in a horseshoe pattern embracing protected parkland views and uphill hiking in the inn's "backyard." The main building of the Southwest-style inn hosts the welcoming lounge with terra-cotta floors, fireplace, art-

PHONE: (760) 767–0311 or (800) 333–5810

FAX: (760) 767–0900

WEB SITE: www.borregovalleyinn.com

FEATURES: inn; 14 casitas; air-conditioning; in-room phones; computer hookups; in-room televisions and VCRs; refrigerators; microwaves; bicycles; pools; spas; croquet court; airport pick-up; fax; in-room workspace

NEARBY: Anza-Borrego Desert State Park Visitor Center; hiking paths; restaurants; golf; Julian; Palm Springs

INNKEEPERS/OWNERS: Allisen Wolever and Grant Rogers

work, rugs, and other Sedona-inspired decor, as well as French doors granting views of the open desertscape. The morning meal is served here and makes for a perfect hiker's buffet, with bagels, sweet breads, English muffins, granola, yogurts, juice, and a variety of fresh fruits. Diners choose from inside tables-for-two overlooking the mountains and open desert or outside patio dining with close-up mountain views. The pueblo-style casitas with adobe tile roofs share one common wall and have been designed for maximum privacy. Some offer fireplaces, whirlpool tubs, a minikitchen with refrigerator, sink, microwave, and dishes, which is particularly inviting to the guest wishing a longer stay. Each room features terra-cotta tile floors, French doors leading to a private rear patio with seating, and bathrooms with vanity areas and spacious tiled showers. The queen-size beds are blanketed with lots of pillows, and some face a cozy fireplace. The grounds, with natural desert plants, a pleasant fountain, and a bird aviary, contain two pools and two spas for soaking under the stars at night or perhaps a brisk morning swim. Mountain bikes are available for exploring; the innkeepers are happy to recommend hikes and special picnic outings. Afternoon refreshments are served.

PELICAN COVE INN

320 Walnut Avenue
Carlsbad, CA 92008

♿ ⊗ $–$$$

▧ Located in the village, just 200 yards from the beach, is this contemporary Cape Cod–style inn painted a light blue with cranberry trim. Fronted by two large palms and bright blooms, the inn offers guests a sunny third-floor sundeck as well as guest rooms with private baths and entrances, queen- or king-size beds, and romantic fireplaces; two rooms contain spa tubs. Each

PHONE: (760) 434–5995 or (888) 735–2683
FAX: (760) 434–7649
WEB SITE: www.pelican-cove.com
FEATURES: inn; 10 rooms; in-room phones; in-room televisions; beach chairs; in-room massages; computer hookups
NEARBY: beach; village shops and restaurants; biplane and hot-air ballooning
INNKEEPERS/OWNERS: Nancy and Kris Nayudu

room is decorated with a pleasant mixture of contemporary and antique furnishings; feather beds and down comforters are available. The breakfast of fresh fruit, juices, and cereals is served in the guest parlor, on the garden patio, or on the sunporch. Extras at the inn include use of beach chairs, towels, and picnic baskets.

PRUFROCK'S GARDEN INN

600 Linden Avenue
Carpinteria, CA 93013

$$$–$$$$

PHONE: (805) 566–9696 or (877) 837–6257
FAX: (805) 566–9404
WEB SITE: www.prufrocks.com
FEATURES: inn; 7 rooms
NEARBY: beach; town shops; Santa Barbara; Lake Casitas; Ojai
INNKEEPERS/OWNERS: Judy and Jim Halvorsen

▪ Tucked between the ocean and the mountain wilderness is the tiny beach community of Carpinteria. Prufrock's, a circa 1904 inn surrounded by gardens, offers a traditional B&B experience with seven comfortable rooms and such amenities as Jacuzzis, fireplaces, sitting rooms, and antiques. The Afternoon Delight is a particularly special offering with two garden patios, one with a fireplace, and a separate bedroom and sitting room. Guests enjoy a home-cooked breakfast each morning, a good book by the living room fireplace, and relaxation on the beach. The inn, named after T. S. Eliot's *Love Song of J. Alfred Prufrock*, is just a stroll from the shops and a short drive from Santa Barbara or Ojai.

CORONADO VICTORIAN HOUSE

1000 Eighth Street
Coronado, CA 92118

♿ 🚭 $$$$

▪ This three-story 1894 Victorian home in the heart of Coronado has been meticulously renovated over three years. The historically designated blue-gray Victorian, with white and burgundy trim, stained-glass doors and windows, and a generous

PHONE: (619) 435–2200 or (888) 299–2822

FAX: (619) 435–4760

WEB SITE: www.coronadovictorian house.com

FEATURES: inn; 7 rooms; in-room televisions; small pets allowed; in-room workspace; computer hookups; catering; meeting areas; dance, exercise instruction

NEARBY: on island; shops; restaurants; beach

INNKEEPER/OWNER: Bonni Marie Kinosian

supply of sunporches and balconies, offers a unique bed-and-breakfast package: an elegant overnight accommodation, a gourmet health/ethnic-food breakfast, and a sample session of dancing or exercise instruction in the 40-foot first-floor dance studio! Dance teacher/innkeeper Bonni Marie Kinosian is the master of dance, as well as chef and hostess in her home filled with fine antiques and sunlit rooms. Guests enjoy a living room, with the original carved wooden fireplace and antique checkerboard, and a dining room that opens to a bilevel patio and sunporch. Guest rooms, all with private baths, include a two-bedroom suite with stained-glass windows, a wet bar, and original beamed ceilings. Special decorator touches in guest rooms include two pre–Civil War step-up sleigh beds and an antique quilt. The generous breakfast includes fresh fruits, juices, homemade rolls, health cereals, homemade yogurt, and such ethnic foods as rolled grape leaves and stuffed zucchini. Guests may choose from social ballroom, ballet, jazz, tap, Hawaiian, swing, salsa, dance workout, and belly dancing as a part of their B&B package; health and fitness walks are offered each morning. Tea, coffee, and healthy snacks are always available.

GLORIETTA BAY INN

1630 Glorietta Boulevard
Coronado, CA 92118

♿ ⊗ $$$–$$$$

▪ Built by sugar-baron John Spreckles in 1908 in the Italianate style, this bayside/beachside mansion with eleven rooms and baths was restored/remodeled in 1998. Many of the original chandeliers, ornate moldings, marble stairs, and brass banisters remain as dramatic reminders of its elegant Edwardian grandeur. The

PHONE: (619) 435–3101 or (800) 283–9383

FAX: (619) 435–6182

WEB SITE: www.gloriettabayinn.com

FEATURES: inn; 100 rooms; air-conditioning; in-room phones; computer hookups; in-room satellite televisions; fax; copier; in-room workspace; small swimming pool; hot tub; library

NEARBY: ocean; bay; water sports; town; restaurants; golf; San Diego Zoo; Sea World

INNKEEPER: Kim Akers

rooftop Penthouse Suite was created in Mr. Spreckles' original solarium; French doors lead to a large private deck. Contemporary buildings adjacent to the mansion house another eighty-nine antiques-filled rooms, all with private baths, refrigerators, televisions, VCRs, and lots of old-world charm. The continental-plus breakfast can be enjoyed in the dining area or patio overlooking the bay. Afternoon refreshments can be enjoyed in the original Music room, featuring a baby grand.

BLUE LANTERN INN

34343 Street of the Blue Lantern
Dana Point, CA 92629

♿ ⊗ $$$–$$$$

▓ This 1990-built Cape Cod–style inn on a bluff is a peaceful retreat on the south Orange County coast. The tan structure with neat white trim is marked by a gabled slate roof and cobblestone paths lined with bright blooms. The interior colors of the inn reflect the dramatic ocean scenery outside with hues of blues, whites, and sand. The twenty-nine guest rooms feature luxury details including period furnishings, original art, print wallcoverings, Jacuzzis, televisions, terry-cloth robes, and refrigerators stocked with complimentary soft drinks. Guests stay warm and cozy in their quarters with romantic fireplaces and fluffy quilts. Balcony rooms are available. The morning breakfast fare is a full country buffet in the dining room; complimentary beverages and cookies are available throughout the day. Breakfast in bed is available for a small service charge. Afternoon tea, wine, and hors d'oeuvres are served from 4:30 to 6:30 P.M. The main level of the inn hosts a book-lined library and an ocean-view dining room; the lower level offers an exercise room and conference rooms for small groups. Bicycles are available for touring the scenic area; several restaurants are within walking distance.

PHONE: (949) 661–1304 or (800) 950–1236

FAX: (949) 496–1483

WEB SITE: www.foursisters.com or www.bluelanterninn.com

FEATURES: inn/hotel; 29 rooms; air-conditioning; in-room phones; computer hookups; in-room televisions; fax; copier; in-room workspace; audio-visual equipment; catering; conferences; refrigerators; exercise room; bicycles

NEARBY: ocean; harbor; tidal pools

INNKEEPER: Patty Olsen

OWNER: Four Sisters Inns

THE INN AT FAWNSKIN

880 Canyon Road
P.O. Box 378
Fawnskin, CA 92333

⊗ $$–$$$$

■ Nestled on the tranquil north shore of Big Bear Lake and surrounded by an acre of pines is this contemporary log bed-and-breakfast inn with knotty pine paneling and beamed ceilings. The cozy living room features a massive rock fireplace and lake-view windows. Guests also enjoy the inn's game room with a full-size pool table, big-screen television (with movie library), and wet bar. Three guest accommodations upstairs offer private baths. The inn's special Garden suite features a jetted tub-for-two, king-size bed, and a piano. Breakfast, served in the dining room (with yet another stone fireplace), is a three-course gourmet affair with freshly squeezed juice, vanilla-baked apples, and a main entree such as almond croissants, French toast with maple syrup, and sausage. Breakfast is served on the patio during summer; hors d'oeuvres and beverages are served evenings.

PHONE: (909) 866–3200 or (888) 329–6754 (California)
FAX: (909) 878–2249
WEB SITE: www.fawnskininn.com
FEATURES: inn; 4 rooms; in-room televisions and VCRs (suites); fax; pool table
NEARBY: Big Bear Lake; skiing; hiking; boating; golf
INNKEEPERS/OWNERS: Nancy and Bill Hazewinkel

WINDY POINT INN

39015 North Shore Drive
P.O. Box 375
Fawnskin, CA 92333

⊗ $$–$$$$

■ Nestled serenely on the north shore of Big Bear Lake is this small, contemporary inn featuring five rooms, all with spectacular unobstructed lakeside views. Just minutes from nature trails, the Discovery Center, and bistros, the inn features suites and rooms with special features such as skylights, walk-in closets, sofas, raised beds, wet bars, and whirlpools.

PHONE: (909) 866–2746
FAX: (909) 866–1593
WEB SITE: www.windypointinn.com
FEATURES: inn; 5 rooms; lakeside
NEARBY: on lake; north shore shops and restaurants; Discovery Center; hiking
INNKEEPERS/OWNERS: Val and Kent Kessler

All include feather-topped beds, private decks, individually controlled heating, refrigerators, wood-burning fireplaces, and DVDs. The Shores and the Coves are the inn's newest suites and feature split-level design with panoramic lake views and breakfast in the room. The inn serves complimentary afternoon hors d'oeuvres by a blazing fireplace and a breakfast featuring caramel-apple-cinnamon French toast or another house specialty on the glass-enclosed deck.

THE ARTISTS' BARN

416 Bard Street
Fillmore, CA 93015

 $

A Ventura County Landmark building, this barn/bed-and-breakfast is a unique lodging experience. In the 1930s and 1940s the barn was host to many art exhibits and demonstrations, drawing famous artists from all over the state. A wall in the barn, the Artist's Wall, remains here as a memento of those days with the celebrated minidrawings and paintings by its artist-guests. When the owners acquired the barn their goal was to preserve it as a historical landmark but also share it carefully with the public, hence the bed-and-breakfast. The spacious quarters, easily big enough for four people, consist of a large living room with rock fireplace; a kitchen where the make-your-own breakfast goodies and snacks are kept; a downstairs bedroom, bath, and sitting room; and a loft sleeping area that is ideal for children. The comfortable quarters are decorated with country treasures, family antiques, and historical items. The cottage is walking distance to old downtown Fillmore and the train station for the popular, vintage Fillmore & Western Railway that runs throughout the year with special tours. The innkeepers give carriage rides.

PHONE: (805) 524–1216
WEB SITE: www.book-on-disc.com/artists.htm
FEATURES: cottage; in-room television; kitchen; carriage rides
NEARBY: old town Fillmore; cafes; movie theater; vintage railroad trips; Santa Paula
INNKEEPERS/OWNERS: Max and Alma Gabaldon

All Aboard for Vintage Fun

Downtown Fillmore, which through its history has been known as a train town, is now host to this fully operational vintage train—the Fillmore & Western. The antique 1920s-style Pullman and restored dining, sleeper, commuter, and baggage cars are all staffed by workers in vintage costume. Even if you have never been to Fillmore, you have probably seen the train, which has been featured in more than 200 movies and countless television programs and ads. Special tours, which basically connect Fillmore with Santa Paula 10 miles away, range from December Christmas tree–cutting expeditions to antiques hunting to murder-mystery dinners. All of the tours follow a citrus-lined path through this rural Sunkist country, and most include a meal and entertainment. For information call (800) 773–8724 (TRAIN) or log on to www.fwry.com.

FERN VALLEY INN

25240 Fern Valley Road
P.O. Box 116
Idyllwild, CA 92549

♿ ⦻ $–$$

■ This compound of eleven red cottages with latticed white trim rests serenely amid carefully trimmed gardens and shading trees. These private and secluded accommodations, with up to two bedrooms, offer queen-size, quilt-covered beds; luxurious linens; cozy down comforters; private baths; fireplaces; refrigerators or complete kitchens; private patios;

PHONE: (909) 659–2205 or (800) 659-7775

FAX: (909) 659-2630

WEB SITE: www.fernvalleyinn.com

FEATURES: inn; 11 cottages; ceiling fans; in-room satellite televisions and VCRs; kitchens or wet bars (some); swimming pool

NEARBY: town; hiking; horseback riding; bicycling; fishing

INNKEEPERS/OWNERS: Theo and Jamie Giannioses

and televisions and VCRs secreted in oak armoires. The makings for a continental breakfast are provided in each cottage. Additional accommodations are available with up to four bedrooms for families or groups.

STRAWBERRY CREEK INN

26370 Highway 243
P.O. Box 1818
Idyllwild, CA 92549

♿ ⊗ $–$$$

 This homey wood-shingled inn with
etched-glass windows and a deck under the towering pines offers a romantic moun-
tain retreat, yet is close to the village. Guests enjoy a spacious living room with cozy
fireplace and a glassed-in sunporch where the full breakfast is served. Guest rooms
are located in the main house as well as
around a sunny courtyard behind the inn
and feature antiques and family memen-
tos. Each courtyard room boasts a queen-
size bed, private bath, small refrigerator,
skylight, and fireplace; the Autumn room
features a Queen Anne–style four-poster
bed and is decorated in fall colors. Deluxe
rooms in the main house offer fireplaces,
small refrigerators, and televisions with
VCRs. The inn's Honeymoon cottage fea-
tures a king-size bed, whirlpool, fireplace,
television and VCR, a fully equipped
kitchen, and sunny glassed-in deck. A full breakfast may include Jim's baked German
French toast with smoked bratwurst or Diana's tasty herb baked eggs.

PHONE: (909) 659–3202 or (800) 262–8969

WEB SITE: www.strawberrycreekinn .com

FEATURES: inn/cottage; 9 rooms, 1 cottage; in-room televisions and VCRs (2 units); refrigerators; fax; copier

NEARBY: village shops, restaurants; hiking

INNKEEPERS/OWNERS: Diana Dugan and Jim Goff

BUTTERFIELD BED & BREAKFAST

2284 Sunset Drive
P.O. Box 1115
Julian, CA 92036

⊗ $$–$$$

 This mountain cottage home is tucked away up a quiet residential road above the
historic gold-rush village of Julian. Pine and oak trees, country shutters, private
patios, waterfalls, and a Victorian gazebo make this bed-and-breakfast a romantic
escape that has the same guests returning each year. The gourmet breakfast
delights, such as crepes and blintzes, are served under the wedding gazebo on warm

PHONE: (760) 765–2179 or (800) 379–4262

FAX: (760) 765–1229

WEB SITE: www.butterfieldbandb.com

FEATURES: inn; 5 rooms; in-room televisions and VCRs; air-conditioning; fax; computer hookups; catering for small meetings/receptions; weddings

NEARBY: downtown Julian shops and restaurants; winery; wild-animal park; Palomar Observatory; state parks; Anza-Borrego Desert State Park

INNKEEPERS/OWNERS: Ed and Dawn Glass

mornings and by a crackling fire in the living room/dining room area on cooler days. Afternoon homemade snacks include "killer brownies" and popcorn, along with teas, ciders, coffee, and cocoa. The five guest accommodations are all unique, but all have private bathrooms and lots of special home-style touches. The suites feature fireplaces. The French bedroom opens to the gazebo patio with its own private entrance, fireplace, and elegant furnishings. The Rose Bud cottage is a favorite with vaulted knotty-pine ceiling, potbellied stove, living room area, and dressing room. It also has a private entrance. The Feather Nest offers spring decor, feather bed, and window seat with country view; this room is accessed down a winding staircase through the main house. Guests at Butterfield may make reservations ahead for the inn's Romantic Candlelight Dinner. Each course is prepared and served in the privacy of the guest room on heirloom china; on summer nights guests may opt to dine under the stars. The inn is happy to arrange horse-drawn carriage rides into the countryside or into town.

Find Your Own "Gold" in Julian

Gold brought early pioneers to settle this town in the mountains above San Diego, but today's "settlers" are happy to "mine" weekend tourists who flock in for the best apple pie in the West, gift-shop browsing, and antiques hunting. The apple industry took off about the same time gold fever reached a pitch in historic Julian, and ancient orchards still flourish.

Wander the late-1800s main street of town on foot, taking in the aroma of apple pies fresh from the oven. Better yet, pamper yourself by touring by horse and carriage with Country Carriages in real old-fashioned style. Snuggle into a goose-down comforter and let the horse-drawn carriage take you into the country to the local Menghini Winery for wine-tasting or over the hill to one of your favorite bed-and-breakfasts. Reserve your romantic carriage ride by calling (760) 765–1471; for more information visit www.julianca.com.

JULIAN HOTEL

2032 Main Street
P.O. Box 1856
Julian, CA 92036

 $$–$$$

■ The only hotel survivor of the area's mining-boom days, the hotel was constructed by freed slaves in 1897 and is listed on the National Register of Historic Places. The inn is completely furnished in authentic American antiques from the turn of the twentieth century (including some original hotel pieces such as the upright piano), and the lobby and some of the guest rooms have ceilings of both pressed tin and redwood railroad-car siding. Guest rooms have Victorian wall coverings, headboard canopies, and cozy comforters or quilts. The Honeymoon House is a one-bedroom cottage with wood-burning fireplace and lots of romantic lace. The complimentary full breakfast of eggs Florentine, apple-filled pancakes, fruit, nut bread, homemade granola, and juice is served in the dining room. Tea is served each evening in the parlor.

PHONE: (760) 765–0201 or (800) 734–5854
FAX: (760) 765–0327
WEB SITE: www.julianhotel.com
FEATURES: inn/hotel/cottage; 13 rooms, 2 cottages; fax; copier; restaurant
NEARBY: town; restaurants; shops; hiking; fishing; orchards
INNKEEPERS/OWNERS: Steve and Gig Ballinger

MOUNTAIN HIGH BED & BREAKFAST

4110 Deer Lake Park Road
P.O. Box 268
Julian, CA 92036

♿ ⦸ $$$

■ Just 3 miles from historic Julian, an 1870s mining town, is this small B&B that is situated at the end of a meadow- and orchard-lined road. The home establishment is nestled on three acres of parklike grounds that hold towering pines, inviting lawns, casual gardens, and a horse paddock with two Arabians. The renovated 1940s home, made of cedar, and the 500-square-foot cottage are situated on a gentle slope facing thirty-five acres of meadows and a scenic pond. The Rose cottage is charmingly cov-

PHONE: (760) 765–1083
WEB SITE: www.mountainhighbnb.com
FEATURES: home; 2 rooms, 1 cottage; air-conditioning; in-room televisions and DVD players; in-room massages; spa
NEARBY: old town Julian; William Hiese Park
INNKEEPERS/OWNERS: Scott and Martha Baker

ered with ivy. The living room has a Swedish woodstove for chilly nights, spring colors and down bedding punctuate the bedroom, and the full kitchen offers a redwood deck. The Woods Room, on a wing of the main house, offers meadow and tree views and has a private French door entry, as well as a private garden patio under the apple trees. The spacious room is outfitted with country provincial furnishings, a stone fireplace, warm wood paneling, a brass queen-size bed, and private bath. The full breakfast, served in the room or in the cottage, includes a variety of innkeeper specialties. The private and peaceful retreat offers a lot of extras: fresh flowers in the rooms, hot cider on chilly nights, or fruit and herbal ice chillers in the summer. The B&B is near numerous hiking trails.

PINE HILLS LODGE

2960 La Posada Way
Julian, CA 92036

$–$$$

The rustic wooden lodge built in 1912 features a giant native-stone fireplace in the lobby and an authentic Western bar. The guest accommoda-

PHONE: (760) 765–1100
FAX: (760) 765–1121
WEB SITE: www.pinehillslodge.com
FEATURES: inn/hotel/cottages; 18 rooms; barbecue/dinner theater; Sunday brunch; pets allowed; copier; conference area; weddings
NEARBY: town; shops; restaurants; hiking; fishing
INNKEEPERS/OWNERS: Terry and Hanna Sheldon

tions include five European-style rooms in the lodge with washbasins (a bath with claw-foot tub is down the hall) and a dozen renovated cottages with private baths, some with fireplaces and patios. A continental breakfast is served to guests weekdays and a full-service breakfast is offered on weekends in the country-style dining room. An all-you-can-eat barbecue dinner theater is offered on weekends in the lodge restaurant.

SHADOW MOUNTAIN RANCH

2771 Frisius Road
Box 791
Julian, CA 92036

♿ ⊗ $$

This ranch-style B&B, formerly an apple orchard and cattle ranch, is surrounded by meadows and pine-covered mountains. The individually decorated guest rooms include such features as wood-burning stoves, antiques, and Native American artifacts. One unusual guest accommodation is actually an "adult" tree house nestled in a century-old oak. Besides the full ranch breakfast, guests may enjoy the hot tub and hiking trails, or even feed ranch animals. The evening brings a fireside glass of sherry or cup of warm vanilla milk. Guests also enjoy a lap pool, horseshoes, and badminton.

PHONE: (760) 765–0323
FAX: (760) 765–0323
WEB SITE: www.shadowmountain ranch.net
FEATURES: home/cottages; 6 rooms, 5 cottages; some air-conditioning; in-room televisions and VCRs; in-room workspace; computer hookups; copier; audiovisual equipment; meeting areas; lap pool; Jacuzzi; horseshoes; badminton; no credit cards
NEARBY: town; shops; restaurants; hiking; fishing
INNKEEPERS/OWNERS: Jim and Loretta Ketcherside

CARRIAGE HOUSE

1322 Catalina Street
Laguna Beach, CA 92651

⊗ $$–$$$

This colonial inn, built in the 1920s in the artistic community of Laguna Beach, offers an array of room decors ranging from English and French country to a tropical Oriental theme. All guest quarters host large sitting rooms and one or two bedrooms; five suites contain kitchens. The Home Sweet Home suite, filled with calicos, ginghams, and antiques, is like a fantasy visit to Grandma's house. Guest-room French doors open to a courtyard and fountain, where guests may enjoy an expanded continental breakfast featuring one of Lesley's famous family recipes. Guests are welcomed with a bottle of wine and fresh fruit in the suite. There is a two-night minimum stay on weekends; three-night minimum during holidays.

PHONE: (949) 494–8945 or (888) 335–8945
WEB SITE: www.carriagehouse.com
FEATURES: inn; 6 rooms; pets allowed; in-room televisions; some kitchens; in-room workspace
NEARBY: village shops, restaurants; ocean; art galleries
INNKEEPERS/OWNERS: Andy and Lesley Kettley

CASA LAGUNA INN AND SPA

2510 South Coast Highway
Laguna Beach, CA 92651

$$$–$$$$

This hillside California Mission–Spanish Revival inn with secluded gardens and meandering paths offers flower-filled patios with spectacular ocean views. Guests also enjoy the grounds' shady terraces, tropical aviary, courtyards, fountains, heated pool, and panoramic ocean views from the bell tower at the restored 1930s villa that boasts hand-painted tile work and wrought-iron touches. The interior of the inn offers guests a library for relaxation and a pleasant mixture of contemporary and antique furnishings. The overnight accommodations include two private cottages, five suites, and fifteen guest rooms. All facilities offer private baths, individual decor, cable television, and clock radios; many have refrigerators, fireplaces, direct-dial telephones, and patios or balconies. The inn serves a generous continental breakfast and afternoon refreshments of wine, hors d'oeuvres, and cheeses. The complimentary repasts are served in the library and may be enjoyed there, by the pool, or in the garden.

PHONE: (949) 494–2996 or (800) 233–0449
FAX: (949) 494–5009
WEB SITE: www.casalaguna.com
FEATURES: inn/hotel/cottages; 20 rooms, 2 cottages; in-room televisions; in-room phones; voice mail; computer hookups; pets allowed; fax; copier; heated swimming pool; in-room refrigerators (some); spa services
NEARBY: ocean; beach; village; art galleries
INNKEEPERS/OWNERS: Francois Leclair and Paul Blank

EILER'S INN

741 South Coast Highway
Laguna Beach, CA 92651

$$–$$$

Situated just steps from the ocean in the heart of Laguna Beach is this European-style inn with French windows, lace curtains, and a courtyard with fountain, fish pond, and gardens. The guest rooms, built around the lush courtyard, are individually furnished in antiques and have private baths. One suite offers a kitchen, fireplace, and ocean view. Guests enjoy a library and living room downstairs as well as an

PHONE: (949) 494–3004 or (866) 617–2696
FAX: (949) 497–2215
WEB SITE: www.eilersinn.com
FEATURES: inn/hotel; 12 rooms; catering; small events, weddings
NEARBY: beach; ocean; village
INNKEEPER/OWNER: Kimberly Silveira

ocean-view sundeck upstairs. The generous continental breakfast is served in the courtyard, as are evening wine and cheese. A classical guitarist is featured during the social period on weekends. Complimentary fresh flowers and fruit baskets are placed in each guest room, and sun tea and coffee are available all day.

THE BED & BREAKFAST INN AT LA JOLLA

7753 Draper Avenue
La Jolla, CA 92037

♿ ⊗ $$$–$$$$

This 1913 Irving Gill–built B&B is a part of the San Diego Historical Registry and was the John Philip Sousa family residence for several years in the 1920s. Cubist-style architecture describes the exterior of the inn, which is surrounded by the original gardens. The main house contains nine of the guest rooms; six are located in the annex. Guest rooms at the inn are elegantly and individually decorated in Laura Ashley or Ralph Lauren fabrics, and each room has either a queen-size bed or two twins; some have fireplaces. Fresh fruit, sherry, and flowers add a nice touch to each guest room. A gourmet breakfast is served on fine china and linen on a tray in the room or in the garden, or the guest may join with others in the dining room; wine and cheese are served in the afternoon. This B&B is located in the heart of La Jolla's cultural complex, just 1½ blocks from the beach.

PHONE: (858) 456–2066 or (800) 582–2466
FAX: (858) 456–1510
WEB SITE: www.innlajolla.com
FEATURES: inn; 15 rooms; air-conditioning; in-room phones; computer hookup; in-room televisions and VCRs (some); in-room workspace (some); fax; copier; catering; small meetings
NEARBY: beach; town; shops; restaurants
INNKEEPER: Gayle Wildowsky

BRACKEN FERN MANOR *Best Buy*

815 Arrowhead Villas Road
P.O. Box 1006
Lake Arrowhead, CA 92352

⊗ $–$$$

Independence Day 1929 marked the opening of this historic-landmark-site inn. It was then known as the Cottage, Lake Arrowhead's first private resort. Movie stars, socialites, and bootleggers found refuge here throughout Prohibition, when the local artesian-well water produced some of the era's finest gin. The well still supplies the inn with excellent drinking water today. After two years of extensive restoration, Bracken Fern opened as Lake Arrowhead's largest B&B in 1993. The English Tudor architecture of the resort was restored to its original charm, and the interiors of the inn are filled with fine antiques from England and Belgium. In addition, the inn maintained most of the resort's original doors, hardware, and flooring. Guests especially enjoy the manor's wine cellar and its game parlor, which contains a restored antique snooker table, along with chess, backgammon, shuffleboard, and classic movies. Ample outside recreation includes a sauna, garden Jacuzzi, and a hammock nestled in a grove of dogwoods. The guest rooms are named after ladies who lived in the inn during Prohibition; the Dahlia features a cabbage-rose design and a queen brass bed and can combine with the Daisy, which hosts a wrought-iron daybed and trundle. The attic suites of the inn include a bridal suite with veiled, hand-carved, four-poster, queen-size oak bed; a skylight view; and Jacuzzi tub-for-two. The cottage has a fireplace and kitchenette and sleeps four. Breakfast is served in the dining room or alfresco on the deck, offering a choice of bran cereals, quiche, fresh fruit, pancakes or baked goods, freshly squeezed juices, and the inn's own special vanilla-nut coffee. Wine and hors d'oeuvres are served during the social hour; hot toddies, hot chocolate, and bun warmers are served in the winter. The William J. Gallery at the inn offers various art showings and sales throughout the year. Bracken Fern Manor specializes in small group functions, such as weddings, conferences, and ski packages.

PHONE: (909) 337–8557 or (888) 244–5612

FAX: (909) 337–3323

WEB SITE: www.brackenfernmanor.com

FEATURES: inn/cottage; 10 rooms, cottage; spa; sauna; fax; copier; audiovisual equipment; computer hookup; catering; conference/meeting areas; weddings

NEARBY: ice skating; bowling; all lake and mountain activities

INNKEEPER/OWNER: Cheryl Weaver

THE ROMANTIQUE LAKEVIEW LODGE

28051 Highway 189
P.O. Box 128
Lake Arrowhead, CA 92352

♿ ⊗ $–$$$

■ This hideaway amid a lush pine forest offers views of Lake Arrowhead and privacy. The white Victorian-feel inn is furnished throughout with antiques and boasts oil paintings and gleaming brass and crystal touches. The uniquely decorated guest rooms and suites feature king- and queen-size beds, romantic fireplaces, luxurious private baths, VCRs, and classic movies. Guests enjoy a continental breakfast, featuring "sinful" cinnamon rolls baked especially for the inn, on the lake-view patio. Located across the street from the village and lake, the lodge is within strolling distance of fine restaurants and shops.

PHONE: (909) 337–6633 or (800) 358–5253
FAX: (909) 337–5966
WEB SITE: www.lakeviewlodge.com
FEATURES: inn; 9 rooms; in-room televisions and VCRs
NEARBY: Lake Arrowhead; village shops and restaurants
INNKEEPERS/OWNERS: Linda Womack and Megan McElrath

LAKE LA QUINTA INN

78–120 Caleo Bay
La Quinta, CA 92253

♿ ⊗ $$–$$$$

■ Located lakeside is this exclusive inn that resembles a fine French chateau. All of the thirteen guest rooms and suites offer views of the lake and mountains and a romantic fireplace. The inn is made up of three types of rooms to delight: the Chateau rooms, the Jacuzzi rooms, and the separate Boathouse rooms, which boast private hot tubs and maximum privacy. All accommodations have private baths with whirlpools for two, king- or queen-size beds, gas fireplaces, discreet televisions and phones, and either patios or balconies overlooking the lake. A full breakfast is served each morning and wine and hors d'oeuvres each evening. The inn has a unique association with Trilogy Golf Club nearby to provide golf to its guests at an exclusive rate. Dinners may be included on Saturday-night stays per a special package.

PHONE: (760) 564–7332 or (888) 226–4546
FAX: (760) 564–6356
WEB SITE: www.lakelaquintainn.com
FEATURES: inn; 13 rooms; hot tubs; golf arrangements; lake activities; Saturday-night dinners; massage facility
NEARBY: lake; golf; shopping; fine restaurants; tennis; polo
INNKEEPER/OWNER: G. Giovanni Giammarco

UNION HOTEL AND VICTORIAN MANSION

362 Bell Street
P.O. Box 817
Los Alamos, CA 93440

$$–$$$

■ This restored 1880s hotel/stage stop, a California Historical Landmark, with 1864-built Victorian Mansion annex is nestled in the heart of the antiques-shop-filled town of Los Alamos. The grounds of the complex are reminiscent of a turn-of-the-twentieth-century park, hosting a hedge maze, Victorian arbor, old-fashioned benches, and street lights; inside diversions include billiard and Ping-Pong rooms. Guests receive fruit baskets with champagne or sparkling cider and may choose from the unique accommodations in both buildings, complete with hand-painted oil murals and appropriate costumelike robes to fit the mood. Victorian Mansion accommodations—with hot tub for two, fireplaces, and televisions and VCRs—range from the whimsical Drive-in Movie room, where guests sleep in a 1956 Cadillac convertible, to the Gypsy room, with an authentic gypsy wagon as a bed and a sunken pool with waterfall as a bath. Bathrooms in the eleven private-bath accommodations are cleverly hidden, as are the televisions. The stay at the inn includes a full breakfast. The inn's restaurant is open Saturday, and the Stagecoach Murder Mysteries are performed there on the last Saturday of the month.

PHONE: (805) 344–2744 or (800) 230–2744
FAX: (805) 344–3125
WEB SITE: www.unionhotelvict mansion.com
FEATURES: inn/hotel; 19 rooms; in-room televisions; in-room VCRs (some); restaurant; bar; weddings; Stagecoach Murder Mysteries
NEARBY: antiques shops; Solvang
INNKEEPER/OWNER: Christine Williams

CASA LARRONDE

P.O. Box 86
Malibu, CA 90265

⊗ $$–$$$

■ A private beach and movie-star neighbors are attractive and unique ingredients of this home B&B in famous Malibu. The spacious two-story home on the ocean offers one guest suite with fireplace, minikitchen, television, sitting area, beamed ceilings, ash paneling, and floor-to-ceiling ocean-view windows. The

PHONE: (310) 456–9333
FAX: (310) 456–0345
WEB SITE: www.bedandbreakfast.com/california/casa-larronde.html
FEATURES: home; 2 rooms; in-room phones; in-room televisions; fax; meeting area; in-room workspace; private beach; no credit cards; closed July through October
NEARBY: on beach; Malibu restaurants
INNKEEPER/OWNER: Charlou Larronde

guest suite also boasts a 40-foot private deck. A downstairs guest room with private bath is also available. The full breakfast may be enjoyed on the deck, and complimentary champagne and hors d'oeuvres are offered in the evening. The B&B is closed during the summer and when the innkeeper is traveling.

DORYMAN'S INN

2102 West Oceanfront
Newport Beach, CA 92663

⊗ $$$–$$$$

This 1892-vintage hotel fronting the ocean has been totally renovated and decorated in carefully selected French-country antique furnishings and wall coverings. Each individually decorated guest room boasts a fireplace and marble sunken bath, and two rooms have Jacuzzis. The deluxe master suite in shades of burgundy offers luxury with a king-size canopy bed facing the fireplace, a cozy sitting area with sofa bed, private bath with marble sunken whirlpool, and spectacular ocean views. An expanded continental breakfast of fresh fruit, cheese and crackers, yogurt, hardboiled eggs, and assorted minipastries is served each morning in the parlor or on the ocean-view rooftop deck. The inn restaurant furnishes dinner in the room or parlor upon request.

PHONE: (949) 675–7300
FAX: (949) 675–7300
WEB SITE: www.dorymansinn.com
FEATURES: inn; 11 rooms; in-room televisions; in-room phones; computer hookups; dinners; restaurant
NEARBY: ocean; Balboa; beach
INNKEEPER/OWNER: Leo Gugasian

PORTOFINO BEACH HOTEL

2306 West Oceanfront
Newport Beach, CA 92663

$$$–$$$$

Nestled on the sand in Newport Beach is this intimate hotel. The luxuriously appointed accommodations, decorated uniquely in hues of dusty rose, cream, burgundy, and green, boast custom-made bedspreads on queen-size beds, fresh flowers, nostalgic wall coverings and

PHONE: (949) 673–7030
FAX: (949) 723–4370
WEB SITE: www.portofinobeachhotel.com
FEATURES: inn/hotel; 20 rooms; limited smoking; air-conditioning; in-room phones; computer hookups; in-room televisions; in-room workspace; fax; copier
NEARBY: beach; shops; restaurants
INNKEEPERS/OWNERS: Ken and Betty Ricamore

draperies, televisions, private baths, and telephones; some rooms feature spa tubs or minipatios. Two front rooms offer panoramic ocean views; five other rooms provide partial views of the ocean and Newport Pier. Guests enjoy an observation parlor with awe-inspiring sunset views over the Pacific. The complimentary continental morning fare of fruit, juice, and croissants is served in the downstairs La Gritta Lounge by a cozy fireplace.

HOTEL NIPTON

72 Nipton Road
P.O. Box 357
Nipton, CA 92364

⊗ $

■ This restored turn-of-the-twentieth-century hotel is a part of the small desert town of Nipton, a former 1885 gold-mining camp. The community (population: 70) in the East Mojave National Scenic Area is also owned by the B&B innkeepers, who purchased the town for restoration in 1986. The carefully renovated hotel maintains the early-1900s desert flavor with foot-thick adobe walls, lobby with wood-burning stove, and historic photos of the town's earlier days. Guests are treated to panoramic views of the desert and mountains from the hotel's front porch surrounded by rock and cactus gardens. The five guest rooms, which share baths, are named after prominent individuals from the hotel's past; room #3 is named after Clara Bow, who stayed in the 1930s. Modern conveniences at the inn include central air-conditioning and heating and two hot tubs for stargazing. Two tented cabins accommodate up to four adults, but they are roomy enough for a family of six. Each cabin is air-cooled and has two double beds, a woodstove, electric lights, and an overhead fan. Community bath facilities are near the cabins. Guests are served a continental breakfast each morning and may help themselves to apricot brandy anytime.

PHONE: (760) 856–2335
FAX: (760) 856–2335
WEB SITE: www.nipton.com
FEATURES: inn; 5 rooms, 2 tented cabins; air-conditioning; computer hookups; fax; catering; meeting area; two hot tubs
NEARBY: desert landmarks; Las Vegas; Death Valley
INNKEEPERS/OWNERS: Roxanne and Jerry Freeman

SNOWLINE CIRCLE INN

39196 Snowline Circle
Oak Glen, CA 92399

⊗ $–$$

▦ This country-home inn is set among
the pine, oak, and apple trees of Oak
Glen—a peaceful spot to picnic and sample apples and cider from the many surrounding farms. All four rooms have a
unique personality, decorated in antiques with modern comforts. The king- and
queen-size beds are covered in cozy down comforters; the Candlelight suite is the
romantic choice with Jacuzzi and private mountain-view balcony. A full breakfast is
offered in the dining room each morning; in warmer months guests may eat on the
deck. Breakfast in bed is always an option.

PHONE: (909) 797–7309
WEB SITE: www.snowlinecircleinn.com
FEATURES: inn; 4 rooms
NEARBY: apple farms
INNKEEPERS/OWNERS: Jon and Sue
Evans

THEODORE WOOLSEY HOUSE

1484 East Ojai Avenue
Ojai, CA 93023

♿ ⊗ $–$$$

▦ This 1887-built, stone and clapboard
residence is reminiscent of a New England
farmhouse. The two-story house with a
70-foot shaded veranda is situated down
a rose-lined country drive on seven oak-
studded acres. On the grounds of the Ojai
Historical Landmark home is a 50-foot,
kidney-shaped pool with spacious deck
and pleasant gardens. The parlor of the
inn provides comfortable seating, a custom-
made walnut piano, fireplace, and a 1950s
jukebox. Guest rooms, with private baths, are individually decorated with floral wall
coverings, lace curtains, wainscoting, and some of the home's original furnishings.
Edith's room is a romantic retreat decorated in hues of mauve and lavender with a

PHONE: (805) 646–9779
FAX: (805) 646–4414
WEB SITE: www.theodorewoolsey
house.com
FEATURES: inn/cottage; 6 rooms; air-
conditioning; in-room phones; in-room
televisions; DVD/VCR players; fax;
copier; swimming pool; small meet-
ings; no credit cards
NEARBY: village; hot springs
INNKEEPER/OWNER: Ana Cross

fireplace, spacious balcony, and private bathroom with stained-glass window and lavender claw-foot tub. An expanded continental breakfast is served each morning in the dining room; guests enjoy a variety of coffee cakes, bread, and bagels, as well as waffles, fresh fruit, yogurt, cereals, and freshly squeezed juices. Early-morning coffee and tea are available near the guest rooms. Other recreation at the inn includes volleyball, croquet, and horseshoes.

CASA CODY B&B COUNTRY INN

175 South Cahuilla Road
Palm Springs, CA 92262

♿ $–$$$$

■ The oldest continuously operating hotel in Palm Springs, Casa Cody was founded in the 1920s by Hollywood pioneer Harriet Cody, Buffalo Bill's cousin. The Santa Fe–style suites and villas have been completely refurbished in tasteful decor and art and offer such amenities as fully equipped kitchens and wood-burning fireplaces in many of the units. Ten suites, with one or two bedrooms, are nestled around an inviting pool area; an adjacent wing, the Apache, offers seven additional guest rooms and suites. A grassy courtyard at the inn provides six additional suites with magnificent mountain views. The adobe cottage has two bedrooms, a large living area, stone fireplace, and a huge stone tub in the bathroom. In addition to the pool, guests may enjoy a secluded, tree-shaded Jacuzzi. The complimentary continental breakfast is served casually at one of the inn's two pools. Casa Cody is a short walk from downtown shops, fine restaurants, and the Desert Museum and is convenient to hiking trails, tennis, and golf.

PHONE: (760) 320–9346 or (800) 231–2639

FAX: (760) 325–8610

WEB SITE: www.casacody.com

FEATURES: inn/cottage; 23 rooms; limited smoking; air-conditioning; in-room phones; in-room televisions and VCRs (some); pets allowed; kitchens; swimming pools; Jacuzzi; fax; copier; in-room workspace; small groups

NEARBY: in town; restaurants; shops; Desert Museum; golf; tennis; hiking trails

INNKEEPERS/OWNERS: Frank Tysen and Therese Hayes

VILLA ROYALE

1620 Indian Trail
Palm Springs, CA 92264

$$-$$$$

▨ This secluded Mediterranean-style
estate is near everything but provides a
wonderfully private getaway. Built in
1947, the historic inn hosts three sets of
buildings that together offer thirty-one
unique guest accommodations with such
amenities as fireplaces, kitchens, down duvets, and thick bathrobes. The rooms are
sprinkled amid the grounds, lush with flowers, fountains, and courtyards that hold
two swimming pools and a large Jacuzzi. The inn's deluxe villas contain one or two
bedrooms and are equipped with a complete dining room, living room with fireplace,
and kitchen. The Royale guest rooms offer kitchens or private patios, as well as fire-
places; the six charming Hideaway guest rooms are furnished in interesting antiques.
The award-winning Europa restaurant and bar at the inn is a romantic choice with
French doors and wood-burning fireplace inside or by the fountain on the patio out-
side under the stars. The bistro serves modern continental fare with all the personal
touches of a fine restaurant. The inn hosts weddings, receptions, and corporate
retreats.

PHONE: (760) 327–2314 or (800) 245–2314

FAX: (760) 322–3794

WEB SITE: www.villaroyale.com

FEATURES: inn; 31 rooms; swimming pools; Jacuzzi; kitchens (some); restaurant and bar; weddings; corporate retreats

NEARBY: village shops and restaurants; Indian Canyons; tram

INNKEEPER/OWNER: Sue Lovato

Metal "Ambassadors" to the Desert

Entering the desert community of Palm Springs on Interstate 10, visitors
are mesmerized by a metalized group of "ambassadors" with spinning
propellers towering 150 feet off the ground. One of the world's largest
such windmill energy-producing centers, this alternative energy solution
is now also a tourist attraction.

Palm Springs Windmill Tours whisks tourgoers in solar-powered cars
into the middle of a "power plant" amid the "whooshing" windmills
while the tour ranger imparts valuable information on anything and
everything relating to wind energy. For information on booking this
unusual tour, call (760) 251–1997; reserve as soon as possible. Hints:
Take sunscreen, water, and a mind ready to absorb interesting facts.

THE WILLOWS HISTORIC PALM SPRINGS INN

412 West Tahquitz Canyon Way
Palm Springs, CA 92262

⊗ $$$$

■ Einstein really slept here, as did honeymooners Carole Lombard and Clark Gable, and Hearst's
mistress Marion Davies, among many other members of the rich and famous. This 1927-built
Mediterranean villa, lovingly embraced by Mount
San Jacinto, was originally the winter estate of
Samuel Untermyer, former U.S. secretary of the treasury. Exquisitely restored to the
near-identical ambience of its 1930s elegance, this private and posh inn is a romantic
delight nestled in the midst of downtown Palm Springs. The interiors are striking:
Mahogany beams grace the great hall,
frescoed ceilings fill the veranda, and the
estate's original 50-foot rock waterfall
spills hypnotically into a pool just outside
the stone-floored dining room. All the
inn's rooms offer views from its perch just
over town and the Desert Museum—
whether of the majestic mountains; the
estate's lush, subtropical, hillside garden
dotted with stately palms that climbs
above the city; or the relaxing and private
heated swimming pool and spa area. The
decor of the inn is a pleasing blend of
antiques and neoclassical elements, com-
plemented by muted walls, coffered and
vaulted ceilings, natural hardwood and
slate floors, and an ample supply of stone
fireplaces. The expansive living room
hosts a grand piano and the evening's offering of complimentary hors d'oeuvres and
wine with a backdrop of live music on weekends. Morning brings gourmet, multicourse fare served in the dining room or on the patio. The eight guest rooms at the
Willows offer uniqueness, privacy, and elegant comfort. Einstein's Garden room was
the original guest room of the house (and where Einstein stayed while visiting); Art
Deco mahogany inlaid furniture, a king-size bed, and French doors that open to a pri-

PHONE: (760) 320–0771 or (800)
966–9597
FAX: (760) 320–0780
WEB SITE: www.thewillowspalm
springs.com
FEATURES: inn; 8 rooms; air-conditioning;
in-room phones; voice mail; computer
hookups; in-room televisions; heated
swimming pool; Jacuzzi; group
retreats/conferences/weddings; catering; fax; copier; in-room workspace;
audiovisual equipment
NEARBY: Desert Museum; village of
Palm Springs; golf; tramway; hiking;
tennis
INNKEEPER: Kimberly Tucker
OWNERS: Tracy Conrad and Paul Marut

vate garden patio highlight this choice. For a romantic escape try the Marion Davies room, with its elegant antique furnishings, fireplace, and "fantasy" bathroom with two-person claw-foot tub, silver chandelier, and marble-floored shower. For ultraprivacy choose the Loft, hidden up a curving set of stairs; this former chauffeur's room is anything but a servant's quarters!

INN AT PLAYA DEL REY

435 Culver Boulevard
Playa del Rey, CA 90293

  ♿ ⊘ $$–$$$$

■ Just 3 blocks from the ocean and five minutes north of LAX, this praiseworthy inn is the only airport-area lodging spot within walking distance to the beach. Add to this its scenic locale overlooking the main channel of Marina del Rey, as well as the 350-acre Ballona Wetlands and bird sanctuary, providing egrets, blue herons, and hawks as welcome backyard "neighbors." The recently built, three-story Cape Cod–style inn is bright and airy. The twenty-one guest rooms cater to both the business traveler and the romantic, combining practical and aesthetic elements—from fresh flowers to phones with dataports. For a romantic escape try an upstairs suite with sunset views of the wetlands and the marina's main channel. Soothing color schemes flow with the view, and custom wall coverings, brocade-upholstered sofa and chairs, and quality linens add elegance. Particularly romantic is Room 208, adorned with lacy canopy bed and white gauze curtains. For a special stay request Room 304, the Romance room. The spacious suite features a large sitting area, four-poster bed, and see-through fireplace that adds ambience to both the sitting area and the two-person Jacuzzi on the other side. The spacious bathrooms in many of the other rooms contain some Jacuzzis for two; some en suite, see-through fireplaces; and all the luxury touches found in top hotels. The inn's large living room with waterfowl motif is a comfortable retreat with overstuffed sofas, library, fireplace, and windows for bird-watching

PHONE: (310) 574–1920
FAX: (310) 574–9920
WEB SITE: www.innatplayadelrey.com
FEATURES: inn/hotel; 21 rooms; hot tub; air-conditioning; in-room phones; computer hookups; in-room televisions and VCRs; fax; copier; in-room workspace; audiovisual equipment; conference/meeting areas; bicycles; covered parking
NEARBY: LAX; beaches; Ballona Wetlands; bicycling; bird-watching
INNKEEPER: Heather Suskin
OWNER: Susan Zolla

(binoculars provided). Outside rose gardens provide fragrant strolling and soothing hot-tubbing after a day at the beach or at work. Breakfast is served in the inn's beach-themed dining room with pleasing hues of sand, yellow, and blue; the hearty buffet includes a full fare of fresh fruit, juices, baskets of breads or cakes, award-winning egg soufflés, cereals, and yogurt. Afternoon wine, hors d'oeuvres, tea, cookies, and lemonade are served in front of a cozy fire in the living room or out on the sun-warmed decks. The inn boasts an elevator.

CHRISTMAS HOUSE BED & BREAKFAST INN

9240 Archibald Avenue
Rancho Cucamonga, CA 91730

⊗ $–$$$

▨ Turn-of-the-twentieth-century gala yuletide gatherings amid intricate wood carvings and a profusion of red and green stained-glass windows inspired the name of this perfectly restored Queen Anne–Victorian that stands as a historical landmark. The interior of the house boasts period furnishings, seven fireplaces, and rich redwood and mahogany throughout; guests are welcome to enjoy the entire house. Guests also enjoy a sweeping veranda and one acre of gardens. The guest rooms are uniquely decorated in antiques and include shared and private baths, each outfitted with thick terry-cloth robes. The renovated carriage-house rooms include a suite with a unique outdoor shower in a secluded atrium, and the Carriage room with a private spa, fireplace, and VCR with classic movies and the popcorn to go with it!

PHONE: (909) 980–6450
FAX: (909) 980–6450
WEB SITE: www.christmashouseinn .com
FEATURES: inn/carriage house; 6 rooms; air-conditioning; in-room phone (1 unit); in-room televisions, fax; computer hookups; catering; meeting areas; mystery/theater events
NEARBY: wineries; San Gabriel Mountains
INNKEEPER/OWNER: Janice Ilsley

The inn serves a generous continental breakfast weekdays and a full fare on weekends; the meal is served elegantly with antique china, white linens, and crystal. During the month of December, the house is decorated extravagantly in Victorian Christmas splendor, and the old-fashioned festivities include a participatory theater performance of Charles Dickens's *A Christmas Carol* at the inn on December 23 and 24. The inn becomes a "dead"-and-breakfast several times a year when it hosts overnight murder mysteries.

CASA TROPICANA B&B INN AND SPA

610 Avenida Victoria
San Clemente, CA 92672

Ⓢ $$–$$$$

▨ This recently built five-story Spanish-style inn across from the beach and pier offers deluxe B&B accommodations on several levels. The first floor of the building contains a restaurant, the Tropicana Bar & Grill. The deluxe rooms carry Spanish names, such as Casita en Cielo—which means "little house in the sky"—and nearly all feature fireplaces, televisions, refrigerators, ice makers, champagne, and Jacuzzis; some have wet bars. The posh Penthouse suite on the fifth floor boasts a private deck with hot tub and wet bar, a three-way fireplace, and "his" and "hers" showers. Rich mahogany and rain-forest green highlight the Casita San Clemente, which also offers a king-size feather bed, a kitchenette, a fireplace, ocean views, and a Jacuzzi for two. Guests enjoy a full complimentary breakfast chosen from an extensive menu of Spanish and American food served on the deck or in the room. Decks located on guest-room floors offer panoramic views of the ocean.

PHONE: (949) 492–1234 or (800) 492–1245

FAX: (949) 492–2423

WEB SITE: www.casatropicana.com

FEATURES: inn; 8 rooms; in-room phones; computer hookups; in-room televisions; refrigerators; restaurant; beach chairs, umbrellas; weddings; spa facilities

NEARBY: on beach; pier; Amtrak

INNKEEPER/OWNER: Rich Anderson

THE COTTAGE

3829 Albatross Street
P.O. Box 3292
San Diego, CA 92163

Ⓢ $–$$

▨ Situated in an older residential and rural canyon area of the city is this Victorian-furnished guesthouse and private guest room. The cottage offers a full kitchen, bathroom, wood-burning stove, and oak pump organ; the small house will accommodate

PHONE: (619) 299–1564

FAX: (619) 299–6213

WEB SITE: www.sandiegobandb.com/cottage.htm

FEATURES: home/cottage; 2 rooms; in-room phones; in-room televisions; fax; copier; in-room workspace; kitchen

NEARBY: San Diego Zoo; Balboa Park

INNKEEPERS/OWNERS: Carol and Robert Emerick

up to three people comfortably with a king-size bed plus a queen-size hide-a-bed in the living room. The Garden room, located in the innkeepers' home, has a private entrance, private bath, and king-size bed. Guests are served a freshly baked continental breakfast each morning. The B&B is less than 2 miles from the San Diego Zoo and Balboa Park.

HARBOR VACATIONS CLUB

1880 Harbor Island Drive, G Dock
San Diego, CA 92101

⊗ $$–$$$$

■ Located on a scenic marina close to all San Diego tourism sites is this unique B&B experience. Harbor Vacations Club is certainly more than just a bed-and-breakfast stay—you can take a bay cruise without ever leaving your room. The individual yachts and dockside villas are all self-contained, with all of the same amenities found at regular inns, such as private baths, phones, and satellite televisions. Guests may choose from a wide variety of vacation experiences, from staying on a sailboat to lounging in a posh, decorator-designed villa. The villas, with upstairs

PHONE: (619) 297–9484 or (800) 922–4836

FAX: (619) 298–6625

WEB SITE: www.harborvacationsclub.com

FEATURES: yachts; 8 villas or yachts; in-room telephones; in-room televisions and VCRs; kitchens/galleys; swimming pool; bicycles; bay cruises; catered sunset cruises; fax; copier; in-room workspace; catering for meetings and receptions; wedding/conference services; children welcome; airport and train pick-up service

NEARBY: Sea World; San Diego Zoo; beaches; airport; golf; charter fishing; Wild Animal Park; Old Town San Diego; Coronado Island

INNKEEPER/OWNER: Shell Vacations Club

decks for sunning and eating, have one or two bedrooms and baths, full kitchens, and living rooms. The *Neva Mae,* a 32-foot sailing catamaran, features two queen-size-bed staterooms, a double stateroom, and a forward trampoline deck for sunning. The *Villa del Mar* has a spacious salon with a hide-a-bed, fully equipped kitchen, panoramic-view windows, master bedroom with plantation shutters, two baths, and a washer/dryer. The villa's 420-square-foot rooftop sundeck has a special UV-protective awning covering most of the decks on the vessel.

HERITAGE PARK BED & BREAKFAST INN

2470 Heritage Park Row
San Diego, CA 92118

♿ ⊘ $$–$$$$

This Queen Anne–Victorian home with a two-story corner tower and encircling veranda sits in San Diego's historical park in the company of other classic structures and is fronted by cobblestone walkways. Totally restored to its original floor plan, this inn offers vintage movies each evening in the antiques-filled parlor. Accommodations—some with fireplaces and all with private baths outfitted with plush terry-cloth robes—are uniquely decorated in period antiques and have Victorian wall coverings or stenciling, polished wooden floors, Oriental rugs, feather beds, and handmade quilts. A full gourmet breakfast may be enjoyed in the formal dining room or on the sunny veranda, where tea is served in the afternoon. Business services include special rates, no-charge fax service, in-room telephones on request, and the daily newspaper.

PHONE: (619) 299–6832 or (800) 995–2470

FAX: (619) 299–9465

WEB SITE: www.heritageparkinn.com

FEATURES: inn; 12 rooms; in-room phones; in-room workspace; fax; copier; computer hookups; in-room televisions and VCRs (some)

NEARBY: in historical park; restaurants; shops; all San Diego attractions; old town trolley (stop); sunset gondola ride

INNKEEPERS/OWNERS: Nancy and Charles Helsper

KEATING HOUSE INN

2331 Second Avenue
San Diego, CA 92101

⊘ $–$$$

This historic 1888-built Queen Anne–Victorian landmark on Bankers Hill above the bay is just 4 blocks from the Balboa Park attractions. Pleasant, sunny gardens and shaded patios provide relaxation around the restored home with stained-glass windows, two-story bay windows, gabled roofs, and tower. The guest rooms, all with pri-

PHONE: (619) 239–8585 or (800) 995–8644
FAX: (619) 239–5774
WEB SITE: www.keatinghouse.com
FEATURES: inn/cottage; 9 rooms; in-room televisions; air-conditioning; fax; copier; computer hookups; in-room workspace; small conferences; weddings
NEARBY: downtown San Diego; Balboa Park; ocean; Sea World
INNKEEPERS/OWNERS: Ben Baltic and Doug Scott

vate baths, are comfortably decorated in antiques and plants; one room has a fireplace. Guests may also stay in the inn's carriage house, rented separately or as one unit. The cottage accommodations have private baths. Guests may enjoy the parlor and sunny garden and porch. The dining room is the site of the full gourmet breakfast. Complimentary beverages are always available.

THE BATH STREET INN

1720 Bath Street
Santa Barbara, CA 93101

♿ ⊗ $$–$$$$

■ This historic Queen Anne–Victorian, located just a few blocks from the heart of downtown, offers distinctive architectural detailing with its "eyelid" balcony and hipped, uneven roof line. Although completely renovated, great care has been taken to maintain the turn-of-the-twentieth-century feeling of the original home; guest rooms at the inn and in the summerhouse annex boast polished hardwood floors or plush carpeting, fine woodwork, traditional wall coverings, some multipaned windows, and antique furnishings. The Partridge room offers an elegant king-size canopy bed, claw-foot tub and shower, and small balcony overlooking the Santa Ynez Mountains; the summerhouse contains four guest rooms, all with gas fireplaces and three with Jacuzzis. The hearty full breakfast is served in the dining room, at a smaller table in the living room, or on the sunny patio. Refreshments at the inn include a light afternoon tea and evening wine and cheese. Guests at Bath Street relax in the third-floor library and VCR room.

PHONE: (805) 682–9680 or (800) 549–2284
FAX: (805) 569–1281
WEB SITE: www.bathstreetinn.com
FEATURES: inn; 12 rooms; air-conditioning; in-room phones; in-room televisions; in-room VCRs (some)
NEARBY: downtown Santa Barbara; shops; restaurants; park; ocean
INNKEEPERS/OWNERS: Marie Christensen and Deborah Gentry

THE CHESHIRE CAT

36 West Valerio Street
Santa Barbara, CA 93101

$$$–$$$$

Two vintage Queen Anne–Victorian homes have been lovingly restored to create a "fairy-tale" B&B with delicate Laura Ashley wall coverings and fabrics, high ceilings, bay windows, and lots of private nooks. The inn and garden coach house offer guest rooms, all with private baths, English antiques, and king- or queen-size brass beds, and some rooms feature a fireplace, patio, or spa. Names of the guest rooms are taken from *Alice's Adventures in Wonderland,* and especially notable is Alice's own suite, with cozy sitting room and private patio overlooking the gardens and mountains. The light and airy Tweedledum suite in the Cheshire Cat coach house also overlooks the gardens and offers a king-size bed, living room with fireplace, television, wet bar, and Jacuzzi installed beside a beautiful bay window. A full gourmet breakfast is served in the dining room on chilly days and on the patio in warm weather; wine and hors d'oeuvres are offered in the evening. Chocolates and liqueurs can be found in the room on weekends. A relaxing courtyard patio is nestled between the two homes of the inn, and an outdoor spa is built into a private gazebo.

PHONE: (805) 569–1610
FAX: (805) 682–1876
WEB SITE: www.cheshirecat.com
FEATURES: inn/coach house; 17 rooms; in-room phones; in-room televisions; in-room VCRs (some); copier; computer hookup; spa; croquet
NEARBY: downtown Santa Barbara; shops; restaurants; ocean; mission
INNKEEPER/OWNER: Christine Dunstan

THE OLD YACHT CLUB INN

431 Corona Del Mar
Santa Barbara, CA 93103

$$–$$$$

Just ½ block from the beach is Santa Barbara's first B&B, composed now of two vintage California Craftsman-style residences that sit side by side. The original B&B structure was the city's yacht club in the 1920s, and the 1925-built home next door became an inn expansion in 1983. Together the homes, comfortably decorated in antiques and colorful fabrics, offer a dozen guest rooms and suites filled with homey touches, decanters of sherry, and Oriental rugs; most rooms offer sitting areas and private entries, and all accommodations have private baths. In the evening, guests

PHONE: (805) 962–1277, (800) 549–1676 (California only), or (800) 676–1676
FAX: (805) 962–3989
WEB SITE: www.oldyachtclubinn.com
FEATURES: inn; 12 rooms; in-room phones; in-room televisions (some); fax; copier; computer hookups; in-room workspace; meeting areas; dinners (Saturday); bicycles; beach towels, chairs
NEARBY: beach; mission; bicycling; downtown Santa Barbara
INNKEEPERS/OWNERS: Eilene Bruce and Vince Pettit

may sip sherry by the parlor fire or on the porch. The inn is well known for its full gourmet breakfasts, featuring omelettes, quiches, or French toast. Candlelight dinners are a tradition on Saturday nights for inn guests and are a five-course feast featuring the finest and freshest local ingredients. Guests are able to use the inn's bicycles, beach towels, and beach chairs.

THE ORCHID INN

420 West Montecito Street
Santa Barbara, CA 93101

⊗ $$–$$$$

■ This cottage-style inn, formerly the Blue Dolphin Inn and now under new ownership, is in a perfect location for enjoying all of Santa Barbara—just 2 blocks from the beach and 4 blocks from State Street's shopping and bistros. The eight guest rooms, furnished in antique decor, offer queen- and king-size beds and private baths; most have fireplaces, and some feature Jacuzzis. The stay includes a full breakfast and evening wine and cheese.

PHONE: (805) 965–2333 or (877) 722–3657
FAX: (805) 962–4907
WEB SITE: www.orchidinnatsb.com
FEATURES: inn; 8 rooms; in-room massage and yoga; in-room fireplaces (some)
NEARBY: beach; harbor; restaurants; shops
INNKEEPERS: Emilie and Towe
OWNER: Susan Spieler

THE SECRET GARDEN

1908 Bath Street
Santa Barbara, CA 93101

⊗ $$–$$$$

■ Nestled among lush gardens and mature trees is this 1915 California-bungalow main house and cottages with peaceful brick patios and meandering paths. English and American country antiques fill the inn, which offers individually decorated guest

PHONE: (805) 687–2300 or (800) 676–1622

FAX: (805) 687–4576

WEB SITE: www.secretgarden.com

FEATURES: inn/cottages; 11 rooms, 2 cottages; in-room televisions (some); fax; computer hookups

NEARBY: beach; town; shops; restaurants; mission

INNKEEPER/OWNER: Dominique Hannaux

rooms and suites, all with private baths. The cottage Nightingale suite features a queen-size bed, a spacious living room with gas fireplace, a private entrance, and Jacuzzi. The Woodthrush, decorated in French country whites, is a totally private cottage accommodation overlooking the lawn and gardens and features a bedroom with king-size bed, sitting room with daybed, a charming living room, and private Jacuzzi. Wine and light hors d'oeuvres are served in the late afternoon; after dinner the inn offers homemade sweets and hot spiced apple cider. The full gourmet breakfast, featuring French-recipe quiches and a special fruit dish, is served in the main house dining room or on the garden patio each morning.

SIMPSON HOUSE INN

121 East Arrellaga
Santa Barbara, CA 93101

♿ ⦻ $$$–$$$$

■ This 1874-built, award-winning B&B is nestled on a secluded acre of grounds with tall hedges, English gardens, curving paths, lawns, and mature shade trees and is within walking distance of town. The restored inn and 1878 barn and quaint cottages are appointed throughout with tasteful antiques and include a spacious

PHONE: (805) 963–7067 or (800) 676–1280

FAX: (805) 564–4811

WEB SITE: www.simpsonhouseinn.com

FEATURES: inn/cottages; 15 rooms, 3 cottages; air-conditioning; in-room phones; voice mail; computer hookups; in-room televisions and VCRs; in-room Jacuzzis; all business and meeting services; spa and health-club services; bicycles; video library

NEARBY: town; shops; restaurants

INNKEEPERS/OWNERS: Glyn and Linda Davies and Janis Clapoff

sitting room with library and fireplace and an adjoining formal dining room. French doors lead to a garden veranda with white wicker seating. Guest rooms, all recently redecorated with hand-printed Victorian wall coverings, offer special features such as English laces, Oriental rugs, fireplaces, televisions and VCRs, Jacuzzis, antiques, and queen- or king-size beds; all units have private baths. The Robert and Julia Simpson room features a private sitting area and French doors that open to a spacious garden deck, and the Parlor room boasts a bay window and small library. Four luxurious suites are located in the barn and feature antique pine floors and French doors leading to private decks; cottages with similar antique elegance offer private brick patios for relaxing garden breakfasts. The full morning meal is served on the veranda, the brick patio, the private decks, or in the dining room and consists of such specialties as apple French toast and Simpson House Savory Eggs. The inn offers an elaborate evening buffet of Mediterranean hors d'oeuvres and local wines as well as afternoon tea on request. Spa services are available to guests as well as health-club and pool privileges at a nearby club.

TIFFANY COUNTRY HOUSE

1323 De la Vina Street
Santa Barbara, CA 93101

⊗ $$$–$$$$

▦ This 1898 Victorian home has been completely restored, with its diamond-paned windows, wood staircase, and authentic bath intact. Guests enjoy an old-fashioned garden with wicker furniture and a lattice-covered porch, as well as evening wine and cheese before a parlor fire. Guest rooms offer turn-of-the-twentieth-century furnishings, king- or queen-size beds, fireplaces, and private baths. A honeymoon suite is also available with Jacuzzi for two, as is a third-floor penthouse suite with private balcony, refrigerator, sitting room, and Jacuzzi; guests in the suites enjoy breakfast in the room. The homemade breakfast, which includes quiche, French toast, muffins, and breads, is served each morning in the dining room or on the old-fashioned porch, as is afternoon wine and cheese.

PHONE: (805) 963–2283 or (800) 999–5672

FAX: (805) 962–0994

WEB SITE: www.tiffanycountryhouse.com

FEATURES: inn; 7 rooms; in-room phones; in-room televisions and VCRs; fax; in-room refrigerators (2 units)

NEARBY: town; shops; restaurants; ocean; mission

INNKEEPER/GENERAL MANAGER: Jan Martin Winn

OWNER: Country House Inns

THE UPHAM HOTEL & GARDEN COTTAGES

1404 De la Vina Street
Santa Barbara, CA 93101

⊗ $$$–$$$$

▦ Claiming to be the "oldest continuously operating hostelry in Southern California,"

PHONE: (805) 962–0058 or (800) 727–0876

FAX: (805) 963–2825

WEB SITE: www.uphamhotel.com

FEATURES: inn/hotel/cottages; 50 rooms; in-room phones; computer hookups; in-room televisions; in-room workspace; fax; copier; audiovisual equipment; catering; conferences/ meeting areas

NEARBY: downtown Santa Barbara; shops; restaurants; mission; ocean

INNKEEPER: Jan Martin Winn

OWNER: Country House Inns

this restored 1871 Victorian and its adjoining cottages are nestled on a garden-filled acre in downtown Santa Barbara. The individually decorated rooms offer period furnishings and antiques and cozy comforters; some accommodations have fireplaces, and many feature private porches or patios. All have private baths. The master suite has a fireplace, Jacuzzi, wet bar, and private yard with a hammock. Guests enjoy wine and cheese around the lobby fireplace in late afternoon; a complimentary continental breakfast is offered each morning in the lobby or on the garden veranda. The breakfast includes seasonal fruits, cereals, and a variety of muffins, breads, and pastries; the morning newspaper is also complimentary. The inn offers banquet and conference facilities.

VILLA ROSA INN

15 Chapala Street
Santa Barbara, CA 93101

⊗ $$–$$$$

▦ Offering "eighteen rooms just eighty-four steps from the beach," this intimate B&B hideaway has a Southwest feel, with rough-hewn beams, plantation shutters, and louvered doors. A lounge adjoins the pool and spa in the manicured garden courtyard. Included is a continental breakfast, and complimentary port, sherry, and coffee are offered in the lobby each evening. Guests are also treated to afternoon wine and cheese. Light and airy

PHONE: (805) 966–0851

FAX: (805) 962–7159

WEB SITE: www.villarosainnsb.com

FEATURES: inn/hotel; 18 rooms; in-room phones; swimming pool; spa; fax; computer hookups; copier; conference areas

NEARBY: beach; restaurants; shops

INNKEEPER/OWNER: Julia Finucin

guest rooms and suites, all with private baths and queen- or king-size beds, and some with fireplaces, are decorated in pastel color schemes and a combination of contemporary and Spanish colonial furnishings. The inn offers impressive small business conference facilities.

WHITE JASMINE INN

1327 Bath Street
Santa Barbara, CA 93101

🚫 $$–$$$$

■ Five unique properties consisting of
two vintage California Craftsman-style
houses, an 1880s summer cottage, and
two turn-of-the-twentieth-century loca-
tions make up this B&B, formerly the Glen-
borough Inn. The main house offers a

PHONE: (805) 966–0589 or (888)
966–0589

WEB SITE: www.glenboroughinn.com

FEATURES: inn/cottages; 14 rooms, 2
cottages; in-room phones; voice mail;
computer hookups; in-room work-
space; minirefrigerators (some); hot
tub; in-room massage

NEARBY: downtown Santa Barbara;
shops; restaurants; mission; ocean

INNKEEPER/OWNER: Marlies Marburg

cozy parlor with a gas fireplace, comfortable antiques, oak floors, guest refrigerator,
and games and reading material. Four upstairs rooms feature different themes, such
as shabby chic, country, Craftsman style, and more. The private garden suite has a
fireplace, sitting room, private entrance, and deck, and a patio with a private Jacuzzi
spa. One of the cottages offers two spacious suites with canopies, fireplaces, private
entrances, and private baths, as well as two additional guest rooms with private
baths and pretty antiques. Accommodations in the inn's White Farm House include
two guest rooms; one of the cheerful rooms offers a view of the coastal mountains.
These rooms and all of the rest have private baths. Guests are treated to a full gour-
met breakfast prepared from scratch and served in the room. A fully enclosed out-
door hot tub may be enjoyed in total privacy, or visit the back garden to enjoy the
gazebo and tranquil fountain. Hot and cold beverages are available at all times in the
refreshment center; hors d'oeuvres are served weekends.

CHANNEL ROAD INN

219 West Channel Road
Santa Monica, CA 90402

♿ 🚫 $$$–$$$$

■ The oldest residence in the city, this
structure was built in 1910 as the
Thomas McCall House. Scottish-born McCall was a successful cattle rancher who
eventually settled in Santa Monica with his family, where he lived until his passing in
1941. The distinctive blue-shingled estate home was carefully moved to this site at
the mouth of Santa Monica Canyon near the beach several years ago. The three-story
Colonial Revival inn has been renovated and decorated to reflect a fine Santa Monica

home in the 1920s, with pastel pink upholstered furnishings, lavender Chinese rug, polished oak floors, birch woodwork, and a stately fireplace. Guests enjoy a sunny library with white wicker and green chintz furnishings. The fourteen guest rooms and suites, all with private baths, are individually decorated, and some rooms boast four-poster beds, lace bed coverings, and Amish quilts. Bathrooms are stocked with bathrobes and bubble bath, and all accommodations offer telephones, armoire-tucked televisions, and fresh fruit and flowers. Several rooms feature Jacuzzis and/or fireplaces, some rooms offer minirefrigerators and/or VCRs, and some have ocean views. Romantic Room #3 at the inn has a cozy sitting room with fireplace and a four-poster canopy bed in the bedroom. Freshly baked cookies are delivered to the rooms each afternoon. Served in the sun-filled breakfast room or in the guest room, the full breakfast includes juice, homemade muffins and breads, fresh fruit, and a hot dish such as egg soufflé or baked bread pudding. Complimentary wine and cheese are served each evening. The inn also offers guests a hillside spa and bicycles for biking to the beach 1 block away.

PHONE: (310) 459–1920
FAX: (310) 454–9920
WEB SITE: www.channelroadinn.com
FEATURES: inn; 14 rooms; in-room phones; computer hookups; in-room televisions; in-room VCRs (some); fax; copier; in-room workspace; in-room refrigerators (some); spa; bicycles; small meetings
NEARBY: beach; restaurants; the Getty Museum; pier
INNKEEPER: Christine Maxwell
OWNER: Susan Zolla

SANTA YNEZ INN

3627 Sagunto Street
P.O. Box 628
Santa Ynez, CA 93460

🚫 $$$$

▥ Opened in the fall of 2000, this luxurious Victorian-style structure, featuring twenty-first-century amenities, is the historic town's first lodging (since its College Hotel burned down in 1935). Surrounded by extensive gardens, the inn features parlor and library meeting rooms, a fitness facility with sauna, and inviting individually decorated rooms with queen- or

PHONE: (805) 688–5588 or (800) 643–5774
FAX: (805) 686–4294
WEB SITE: www.santaynezinn.com
FEATURES: inn; 14 rooms; air-conditioning; in-room televisions and DVD/CDs; two in-room phones; voice mail; computer hookups; in-room refrigerators; in-room workspace; fax; copier; audiovisual equipment; bicycles; fitness facility; spa; meetings; weddings
NEARBY: wineries; antiquing; Solvang; golf; horseback riding; flight-seeing (sightseeing by air); casino; mission; restaurant
GENERAL MANAGER: John Martino
OWNERS: Douglas and Christine Ziegler

king-size beds, luxury Frette linens, unique antiques, some fireplaces, refrigerators, and private baths with double steam showers and whirlpools. Afternoon tea, early-evening wine and hors d'oeuvres, and a full gourmet breakfast are included. Bicycles are available for rent. The Vineyard House restaurant is adjacent to the inn.

THE SEAL BEACH INN AND GARDENS

212 Fifth Street
Seal Beach, CA 90740

♿ ⊘ $–$$$$

■ This romantic, classic country inn with lush, colorful gardens sits in the charming village of Seal Beach. In a quiet residential neighborhood 1 block from the beach, the old-world B&B with blue canopies, window boxes, shutters, and brick courtyard offers twenty-four guest rooms, no two alike. The inn, more like a Mediterranean villa, was Southern California's first B&B and has been redecorated with some new artwork and furnishings. Most guest rooms have kitchens, fireplaces, and sitting areas, and all have private baths (some with Jacuzzis for two), antiques, televisions, and telephones. Guests enjoy a library with tiled fireplace, brass chandeliers, an ornate antique tin ceiling, lace curtains, and vintage furnishings. The generous morning fare is served in the spacious tea room with a fireplace, by the pool, or in the gardens that are dotted with interesting art and remain abloom year-round. Special packages are available.

PHONE: (562) 493–2416 or (800) HIDE-AWAY

FAX: (562) 799–0483

WEB SITE: www.sealbeachinn.com

FEATURES: inn/hotel; 24 rooms; in-room phones; computer hookups; in-room televisions; air-conditioning (some); kitchens (some); swimming pool; all business and meeting services by arrangement

NEARBY: beach; village; shops; restaurants

INNKEEPER/OWNER: Marjorie Bettenhausen-Schmaehl

PETERSEN VILLAGE INN

1576 Mission Drive
Solvang, CA 93463

🚫 $$$–$$$$

▣ This Danish-style hotel is a part of a "village" in the heart of Solvang. The B&B rooms are scattered throughout the "village" on the second floor of many of the dozen buildings and offer views of the quaint Danish streets, shops, and courtyard. Each hotel minisuite is decorated individually, and many have wall coverings, authentic canopy beds, sitting areas with couches, down pillows, and balconies. A complimentary European-style buffet breakfast is served in the inn's courtyard lounge each morning, and guests may enjoy wine, cheese, and desserts in the wine bar each evening. This family-owned hotel offers a European touch and personal services as well as large hotel amenities such as dining and conference facilities.

PHONE: (805) 688–3121 or (800) 321–8985
FAX: (805) 688–5732
WEB SITE: www.peterseninn.com
FEATURES: inn/hotel; 39 rooms; air-conditioning; in-room phones; in-room televisions; fax; copier; computer hookups; in-room workspace; conference areas
NEARBY: in village; shops; restaurants
INNKEEPER: Jim Colvin
OWNER: Earl Petersen

THE STORYBOOK INN

409 First Street
Solvang, CA 93463

🚫 $$–$$$$

▣ A true family operation, this three-level bed-and-breakfast in the heart of the charming Danish village of Solvang captures the quaintness and hospitality of the area. The European-style villa features nine rooms decorated in family antiques with both marble fireplaces and either a canopy, sleigh, four-poster, or Victorian bed; the deluxe suites, the Little Mermaid and the Swan's Nest, feature Jacuzzis. Breakfast is a Danish delight with such notable local dishes as *aebelskivers*, Danish pastries, homemade breads, and egg entrees. Afternoon wine and cheese are served in the parlor.

PHONE: (805) 688–1703 or (800) 786–7925
WEB SITE: www.solvangstorybook.com
FEATURES: inn; 9 rooms
NEARBY: village shops, restaurants, and attractions; wine tasting
INNKEEPERS/OWNERS: the Orton family

THE ARTISTS' INN AND COTTAGE

1038 Magnolia Street
South Pasadena, CA 91030

⊗ $$–$$$$

▓ Built in 1895 with the ambience of a Midwest-style Victorian farmhouse, this original home, which was the focal point of a poultry ranch, has been restored with elegance and yesteryear in mind. The loving restoration began in 1989 with some additional square footage and interior work that included fine art, antiques, rich fabrics, and original picture moldings. The pale yellow clapboard Victorian features an old-fashioned front porch, used almost daily for breakfast, reading, and relaxing. The garden is patterned after a typical turn-of-the-twentieth-century garden, with an abundance of rosebushes, geraniums, nasturtiums, daisies, and dusty miller. A white picket fence borders the garden. The living room of the inn features a cozy fireplace and Turkish rug; complimentary English teas are offered every afternoon here or on the porch. Each guest room or suite of the inn is designed to reflect an art period or the work of a specific artist. The Eighteenth-Century English room is filled with reproductions of works by Gainsborough, Reynolds, and Constable; a king-size canopy bed and rose-patterned wall covering highlight the room. The inn has added a 1908-built cottage annex at the rear of the house, adding five imaginative room offerings, all with Jacuzzis and private entrances. Continuing the art theme, the Degas suite features a bedroom with king-size canopy bed and sitting area with fireplace, sofa, and desk. The Georgia O'Keeffe room is distinctive, with bright Southwest colors and kiva fireplace. Most impressive is the Expressionist suite, with queen-size canopy bed, fireplace, an oversize red Jacuzzi, and the art of Matisse, Dufy, and Picasso. Guests receive breakfast slips each night for choosing a custom morning dining experience. A full gourmet breakfast,

PHONE: (626) 799–5668 or (888) 799–5668

FAX: (626) 799–3678

WEB SITE: www.artistsinns.com

FEATURES: inn; 9 rooms; air-conditioning; in-room television (on request); in-room phones; computer hookups; fax; catering; meeting areas

NEARBY: old town Pasadena; Rose Bowl; Norton Simon Museum

INNKEEPERS: Jody Schmoll and Dennis Hayden

OWNER: Janet Marangi

prepared by a chef from the California Culinary School, is served on the front porch, in the dining room, or in the guest room, if preferred. Guests choose from an assortment of coffees, teas, juice, fresh fruit, home-baked breads and muffins, granola, cereal, and a special main entree. The Artists' Inn caramelized French toast is a special treat.

THE BISSELL HOUSE

201 Orange Grove Avenue
South Pasadena, CA 91030

⊗ $$–$$$

▓ The name Bissell makes one think of vacuum cleaners, and so it is that this Victorian estate was formerly the home of the vacuum magnate's philanthropist daughter, Anna Bissell McCay. Known today as the Bissell House, the three-story 1887 home is situated on a half-acre corner behind a 40-foot hedge in the area at one time referred to as the Orange Grove Mansion District. These days the area is more popularly referred to as Millionaires' Row, and the estate keeps good company with other local historical landmarks. The B&B offers five guest rooms, each with a private bath and individual heating and air-conditioning. The Garden room is a spacious third-floor suite with an antique, carved, queen-size bed draped in floral chintz fabrics; it offers a down-filled sofa in the sitting area for lounging while enjoying complimentary wine and cheese, as well as a Jacuzzi for two. The Morning Glory room offers a view of towering trees and tall mountain peaks from the antique white iron-and-brass bed. The claw-foot tub in the bathroom is accompanied by fluffy towels, bathrobes, and toiletries. Guests discover their rooms stocked with a wide array of complimentary beverages,

PHONE: (626) 441–3535 or (800) 441–3530
FAX: (626) 441–3671
WEB SITE: www.bissellhouse.com
FEATURES: inn; 5 rooms; air-conditioning; swimming pool (unheated); spa; fax; in-room workspace
NEARBY: old town Pasadena; Wrigley Mansion; Norton Simon Museum; Rose Bowl; Huntington Library
INNKEEPERS/OWNERS: Russ and Leonore Butcher

as well as cookies, crackers, fruit, and more. A full gourmet breakfast awaits guests on the weekend; weekday guests enjoy a hearty continental fare. Freshly roasted coffee and homemade bread highlight all the breakfasts, and the owners vary the special dishes that accompany them. An unheated swimming pool and a spa are available to guests.

INN ON SUMMER HILL

2520 Lillie Avenue
Summerland, CA 93067

♿ Ⓧ $$$–$$$$

■ This award-winning California Craftsman–
style inn, built in 1989, has been designed
with arbors, balconies, and river-rock columns and walkways. English flower gardens
and local tropical vegetation are lush; the pansy is the inn's signature flower, planted
extensively throughout the gardens. The interior of the B&B is a romantic delight,
filled with an enjoyable extravagance of prints, colors, and keepsakes in an elegant
European-country decor. Each of the sixteen suites offers a totally different style of
furnishings, but each accommodation boasts fresh flowers, down comforters, quilts,
chaise, love seat, chairs, refrigerator, and an armoire filled with VCR, television, and stereo. The private baths include Jacuzzis, hair dryers, telephones, hand-painted porcelain laundry hampers, and thick terry-cloth robes. The canopy beds of the inn are draped in varying floral, striped, and gingham fabrics; in some rooms the beds are so high that pine stepping stools are provided. Every room has French doors leading to a patio or balcony view of the sea at this inn, which is near the exclusive community of Montecito.

PHONE: (805) 969–9998 or (800) 845–5566
FAX: (805) 565–9946
WEB SITE: www.innonsummerhill.com
FEATURES: inn; 16 units; air-conditioning; in-room phones; in-room televisions and VCRs; in-room refrigerators; fax; copier; spa
NEARBY: beach; Montecito; Santa Barbara
INNKEEPER: Camellia Fernando
OWNERS: Paul and Mabel Shults

Breakfast, served in bed or on the patio, consists of fresh fruits, juice, choices of breakfast breads, and a special hot entree such as gourmet omelettes and quiches. Guests also enjoy afternoon wine, cheese, special hors d'oeuvres, and fruit, as well as evening desserts, served fireside in the country dining room.

INN AT CHURON WINERY BED & BREAKFAST

33233 Rancho California Road
Temecula, CA 92591

♿ Ⓢ $$–$$$$

▪ This French chateau–style inn is situ-
ated on the Churon Winery grounds and
hosts the inn's stately tasting room in its
basement level. The sixteen rooms and six luxurious suites are perched on a hillside
overlooking the vineyards and rolling hills. Rooms and suites feature gas fireplaces,
Jacuzzis for two, elegant furnishings, and either a balcony or terrace with views of
the gardens, fountains, and vineyards of the estate. The Zinfandel suite offers 900
square feet of living space. Guests are treated to a special, private wine tasting in the
basement winery and gift shop each evening and to a full breakfast in the vineyard-
view breakfast room or in the room. Hot-air balloon packages are available with pick-
up at the inn.

PHONE: (909) 694–9070
FAX: (909) 676–8634
WEB SITE: www.temeculabedand
breakfast.com
FEATURES: inn; 22 rooms; winery;
wine-tasting room; hot-air ballooning;
weddings
INNKEEPERS/OWNERS: Ron Thompson
and Chuck Johnson

LOMA VISTA BED AND BREAKFAST

33350 La Serena Way
Temecula, CA 92591

Ⓢ $$–$$$

▪ Surrounded by area wineries on a private hilltop is this Mission-style bed-and-
breakfast, built in 1987, offering panoramic views of lush citrus groves, flowing
vineyards, and mountains. Guests may choose from ten guest rooms, all with air-
conditioning and private baths. The
Champagne Room features a king-size
bed and Art Deco decor, and the Caber-
net Sauvignon has a fireplace, king-size
bed, and a corner Jacuzzi tub. The Sauvi-
gnon Blanc Room is decorated in light
desert hues and boasts a private balcony
overlooking Temecula Valley. A continen-
tal breakfast is served.

PHONE: (951) 676–7047
FAX: (951) 676–0077
WEB SITE: www.lomavistabb.com
FEATURES: inn; 10 rooms; air-
conditioning
NEARBY: wineries; restaurants; golf;
hot-air ballooning; casino
INNKEEPERS/OWNERS: Walt and Sheila
Kurczynski

ROUGHLEY MANOR BED & BREAKFAST INN

74744 Joe Davis Road
Twentynine Palms, CA 92277

⊘ $$

■ Young homesteaders Bill and Elizabeth Campbell built their sanctuary with endless vistas of desert beauty in 1924. The native-stone homestead that was the original Campbell Ranch became a bed-and-breakfast inn in 1994 when current owners Jan and Gary Peters purchased the twenty-five-acre property 2 miles from the entrance to Joshua Tree National Park. Surrounded by Washingtonian palms and flower gardens, the inn is bathed in natural desert vistas. The three-story house with distinctive Vermont maple flooring throughout offers two antiques-filled suites in the main house, five rooms in two detached cottages nearby, and two additional cottages. The Campbell room is the original room of Bill and Elizabeth and is elegantly furnished with a large king-size four-poster bed and hosts a fireplace. The Sunrise room is surrounded by windows on two sides; the cottage offers a sitting room, bedroom with queen-size bed, private bath with antique bathtub, television, small refrigerator, and microwave. The stay includes a full breakfast, served in the dining area of the great room or outside on the patio around the fountain, weather permitting. Breakfast begins with fresh fruits, which might include the inn favorites, pears stuffed with granola mix and baked to perfection or pumpkin pudding served with heavy cream. Entrees are very imaginative and range from gingerbread pancakes served with a lemon topping to a stuffed twice-baked potato topped with scrambled eggs and crisp bacon and covered with cheddar cheese. At 6:30 each evening the manor offers coffee and tea and a special dessert such as Jan's famous banana cream pie.

PHONE: (760) 367–3238
FAX: (760) 367–6261
WEB SITE: www.roughleymanor.com
FEATURES: inn/cottage; 9 rooms; air-conditioning; in-room televisions (some); children welcome with prior arrangement; spa; fax; copier; computer hookups; meeting area; catering for small meetings/receptions; wedding services
NEARBY: Joshua Tree National Park; Morongo Bird Sanctuary; Palm Springs
INNKEEPERS/OWNERS: Jan and Gary Peters

THE 29 PALMS INN

73950 Inn Avenue
Twentynine Palms, CA 92277

$–$$$

◼ The inn was built in 1928 on a California palm fan oasis in the Southern California high desert and, today, is submerged in palm, palo verde, and mesquite trees. An interesting collection of unique adobe bungalows and wood-frame cabins dot the grounds, many around an oasis lagoon that is home to a number of wildlife species. The cabins range in size, but many are suitable for larger groups or families. Guests relax by the pool or on the patio and enjoy a complimentary morning meal of sweet breads, muffins, coffee, and juice poolside. Vegetables from the inn's garden are used in the restaurant, which specializes in homemade sourdough bread and healthful cuisine.

PHONE: (760) 367–3505
FAX: (760) 367–4425
WEB SITE: www.29palmsinn.com
FEATURES: inn/cabins; 24 rooms and cabins; swimming pool; hot tub; picnic lunches; Sunday brunch; in-room massages; vegetable garden; restaurant; pets (by arrangement)
NEARBY: Joshua Tree National Park; town/murals; hiking; rock climbing
INNKEEPERS/OWNERS: Jane and Paul Smith and Heidi Grunt

THE VENICE BEACH HOUSE

No. 15, Thirtieth Avenue
Venice, CA 90291

⊘ $$–$$$$

◼ This circa-1911 historical landmark, once a private celebrity beach hideaway, is located just steps from famed Venice Beach and within walking distance of many fine restaurants and shops. Guest rooms, with both private and shared baths, are elegantly furnished with period antiques and offer telephones and cable television; some accommodations feature private balconies, double Jacuzzis, or wood-burning fireplaces. The inn's Pier suite boasts a king-size bed, fireplace, and sitting room. A hearty European-style breakfast buffet featuring homemade breads and granola may be enjoyed on the veranda, in the sunny parlor, or by the cozy fire in the main living room. Afternoon tea is served daily. Parking is provided on the premises.

PHONE: (310) 823–1966
FAX: (310) 823–1842
WEB SITE: www.venicebeachhouse .com
FEATURES: inn; 9 rooms; in-room phones; computer hookups; in-room televisions; in-room workspace; fax; on-site parking
NEARBY: Venice Beach; shops; restaurants
INNKEEPER: Brian Gannon
OWNERS: Phil and Vivian Boesch

BELLA MAGGIORE INN

67 South California Street
Ventura, CA 93001

♿ $–$$$

■ As a part of the Ventura Historic Walking Tour, this B&B stands out with its classical Italian facade of stone and umbrella awnings. The downstairs area of the inn, its lobby, features antiques, a baby grand piano, and fresh flowers from the garden. Guests may enjoy the afternoon refreshments and appetizers in this pleasant area. The picturesque patio courtyard with Roman fountain is surrounded by flowers and greenery and is a breakfast locale. The morning meal may be selected from a menu with a broad range of choices from the popular restaurant operated here, Nona's Courtyard Café, which serves full breakfasts, lunches, and dinners to the public as well; dinner is not served on Monday and Tuesday. The guest rooms at the inn feature private baths, ceiling fans, shutters, fresh flowers, candy, Italian Capuan beds, and a variety of color schemes. The inn's newest wing features three-room suites with fireplaces, wet bars, microwave ovens, refrigerators, skylights, Jacuzzis, and elegant decor. Some guest rooms open to the patio or sundeck at this European-style inn just blocks from the beach.

PHONE: (805) 652–0277 or (800) 523–8479

FAX: (805) 648–5670

FEATURES: inn; 24 rooms; limited smoking; air-conditioning (some); in-room phones; in-room televisions; in-room refrigerators (some), microwaves (some); catering; computer hookups; conferences; restaurant on premises

NEARBY: downtown shops; restaurants; beach

INNKEEPER/OWNER: Thomas J. Wood

THE BRAKEY HOUSE BED AND BREAKFAST

411 Poli Street
Ventura, CA 93001

⊗ $–$$$

■ This 1890-built Cape Cod–style B&B is nestled on a hillside a few blocks from town and grants inspiring views of the ocean. Even though the inn is walking

PHONE: (805) 643–3600
FAX: (805) 653–7329
WEB SITE: www.brakeyhouse.com
FEATURES: inn; 7 rooms; computer hookups; in-room televisions and DVD players
NEARBY: town; shops; restaurants; beach
INNKEEPER/OWNER: Anthony Rhine

distance to city antiques shops, bistros, and theaters, it has a country feel created by its hilly perch next to the historic old courthouse building. The Santa Barbara room is romantic and spacious with an antique bed, Jacuzzi, sitting area facing a wood-burning fireplace, and window seat facing the Pacific Ocean. The distinctive guest rooms, all with private baths, are each named after the Channel Islands, such as the Santa Catalina room. The guest rooms feature antiques, cozy European comforters, and complimentary wine; all but one room have private entrances. A sumptuous breakfast buffet is served in the Bavarian-style dining room. Guests at this old-world B&B have use of a turn-of-the-twentieth-century lounge.

Absolutely No B&Bs Allowed

Just a short boat ride from Ventura is California's own chain of islands, still much as they have always been. The Channel Islands National Park, operated by the National Park Service, comprises the Anacapa, Santa Cruz, Santa Rosa, San Miguel, and Santa Barbara Islands. Santa Rosa Island, the most recent addition, was purchased in 1987.

The islands, a precious ecological and historical park area, can be visited. However, only one authorized company takes visitors to the Channel Islands for the day or overnight camping visits. Next door to the park headquarters at the harbor is the office and launching spot for Island Packers, which offers an array of tours. Try to book a tour that includes some real island exploring—to Anacapa Island to view marine life or to Santa Cruz Island to the historic Scorpion Ranch.

Call Island Packers at (805) 642–1393, e-mail ipco@isle.net, or log on to www.islandpackers.com. The office is located at 1867 Spinnaker Drive in the Ventura Harbor.

APPENDIX

Reservation and/or Referral Agencies and B&B Associations in California

A majority of the following reservation and/or referral agencies and associations request that a self-addressed, stamped envelope accompany any requests for information.

RESERVATION AND/OR REFERRAL AGENCIES

American Family Inn/Bed & Breakfast
San Francisco
P.O. Box 420009
San Francisco, CA 94142
(415) 899–0060 or (800) 452–8249
Fax: (415) 899–9923
Web site: www.bbsf.com
Serving: San Francisco, Carmel/
    Monterey, Marin County, Wine
    Country

Bed & Breakfast Exchange of Marin
45 Entrata Avenue
San Anselmo, CA 94960
(415) 485–1971
Fax: (415) 454–7179
Serving: Marin County

Bed & Breakfast Homestay
P.O. Box 326

Cambria, CA 93428
(805) 927–4613
Fax: (805) 927–4616
Web site:
www.whisperingpinesbedandbreakfast
    .com
Serving: Cambria

California Riviera
1590 North Coast Highway, Unit 8
Laguna Beach, CA 92651
(949) 376–0305 or (800) 621–0500
Serving: California coastline from San
Francisco through San Diego

Wine Country Bed & Breakfast
P.O. Box 3211
Santa Rosa, CA 95402
(707) 578–1661
Serving: Wine Country

ASSOCIATIONS

Bed & Breakfast Inns of California, A Division of the California Lodging Industry Association
P.O. Box 15918
Sacramento, CA 95852
(916) 925–2915 or (800) 637–4664
Fax: (916) 925–0785
Web site: www.clia.org
Serving: California

California Association of Bed & Breakfast Inns
2715 Porter Street
Soquel, CA 95073
(800) 373–9251
Fax: (831) 462–0402
Web site: www.innaccess.com
Serving: California

Gold Country Inns of Tuolumne County
P.O. Box 462
Sonora, CA 95370
(209) 533–1845 or (888) 465–1849
Web site: www.goldbnbs.com
Serving: Tuolumne County

Historic Bed & Breakfast Inns of Grass Valley & Nevada City
P.O. Box 2060
Nevada City, CA 95959
(530) 477–6634 or (800) 250–5808
Serving: Grass Valley, Nevada City

Julian Bed & Breakfast Guild
P.O. Box 1711

Julian, CA 92036
(760) 765–1555
Web site: www.julianbnbguild.com
Serving: Julian

Northern Redwoods Bed & Breakfasts
(707) 441–1215
Web site: www.northernredwoods.com
Serving: Humboldt County coastal area

Professional Association of Innkeepers
P.O. Box 90710
Santa Barbara, CA 93190
(856) 310–1102
Fax: (856) 310–1105
Web site: www.paii.org
Serving: California

San Diego Bed & Breakfast Guild
(800) 619–7666
Web site: www.bandbguildsandiego.org
Serving: San Diego

Wine Country Inns of Sonoma County
(707) 433–INNS or (800) 946–3268
Web site: www.winecountryinns.com
Serving: Sonoma County, Wine Country

Yosemite-Mariposa Bed & Breakfast Association
P.O. Box 1100
Mariposa, CA 95338
(209) 742–ROOM
Serving: Yosemite Park, Mariposa County (Gold Country)

RESERVATIONS VIA INTERNET

www.sanfrancisco.com/visiting/index

www.bnbinns.com

www.innaccess.com

www.bedandbreakfast.com/usa/
california

www.sonoma.com/lodging/bandbs_
innslistings

www.mendocino.com

INDEXES

Alphabetical Index

wheelchair-accessible accommodations, 9, 25

Whitegate Inn, 63–64

White Jasmine Inn, 293

White Swan Inn, 199–200

Wicky-Up Ranch Bed & Breakfast, 249

Willows Historic Palm Springs Inn, The, 281–82

Willows Inn, The, 200

Windsor, 119–20

Windy Point Inn, 263–64

Wine Country Bed & Breakfast, 305

Wine Country Inns of Sonoma County, 306

Wine Country Inn, The, 111

Wine Way Inn, 81

Woodlake, 249

Yosemite Fish Camp B&B Inn, 243

Yosemite-Mariposa Bed & Breakfast Association, 306

Yountville, 120–21

Yuba City, 165

Zaballa House, 175

Zinfandel House, 82

Zinfandel Inn, 112

B&Bs WITH WHEELCHAIR ACCESS

Northern California

Agate Cove Inn, 55

Albion River Inn, 28

Anderson Creek Inn, 29

Applewood Inn & Restaurant, 48–49

Arbor Guest House, 96

Auberge Mendocino Bed and Breakfast, 50–51

Blue Violet Mansion, 97–98

Brewery Gulch Inn, 56

Carter House, The, 34–35

Cleone Gardens Inn, 41–42

Country Inn, 42–43

Dream Inn, 64

Glass Beach Inn, 43

Grand View Inn, 229

Greenwood Pier Inn, 31

Grey Whale Inn, The, 43–44

Gualala Country Inn, 46

Halcyon Inn Bed and Breakfast, 36

Harbor House Inn, 32

Headlands Inn, The, 57

Homestead Cottages, 248

Hotel Carter, 37

Inn at Benicia Bay, The, 168–69

Inn at Occidental, The, 65

Jenner Inn & Cottages, 50

Landis Shores Oceanfront Inn, 172

Lodge at Noyo River, The, 44

McCloud B&B Hotel, 53–54

Mendocino Hotel & Garden Suites, 59–60

Mendocino Village Inn, 60

Music Express Inn, 128–29

St. George Hotel, 164

St. Orres, 47–48

Sea Gull Inn, 61

Stanford Inn and Spa by the Sea, The, 62

Stevenswood Lodge, 63

Vichy Hot Springs Resort & Inn, 70–71

Whale Watch Inn, 48

California Wine Country

Arbor Guest House, 96

Bartels Ranch & Country Inn, 106–7

Beazley House, 96–97

Blue Violet Mansion, 97–98

Camellia Inn, 88–89

**B&Bs WITH RESTAURANTS, BARS,
OR OTHER MEAL SERVICES**

Northern California

California Wine Country

California Gold Country

San Francisco Bay Area

B&Bs THAT ALLOW PETS

ABOUT THE AUTHOR

Also the author of *Recommended Island Inns: The Caribbean, Southern California Off the Beaten Path, The Seattle Guidebook, Driving the Pacific Coast: California,* and *Driving the Pacific Coast: Washington and Oregon,* Ms. Strong created and ran a nine-guest-room, turn-of-the-twentieth-century B&B inn in central California. Ms. Strong originally began work on this publication at the request of inn guests who were constantly inquiring about a book that would include descriptions of all the state's offerings. This eleventh thoroughly updated edition follows highly successful previous editions and offers close to 400 bed-and-breakfast establishments throughout California. She hopes the book will not only better serve experienced B&B fans, but also convince timid first-timers to give this delightful kind of accommodation a try.

HELP US KEEP THIS GUIDE
UP TO DATE

Every effort has been made by the author and editors to make this guide as accurate and useful as possible. However, many things can change after a guide is published—establishments close, phone numbers change, facilities come under new management, etc.

We would love to hear from you concerning your experiences with this guide and how you feel it could be made better and be kept up to date. While we may not be able to respond to all comments and suggestions, we'll take them to heart, and we'll also make certain to share them with the author. Please send your comments and suggestions to the following address:

The Globe Pequot Press
Reader Response/Editorial Department
P.O. Box 480
Guilford, CT 06437

Or you may e-mail us at:
editorial@GlobePequot.com

Thanks for your input, and happy travels!